PETRARCH'S *SONGBOOK*

Rerum Vulgarium Fragmenta

A VERSE TRANSLATION

by

James Wyatt Cook

PETRARCH'S
SONGBOOK

Rerum Vulgarium Fragmenta

A VERSE TRANSLATION

by

James Wyatt Cook

Italian text by Gianfranco Contini

Introduction by Germaine Warkentin

MEDIEVAL & RENAISSANCE TEXTS & STUDIES
Binghamton, New York
1996

Library of Congress Cataloging-in-Publication Data

Petrarca, Francesco, 1304–1374.
 [Rime. English]
 Petrarch's songbook : a verse translation of the Rerum vulgarium fragmenta
/ translated into English verse, annotated and edited by James Wyatt Cook ; with
an introduction by Germaine Warkentin.
  p.   cm. — (Medieval & Renaissance Texts & Studies ; v. 151)
 Includes bibliographical references and index.
 ISBN 0–86698–191–8 (hc : alk. paper). — ISBN 0–86698–192–6 (pbk. : alk.
paper)
  I. Cook, James Wyatt, 1932– . II. Title. III. Series.
 PQ4496.E23C66 1995
 851'.1—dc20   95–35500
                                                                                  CIP

⊗

This book is made to last.
It is set in Bembo,
smythe-sewn and printed on acid-free paper
to library specifications

Printed in the United States of America

Table of Contents

Acknowledgements

Like any work of considerable magnitude, this project owes much to many. Yet it and I owe an extraordinarily profound debt of gratitude to Professor Germaine Warkentin of the University of Toronto—first a collaborator in, and later a consultant to, this project. Professor Warkentin's taste, counsel, and poetic sensitivity are everywhere evident in this text. Many of the felicities in this translation are directly attributable to her suggestions. Whatever imperfections remain, I fear, are all my own. Extraordinary, too, is the debt I owe Professor Amilcare Iannucci who supported this project with help, advice, and counsel from its outset.

Material assistance for this project has come from many sources. A Newberry Library short-term fellowship made possible project initiation. Grants from the Albion College Hewlett-Mellon Faculty Development Fund and Faculty Development Committee and from the Marguerite Eyer Wilbur Foundation made possible time at the Correr and Marciana libraries in Venice, the British Library, and the Fiske Rare Book Library at Cornell University for the examination of manuscripts and early printed editions of the text, and for the study of the long tradition of Italian textual commentary from the fifteenth century to the present. Albion College also generously underwrote the acquisition of the *Grande Dizionario Italiano* to facilitate the etymological research in which much of this translation is grounded. The organizations mentioned above, together with support from the National Endowment for the Humanities' Translation Division and a sabbatical leave from Albion College, made possible a year's work at the University of Toronto during which the translation was revised to its almost final form. The generosity of the late Mrs. Lily Stanick and of Dr. James Horner defrayed some of the attendant expense. The Centre for Reformation and Renaissance Studies and The Pontifical Institute for Mediaeval Studies at the University of Toronto provided non-stipendiary fellowships, project office space, and some supplies. The Records of Early English Drama (REED) Project of the University of Toronto and its director, Professor Alexandra Johnston, provided access to its computer terminal, and Dean Richard Van Fossen and Erindale College in the University of Toronto supported the computer processing and printing of the penultimate version of the manuscript.

Welcome encouragement has also come from many quarters. Professors Aldo Bernardo, Robert Hollander, Mark Musa, John Tedeschi and the late Fredi Chiapelli were among those lending early advice and advocacy. Later on, feedback from Professors Albert Ascoli, Dino Cervigni, Charles Crupi, Carol Kaske and the late Robert Kaske, Victoria Kirkham, Janet Smarr and Peter Wiggins, and the kind interest of Professor Elissa Weaver and of Evalyn Lindsay and C. Thomas and Frances Wilson helped provide the necessary motivation to keep at it. I cannot well express my gratitude to the staffs of the libraries listed above. All were genuinely splendid in their patience and diligence, but in particular those at the Newberry Library and the Fiske Rare Book Room of the Cornell University Library did signal service in support of my many requests. Professor Amilcare Iannucci read the penultimate version critically and offered many useful suggestions, and Professor Konrad Eisenbichler spent three-and-a-half long days (and evenings) with me as we read aloud the English against the Italian text in search of gaffes that only a native speaker with training in Renaissance Tuscan might catch. Ms. Ilene Crawford of MRTS made many useful suggestions for the notes accompanying this text, and Professor John Williams of Albion College checked the mid-thirteenth century alignments of certain stars and constellations.

Finally, my family supported me through all my laborious days and nights without complaint at my distraction. To them I owe the greatest debt of all, and it is to them, to my wife Barbara, my children Christopher, Kathleen and David and their spouses and beloveds, to my grandchildren Samuel James Dauphinais and Riley Leigh Cook, and to the memory of my late uncle, John D. Wyatt, that I dedicate that effort and this translation.

Translator's Preface

In our 1980 article, "Toward Making a New English Verse Canzoniere" (*Yale Italian Studies* 1:2, 23–43), Germaine Warkentin and I traced the history of the English translation of Petrarch's vernacular lyrics and enunciated the principles on which this translation is based. I do not, therefore, wish to reconsider here all the issues discussed in that extensive treatment. Because accidents of history have long delayed the publication of this translation, however, I do feel obliged first, to acknowledge the appearance in the past thirteen years of a number of new translations of selections from the *Rerum vulgarium fragmenta* (hereafter *Rvf.*) and second, to restate the central concerns that have guided me in bringing forth this translation of the whole work.

Those intervening years have seen the publication of selections by Nicholas Kilmer: *Francis Petrarch: Songs and Sonnets from Laura's Lifetime* (San Francisco: North Point Press, 1981); by G. R. Nicholson: *Sonnets for Laura* (London: Autolycus, ca. 1981); by Marion Shore: *For Love of Laura: Poetry of Petrarch* (Fayetteville: Univ. Arkansas Press, 1987); and, after having changed his mind about undertaking a Petrarch translation at all, by Mark Musa: *Selections from the Canzoniere and Other Works* (Oxford: Oxford Univ. Press, 1985).

Kilmer's selections might better be described by the term P. Lal chose to describe his rendering of the *Mahabharata*—"transcreations." Quirky and often brilliant, Kilmer's free and free-verse translations sometimes offer a nearly literal rendering and sometimes a highly impressionistic interpretation of the facing-page Italian. A clear example of the latter appears in his version of *Rvf* 6. For the Italian:

> Si travïato è 'l folle mi' disio
> A seguitar costei che 'n fuga è volta
> E de' lacci d'Amor leggiera e sciolta
> Vola dinanzi al lento correr mio....   (Kilmer, 6)

Kilmer transcreates:

> I've come this far. My foolhardy desire
> Follows her escape. She is airborne,
> Careless. I can hear the four feet under me.

(Kilmer, 7)

In contrast to this free-wheeling approach, Shore and Nicholson both return to the mainstream tradition of Petrarch translation by doing rhymed versions. Shore's selections are both faithful to Petrarch's Italian and charming as English poems. Nicholson's vary widely in their degree of faithfulness to the original and often strain the capacity of English to tolerate ingenious rhyme. Both illustrate once again, however, Warkentin's conviction and mine that, though it is certainly possible to arrive at polished, rhymed translations of Petrarch's vernacular lyrics when one can pick and choose one's poems to preserve both poetic locus and formal convention, it is quite another matter to produce a rhymed version that sustains both qualities.

Mark Musa's selections continue his practice, followed earlier in his translations from Dante's *La Vita Nuova* (New Brunswick: The Rutgers Univ. Press, 1957), and Dante's *Inferno* (Bloomington: Indiana Univ. Press, 1971), of employing blank verse to render Italian hendecasyllables. Not surprisingly, Warkentin and I concur entirely in his reasons for doing so since we independently and earlier arrived at a similar solution and, indeed, profited from Musa's encouragement and advice in the late 1970s when we sent him preliminary versions of some of our work for his comment.

Any set of selections, whatever might be its author's motives, loses sight of the important truth that the whole of Petrarch's collection is itself carefully crafted as a unified poem and that each of the individual poems—sonnets, *canzoni*, madrigals, sestinas, and *ballate*—stands in a consciously situated and complex relation both to the subordinate units within the collection and to the entire work. That unity I have tried to bear firmly in mind as I have polished this translation.

I have also tried to bear in mind the advice of dozens of teachers and readers of Petrarch who have told me they want an English translation to do two things: first, to present a version recognizable to a bilingual reader as an acceptable linguistic simulacrum of the original and second, to present a version readable as poetry. Robert Durling's prose version of *Petrarch's Lyric Poems* (Cambridge Mass.: Harvard Univ. Press, 1976) has accomplished the first objective satisfactorily for the past two decades. I had begun my verse translation shortly before Durling's prose version appeared, and was tempted to discontinue my project when it was published. Admirable as Durling's prose versions are, however, and as useful as they have proved to be for me in checking my own understanding of thorny passages, in their virtually exclusive pursuit of lexical fidelity, much that I hoped to achieve was lost, so I persevered. Working from the critical text edited by Gianfranco Contini (Turin: Einaudi, 1964), in this translation I have tried to offer nearly as literal a reading as Durling's. Occasionally, perhaps, it becomes even a bit more so. Sometimes, to convey to the English reader elements of implication that exist in the Italian, I have exploited the interstices occasioned by moving from a more to a less inflected language by twice, and, on one occasion, even thrice translating a term. Very rarely, I have permitted myself a flight of poetic fancy that I feel justified by context, as when I render *"seguaci"* (followers or disciples) as "rag-tag creatures." Occasionally I have transposed grammatical elements and even whole lines to catch as fully as possible Petrarch's nuances without sacrificing English prosody. On one or two occasions in tightly packed poems, I confess, I was reluctantly constrained to employ an alexandrine to catch the full lexical meaning of a passage. Almost everywhere, however, I have repressed such tendencies with a view to providing an English reader with an experience that approximates as closely as possible that of reading Petrarch's Italian.

To help achieve that goal, I strive also to meet the second requirement that Italianists, English professors, and general readers of poetry in translation alike have pressed upon me. They want an English version readable *as poetry.* "I have trouble," said one user of Durling's prose translation, "getting my students to see in the prose version why anyone ever got excited about Petrarch as a poet." Meeting this second requirement in terms of style, of emotional tone, of mirroring poetic device and effect, and of poetic texture has been my constant concern and, in producing this translation, a value for me fully equivalent to that of fidelity to the lexical meaning of Petrarch's making. Employing blank verse or—as Petrarch's line length required in mirroring his practice in the *canzoni*—a shorter iambic line, has served the turn admirably. As Warkentin and I said in our *Yale Italian Studies* article:

> The function of a poem's prosody is of course to establish a pattern of metrical expectation . . . [that] the poet can fulfill or interrupt depending on the effect he wishes to create, but . . . [that] is fundamentally consistent for the poem as a whole. [Though] in Petrarch's case the prosodic choices are deliberately varied . . . it is the sonnet that dominates . . . , and we felt we could emphasize the conceptual split between octave and sestet, if need be by the arrangement of lines upon the page. This . . . system . . . also works for exhibiting the division between the *ripresa*

and the *stanza* of the *ballata*. A second advantage of blank
verse is that its basic metrical unit—the iambic foot—falls
naturally into English speech patterns and lends itself easily
to rendering the varying line lengths found in *canzoni, bal-
late*, and madrigals. This seemed important to us because
we were aware that in abandoning the over-familiar
rhyme scheme of the Petrarchan sonnet we would also be
casting away the complex network of interlocking rhymes
designed to emphasize the *fronte, chiave*, and *sìrima* of the
canzone. Our *canzoni* substitute for these the illusion of
looseness and freedom traditional in the English ode while
faithfully mirroring Petrarch's metrical patterns.[1]

In pursuing Petrarch's poetic texture, and to acquire a sense of the sub-
texts informing his poems, I have studied the work of many commentators
across the centuries, from Filelfo and Gesualdo, through Bembo, Tassoni
and Muratori, Leopardi, Carducci-Ferrari, and Chiorboli, to Zingarelli and
Contini-Ponchioroli, to list a representative though far from exhaustive
sample. This experience has informed both Professor Warkentin's forth-
coming notes and commentary that will be keyed to this translation, and
the translation itself with a sense of the densely woven web of classical,
Christian, and amorous-vernacular poetic allusion and convention that
underpins the deceptively simple surface of Petrarch's idiom. This tapestry
I have tried, if not to mirror, at least to suggest.

Fidelity, then, both to the linguistic and, rhyme excepted, to the poetic
values of Petrarch's text, has been the guiding principle of this translation.
In following that principle, I have come increasingly to understand, as I
hope my readers will, the unity that makes the title of this carefully crafted
gathering together of these *Rerum vulgarium fragmenta* (fragments in the lan-
guage of ordinary life)—this collection of poems whose composition scat-
tered them across a lifetime—an example of Petrarch's sense of self-referen-
tial irony and of his view of the way that unity arises from diversity.

---

[1] In making this choice we followed the example of Edmund Spenser, whose blank-
verse renderings of Petrarch appear in Jan Van Der Noot's *Theatre* ... *[for]* ... *Worldlings*
(London, 1569).

INTRODUCTION

Introduction

Late in 1344, when he was living temporarily at Selvapiana near Parma, the Italian poet Francesco Petrarca became an unwilling witness to the carnage that attended his friend and patron Azzo da Correggio's liberation of that city from the tyranny of Mastino della Scala. The peoples of Parma, Reggio, Ferrara, Mantua, Milan, Verona, Bologna, and Ravenna found themselves warring on one side or the other, while German mercenaries of uncertain loyalty despoiled the countryside. Up to the moment of his inevitable flight from the region, work for Petrarch continued as always: in Italian, an exquisite madrigal, four sonnets, three *canzoni* (two of them among his finest), a segment of the *Trionfi*; in Latin, half a dozen verse epistles, the polishing of his epic *Africa* and his encyclopedia of the sayings and acts of great men, the *Rerum memorandarum libri*, as well as the careful drafting of various prose letters. Even amidst the strife he must have been contemplating making a collection of his Italian lyrics; late in his life he would send another patron a manuscript copy of it, with a letter referring to the poems dismissively as trifles. Upon these trifles, however, he had lavished three decades of care. His "canzoniere" or book of songs (to use the term Petrarch's contemporaries would likely have applied to it) is today the foundation text of modern lyric poetry in the European languages, immeasurably more influential than his Latin epistles in verse or prose, his never-completed epic, or his encyclopedia consulted only by scholars. Petrarch's own copy, with his last emendations, is in the Vatican Library in Rome (MS. Vatican Latinus 3195); with the same dismissiveness, it is headed *Rerum vulgarium fragmenta*, "fragments in the language of ordinary life."

One of the poems written at Selvapiana, a *canzone* or song (*Rvf.* 127), considers the problem of how to assemble such a collection while tormented by the very passion that provokes the poems:

> Wherever I am spurred by Love I must
> Urge on these doleful rhymes, which are
> The rag-tag creatures of my troubled mind.
> Which should be last, ah me! and which come first?
>
> (lines 1–4)

As he hovers over his poems, the poet engages in a frustrating debate with Love: "he who discourses with me of my pain / Leaves me in doubt with his confused advice." Yet, he continues, . . . since I find inscribed in his own hand

> Within my heart the history of all
> My martyrdom (which often I consult),
> I'll speak, because sighs uttered
> Declare an armistice and ease my pain.
>
> (lines 7–11)

The record of the poet's martyrdom has been written in his heart by the hand of Love, but in such a way that the poet can release his pain by returning to it again and again. In a display of rhetorical skill unrivalled in his age, Petrarch does just this, creating a virtuoso set of meditations in which the disruptive effects of his experience are envisioned and reenvisioned as if through an ever-revolving prism. The resulting confrontation between the diverse and the singular, between the proliferating poems and the centrifugal force of their relationship with each other, is at the heart of the poetics of the *Rerum vulgarium fragmenta*.

For if Petrarch is thrown into confusion by the fragmenting effects of love, at the same time his creativity has a single focus:I'll say, though raptly gazing

> Upon a thousand varied things, I saw
> One lady only—and her lovely face.
>
> (*Rvf.* 127, lines 12–14)

As the *canzone* develops, the poet's experience of his beloved Laura, from her youth to the full maturity of her present beauty, is compared to the passage of time in nature itself. In the same way the light of day passes over mountain snow, and the flowers of spring give way to those of summer, Petrarch has watched "the lovely girl who is a lady now (line 23)." The vision of all creation's drive towards unity which had been expressed by Dante in his *Commedia*—the greatest Italian poetic work of the generation before Petrarch—is set aside for another way of seeing, one infatuated with the materiality of earth itself, and of things earthly: flowers and flesh, grass and snow. This mode of vision is created by the very power of the poet's awareness of opposites, by his ability to juxtapose the girl and the

[2]

flower, to envision the past in the present, and even with ironic innocence to foreshadow in the whiteness of snow a death which he will later attempt in his sorrow to write, to rewrite, and to rewrite yet again. The capacity to weave a fabric from such oppositions comes (as the *canzone* itself points out) from the very experience of loss, disruption, and doubt which the poet is enduring. As the *Rerum vulgarium fragmenta* is composed and recomposed over the years, this dialectic of loss is absorbed into larger and larger cultural images of separation and fragmentation, and by technical challenges unenvisioned by European vernacular lyric before Petrarch's time.

The poems Petrarch wrote during his residence near Parma show this process already at work. Among them is the famous political *canzone* "My Italy" ["Italia mia"], (*Rvf.* 128), in which the vocabulary he had been developing in his amorous lyrics—the restraining "reins" of line 18; the "verdant earth" of line 21; the "error vain" of line 23; the "blind desire" of line 36—is refashioned to produce a hymn of passionate sorrow at the carnage wrought by the medieval warlords who were battling all about him. It is evident too in the relationship which "My Italy" bears in its turn to a political *canzone* of a decade earlier, "Oh fair and blessed soul whom heaven awaits," (*Rvf.* 28). The earlier poem had been written to Giacomo Colonna, who was bishop of Lombez and the brother of Giovanni, Cardinal Colonna, Petrarch's most important patron, on the occasion of the crusade proposed by Philip VI in the 1330s but never carried out. In a consummate display of structural control by the then thirty-year old poet, *Rvf.* 28 was organized in four different ways: as a description of the world and its peoples, as a typologically structured history of classical and modern Italy designed to encourage in contemporary Romans the achievements of the ancients, as a prophetic instruction to the orator whose words must bring this about, and as a *sirventes,* a genre of Provençal poetry often directed to public issues. But in that *canzone* (*Rvf.* 28), the poet could not disentangle himself from the snares of love, and thus the active role, and the task of prophesying a new era for Rome, fell to Giacomo Colonna. In *Rvf.* 128, however, poetry and prophecy are one, and it is the poet who has become the man of action, though tragically isolated by the power of his insight.

Situating these poems in their context and in relationship to each other reveals at once the range and variety of a poet who in English has unfortunately always been thought of as writing in a single key. Petrarch's name became synonymous with love lyric even in his own lifetime, but for a Renaissance reader he was also the author of another important vernacular poem, the *Trionfi*, and a substantial folio volume of Latin works. But despite a revival of interest among Italianizing Romantic poets in the early nineteenth century, the Petrarchan sonnet (by no means the only form he exploited, and by no means always a love-sonnet) has remained a by-word for artifice and conventionality. There have been more than fifty translations of Dante's *Commedia* into English, and at least fifteen of Boccaccio's *Decamerone*, but despite many successful versions of individual poems, only half a dozen complete versions of the *Rerum vulgarium fragmenta*. Yet Petrarch's artifice, and his exploitation of convention, are products of a powerful engagement with the forms of poetry in his age at both the technical and visionary level, and the ways of writing poetry which his experimentalism generated were to shape the entire course of modern lyric.

Even the earliest of Petrarch's poems—"Had not those honored leaves that tame the wrath" (*Rvf.* 24), "A youthful lady under a green laurel" (*Rvf.* 30), "Diana did not please her lover more" (*Rvf.* 52)—are among the most extraordinary products of late medieval courtly culture: learned in both classical and contemporary lyric, expert in their rhetorical play, resourceful in their exploration of genre, and in the case of his sonnets, melodious beyond any yet written in Italian. Petrarch's sense of his own position in the tradition within which he was writing is apparent in the early *canzone* "Ah wretched me, for I know not on what / To pin my hope," (*Rvf.* 70), where each stanza terminates in a line from an eminent poet of the vernacular tradition. These are not the antique members of the "bella scuola" into which Dante is admitted in the fourth canto of the *Inferno*— Homer, Virgil, Horace, Ovid, and Lucan—but the contemporary masters among whom Petrarch wishes to be weighed: Arnaut Daniel (as Petrarch thought), Guido Cavalcanti, Dante, Cino da Pistoia, and in the triumphal concluding position, the poet himself, represented by what was to become (though it was still unfinished) his most arduous and comprehensive *canzone*, "In the sweet season of my early youth" (*Rvf.* 23).

The careful structural relationships Petrarch early developed between individual sonnets (see for example *Rvf.* 41–43[1]) and evident in the *canzoni* as well (the numerological *Rvf.* 30, the climactic list of poets in *Rvf.* 70, the careful framing of the *canzoni* known as the "three sisters," (*Rvf.* 71, 72, 73) indicate not only his mastery of genre but hint at a transformative capacity which is, though ironically, the very subject of "In the sweet season of my early youth." In this formidable *canzone*, proleptic of the whole of the *Rerum vulgarium fragmenta*, Petrarch sings of how in youth he resisted Love. This transgression against Love's power leads to six encounters with Laura, in each of which he is punished by suffering a

---

[1] For a close study of the relationships among these three sonnets see Peter Hainsworth, *Petrarch the Poet: An Introduction to the "Rerum vulgarium fragmenta"* (London and New York: Routledge, 1988), 65–69.

[4]

transformation based on one of the stories in Ovid's *Metamorphoses*: into a laurel, a swan, a stone, a fountain, an echo, and a deer. Yet as he changes he grows in understanding and poetic power, and at the final metamorphosis is able to cast aside less worthy images of Jupiter (who had come to Danae in a shower of gold and Aegina as a flame) for the noble symbol of the Jovian eagle, which soars upward in praise of Laura, and represents Petrarch's triumphant claim to have mastered the secular art of poetry. But if the central allusions of the poem are Ovidian, Petrarch also exploits biblical and theological parallels, of which the most suggestive may be the likeness in lines 111–13 between Byblis prostrate under the beech and St. Augustine weeping beneath the fig tree at the moment of his conversion. At the same time as the *canzone* dramatizes this crisis, however, it illustrates the immense control he was able to wield as the poem developed, both over its internal economy and its setting in the collection. This *canzone* was actually composed over a period of twenty years; lines 1–89 were written out (probably from an earlier draft, ca. 1333) in late 1337, and in 1350 he returned to the poem and worked on it with increasing intensity until 1356.[2] In the late 1360s he would devise a *canzone* to parallel it and stand near the end of the collection, "While one day at my window as I stood," (*Rvf.* 323). These late visions—a deer, a ship "with silken rigging and a sail of gold," a laurel, a fountain, a phoenix—are all versions of the "pensive lady . . . graceful, fair" whose death the poem recapitulates as Petrarch's entrapment had been recapitulated in the early *canzone*; this time, however, the poem concludes not in Jovian confidence, but in the bitter reflection "All things to their end take flight" (line 55).

This awareness of the relationships between poems—between the poems of the ancients and his own, between those of his contemporaries among whom he sought a place, and in particular between the poems of the *Rerum vulgarium fragmenta* itself—is a feature which differentiates Petrarch markedly from his fellow poets. With the Provençal troubadours he had paid tribute to in *Rvf.* 70, he shared a sense of the fertility of the new vernacular genres: *canso*, *sirventes*, *descort*, and in Italy the sonnet, madrigal and *ballata*—through which a single situation could be variously explored using different generic principles. But the formal repertoire of Roman poetry also fascinated him; the *Rerum vulgarium fragmenta* is deeply marked by his fresh and philologically acute attention to classical *topoi*, genres, and verbal devices. And his method of reading encouraged the search for dimensions of allusiveness which would deepen even further the relationships between poems. To judge from his own account in *Familiares*

---

[2] See Dennis Dutschke, *Francesco Petrarca: Canzone XXIII from First to Final Version* (Ravenna: Longo editore, 1977).

3.18, he explored classical and late Latin writers in the same way, reading through St. Augustine to aspects of Virgil he would not otherwise have perceived, and through Cicero to Plato, whom he could not know directly because he lacked the necessary Greek.

At the same time, however, he was constructing a powerful fiction of the self who possessed this learning and this artistry. The solitary figure who speaks as prophet at the end of "My Italy" reappears everywhere in the *Rerum vulgarium fragmenta*, wandering the fields pursued by Love in "Alone in thought with lagging paces slow" (*Rvf.* 35), watching from the periphery a crowd of ladies around his beloved Laura in "Amidst a thousand ladies I saw one" (*Rvf.* 335), mourning the deaths in the same year of Laura and his patron Giovanni Colonna in "That column high, that laurel green as well" (*Rvf.* 269), remembering in aging solitude the Laura of his youth in "To my mind she returns—in fact, dwells there" (*Rvf.* 336). Yet in reality Petrarch was anything but solitary. The chief Italian poet of his age, he was a scholar of singular gifts, and throughout much of his life princes sought him as a counsellor. As a young man in Avignon, he had curried favor at what has been called the first modern court, and his political poems, above all the notorious Babylonian sonnets (*Rvf.* 136–38), make it clear that his repudiation of court life arose from an insider's knowledge of its workings.[3] Nevertheless, in later life he shocked his friends by spending eight years in the service of the despotic rulers of Milan, the Visconti, and this suggests that his incessant wanderings were controlled by a shrewd sense of when to enter public life and when to step aside from it. Yet in *Familiares* 1.1 (so rich a source for Petrarch's mythology of himself) he writes, "Compare my wanderings to those of Ulysses. . . . I, begotten in exile, was born in exile. . . . I approached the very threshold of life under the auspices of death." It is plain that his constant presentation of himself as one hovering on such a threshold—between life and death (*Rvf.* 36), between achievement and failure (*Rvf.* 40), between possession and loss (*Rvf.* 139), between hell and heaven (*Rvf.* 366)—is the central fiction of a complex, worldly personality.

When he wrote in Latin, Petrarch was employing what was still, despite the example of the *Commedia*, the only language in which a learned man could attempt poetry of high seriousness. But his disdain for the Latin poets of the late medieval period was immense. His own philological interests had early led him to search assiduously for the works of lost or forgotten classical writers; we owe our knowledge of a substantial portion of

---

[3] On Avignon as the first modern court see Norbert Elias, *The Court Society*, trans. Edmund Jephcott (Oxford: Basil Blackwell, 1983), 39, citing Werner Sombart, *Der moderne Kapitalismus*, 3 vols. in 6 (Munich: Dunker und Humblot, 1922).

Livy to his scholarship, as well as the letters of Cicero to Atticus, and very likely the elegies of Propertius. Petrarch's specific interest in the shape of poetic books seems to have first emerged in the setting of his classical studies; as early as 1325 the young poet carefully marked in a manuscript of Horace's *Odes* (now Pierpont Morgan Library MS. 404) the book divisions which the copyist had omitted. The motive for his interest is revealed by an annotation in the same copy, where, as Giuseppe Billanovich has observed, he wrote beside *Odes* 2.9, lines 11–12, with its reference to an unceasing flow of love poems, "note regarding *amantes sine intermissione* [unceasing love-poems]: he does the same as we will write in a little book [*libello*]."[4]

Throughout his life, but most intensely in the period before 1350, Petrarch sought to recapture the stylistic elegance and linguistic purity of the ancient writers: the elegists, Horace, and, above all, Virgil. When he was about twenty-one, he and his father worked together to assemble a beautiful and scholarly manuscript of the works of Virgil. The result, with its great frontispiece by Simone Martini, was long treasured by Petrarch and reposes today in the Biblioteca Ambrosiana, Milan. It is full of annotations on the poems, and contains several important memoranda on Petrarch's own life.[5] In reading the intensely-contemplated Italian poems of the *Rerum vulgarium fragmenta* it is well to keep in mind this "Latin" Petrarch, laboring with equal care over his volume of pastoral poetry, the *Bucolicum carmen*, the ever-frustrating text of the *Africa*, and especially his collections of prose letters, the *Familiares* ("familiar letters") and the *Seniles* ("letters of old age").

He labored not as an antiquarian, but (as he wrote in *Rvf.* 40, "If Love or Death does not create some flaw") as one who sought to shape a work

> Between the moderns' style and ancient tongue
> That (and I dare to say this fearfully)
> At length you'll hear it noised abroad in Rome.
>
> (lines 6–8)

In 1341, having been examined by King Robert of Naples, he was

---

[4] See Giuseppe Billanovich, "L'Orazio Morgan e gli studi del giovane Petrarca," in *Tradizione classica e letteratura umanistica per Alessandro Perosa*, ed. Roberto Cardini, Eugenio Garin, Lucia Cesarini Martinelli, and Giovanni Pascucci (Rome: Bulzoni editore, 1985), 121–38; see esp. 129–31.

[5] There is a facsimile: *Francisci Petrarcae Vergilianus codex* . . . with a prefatory pamphlet by Giovanni Galbiati (Milan: U. Hoepli, 1930). The details of its compilation were finally assembled and edited by Giuseppe Billanovich, "Da Dante al Petrarca," in *Accademia Nazionale dei Lincei (Adunanze Straordinarie per il conferimento dei premi della Fondazione A. Feltrinelli)* vol. 1, fasc. 3 (1966) 63–67.

crowned with laurel on the Capitoline Hill in Rome. Though he was thirty-seven, Petrarch had as yet produced very little, and it has been suggested that he manoeuvered himself into the good fortune of receiving on the same day two invitations to accept the laureateship, one from Paris and one from Rome. It was the Roman one he accepted, and the oration he delivered at the time was heavily freighted with allusions to the classics. It was heavy also with his own sense of mission:

> While there are some who think it shameful to follow in the footsteps of others, there are far more who fear to essay a hard road unless they have a sure guide. Many such men have I known, especially in Italy: learned and gifted men, devoted to the same studies, thirsting with the same desires, who as yet ... have not entered upon this road. Boldly therefore, but—to the best of my belief— with no unworthy intention, since others are holding back I am venturing to offer myself as a guide for this toilsome and dangerous path; and I trust that there may be many followers.[6]

By the late fifteenth century the purified Latin he sought (which, unlike his intellectual heirs Lorenzo Valla, Angelo Poliziano, and Desiderius Erasmus, Petrarch himself would never write terribly well) was to become the *lingua franca* of the new intellectual movement of Humanism.

When he turned to the vernacular, Petrarch was one of a triumvirate of European poets whose shared cultural significance has never been fully examined: Petrarch himself, the brilliant French musician and lyricist Guillaume de Machaut (1300–1377), and the English poet Geoffrey Chaucer (1345?–1400). Different as their careers and national significance may have been, all three were attempting to shape the possibility of a subjective position for the vernacular poet outside the then-dominant mode of romance verse narrative.[7] As a specifically Italian poet, Petrarch was also part of a triumvirate, a group early saluted as the "tre corone" (three crowns) of the emergent Italian literature: Dante, Petrarch, and Boccaccio. Petrarch

---

[6] E. H. Wilkins, "Petrarch's Coronation Oration," in *Studies in the Life and Works of Petrarch* (Cambridge, Mass.: Medieval Academy of America, 1955), 306.

[7] For Machaut, see Jacqueline Cerquiglini, *"Un engin si soutil": Guillaume de Machaut et l'écriture au XIV siècle* (Geneva-Paris: Editions Slatkine, 1985), and her essay "Ethique de la totalisation et esthetique de la rupture dans le *Voir-Dit* de Guillaume de Machaut," in *Guillaume de Machaut, Colloque-Table Ronde, Université de Reims, 19–22 avril, 1978* (Paris: Editions Klincksieck, 1982), 253–62. With respect to Chaucer (and a different approach to the same problem) see Lee Patterson, *Chaucer and the Subject of History* (Madison: Univ. of Wisconsin Press, 1991).

met Boccaccio (with whom he had already corresponded) in 1350; they remained close friends, and the earliest extant version of the *Rerum vulgarium fragmenta*, MS. Chigi L. V. 176 (ca. 1362) in the Vatican Library, is in the younger poet's hand.[8] But Boccaccio tended to regard Petrarch as a mentor, and his medium was prose.[9] Dante, however, was the most eminent poet of the age just past; he had been a friend of Petrarch's father Ser Petracco dell'Incisa, and the younger poet may in youth have briefly encountered Dante himself.

The challenge to his art posed by such an eminent predecessor haunted much of Petrarch's life. To Boccaccio he insisted he had never possessed a copy of the *Commedia*, but as Marco Santagata has demonstrated, multiple allusions in the *Rerum vulgarium fragmenta* show that he studied it intensively early in his career, and, after a gap of decades, returned to it late in life.[10] In the *Rerum vulgarium fragmenta* we encounter an inversion—at once hostile and fiercely emulative—of all that Dante represents. In Dante there is a powerful sense of the ordered hierarchy of all created things, which—despite the deepest historical and ethical ironies—represents in the ascending three-part structure of the work the capacity of its fabricator to attain a higher vision. But in the *Rerum vulgarium fragmenta* we find a compelling need to review, revise, and remake; and we discover a vision of the poet's book as a storehouse of such opportunities. In *Paradiso* 33, Dante has a vision in which "I saw ingathered, bound by love in one single volume, that which is dispersed in leaves throughout the universe...." In the *Rerum vulgarium fragmenta* this volume becomes Petrarch's "many leaves" ["mille carte"], Dante's upward *itinerarium*, Petrarch's winding labyrinth; his eternally creating Word, Petrarch's earthly, temporal Laurel. If Dante in the *Vita Nuova* tells us he met Beatrice at the age of nine, a number which signifies the miraculous form and spiritual significance of his experience, Petrarch meets Laura at twenty-three, an age of earthly significance; according to Censorinus, whose writings Petrarch knew, it is in this stage of life that men are physiologically most suited for love.[11] In the

---

[8] There is a facsimile edition: *Il Codice Chigiano L. V. 176: Autografo di Giovanni Boccaccio*, intro. Domenico de Robertis (Rome: Archivi edizioni, 1974).

[9] Boccaccio's indifference to the compilation of his lyrics (compared with his concern about the fate of his other works) is discussed by Vittorio Branca, *Tradizione delle opere di Giovanni Boccaccio* (Rome: Edizioni di storia e letteratura, 1958), 1:288–89.

[10] Marco Santagata, "Presenze di Dante 'Comico' nel 'Canzoniere' del Petrarca," *Giornale Storico della Letteratura Italiana* 146 (1969): 163–211.

[11] Petrarch (born in 1304), dates his meeting with Laura as 1327 in *Rvf.* 211. In *Rvf.* 23, line 23, he reports that this happened when "my youthful countenance was changed," that is, when his beard appeared. Censorinus (*De die natali* 14.7) describes the physiological signs which distinguish the seven-year periods of man's life; the beard is the sign of the

Commedia, Dante portrays himself as the citizen of a specific city, Florence, though unjustly exiled. Petrarch, as a result of the psychological wound inflicted on him by Love, is by nature a solitary; within the historical fact of Dante's exile he makes himself a greater exile yet. In the *Commedia* we are presented with a densely crowded human scene; in the *Rerum vulgarium fragmenta* Petrarch retreats to nature; *"solo e pensoso,"* he wanders the empty fields, fleeing every trace of man and followed only by Love (*Rvf.* 35). And Dante's confidence in language is countered by Petrarch's linguistic duplicity, in which every form of words seems at the same time to state and negate, and the search for eloquence produces a language so packed with allusion that a single word can flower with three, four, and five meanings. Petrarch's response to the most important work in his own language in his own age was thus a virtual turning inside-out of its terms of existence, both thematic and formal. This act was to take him nearly a lifetime, and to transform the youthful poet's *"libello"* into a complex artifact over which the aged giant would still hover, planning the reorganization of its last thirty poems, fifty years later.

★ ★ ★

Petrarch was indeed born in exile; his father, a friend and ally of the White Guelph (that is, conservative) Dante, had been banished from Florence in 1302, and Petrarch was born in Arezzo in 1304. In 1312 Ser Petracco, who was a notary, transported his family to Provence, where the papal court had taken up residence in Avignon, and it was there, at Carpentras under the shadow of Mont Ventoux, that his son was raised and educated, along with his younger brother Gherardo. At the age of twelve Petrarch was sent to Montpellier, where he spent four years studying civil law, and between 1321 and 1326 he spent extended periods at the prestigious law school at Bologna, across the mountains in Italy. His father had destined his sons for legal careers at the papal court, though both were eventually to repudiate this scheme, Petrarch for a literary career eternally dependent on the patronage of the great, Gherardo for the cloister. But the sites of his youthful education and the eleven years he spent as a courtier in Avignon marked Petrarch's later career as a poet in two important respects, one vernacular, one classicizing.

Avignon was geographically near the centre of the literary culture from which much that was important to the poetry of modern continental Europe had emerged, that of the Provençal troubadours. In addition to his na-

---

third of these. Petrarch was well acquainted with Censorinus; *De die natali* is mentioned under two different titles in the marginal notes in his Virgil; see Pierre de Nolhac, *Pétrarque et l'Humanisme* (Paris: Librairie Honoré Champion, 1965) 1:156, and 2:105.

tive Italian, Petrarch must have spoken Provençal as a youth in Carpentras; the contemporary vernacular poetry of his student years would have been the *cansos*, *sirventes*, and *descorts* of the courtly repertoire, and in Bologna he would have encountered the powerful influence which Provençal poetry still exercised over the emerging vernacular lyric of Italy. Not merely in its prevailing theme of love-service, but in its genres and its allusions to Provençal poets, the earlier lyrics of the *Rerum vulgarium fragmenta* reveal Petrarch's alertness to what had, in the past two centuries, become the master school of vernacular lyric in Europe. In this respect he was like most of the Italian poets of this and the preceding age: Guido Guinizelli, Dante, Guido Cavalcanti, and Cino da Pistoia.

He differed from them, however, in an important respect which his situation in Avignon made possible. Though Petrarch fretted at the futility of court life and was eventually to castigate Avignon as a new Babylon, a "school of wrongs and shrine of heresy" (*Rvf.* 138), it was among the books of the patrons he encountered at court, that he found the tools which would shape his philological studies and, as a consequence, his rapid and deep absorption, not merely of classical ideals, but of sheer information about Roman life and literature. This early period of apprenticeship (1325–1337) was intense and fruitful. Even as a young law student, Petrarch had rediscovered and edited several of the lost books of Livy's history of Rome; by 1333 he had found in Paris and copied in his own hand a manuscript of Propertius, a poet Dante had referred to with respect, but whose elegies he could not have known. If an immersion in Provençal lyric had given Petrarch an instinct for the subtlety, music, and generic richness possible in vernacular poetry, his exploration of Horace, the elegists, and Virgil stretched his technical skills even further while at the same time legitimizing, with the authority of the classic past, his own poetic experiments. Petrarch must have sensed, furthermore, the resemblance between the ambition with which Provençal lyric asserted its presence on the literary scene, and the fierce aspiration of Roman poetry: "I have built a monument more lasting than bronze," Horace had written in *Odes* 3.30, a *topos* which Petrarch would both adopt and subject to ironic scrutiny in the "scattered rhymes" of his own book. The balance required to maintain this contrast between aspiration and loss was to haunt the *Rerum vulgarium fragmenta* in all its forms.

The visionary framework in which Petrarch's conception of poetry and his fiction of himself would be developed is suggested by another book he acquired in youth: a treasured manuscript of St. Augustine's *Confessions* presented to him by the Augustinian monk Dionigi da Borgo San Sepolcro in 1333, the same year in which Petrarch transcribed the Parisian manuscript of Propertius. The *Confessions* would become a crucial impetus for the subjectivity of the *Rerum vulgarium fragmenta*, with its presentation of the life of a wanderer riven by the conflict between opposing ideals. For St. Augustine the world of sense is fallen, yet still urgent with the need to possess: "I loved not yet, yet I loved to love, and out of a deep-seated want, I hated myself for wanting not," he writes, producing an almost Ovidian oxymoron to express the fixity of his youthful obsession.[12] Though in his writings on discourse Augustine emphasized the harmony necessary to the literary work and the way in which that harmony expressed the order of creation, in his spiritual life he constantly thought of himself as a "peregrinus": the foreign resident of a greater power, a sojourner from outside the wall, a wandering pilgrim.[13] He saw himself as a restless traveller and his life as an incessant journey, his fallen state providing the very condition "of not-having, of not-seeing," which drove him towards insight.[14] But mindful of Christ's words in John 14:6 he wrote, "for there is hope to attain a journey's end when there is a path which stretches between the traveller and his goal . . . this road is provided by one who is himself both God and Man. As God, he is the goal; as man, he is the way."[15] The image of the "way" made it possible for Augustine to maintain an unceasing dialectic between the perfect and the deficient, the one and the multiple, the harmony of the centre and the anxiety endured at the periphery. It is an image which recurs again and again in the poems of the *Rerum vulgarium fragmenta*.

Petrarch's repudiation of court life in 1337 did not mean his departure from Provence. He had visited Paris in 1333 and Rome in 1336–1337, and when he returned from the latter journey, it was to settle in the little valley of Vaucluse, close to Carpentras where he had lived as a child, close also to the Avignonese matron Laure de Noves, wife of Hugues de Sade.[16] In a gesture which reveals his saturation in the courtly ethos of Provençal lyric, he had already made this woman—several years younger than himself, and already the mother of children—the subject of his amorous poetry. In a note written in his precious copy of Virgil at the time of her death in the plague of 1348, Petrarch tells us that he first saw Laura in

---

[12] *Confessions* 3.1.1, trans. E. B. Pusey (London: J. M. Dent, 1838). The passage may echo Ovid *Amores* 3.4.5: "Odi, nec possum, cupiens, non esse quod odi" ("I hate what I am, and yet, for all my desiring, I cannot but be what I hate").

[13] On the nuances of *peregrinatio* in Augustine, see Peter Brown, *Augustine of Hippo* (London: Faber and Faber, 1967), 323–24.

[14] Terence Cave, *The Cornucopian Text: Problems of Reading and Writing in the French Renaissance* (Oxford: Clarendon Press, 1979), 102.

[15] *The City of God*, trans. Henry Bettenson (Harmondsworth: Penguin, 1967), 11.3.

[16] For the history of this identification and its probable confirmation, see F. J. Jones, "Further Evidence of the Identity of Petrarch's Laura," *Italian Studies* 39 (1984): 27–46.

the church of Santa Clara in Avignon on the sixth of April, 1327; the note records her death, on the same day, in 1348 "while I, as it chanced, was in Verona, unaware of my fate."[17] Their first encounter (he deals with it in sonnets from differing amorous and Christian perspectives in *Rvf.* 2 and *Rvf.* 3) evokes an archetypal situation of Provençal and Italian courtly poetry, one which had already been exploited by Dante in the *Vita Nuova*: the watching youth, the beauteous woman, the piercing glance with which a beam from her eye, in the form of Love's arrow, penetrates his heart and marks him forever, and (as events transpired in both works) the inevitable averting or veiling of the lady's gaze which plunges her lover first into despair, and then into an attempt to recapture, or at least to become worthy of, her glance. In Petrarch, as well as in Dante, the poet must endure not only this repudiation, but the actual loss of his beloved. Laura's death in the Black Death, the terrible plague of 1348, divides Petrarch's life as it divides his lyric book. After several years of vacillation, he left Provence for good in 1353. Until he settled at Arquà near Padua four years before his own death in 1374, he was to travel from one city to another: eight years in Milan, another nine in Venice, Padua, and Pavia, becoming in the course of time the foremost scholar-poet of his age. A transformation, however, had already been taking place in him even before Laura fell victim to the Black Death, and it is closely associated with his inception, about 1349–1353, of definitive collections of several of his works.

★ ★ ★

In the four years after the Black Death, the poet, now in mid-life, was to move beyond—if never entirely set aside—his earlier pursuit of classical ideals in order to saturate himself in the writings of the Fathers of the Church. After 1345 Petrarch did almost no work on the *Africa*, and he never released it for publication. Instead, he turned to the ordering of a series of collections in prose and verse—the *Bucolicum carmen*, the *Epistolae metricae*, and the *Familiares*—the elements of which he had been assembling for some years. In the opening letter of the *Familiares* he writes of

> the great number of writings of different kinds that lie
> scattered and neglected throughout my house. I searched
> in squalid containers lying in hidden places, and pulled
> out dusty writings half destroyed by decay.

"Beset and encircled by confused heaps of letters and formless piles of paper," he resolves to throw everything into the fire, for

---

[17] The famous note is given in full by Wilkins, *Life*, 77.

when I began turning over the papers piled at random in no particular order, I was astonished to notice how varied and disordered their general aspect appeared. I could hardly recognize certain ones, not so much because of their form but because of the changed nature of my understanding.

Close verbal echoes link this letter with the "scattered rhymes" of the *Rerum vulgarium fragmenta*'s first poem, "O you that hear in scattered rhymes the sound," composed, we now know, in 1349.[18] In the following decades the ordering of fragments would acquire a compelling significance for Petrarch; upon it eventually turned his very capacity for the transformation and reintegration of a continuously troubled soul.

His spiritual crisis of the early 1350s—for such it seems to have been—thus led Petrarch on the one hand to a fierce inner debate over his poetic future, and on the other to plan that future by beginning the orderly disposition of his works. Petrarch framed its issues in the three dialogues known as the *Secretum*, which he was also working on at about this time. There he presents himself arguing his spiritual health with St. Augustine; will his love for Laura and his passion for poetry close the gates of heaven to him? Augustinus argues (and his doctrine is sound) that unless Franciscus abandons his desire for worldly fame, he will be turning away from God, but Franciscus as usual wants to have it both ways:

> I return to attend to those other concerns only in order
>   that, when they are discharged, I may attend to these....
> I have not strength enough to resist that old bent for study altogether.[19]

Despite this final equivocal response, however, he had already spoken of gathering up the scattered fragments of his soul,[20] in a plain allusion to Christ's "Gather up the fragments that remain, that nothing be lost" (John 6: 12), an allusion which also lies behind the Latin title, *Rerum vulgarium fragmenta* of his lyric book.[21] A similar stubbornness seems to have led in

---

[18] See Francisco Rico, " 'Rime Sparse,' 'Rerum vulgarium fragmenta.' Para el titulo y el primer sonetto del 'Canzoniere,' " *Medioevo Romanzo* 3 (1976); 101–38. Rico proposes a date very shortly after November 30, 1349, when what he believes to be the first nucleus of the poem appears in VL 3196.

[19] *Petrarch's Secret: or The Soul's Conflict With Passion*, trans. William H. Draper (London: Chatto and Windus, 1911), 192.

[20] Draper, 191, but "animae" is wrongly translated by Draper as "wits"; the Latin reads "et sparsa anime fragmenta recolligam." The Vulgate text of John 6:12 is: "Colligite quae superaverunt fragmenta, ne pereant."

[21] See Robert M. Durling's introduction to his prose translation of the *Canzoniere*,

this period to a gathering of his forces, and a fresh and transformed creativity. Out of the papers scattered on his study floor in 1349–1351 may have come the half-finished draft of "In the sweet season of my early youth" (*Rvf.* 23); certainly he returned to this *canzone* with intense concentration during the next five years, and completed it in 1356 with the lines that express his soaring confidence in the power of his verse:

> Oh song, I never was that cloud of gold
> Which in a priceless rain came falling once—
> The one in which Jove's fire, in part, was spent—
> But, lit by one sweet look, I've been a flame,
> Yes, and that bird which shears the upper air,
> Bearing her high whom my words celebrate;
> Nor could I from a new form learn to part
> From that first laurel whose sweet shade yet sweeps
> Every delight less lovely from my heart.
>
> (lines 161–69)

And in these years—in the late 1340s and again in 1356–1358, this time perhaps for Azzo da Correggio, his old friend at Parma—he returned to the making of a collected book of verse.

Petrarch would not have encountered any purely technical problems in developing a formal collection out of the "ragtag creatures of my troubled mind." Behind the assemblages of individual poets' writings which appear in the great Provençal and Italian anthologies in which poetry was circulated in the early fourteenth century there lie personal notebooks or collections of drafts which a given poet would have treated as a kind of archive. Indeed, there is increasing evidence that the *Rerum vulgarium fragmenta* emerged from an eclectic and since-forgotten tradition of composed collection. The conceptualizing of the manuscript archive itself as embodying a formal possibility, as a genre to be explored, transformed, and transmitted to others, was being actively investigated in the thirteenth and fourteenth centuries, possibly by certain late troubadours such as Guiraut Riquier, certainly by Dante and his contemporaries, and by poets abroad as well: Guillaume de Machaut in France and John Gower in England.[22] Thus

---

Petrarch's Lyric Poems: the Rime Sparse and Other Lyrics (Cambridge, Mass.: Harvard Univ. Press, 1976), 26.

[22] On Italian poets of the period see Furio Brugnolo, "Il libro di poesia nel trecento," in *Il libro di poesie dal copista al tipografo: Ferrara, 29–31 May 1987*, edited by, Marco Santagata and Amedeo Quondam (Modena: Edizioni Panini, 1989), 9–23; for French poetry see Sylvia Huot, *From Song to Book: The Poetics of Writing in Old French Lyric and Lyrical Narrative Poetry*, (Ithaca and London: Cornell Univ. Press, 1987). For Machaut, see the studies by Cerquiglini mentioned in n. 7; for Gower and his manuscripts, see R. F.

from one point of view, Petrarch was no innovator. But his life-long transformation of his personal archive of poems into a series of "editions" of his lyric collection was eventually to generate one of the most influential practices of European lyric poetry, the making of a subjective lyric book in which, besides the sonneteers of the Renaissance, his heirs would be George Herbert, Goethe, Baudelaire, Whitman, and Rilke. To achieve it he would assimilate the material realities of the archive itself—its many sheets of paper (no less than sixteen references to "carta") pens (thirteen) and ink (five)—to the theological *topos* of the book of nature, and then use the result to explore the problem of his own evolving subjectivity. It was not by chance that in the sixteenth century, the constantly reissued texts of the *Rerum vulgarium fragmenta* were referred to simply as "Il Petrarcha"; the man and the book had become totally identified with each other.

A portion of his archive, the famous "codice degli abbozzi" or "book of sketches," still exists in the Vatican Library (MS. Vatican Latinus 3196).[23] This manuscript is an assemblage of only twenty leaves of poems in various stages of composition, but they come from all periods of Petrarch's life, and show the immense care with which he polished each poem, sometimes over many years, until he was satisfied. This satisfaction was made the more attainable by Petrarch's manifest attraction to shorter literary units such as eclogue, letter, sonnet, *canzone*, and dialogue, as well as by his general interest in the amassing of compilations. Likewise, the series of "editions" of the *Rerum vulgarium fragmenta* Petrarch issued from the late 1350s onwards represents the typical creative manoeuverings of an imagination which is as deeply satisfied by the act of revision as by the completion of the poem. As the poet's frequent marginal annotations indicate, once polished, a poem was usually transcribed *in ordine,* that is, into a fair copy with an organized plan to it. It is in the making of such a copy that the ambition of composing a coherent work made up of shorter poems would have taken practical form. This copy and its successive versions are long since lost, but careful scholarship has been able to hypothesize their shape and direction from the pages of MS. VL 3195 and MS. VL 3196, and from the evidence of copies made by others.[24]

The stages through which Petrarch's book probably developed are

---

Yeager, *John Gower's Poetic: The Search for a New Arion* (Cambridge: D. S. Brewer, 1990).

[23] There is a facsimile: *Il codice vaticano lat. 3196 autografo del Petrarca*, ed. M. Porena (Rome: R. Accademia d'Italia, 1941).

[24] The standard study of this subject, still essential though it urgently needs reassessment, is Ernest Hatch Wilkins, *The Making of the Canzoniere and Other Petrarchan Studies* (Rome: Edizioni di storia e letteratura, 1951), from which the following summary is derived.

these. In 1342 he organized from among his earlier drafts a "first form" of the collection, beginning with the sonnet that now stands thirty-fourth, "Apollo, if that fair desire still lives," and consisting of a single body of perhaps a hundred poems. A second form, probably much larger, dates from the years just after the Black Death; scholars argue over whether this version was yet divided into two parts (in my view, it was). Between 1356 and 1358 Petrarch was again at work on a third version of the collection, the one he sent to Azzo da Correggio in Parma sometime after November 1357. This was followed by the Chigi version, begun in 1359, and copied out by Boccaccio no later than 1362. The final form as it stands in Petrarch's own manuscript, MS. VL 3195, was begun in 1366, first by his favorite scribe Giovanni Malpaghini and then, when that tempestuous young man left his service, in the poet's own hand. Even here different stages of development can be discerned: that of the text as it was when Giovanni abandoned work on it, Petrarch's own years of labor on the same manuscript, and two slightly variant forms which can be surmised from the descendants of copies which Petrarch released around 1371–1373.

The evolution of the *Rerum vulgarium fragmenta* thus took place in the public eye, so to speak. Rather than presenting his friends and patrons with diverse poems organized in a single confident design, like Dante's *Vita Nuova*, we find Petrarch unfolding before them ever more suggestive editions of a single book, one which remained an "open text" as long as he himself lived to continue work upon it. And to the manuscript which contained the latest version of this text, he gave the attention of a lover throughout the final decade of his life. Just as Petrarch searched relentlessly for logic of form in individual poems, often revising over a period of many years in his search for rhetorical control, so too he subjected the collection as a whole to the same intense scrutiny, returning persistently, though in contrasting, ever-evolving ways, to the central situation which had been deeded to him by the legacy of Roman elegy and Provençal poetry: the conflict between the poet's devotion to an unattainable woman, and his search for a way to breach the barrier between them, whether raised by disdain or death.

From the mid-1330s, when Petrarch began to explore the complex ways in which Italian makes it possible to play on Laura's name—*lauro* (both the mythological tree and the conqueror's crown), *l'oro* (the gold of her hair), and *l'aura* (the breeze that surrounds her)—he had focussed his dialectic of aspiration and loss on the Ovidian story of Apollo and Daphne. The result was not only to stress the connection between the distance Laura resolutely maintained from him, and the girl who fled the god only to be transformed into a laurel tree, but to forge a link between the poet and Apollo, and with the Christian ideal of achievement in poetry. In contrast with the medieval tendency to demonize Apollo, Petrarch, in explaining the first eclogue of the *Bucolicum carmen* to his brother Gherardo, identified Apollo with Christ.[25] Thus the collection of 1342, though fraught with themes that reappear in later versions of the *Rerum vulgarium fragmenta*, does not commence as they do with the poet in penitential stance, begging the reader's pardon for his errant life and his varied rhymes. Rather, it opens with a prayer to Apollo (*Rvf.* 34), begging the god not only to protect the "honored, sacred fronds" of the laurel tree they both love, but to

> ... clear the air of these obscuring mists;
> Thus you and I will see a wondrous sight:
> Our lady sitting down upon the grass
> And making, with her arms, shade for herself.
>
> (lines 11–14)

This sonnet (which, as an opening or programming poem, has a long ancestry among the opening poems of the Roman elegists and Horace) foretells a collection in which the resources of a Christian yet Apollonian poetry endows the poet with intense visionary power, a collection which was not, so far as we can tell, divided in two.

But when the poet returned to work on his lyric book a few years later he was in search of larger structural resources to express the dialectic of desire and loss which the Apollo/Daphne myth empowered. He began to develop the *Rerum vulgarium fragmenta* as a collection in two parts, separated ostensibly by Laura's death, but divided also by the crisis of conscience recorded in the magisterial *canzone* that he wrote to open the second part, *Rvf.* 264, "I wander thinking, and within my thoughts":

> One thought discourses with my mind, and says,
> "What do you covet still? Whence succor wait?
> Wretch, do you fathom not
> With what dishonor to you time goes by?
> With wisdom make your mind up! Make it up!
>
> (lines 19–23)

Petrarch's structural task was to subordinate the poems yielded by this kind of vacillation to some kind of over-all control.

Late in life Petrarch explained what he had attempted to do with the

---

[25] The letter to Gherardo is *Fam.* 10.4. See Aldo Bernardo, trans., *Rerum familiarium libri, IX–XVI* (Baltimore: John Hopkins Univ. Press, 1982). For Petrarch's interpretation of Apollo see Marjorie O'Rourke Boyle, *Petrarch's Genius: Pentimento and Prophecy* (Berkeley: Univ. of California Press, 1991), 11–43.

poems in a letter of 1373, sent to Pandolfo Malatesta with a copy of the *Rerum vulgarium fragmenta*; there he referred to the poems as "my vernacular trifles," observing "let the rambling madness of lovers, which is the subject right at the outset, above all excuse the variety of the work"[26]— that is, those lines of the opening poem where the poet-lover identifies the "scattered rhymes" and "various style" of the work with the unhappy condition of the lover, wandering between vain hope and weeping, whose plea for pity we are about to hear. Petrarch was well acquainted with the standard descriptions of what the ancients regarded as "love-malady": alternating fever and chills, erratic behavior, a penchant for solitude.[27] The familiar symptoms afflict Massinissa in Book 5 of the *Africa*; in *Secretum* 3, St. Augustine observes their presence in the poet himself, and in *De remediis utriusque fortunae* 1.69, their consequences are ruthlessly satirized. Petrarch's missive to Pandolfo makes perfectly explicit that he identified the *varietas* of his poems with what medieval medical knowledge regarded as the variability of the lover, and that it was a self-explanatory structural device which needed only to be pointed out. *Varietas* itself was a classical rhetorical concept; Quintilian takes almost for granted the desirability of variety in the oration (*Inst. Orat.* 2.12.10); the ease and mobility it creates is stressed (2.13.8–11), and he thinks it natural for structural variety to mirror variety of subject and intention (11.3.152).[28] But Petrarch both exploits and transcends this rhetorical foundation: just as the familiar physiological symptoms of love-sickness are transformed into a vision of the moral self, so too the very fragmentation of the poet's experience becomes an operative principle by which the text is generated.

---

[26] *Sen.* 13, 11, in *Letters of Old Age: Rerum senilium libri I–XVII*, trans. Aldo S. Bernardo, Saul Levin, and Reta A. Bernardo, 2 vols. (Baltimore and London: The Johns Hopkins Univ. Press, 1992), 1:499. The connection between the letter and "You that hear in scattered rhymes the sound" (*Rvf.* 1) is noted by Robert Durling, *The Figure of the Poet in Renaissance Epic* (Cambridge, Mass.: Harvard Univ. Press, 1965), 86.

[27] Among a number of recent studies, see especially Mary Frances Wack, *Lovesickness in the Middle Ages: the Viaticum and its Commentaries* (Philadelphia: Univ. of Pennsylvania Press, 1990). Quite apart from his contemporaries' interest in love-malady, Petrarch was a life-long reader of Cicero's *Tusculan Disputations*, where the classical attitude to such passions is fully set forth.

[28] Varro, discussing grammar in *De Lingua Latina* (9.33, 46–47), suggests what a Roman would have meant by "variety": "if variety is a pleasure, then there is greater variety in that in which some things are alike and others are not; and just as a side-table is adorned with silver in such a way that some ornaments are alike and others are unlike, so also is speech adorned." Horace's elegant architectonic sense yields a specific reproof to him who "tries to vary a single subject in monstrous fashion" (*Epistle to the Pisos* 29). And in *The Consolation of Philosophy* 4.6, Boethius proposes a change of genres to offer the reader "refreshment."

Petrarch investigates the meaning of *varietas* with every resource at his command. On one hand he presents himself as an *auctor*, a poet of established prestige who, because he speaks in his own person, invites our assent to his account of his situation. Yet at the same time he has suffered a wound which specifically prevents him from narrating its history, its *storia*. In obedience to the pathology of love-malady, submission to such a love results in the impairment of the lover's capacity to discern false semblances from true perceptions. The poet's wound manifests itself as a disruption of the poetic process: "How many times I've started to write verse / To find that pen and hand and intellect / Remain still conquered by the first assault" (*Rvf.* 20, 12–14). In reality the wound has come not from Love, but from within himself, because he has been unable to muster sufficient strength to withstand his assailant (*Rvf.* 2). In *Rvf.* 152, he writes, "Nor can my frail and worn-out virtue stand / Henceforth, so much variety; at once / It burns and ices, reddens and grows pale." As a result, the aesthetic rationale of the text is grounded in a disrupted moral order of which the lover's pathological condition—and the profusion of papers, the "mille carte" to which it gives rise—is merely a symptom. Yet by the very virtue of the opposites it can contain, the work constantly generates alternatives to its own disorder. In *Rvf.* 351, we find that the confusion of the love experience has been reimagined as a process which literally tempers the lover, like a blade first heated and then cooled:

> Those sweet severities and mild reproofs,
> With chaste love filled, and piety as well,
> That gracious scorn which tempered my desires,
> Inflamed and witless (as I'm now aware),
> . . . .
> This sweet variety became the root
> Of my soul's health, which otherwise had failed.
>
> (lines 1–4, 13–14)

The principle of difference which the poet has so rigorously pursued has become the very source out of which his soul repairs itself.

★ ★ ★

In the *Rerum vulgarium fragmenta*'s creation of variety, the lyric genres Petrarch uses—chiefly sonnets and *canzoni*, with a few *ballate* and madrigals—play an important role. The longer *canzoni* (which includes the *sestine*) are offset by sonnets in their hundreds: sonnets alone and sonnets in groups, sonnets linked by rhyme play and sonnets linked by theme, sonnets with important structural functions and sonnets which are mere exercises, sonnets to Laura of course, but sonnets also to friends, patrons, and indeed enemies. The very likeness of this flood of sonnets, one to another, reminds us that *varietas* is paradoxically an aesthetic of similarity, one which depends for its creation of difference on the fact that all these poems resemble each other even when, through glittering displays of the art of inversion, they appear to be contradictory (for example, the case of the two versions of the moment when the poet fell in love, *Rvf.* 2 and *Rvf.* 3). In the *Rerum vulgarium fragmenta* transformation occurs ceaselessly everywhere, as in sonnet after sonnet the iron-clad fourteen-line form requires change to be internalized to the technique and content of the poem itself. And if sonnets at first seem inherently alike, *canzoni* are by definition various. The *canzone* is not a fixed form like the sonnet; it uses a two-part module (the romance *frons* and *sirima*) to build stanzas that vary in length and rhyme scheme from poem to poem. Except in the case of those which are grouped by theme (*Rvf.* 71–73; *Rvf.* 125 and 126), Petrarch's *canzoni* vary greatly in their rhyme schemes. The effect is to provide a field of radically different thematic and formal possibilities against which the fixity of the sonnet is constantly asserting its own reduplicative power. The tensile strength which comes from such interaction is immense.

The final aesthetic effect of the Petrarchan poem, and of the *Rerum vulgarium fragmenta* itself, is that of the weaving of a fabric of great richness and refinement in which many elements play their role: thematic and linguistic allusiveness, verbal music, the presence of other poems—and other poets—as context. It is this weaving which makes possible the coexistence in the collection at one and the same time of the symbols of unity as well as the dissipating forces of disunity. The largest of these symbols is the calendar, which evidently underlies the poet's selection of precisely 366 poems to compose his book. Petrarch's sense of the overall pattern which should govern the *Rerum vulgarium fragmenta* seems to have changed several times during the more than three decades of its compilation; the undivided collection of 1342 is succeeded by the two-part collection initiated in 1349–51 and copied by Boccaccio in the Chigi manuscript. Then, in about 1366, when the copying of MS. VL 3185 began, Petrarch apparently determined that the two parts should make up a calendrical 366 poems, and it was in this form that the collection remained at his death.

The significance of this calendrical pattern, and the strictness with which it was exploited, is a matter of controversy. Thomas P. Roche, Jr. argues its detailed relationship to the Christian year, Wilhelm Pötters sees an intricate mathematical device related to the name of Laura, and F. J. Jones has suggested it is a loosely-knit personal calendar marking some dates important to the poet. Jones, who has carefully investigated Petrarch's system of dating and telling time, points out that "a complete calendrical structure does not emerge until the writing of MS. VL 3195 ... towards the end of the poet's life, and perhaps even then it appears only in a general and schematic form."[29] And any theory which explains the very evident calendrical elements in the *Rerum vulgarium fragmenta* has also to explain their emergence during the evolving manuscript tradition of the work, during what Alfredo Schiaffini (alluding to a phrase of Carducci's) calls the "lavorio della forma" which expresses Petrarch's unalloyed joy in revision.[30] It must also contend with what Petrarch said about the work and its compilation to his correspondents. In the unrevised version of his 1373 letter to Pandolfo Malatesta he complains of the difficulty of finding good binders in Padua; he has sent Pandolfo a copy of the *Rerum vulgarium fragmenta* in two parts, with a "good space" [*"bona spatia"*] left for later additions, in case he should be able to send any.[31] There is just such an "added" fascicle at the end of part one of MS. VL 3195; it contains the magnificent sonnet "O you victorious and triumphal tree" (*Rvf.* 263), the late-achieved "programming" poem which concludes part one of the collection. But it also contains three empty leaves, when a single folded sheet would have been sufficient to hold the additions.[32] The same restless confidence in his poetic fertility is evident in the late annotations (1373–1374) by which the aging poet reordered thirty of the poems at the end of the manuscript on a penitential pattern more appropriate to the conclusion of a life in art.

But though even at the end of his life Petrarch's work on the *Rerum vulgarium fragmenta* was remorselessly subjected to his vision of the disjunctive power of change, at the same time this very vision is made a subject of contemplation: provisional as it is, the arrangement of the poems as it stands frames the poems "in vita"—those represented as written in Laura's lifetime—by two sonnets, that is, by a fixed form; in contrast the poems "in morte" are framed by two *canzoni*, a variable form. This "structural chiasmus" is indescribably ironic, for by its means the fixed form is equated

---

[29] F. F. J. Jones, "Petrarch's Methods of Dating and Time-Telling in Vat. Lat. 3196 and in his Correspondence," *Modern Language Review* 80 (1985): 586–93; I cite p. 593. See also Thomas P. Roche, Jr., "The Calendrical Structure of Petrarch's Canzoniere," *Studies in Philoglogy* 71 (1974): 152–72, and his *Petrarch and the English Sonnet Sequences* (New York: AMS Press, 1989), 1–70; see also Wilhelm Pötters, *Chi era Laura? Strutture linguistiche e matematiche nel "Canzoniere" di Francesco Petrarca* (Bologna: Società editrice il Mulino, 1987).

[30] Alfredo Schiaffini, "Il lavorio della forma in Francesco Petrarca," in his *Momenti di storia della lingua italiana*, 2d ed. (Rome: Editrice Studium, 1953), 67.

[31] The final version of this letter, without the footnote containing this phrase, is *Sen.* 13.11, referred to above. The unrevised version is *Variae* 9, in Francisci Petrarcae, *Epistolae de rebus familiaribus et variae*, ed. Joseph Fracassetti (Florence: Le Monnier, 1859–63), 3:323.

[32] For Petrarch's habit of circulating additions to his works among his friends see Nicolas Mann, "'O Deus, Qualis Epistola!': A New Petrarch Letter," *Italia Medioevale e Umanistica* 17 (1974): 207–43.

with the fallen world of mutability, and the variable form with the freedom of eternal life.[33]

★ ★ ★

At the centre of this web of words is situated the poet himself, the central figure in a mythos of loss and exclusion which by his very eloquence he seeks to ratify and make persuasive. To do so he must become master not of cognition, but of recognition, not of the passage through unknowing to knowledge, but of the sundering of all bonds so that new and more substantial ones can be spun out. Typically, Petrarch envisions this task in terms of a series of oppositions: how, for example, is he to correlate the regenerating solitude he enjoys at Vaucluse with the public obligations of the political counsellor? Is the exclusion of the lover from his lady's grace, so productive of poetic glory, at the same time the vanity of a sinner who may because of his passion be excluded from God's mercy? The contemplation of these alternatives and others like them is what forces the poet into the wanderings in which we find him in *Rvf.* 35, pacing the empty landscape pursued by Love, alone in his search and alone in his will to search. As this suggests, the *Rerum vulgarium fragmenta* presents less a model of Creation, such as Dante had developed in the tripartite structure of the *Commedia*, than a model of the human psyche limited to the perimeters of its own consciousness. The result is an intense evocation of the variability, fragmentation, and privacy of human experience. Petrarch revels in his selfhood. In him the emerging Romance fascination with the individual as subject instantly fuses with a revived Romanism which rejoices in the evocation of individual personality.

In a way, Petrarch is less a poet at work than a text being written by the hand of Love, and his only protection in such a state of vulnerability is to assert the power of his own voice. This assertion, as his other works make clear, is a deeply instinctive one. Petrarch is one of the greatest of all poets of the speaking voice; though in the *Rerum vulgarium fragmenta* we hear one voice alone, it is always engaged in debate, whether with Love as in *Rvf.* 35, or lamenting in a late sonnet (*Rvf.* 315) the lost opportunity for talk with Laura:

> All my green, flow'ring years were passing by;
> Indeed, I felt the fire that burned my heart

---

[33] Christopher Kleinhenz, "Petrarch and the Art of the Sonnet," in *Francis Petrarch, Six Centuries Later*, ed. Aldo Scaglione (Chapel Hill: Department of Romance Languages, Univ. of North Carolina; and Chicago: Newberry Library, 1975), 189–90; also noted from a different perspective by Guglielmo Gorni, "Metamorfosi e redenzione in Petrarca. Il senso della forma Correggio del Canzoniere," *Lettere italiane* 30 (1983): 4.

Grow cool, and I had come to that place where
Life slips away, till at the end it fails.
Already, bit by bit, my precious foe
Began to feel more trust, despite her doubts.
And into playfulness her virtue sweet
Had started to transform my bitter pain.
That time when chastity falls in with Love
Was near, and when together lovers may
Sit down to talk of anything they like.
Death envied me this happy state—that is,
The hope of it—and, like a well-armed foe,
Fell on it as it went along its way.

In his letters, in the pastoral dialogues of the *Bucolicum carmen*, even in *De remediis*, we are made aware of the illusion of speech, created by the immediacy of monologue and dialogue.[34] Thus, insofar as Petrarch commands his authorial role, it is as a voice that speaks, a style achieved, a dramatic image. If the "history of all my martyrdom" referred to in *Rvf.* 127 is to be told, it cannot be in the form of an extended and complete narration, for the voice of the poet—whether the notorious sinner of the opening sonnet, or unregarded prophet, the stance he adopts in "My Italy" (*Rvf.* 128)—has become the single stable point around which the concept of a text can consolidate. It is only when he turns to the Virgin in the last *canzone*—that "window of heaven" who is both earthly mother of God and transfigured woman—that he permits these barriers, insofar as they ever do, to collapse. The status of the *Rerum vulgarium fragmenta* as personal testimony, and its rhetorical stress on *pronuntiatio*, the illusion of speech, thus become of first importance. As Dante had done before him, Petrarch speaks *in propria persona*, but this time he has stripped himself of every device which validates that utterance except his personal authority and the eloquence with which he speaks.

When questioned by others, Petrarch insisted that Laura was a real woman and not a philosophical abstraction, but this is actually an aspect of his insistence on the primacy of his own world and his response to it. Thus, when he writes in his manuscript of Virgil the note on Laura's death, it is less her death we confront than his own experience of that death, and when he refers dryly in a letter to one of the Colonna to "that other fiction of mine, Augustine," (*Familiares* 2.9) his sarcasm is not di-

---

[34] On Petrarch's exploitation of voice, see Aldo Bernardo, "Dramatic Dialogue in the Prose Letters of Petrarch," *Symposium* 5 (1951): 302–316, and "Dramatic Dialogue and Monologue in Petrarch's Works—II," *Symposium* 7 (1953): 92–119.

rected at confirming the existence of Augustine (which is beyond doubt), but at the validity of the experience of that Petrarch who now imagines the theologian engaging in the debate of the *Secretum*. The result is to set up a plangent, and for later critics deeply problematic, interplay between the artful weaving of the poems and the historicity of the man who utters them. Despite the way each poem seeks the impersonal abstraction of ideal and timeless form, the ground of each is a cognitive process completely rooted in the individual, the particular, the natural.

Thus when in the *Rerum vulgarium fragmenta* we witness the green and gold of the youthful poems give way to the gray-haired manner, the "stile canuto" of old age, it is the poet's personal sense of loss which remains the central experience of the work as a whole even when, as a result of age and grief, loss itself ought to have been conquered completely. In *Rvf*. 315, "All my green, flow'ring years," and other poems like it, Petrarch drives himself to recreate in age the now irretrievable past, to imagine the conversations he and Laura might once have had, and the riverbank still haunted by her memory. It is this persistent recreation of a threshold before which the poet must wait, yet which he always hopes to cross, which nurtures the ever exfoliating forms of the work itself, and constitutes the mythopoeic ground of its unity.

From an early date, Petrarch's central image had been the antique one of Apollo's pursuit of the laurel, but this classical myth of flight and transformation was permeated with the Biblical interplay between scattering and gathering which operates on the one hand to disperse the enemies of the Lord and, on the other, to signify the miraculous multiplication of one into many by which He fed the multitude. If the "scattered rhymes" of the opening poem (the "fragmenta" of its Latin title) evoke Christ's admonition in John 6:12: "Gather up the fragments that remain, that nothing be lost," the poems of the collection are thus at one and the same time *disjecta membra* and sustaining bread, and insofar as they have been gathered up from the Lord's feast, they call to mind St. Augustine's conception of the preacher as one who feeds the multitude by expounding the Scripture.[35] It is in this spirit that in the *De doctrina Christiana* Augustine writes of the debasement of one language into many marked by the building of the tower of Babel:

> Thus it happened that even the Sacred Scripture, by which so many maladies of the human will are cured, was set forth in one language, but so that it could be spread

---

[35] Peter Brown, *Augustine of Hippo* (Berkeley: Univ. of California Press, 1967), 252, citing St. Augustine, *Serm.* 95.1.

conveniently through all the world it was scattered far and wide in the various languages of translators that it might be known for the salvation of peoples who desired to find in it nothing more than the thoughts and desires of those who wrote it and through these the will of God, according to which we believe those writers spoke.[36]

Here in the face of time, the decay of language, and the impercipience of the reader, is asserted nonetheless that power of speech which triumphs even as it is dispersed into the experience of humankind.

★ ★ ★

Petrarch has sometimes been called the first modern man, and it is true, as Thomas M. Greene writes, that he "took more or less alone the step an archaic society must take to reach maturity; he recognized *the possibility of a cultural alternative.*"[37] It was Petrarch's thoughtfulness about the process of composition, a mental set not unlike his discrimination as a scholar, which revealed to him a diversity of options not always evident to his contemporaries, and which in turn proclaimed—by his very ability to choose among them—his authority as a master-poet. His avoidance of the linearity of romance narrative, his use of classical allusions ranging widely beyond the Ovid who had served as schoolmaster to his medieval predecessors, his capacity for structural innovation, and the looseness and ease with which he could work within an apparently closed schema all constitute a rich commentary on the tradition of the lyric book as he received it, and the shaping forces of that book as he transmitted it to the generations of "Petrarchists" who, over the next two centuries, were to imitate his example.

But the Renaissance reputation of Petrarch's *Rerum vulgarium fragmenta* as the archetype of the private lyric collection has other sources as well, among them its powerful fiction of solitary subjectivity. When Petrarch makes his collection a mimesis of his own imperfect humanity, he presents us with a Promethean act: to the evolving concept of the poet as text, he assimilates something which lesser poets tended to exclude from the courtly idea of perfect service: the possibility of rebellion. When the "Canzoniere" or the book of songs he fashioned renounces the reassuring medieval framework of analogy for a more perilous task, it opens the poet fully to the significance of his mortal experience, and to all the implications of his

---

[36] *De doctrina Christiana* 2.5.6 (*On Christian Doctrine*, trans. D. W. Robertson Jr. (Indianapolis: Bobbs-Merrill, 1958), 35.

[37] Thomas M. Greene, *The Light in Troy: Imitation and Discovery in Renaissance Poetry* (New Haven: Yale Univ. Press, 1982), 90.

own humanity; the collection of fragments welcomes us into the concreteness of the private world and gives it explanatory power.

Yet what made it possible for Petrarch to dominate the example of his own predecessors in the history of the poet's book was, paradoxically, his ability to connect rather than to sever. In the possibilities of *rime sparse* he sensed an instrument for exploring the metaphysical problematics of his age, the conflict between a Christian theology at its summit of perfection and an emerging vision of nature which challenged that theology's relevance. Such a work facilitates at one and the same time the recognition of completeness and loss, cosmic order, and natural *varietas*. The form of the *Rerum vulgarium fragmenta* is thus heuristic in character, provoking for later poets—as it did for Petrarch—the further investigation of meaning, yet at the same time affording points of rest and local possibilities of closure. The collection provides both a performative model and a technique which others can use to undergo Petrarch's experience. Between the opposed terms of closed valley and tumultuous city, the timeless solitude of the contemplative and the history-bound nature of civic duty, the desire for spiritual health and the malady of physical passion, Petrarch's poetics establishes a place of transition. This place is occupied by the solitary poet-prophet, whose desire to possess his "other" breaks through the barriers between different social, psychological, and metaphysical planes to insist, if not on the achievement of their union, at least on its possibility.

PETRARCH'S SONGBOOK

Rerum Vulgarium Fragmenta

A VERSE TRANSLATION

by

James Wyatt Cook

1

Voi ch'ascoltate in rime sparse il suono
di quei sospiri ond'io nudriva 'l core
in sul mio primo giovenile errore
quand'era in parte altr'uom da quel ch'i' sono,

del vario stile in ch'io piango et ragiono   5
fra le vane speranze e 'l van dolore,
ove sia chi per prova intenda amore,
spero trovar pietà, nonché perdono.

Ma ben veggio or sí come al popol tutto
favola fui gran tempo, onde sovente   10
di me medesmo meco mi vergogno;

et del mio vaneggiar vergogna è 'l frutto,
e 'l pentersi, e 'l conoscer chiaramente
che quanto piace al mondo è breve sogno.

2

Per fare una leggiadra sua vendetta,
et punire in un dí ben mille offese,
celatamente Amor l'arco riprese,
come huom ch'a nocer luogo et tempo aspetta.

Era la mia virtute al cor ristretta   5
per far ivi et negli occhi sue difese,
quando, 'l colpo mortal là giú discese
ove solea spuntarsi ogni saetta.

Però, turbata nel primiero assalto,
non ebbe tanto né vigor né spazio   10
che potesse al bisogno prender l'arme,

overo al poggio faticoso et alto
ritrarmi accortamente da lo strazio
del quale oggi vorrebbe, et non pò, aitarme.

3

Era il giorno ch'al sol si scoloraro
per la pietà del suo factore i rai,
quando i' fui preso, et non me ne guardai,
ché i be' vostr'occhi, donna, mi legaro.

Tempo non mi parea da far riparo   5
contra colpi d'Amor: però m'andai
secur, senza sospetto; onde i miei guai
nel commune dolor s'incominciaro.

Trovommi Amor del tutto disarmato
et aperta la via per gli occhi al core,   10
che di lagrime son fatti uscio et varco:

1

O you that hear in scattered rhymes the sound°
Of those sighs that I used to feed my heart
In my first youthful error, when I was
In part a different man than now I am,
    Whoever knows of love by trial, from him   5
If pardon none, compassion then I hope
To find, for this the various style in which
I weep, debate these vain hopes, this vain woe.
    Now I see clearly how to everyone
I long have been a fable, and of that   10
Deep in myself I often am ashamed;
    Shame is the fruit of my delirium;
As is repentance, and the knowledge sure
That worldly joy is but a passing dream.

2

To make a graceful one his fit revenge°
And punish in one day a thousand crimes,
Love stealthily took up his bow again°
Like one who waits his time and place to harm.
    My Virtue massed her forces in my heart°   5
To raise defences there, and in my eyes,
When suddenly the mortal arrow fell
Where she had always blunted every shot;
    Plunged into turmoil at this first assault
She had not time nor strength enough to seize   10
Weapons with power sufficient to her need,
    Nor to ascend her high and weary hill°
And wisely lead me out of that affray
Whence she today would save me, but cannot.

3

It was the day on which the sun's rays paled°
At their Creator's passion when, off guard,
All unaware, I taken was and bound,
Tied fast, my lady, by your lovely eyes.
    No need in such a season, so I thought,   5
To frame defence against Love's battery;
Thus, unsuspecting and secure I walked,
When 'midst the common sorrow came my woe.
    Love found me out, defenceless, all disarmed,
Found open wide the way from eyes to heart   10
Through gaps and crazings channeled there by tears;

però al mio parer non li fu honore
ferir me de saetta in quello stato,
a voi armata non mostrar pur l'arco.

4

Que' ch'infinita providentia et arte
mostrò nel suo mirabil magistero,
che crïò questo et quell'altro hemispero,
et mansüeto piú Giove che Marte,
    vegnendo in terra a 'lluminar le carte   5
ch'avean molt'anni già celato il vero,
tolse Giovanni da la rete et Piero,
et nel regno del ciel fece lor parte.
    Di sé nascendo a Roma non fe' gratia,
a Giudea sí, tanto sovr'ogni stato   10
humiltate exaltar sempre gli piacque;
    ed or di picciol borgo un sol n'à dato,
tal che natura e 'l luogo si ringratia
onde sí bella donna al mondo nacque.

5

Quando io movo i sospiri a chiamar voi,
e 'l nome che nel cor mi scrisse Amore,
LAUdando s'incomincia udir di fore
il suon de' primi dolci accenti suoi.
    Vostro stato REal, che 'ncontro poi,   5
raddoppia a l'alta impresa il mio valore;
ma: TAci, grida il fin, ché farle honore
è d'altri homeri soma che da' tuoi.
    Cosí LAUdare et REverire insegna
la voce stessa, pur ch'altri vi chiami,   10
o d'ogni reverenza et d'onor degna:
    se non che forse Apollo si disdegna
ch'a parlar de' suoi sempre verdi rami
lingua morTAl presumptüosa vegna.

6

Sí travïato è 'l folle mi' desio
a seguitar costei che 'n fuga è volta,
et de' lacci d'Amor leggiera et sciolta
vola dinanzi al lento correr mio,
    che quanto richiamando piú l'envio   5
per la secura strada, men m'ascolta:
né mi vale spronarlo, o dargli volta,

No honor, though, to him, or so it seems,
To wound me in that state with passion's dart
And never show the bow to you, all armed.

4

He who with infinite providence and art
Revealed the wondrous mastery of his work,
Who shaped this, and that other hemisphere
And framed more gentle Jupiter than Mars,°
    To earth came, to illuminate the leaves°   5
That had for ages past concealed the truth,
And John and Peter from their nets he took
And made them citizens of heaven's realm.
    Not on proud Rome but on Judea, God
Pleased ever to exalt humility,   10
The grace of his nativity conferred,
    And now a small town gives to us a sun,°
And one that blesses nature and the place
That brought so fair a lady forth on earth.

5°

When I breathe forth my sighs to call on you,
And sound that name which Love wrote in my heart,
Outside, one starts to hear the notes of LAUd,
First accents of a swelling music sweet.
    Your REgal state which I encounter then,   5
Doubles my prowess for the lofty task;
But "sTAy," the end cries out, "to honor her
Must burden shoulders worthier than yours."
    Thus does the word itself instruct those who
Invoke your name, to LAUd and to REvere,   10
O worthy of all reverence, honor's prize;
    Only Apollo himself, perhaps, disdains
Whatever rash, presuming, morTAl tongue
Bespeaks his laurel branches, always green.°

6

So wayward and so crazed is my desire°
That he pursues a girl who's turned to flee,
Who, lightly slipping through Love's snares, flies off
Before the labored slowness of my race.
    The more I call him back, direct his course   5
To the safe road, the less he pays me heed.
No use to spur him or to turn him round;

ch'Amor per sua natura il fa restio.

    Et poi che 'l fren per forza a sé raccoglie,
i' mi rimango in signoria di lui,   10
che mal mio grado a morte mi trasporta:

    sol per venir al lauro onde si coglie
acerbo frutto, che le piaghe altrui
gustando afflige piú che non conforta.

7

    La gola e 'l somno et l'otïose piume
ànno del mondo ogni vertú sbandita,
ond'è dal corso suo quasi smarrita
nostra natura vinta dal costume;

    et è sí spento ogni benigno lume   5
del ciel, per cui s'informa humana vita,
che per cosa mirabile s'addita
chi vòl far d'Elicona nascer fiume.

    Qual vaghezza di lauro, qual di mirto?
Povera et nuda vai philosophia,   10
dice la turba al vil guadagno intesa.

    Pochi compagni avrai per l'altra via:
tanto ti prego piú, gentile spirto,
non lassar la magnanima tua impresa.

8

    A pie' de' colli ove la bella vesta
prese de le terrene membra pria
la donna che colui ch'a te ne 'nvia
spesso dal somno lagrimando desta,

    libere in pace passavam per questa   5
vita mortal, ch'ogni animal desia,
senza sospetto di trovar fra via
cosa ch'al nostr'andar fosse molesta.

    Ma del misero stato ove noi semo
condotte da la vita altra serena   10
un sol conforto, et de la morte, avemo:

    che vendetta è di lui ch'a ciò ne mena,
lo qual in forza altrui presso a l'extremo
riman legato con maggior catena.

9

    Quando 'l pianeta che distingue l'ore
ad albergar col Tauro si ritorna,
cade vertú da l'infiammate corna

Love's nature makes him skittish and perverse.
　　Then when he takes the bit by force himself,
It's he who has the lordship over me;　　　　　　　　10
Spiting my will, he carries me towards death,
　　Only to bring me to the laurel, where
One picks a bitter fruit, the taste of which
Brings greater pain than comfort to one's wounds.

7

　　Gorging and sleep and lazy feather-beds
Have banished every virtue from the world,
And thus our nature, almost overcome
By habit, from its course is led astray.
　　And all the heavens' good influence is spent　　　5
By which a human life could shape itself,
For as a prodigy folk point to one
Who bids a stream spring forth from Helicon.
　　What charm has laurel? What has myrtle now?
"Naked and poor go forth, Philosophy,"　　　　　　10
The rabble cries, intent on paltry gain.
　　Few friends will go that other way with you;
So much the more I pray you, gentle soul,°
Do not forsake your noble enterprise.

8

　　Below the hills where first that lovely one
Put on at birth the garb of earthly limbs—
That lady who so often wakens him
In tears, him who despatches us to you,°
　　We led this mortal life at peace, and free,　　　　5
As every animal desires to do,
Without suspicion that along the way
Something might harm us as we travelled on.
　　But in this wretched plight in which we wait
Since taken from that other life serene,　　　　　　10
We have one solace as we face our death:
　　For vengeance visits him who brought us low.
That one, snared by another's power, lies bound
With greater chains and in extremity.

9

　　When the planet that distinguishes the hours
Returns to house itself in Taurus' sign,
A virtue drops down from his flaming horn

che veste il mondo di novel colore;
et non pur quel che s'apre a noi di fore,   5
le rive e i colli, di fioretti adorna,
ma dentro dove già mai non s'aggiorna
gravido fa di sé il terrestro humore,
    onde tal fructo et simile si colga:
così costei, ch'è tra le donne un sole,   10
in me movendo de' begli occhi i rai
    crïa d'amor penseri, atti et parole;
ma come ch'ella gli governi o volga,
primavera per me pur non è mai.

10

    Glorïosa columna in cui s'appoggia
nostra speranza e 'l gran nome latino,
ch'ancor non torse del vero camino
l'ira di Giove per ventosa pioggia,
    qui non palazzi, non theatro o loggia,   5
ma 'n lor vece un abete, un faggio, un pino,
tra l'erba verde e 'l bel monte vicino,
onde si scende poetando et poggia,
    levan di terra al ciel nostr'intellecto;
e 'l rosigniuol che dolcemente all'ombra   10
tutte le notti si lamenta et piagne,
    d'amorosi penseri il cor ne 'ngombra:
ma tanto ben sol tronchi, et fai imperfecto,
tu che da noi, signor mio, ti scompagne.

11

    Lassare il velo o per sole o per ombra,
donna, non vi vid'io
poi che in me conosceste il gran desio
ch'ogni altra voglia d'entr'al cor mi sgombra.
    Mentr'io portava i be' pensier' celati,   5
ch'ànno la mente desïando morta,
vidivi di pietate ornare il volto;
ma poi ch'Amor di me vi fece accorta,
fuor i biondi capelli allor velati,
et l'amoroso sguardo in sé raccolto.   10
Quel ch'i' piú desïava in voi m'è tolto:
sí mi governa il velo
che per mia morte, et al caldo et al gielo,
de' be' vostr'occhi il dolce lume adombra.

That dresses all the world in freshened hues—°
    Not just those parts that open forth to us,   5
The shores and hills adorned with flowerets—
But deep within where day's light never breaks,
He makes the earthly humor pregnant too,
    Brings forth for harvest this fruit and its kind;°
Thus she who among women is a sun,   10
Creates the thoughts and deeds and words of love,
    Stirring me with the rays from her fair eyes;
But any way she guides or governs them
For me, no matter, spring will never come.

10

    O Column glorious, on whom depends°
Our hope, and that great Latin name which Jove's
Own wrath cannot with blowing tempest yet
Make deviate from its appointed path:
    Here stands no palace, theater, arcade,   5
But in their place a fir, a beech, a pine;
Amidst green grass and, nearby, pleasant hills
Where one descends and climbs and shapes one's verse.
    Our intellects rise up from earth to heaven;
The nightingale that sweetly in the shade   10
Each eve laments and weeps, enraptures all
    Our hearts with amorous thoughts; but you alone
Break off such happiness, and leave it flawed,
You who absent yourself, my lord, from us.

11

    I have not seen you draw aside your veil,
Lady—not for sun or shade—
Since first you recognized the grand desire
That drives all other longings from my heart.
    While I bore secretly those lovely thoughts   5
That have decreed the death of sanity,
I saw compassion grace your countenance,
But from the time Love made you notice me,
Your golden hair has been forever veiled,
Your amorous glance withdrawn into itself;   10
What I most longed for in you I'm denied;
So that veil governs me
Which by my death—in cold as well as heat—
Will darken the sweet light of your fair eyes.°

12

Se la mia vita da l'aspro tormento
si può tanto schermire, et dagli affanni,
ch'i' veggia per vertú degli ultimi anni,
donna, de' be' vostr'occhi il lume spento,

e i cape' d'oro fin farsi d'argento,   5
et lassar le ghirlande e i verdi panni,
e 'l viso scolorir che ne' miei danni
a·llamentar mi fa pauroso et lento:

pur mi darà tanta baldanza Amore
chi'i' vi discovrirò de' mei martiri   10
qua' sono stati gli anni, e i giorni et l'ore;

et se 'l tempo è contrario ai be' desiri,
non fia ch'almen non giunga al mio dolore
alcun soccorso di tardi sospiri.

13

Quando fra l'altre donne ad ora ad ora
Amor vien nel bel viso di costei,
quanto ciascuna è men bella di lei
tanto cresce 'l desio che m'innamora.

I' benedico il loco e 'l tempo et l'ora   5
che sí alto miraron gli occhi mei,
et dico: Anima, assai ringratiar dêi
che fosti a tanto honor degnata allora.

Da lei ti vèn l'amoroso pensero,
che mentre 'l segui al sommo ben t'invia,   10
pocho prezando quel ch'ogni huom desia;

da lei vien l'animosa leggiadria
ch'al ciel ti scorge per destro sentero,
sí ch'i' vo già de la speranza altero.

14

Occhi miei lassi, mentre ch'io vi giro
nel bel viso di quella che v'à morti,
pregovi siate accorti,
ché già vi sfida Amore, ond'io sospiro.

Morte pò chiuder sola a' miei penseri   5
l'amoroso camin che gli conduce
al dolce porto de la lor salute;
ma puossi a voi celar la vostra luce
per meno obgetto, perché meno interi
siete formati, et di minor virtute.   10
Però, dolenti, anzi che sian venute

12

If long enough my life can hold at bay
This torment harsh, my lady, and these pangs
So that I see the light of your bright eyes
Grow dim because of your declining years,
    See turn to silver all your fine gold hair,   5
See laid aside your garlands and fresh clothes,
See color fading from that face which makes
Me slow and fearful to lament my griefs,
    Then, Love will give me dauntlessness so great
That I'll unfold my sufferings to you—   10
Woes that have shaped my years, and days, and hours;
    If time to lovely wishes proves adverse,
At least it will not be that, in my woe,
Belated sighs won't bring me some relief.

13

    When 'midst the other ladies now and then
Love visits that one's lovely countenance,
As much as each is far less fair than she,
This passion grows that makes me fall in love.
    I gladly bless the place, the time, the hour   5
My eyes raised to those heights their wondering gaze
And say: "Soul, give most fervent thanks that you
Were then deemed worthy of such honor great.
    "From her, there comes to you that loving thought
Which, while you follow, leads to highest good—   10
To prize but little what each man desires;
    "And from her springs that valiant grace which will
Mark out for you the proper path to heaven,"
Thus I go forth already, high in hope.

14

    My weary eyes, while I cast you upon
The fair face of that one who murdered you,
I pray you to be careful, for
Already Love betrays you, whence I sigh.
    That amorous way by Death alone can be   5
Closed to my thoughts—that way which takes them to
The harbor sweet where their well-being waits.
But eyes, a lesser object can conceal
Your light from you because you have been formed
A lesser whole with strength inadequate.   10
Therefore, you're filled with grief before the hour

l'ore del pianto, che son già vicine,
prendete or a la fine
breve conforto a sí lungo martiro.

15

Io mi rivolgo indietro a ciascun passo
col corpo stancho ch'a gran pena porto,
et prendo allor del vostr'aere conforto
che 'l fa gir oltra dicendo: Oimè lasso!
Poi ripensando al dolce ben ch'io lasso,   5
al camin lungo et al mio viver corto,
fermo le piante sbigottito et smorto,
et gli occhi in terra lagrimando abasso.
Talor m'assale in mezzo a' tristi pianti
un dubbio: come posson queste membra   10
da lo spirito lor viver lontane?
Ma rispondemi Amor: Non ti rimembra
che questo è privilegio degli amanti,
sciolti da tutte qualitati humane?

16

Movesi il vecchierel canuto et bianco
del dolce loco ov'à sua età fornita
et da la famigliuola sbigottita
che vede il caro padre venir manco;
indi trahendo poi l'antiquo fianco   5
per l'extreme giornate di sua vita,
quanto piú pò, col buon voler s'aita,
rotto dagli anni, et dal camino stanco;
et viene a Roma, seguendo 'l desio,
per mirar la sembianza di colui   10
ch'ancor lassú nel ciel vedere spera:
cosí, lasso, talor vo cerchand'io,
donna, quanto è possibile, in altrui
la disïata vostra forma vera.

17

Piovonmi amare lagrime dal viso
con un vento angoscioso di sospiri,
quando in voi adiven che gli occhi giri
per cui sola dal mondo i' son diviso.
Vero è che 'l dolce mansüeto riso   5
pur acqueta gli ardenti miei desiri,
et mi sottragge al foco de' martiri,

For tears has come—and it is near at hand—
Take now in your extremity
Brief comfort in such lengthy suffering.°

15

At every step I turn around again,
Bearing my worn-out body with great pain;
But I take solace from your ambient glow
That makes me press on crying, "Woe, alas."
     Recalling then the blessings sweet I left,   5
The lengthy road, and my own life so brief,
I halt my feeble and discouraged steps,
And bend my weeping eyes upon the earth.
     At times a single doubt besieges me
Amidst my woeful plaints: how can these limbs   10
So distant from their spirit be alive?
     Love answers, though, "Do you not recollect
That this a privilege of lovers is,
Set free from all their human attributes?"

16

The good old man, gray-haired and pale, stirs forth
From that sweet place where he has passed his life,
And from his little family, dismayed
To see their father dear diminishing;
     From there, upon the final journey of   5
His life, dragging along his ancient flanks
As he is able, by good will helped on,
Ravaged with years, and wearied by the road,
     He comes to Rome, pursuing his desire
To gaze on the true likeness of that One°   10
Whom yet he hopes to see in heaven above;
     Just so, worn out, I wander questing too
Seeking in others, if it's possible,
Lady, your true form, yearned-for and desired.

17

What bitter tears fall raining from my face
Whenever, with an anguished storm of sighs,
It happens that I turn my eyes on you
By whom, alone, I'm cut off from the world.
     Your sweet and gentle laughter, it is true,   5
At last abates the flames of my desire
And from the martyr's fire delivers me,

mentr'io son mirarvi intento et fiso.

    Ma gli spiriti miei s'aghiaccian poi
ch'i' veggio al departir gli atti soavi
torcer da me le mie fatali stelle.

    Largata alfin co l'amorose chiavi
l'anima esce del cor per seguir voi;
et con molto pensiero indi si svelle.

18

    Quand'io son tutto vòlto in quella parte
ove 'l bel viso di mandonna luce,
et m'è rimasa nel pensier la luce
che m'arde et strugge dentro a parte a parte,

    i' che temo del cor che mi si parte,
et veggio presso il fin de la mia luce,
vommene in guisa d'orbo, senza luce,
che non sa ove si vada et pur si parte.

    Cosí davanti ai colpi de la morte
fuggo: ma non sí ratto che 'l desio
meco non venga come venir sòle.

    Tacito vo, ché le parole morte
farian pianger la gente; et i' desio
che le lagrime mie si spargan sole.

19

    Son animali al mondo de sí altera
vista che 'ncontra 'l sol pur si difende;
altri, però che 'l gran lume gli offende,
non escon fuor se non verso la sera;

    et altri, col desio folle che spera
gioir forse nel foco, perché splende,
provan l'altra vertú, quella che 'ncende:
lasso, e 'l mio loco è 'n questa ultima schera.

    Ch'i' non son forte ad aspectar la luce
di questa donna, et non so fare schermi
di luoghi tenebrosi, o d'ore tarde:

    però con gli occhi lagrimosi e 'nfermi
mio destino a vederla mi conduce;
et so ben ch'i' vo dietro a quel che m'arde.

20

    Vergognando talor ch'ancor si taccia,
donna, per me vostra bellezza in rima,
ricorro al tempo ch'i' vi vidi prima,

While earnestly on you I fix my gaze.
    But then my spirits are transformed to ice,
For, when we part, I see those gentle deeds   10
All wrested from me by my fatal stars.
    With amorous keys released at length, my soul
From my heart issues forth to follow you,
And with great trouble is it plucked from there.

18

    When I am wholly oriented toward
That region where my lady's fair face shines,
And in my thought her light remains behind
To burn me and consume me piece by piece,
    I fear then for my heart, which breaks in two,   5
And see at hand the end of my own light,
And start forth like one blind, without a lamp,
Who knows not where he goes yet still sets out.
    Thus I flee on before the blows of death,
But not so quickly that desire does not   10
Companion me, as it is wont to do.
    In silence I pass by, for my dead words
Will make the people weep, and I desire
That only tears of mine be shed for her.

19

    The world has creatures with such lofty sight
That it holds steady though it braves the sun;°
Some others, though, whom that great light offends,
Do not, until the dusk comes, venture forth.
    Still others, maddened by desire, who hope   5
Perhaps to joy in fire because it shines—
They prove its other power, that which burns;
Alas, my place is in the latter rank.
    I have no strength to look upon the light
This lady sheds, nor can I shield myself   10
In sombre places or in hours late;
    Yet nonetheless, with weeping eyes infirm
I'm led by destiny to look on her,
And well I know, I follow to be burned.

20

    Ashamed sometimes that I keep silent still
About your beauty, Lady, in my rhyme,
I call to mind the time I saw you first,

tal che null'altra fia mai che mi piaccia.

    Ma trovo peso non da le mie braccia,   5
né ovra da polir colla mia lima:
però l'ingegno che sua forza extima
ne l'operation tutto s'agghiaccia.

    Piú volte già per dir le labbra apersi,
poi rimase la voce in mezzo 'l pecto: 10
ma qual sòn poria mai salir tant'alto?

    Piú volte incominciai di scriver versi:
ma la penna et la mano et l'intellecto
rimaser vinti nel primier assalto.

21

    Mille fïate, o dolce mia guerrera,
per aver co' begli occhi vostri pace
v'aggio proferto il cor; mâ voi non piace
mirar sí basso colla mente altera.

    Et se di lui fors'altra donna spera,   5
vive in speranza debile et fallace:
mio, perché sdegno ciò ch'a voi dispiace,
esser non può già mai cosí com'era.

    Or s'io lo scaccio, et e' non trova in voi
ne l'exilio infelice alcun soccorso,   10
né sa star sol, né gire ov'altri il chiama,

    poria smarrire il suo natural corso:
che grave colpa fia d'ambeduo noi,
et tanto piú de voi, quanto piú v'ama.

22

    A qualunque animale alberga in terra,
se non se alquanti ch'ànno in odio il sole,
tempo da travagliare è quanto è 'l giorno;
ma poi che 'l ciel accende le sue stelle,
qual torna a casa et qual s'anida in selva   5
per aver posa almeno infin a l'alba.

    Et io, da che comincia la bella alba
a scuoter l'ombra intorno de la terra
svegliando gli animali in ogni selva,
non ò mai triegua di sospir' col sole;   10
poi quand'io veggio fiammeggiar le stelle
vo lagrimando, et disïando il giorno.

    Quando la sera scaccia il chiaro giorno,
et le tenebre nostre altrui fanno alba,
miro pensoso le crudeli stelle,   15

So fair no other ever pleases me.
    But neither weight that's suited to my strength   5
Nor work for my file's polishing I find;
And so creative skill that knows its power
Remains in this pursuit all frozen fast.
    How often when I part my lips to speak,
My voice remains in silence in my breast—   10
What sound, indeed, could ever climb so high?
    How many times I've started to write verse
To find that pen and hand and intellect
Remain still vanquished by the first assault.

21

    A thousand times, O my sweet enemy,
To treat with your fair eyes for armistice
I've proferred you my Heart; but you despise
With your proud mind to cast your gaze so low;
    And should some other lady hope for him°   5
She lives in aspiration weak and vain;
Because I scorn all that displeases you,
My Heart can never be, as once, my own.
    Thus, if I banish him, and he find not
In you, in his sad exile, some relief,   10
And cannot learn to live alone or go
    Where others call, he'll miss his natural course.
For us, what a grave error that will be,
And greater far for you, whom he loves more.

22

    Among such creatures as dwell on this earth,
Except for all those who despise the sun,
For most, the time of travail is the day;
But then, when heaven sets alight its stars,
Some turn for home, and some nest in the woods,   5
To have at least some rest before the dawn.
    And I—the instant that the lovely dawn
Dispels the shadows that enfold the earth,
Awakening the beasts in every woods—
From sighing find no respite with the sun;   10
When next I see appear the blazing stars,
In tears I wander, wishing for the day.
    And when the evening drives away clear day
And makes our darkness from the others' dawn,
I gaze reflectively on those cruel stars   15

che m'ànno facto di sensibil terra;
et maledico il dí ch'i' vidi 'l sole,
che mi fa in vista un huom nudrito in selva.

Non credo che pascesse mai per selva
sí aspra fera, o di nocte o di giorno,   20
come costei ch'i' piango a l'ombra e al sole;
et non mi stancha primo sonno od alba:
ché, bench'i' sia mortal corpo di terra,
lo mio fermo desir vien da le stelle.

Prima ch'i' torni a voi, lucenti stelle,   25
o tomi giú ne l'amorosa selva,
lassando il corpo che fia trita terra,
vedess'io in lei pietà, che 'n un sol giorno
può ristorar molt'anni, e 'nanzi l'alba
puommi arichir dal tramontar del sole.   30

Con lei foss'io da che si parte il sole,
et non ci vedess'altri che le stelle,
sol una nocte, et mai non fosse l'alba;
et non se transformasse in verde selva
per uscirmi di braccia, come il giorno   35
ch'Apollo la seguia qua giú per terra.

Ma io sarò sotterra in secca selva
e 'l giorno andrà pien di minute stelle
prima ch'a sí dolce alba arrivi il sole.

23

Nel dolce tempo de la prima etade,
che nascer vide et anchor quasi in herba
la fera voglia che per mio mal crebbe,
perché cantando il duol si disacerba,
canterò com'io vissi in libertade,   5
mentre Amor nel mio albergo a sdegno s'ebbe.
Poi seguirò sí come a lui ne 'ncrebbe
troppo altamente, e che di ciò m'avenne,
di ch'io son facto a molta gente exempio:
benché 'l mio duro scempio   10
sia scripto altrove, sí che mille penne
ne son già stanche, et quasi in ogni valle
rimbombi il suon de' miei gravi sospiri,
ch'aquistan fede a la penosa vita.
E se qui la memoria non m'aita   15
come suol fare, iscúsilla i martiri,
et un penser che solo angoscia dàlle,
tal ch'ad ogni altro fa voltar le spalle,

That shaped and fashioned me from sentient earth.
And curse the day when first I saw the sun
That makes me seem a savage in the woods.

    I'll never think that, nurtured by the woods
As harsh a creature could be, night or day,   20
As she for whom I weep in shade and sun,
Nor staunch my tears with first sleep or at dawn,
Thus, though I be the mortal flesh of earth,
My love unchanging takes life from the stars.

    Ere I return to you, O shining stars,   25
Or tumble down amidst the amorous woods,
And leave behind this flesh, this crumbling earth,
I would see mercy in her: Just one day
Could give back many years and, toward the dawn,
Could make me happy at the fading sun.   30

    Oh, might I be with her from set of sun
And let no others see us but the stars—
One night alone: And never come the dawn,
Nor let her be transformed into green woods
To issue from my arms as on that day   35
Apollo gave her chase here on the earth.

    But under earth I'll be in withered woods,
And day will pass by filled with little stars
Before, on that sweet dawn, forth shines the sun.°

23

    In the sweet season of my early youth
That saw break forth, almost in grasstime still,°
The passion wild that grew into my bane—
Because my singing sweetens bitter grief,
I'll sing how once I lived in liberty   5
While in my dwelling place Love was disdained.
Next I shall tell how scorn vexed Love too sorely;
Recount, in turn, what chance befell and why,
How I was made a warning to the world.
Although elsewhere my torture   10
Cruel is penned—indeed, it's wearied now
A thousand quills—in almost every vale
The sound of my grave sighs reverberates
And testifies my life is full of pain.
And if my memory fails to serve me here   15
As well as once it used to do, let my
Woes pardon that, and one thought that alone
So grieves it that I'm made to turn my back

e mi face oblïar me stesso a forza:
ché tèn di me quel d'entro, et io la scorza.   20
    I' dico che dal dí che 'l primo assalto
mi diede Amor, molt'anni eran passati,
sí ch'io cangiava il giovenil aspetto;
e d'intorno al mio cor pensier' gelati
facto avean quasi adamantino smalto   25
ch'allentar non lassava il duro affetto.
Lagrima anchor non mi bagnava il petto
né rompea il sonno, et quel che in me non era,
mi pareva un miracolo in altrui.
Lasso, che son! che fui!   30
La vita el fin, e 'l dí loda la sera.
Ché sentendo il crudel di ch'io ragiono
infin allor percossa di suo strale
non essermi passato oltra la gonna,
prese in sua scorta una possente donna,   35
ver' cui poco già mai mi valse o vale
ingegno, o forza, o dimandar perdono;
e i duo mi trasformaro in quel ch'i' sono,
facendomi d'uom vivo un lauro verde,
che per fredda stagion foglia non perde.   40
    Qual mi fec'io quando primer m'accorsi
de la trasfigurata mia persona,
e i capei vidi far di quella fronde
di che sperato avea già lor corona,
e i piedi in ch'io mi stetti, et mossi, et corsi,   45
com'ogni membro a l'anima risponde,
diventar due radici sovra l'onde
non di Peneo, ma d'un piú altero fiume,
e 'n duo rami mutarsi ambe le braccia!
Né meno anchor m'agghiaccia   50
l'esser coverto poi di bianche piume
allor che folminato et morto giacque
il mio sperar che tropp'alto montava:
ché perch'io non sapea dove né quando
me 'l ritrovasse, solo lagrimando   55
là 've tolto mi fu, dí e nocte andava,
ricercando dallato, et dentro a l'acque;
et già mai poi la mia lingua non tacque
mentre poteo del suo cader maligno:
ond'io presi col suon color d'un cigno.   60
    Cosí lungo l'amate rive andai,
che volendo parlar, cantava sempre

On all thoughts else, forget myself perforce;
That thought my being holds, and I the husk. 20
 Since that day Love at first laid seige to me,
Indeed, I tell you, many years had passed
So that my youthful countenance was changed,
And frozen thoughts had hardened round my heart
To make an almost adamantine glaze 25
That would not let the hard effect abate.
No tear yet bathed my breast; none slumber broke,
And that which in myself I could not find,
In others seemed a miracle to me.
Woe: What I am: What I was: 30
Praise life at end; at evening praise the day.
The cruel one of whom I tell, aware
That, after all, no arrow's point of his
Had even penetrated past my robe,
A powerful lady took into his train 35
'Gainst whom not skill, nor strength, nor begging grace,
Availed me then nor yet avails me now.
Those two transformed me into what I am,
Turned me a man alive, to laurel green
That shed no leaf for all the winter's chill. 40
 What I became when first awareness dawned
Of this transfiguration of my self:
I saw my locks become that laurel frond
That I had hoped, indeed, would be their crown;
The feet I stood and walked and ran upon, 45
As to the spirit every limb responds
I sensed become two roots beside the waves—
Not of Peneus—of a statelier stream;°
Felt arms transmute themselves, become two boughs:
My blood runs no less cold 50
Than did it when, arrayed in plumage white,
My hope plunged stricken by a thunderbolt,
Lay dead because he'd risen far too high.
Thus, since I knew not where or when I might
Recover him, by night and day, in tears, 55
Where hope was reft from me, I went alone,
Searching along the banks and in the deeps,
And never more did my tongue cease to tell,
While it could do so, of his dreadful fall.
Hence I, with the swan's song, its color took. 60
 Thus I drifted past those banks well-loved,
And though I wished to speak, went singing ever,

mercé chiamando con estrania voce;
né mai in sí dolci o in sí soavi tempre
risonar seppi gli amorosi guai,   65
che 'l cor s'umilïasse aspro et feroce.
Qual fu a sentir? ché 'l ricordar mi coce:
ma molto piú di quel, che per inanzi
de la dolce et acerba mia nemica
è bisogno ch'io dica,   70
benché sia tal ch'ogni parlare avanzi.
Questa che col mirar gli animi fura,
m'aperse il petto, e 'l cor prese con mano,
dicendo a me: Di ciò non far parola.
Poi la rividi in altro habito sola,   75
tal ch'i' non la conobbi, oh senso humano,
anzi le dissi 'l ver pien di paura;
ed ella ne l'usata sua figura
tosto tornando, fecemi, oimè lasso,
d'un quasi vivo et sbigottito sasso.   80
    Ella parlava sí turbata in vista,
che tremar mi fea dentro a quella petra,
udendo: I' non son forse chi tu credi.
E dicea meco: Se costei mi spetra,
nulla vita mi fia noiosa o trista;   85
a farmi lagrimar, signor mio, riedi.
Come non so: pur io mossi indi i piedi,
non altrui incolpando che me stesso,
mezzo tutto quel dí tra vivo et morto.
Ma perché 'l tempo è corto,   90
la penna al buon voler non pò gir presso:
onde piú cose ne la mente scritte
vo trapassando, et sol d'alcune parlo
che meraviglia fanno a chi l'ascolta.
Morte mi s'era intorno al cor avolta,   95
né tacendo potea di sua man trarlo,
o dar soccorso a le vertuti afflitte;
le vive voci m'erano interditte;
ond'io gridai con carta et con incostro:
Non son mio, no. S'io moro, il danno è vostro.   100
    Ben mi credea dinanzi agli occhi suoi
d'indegno far cosí di mercé degno,
 . et questa spene m'avea fatto ardito:
ma talora humiltà spegne disdegno,
talor l'enfiamma; et ciò sepp'io da poi,   105
lunga stagion di tenebre vestito:

Crying "Mercy" in that alien voice;°
Nor could I ever harmonize the notes—
Now sweet, now soft—of amorous lament   65
So that her stern, fierce heart would yield to me.
For what was there to hear? How memory sears me:
But even more of this—or rather more
About that sweet and bitter foe of mine
Necessity bids me tell,   70
Though such as she transcends the power of speech.
That girl, who with a look rips souls away,
Unsealed my breast, seized with her hand my heart,
Instructing me: "Breathe not a word of this:"
I saw her next in altered guise, alone   75
So that, mistaking her—oh human sense—
I, fearful, spoke the truth to her instead,
At once, then, she resumed her former face
And made of me—alas, poor wretch—a stone,
One half alive, disheartened and dismayed.   80
    She spoke with such a troubled countenance,
It made me tremble there within that rock
To hear: "I am perhaps, not whom you think;"
And to myself I said: "If she frees me
From stone, no life can sadden or annoy."   85
(To make me weep, my Lord, return, I pray)
I know not how, but thence I dragged my feet,
Accusing no one other than myself,
Suspended between life and death all day.
But, since my time grows short,   90
And with desire my pen cannot keep pace,
Much written in my mind I shall omit,
And only speak of certain things that will
Be wonders to whoever hears of them.
Death was within me, coiled about my heart;   95
Nor could my silence free it from her hand,
Nor succor give to my enfeebled powers;
To speak aloud had been forbidden me,
So I cried out with paper and with ink:
"No: I'm not mine; if I die, yours the cost."   100
    I thought in her eyes surely I would change
From one disdained to one deserving grace,
And this hope had made me presumptuous.
But humbleness will sometimes blow out scorn,
Sometimes inflame it: this I quickly learned   105
In darkness shrouded for a season long,

ch'a quei preghi il mio lume era sparito.
Ed io non ritrovando intorno intorno
ombra di lei, né pur de' suoi piedi orma,
come huom che tra via dorma,   110
gittaimi stanco sovra l'erba un giorno.
Ivi accusando il fugitivo raggio,
a le lagrime triste allargai 'l freno,
et lasciaile cader come a lor parve;
né già mai neve sotto al sol disparve   115
com'io sentí' me tutto venir meno,
et farmi una fontana a pie' d'un faggio.
Gran tempo humido tenni quel viaggio.
Chi udí mai d'uom vero nascer fonte?
E parlo cose manifeste et conte.   120
    L'alma ch'è sol da Dio facta gentile,
ché già d'altrui non pò venir tal gratia,
simile al suo factor stato ritene:
però di perdonar mai non è sacia
a chi col core et col sembiante humile   125
dopo quantunque offese a mercé vène.
Et se contra suo stile ella sostene
d'esser molto pregata, in Lui si speccia,
et fal perché 'l peccar piú si pavente:
ché non ben si ripente   130
de l'un mal chi de l'altro s'apparecchia.
Poi che madonna da pietà commossa
degnò mirarme, et ricognovve et vide
gir di pari la pena col peccato,
benigna mi redusse al primo stato.   135
Ma nulla à 'l mondo in ch'uom saggio si fide:
ch'ancor poi ripregando, i nervi et l'ossa
mi volse in dura selce; et cosí scossa
voce rimasi de l'antiche some,
chiamando Morte, et lei sola per nome.   140
    Spirto doglioso errante (mi rimembra)
per spelunche deserte et pellegrine,
piansi molt'anni il mio sfrenato ardire:
et anchor poi trovai di quel mal fine,
et ritornai ne le terrene membra,   145
credo per piú dolore ivi sentire.
I' seguí' tanto avanti il mio desire
ch'un dí cacciando sí com'io solea
mi mossi; e quella fera bella et cruda
in una fonte ignuda   150

For at those prayers my candle had gone out,
And I could not recover anywhere
Her shadow or some vestige of her feet.
Like one who sleeps along   110
His way, one day I weary fell upon
The grass; accusing there that ray of light
Which fled, I gave free rein to woeful tears,
Allowing them to fall just as they would.
And never did snow melt beneath the sun   115
The way I felt myself grow faint and change
Into a fountain underneath a beech.
A long and tearful time I held that course.
Who's heard of fountains born from mortal man?
I speak of things undoubted and well known.   120
      God only shapes the soul's nobility;
From no one else can she attain such grace.
She keeps her likeness to her Maker's state;
And thus she's never weary of forgiving
Whoever with a contrite mien and heart   125
Comes seeking mercy after many faults.
And if against her nature she endures
Long importunity, she mirrors Him—
Does so that sin may be more greatly feared;
One does not honestly repent   130
Of one ill-deed who's ready to do more.
Since, by compassion touched, my lady deigned
To look on me, she saw and understood
My penance had been equal to my sin;
Benign, she led me back to my first state.   135
But nothing on this earth a wise man trusts:
For when I pled once more, my nerves and bones
Were turned to hardest flint; and, shaken thus,
I lived a voice, still burdened as of old,
Calling on Death, and her alone by name.   140
      An errant, doleful spirit (I recall)
Through caverns tenantless, unvisited
I wept my uncurbed daring many years
And found at length the end of that disease,
And turned again from flint to earthly limbs—   145
To make me feel the sorrow more, I think.
How far afield my passion I pursued:
One day, as usual, I went to hunt;
There that untamed one, lovely and severe,
Stood naked in a fount,   150

si stava, quando 'l sol piú forte ardea.
Io, perché d'altra vista non m'appago,
stetti a mirarla: ond'ella ebbe vergogna;
et per farne vendetta, o per celarse,
l'acqua nel viso co le man' mi sparse.   155
Vero dirò (forse e' parrà menzogna)
ch'i' sentí' trarmi de la propria imago,
et in un cervo solitario et vago
di selva in selva ratto mi transformo
et anchor de' miei can' fuggo lo stormo.   160
    Canzon, i' non fu' mai quel nuvol d'oro
che poi discese in pretïosa pioggia,
sí che 'l foco di Giove in parte spense;
ma fui ben fiamma ch'un bel guardo accense,
et fui l'uccel che piú per l'aere poggia,   165
alzando lei che ne' miei detti honoro:
né per nova figura il primo alloro
seppi lassar, ché pur la sua dolce ombra
ogni men bel piacer del cor mi sgombra.

24
    Se l'onorata fronde che prescrive
l'ira del ciel, quando 'l gran Giove tona,
non m'avesse disdetta la corona
che suole ornar chi poetando scrive,
    i' era amico a queste vostre dive   5
le qua' vilmente il secolo abandona;
ma quella ingiuria già lunge mi sprona
da l'inventrice de le prime olive:
    ché non bolle la polver d'Ethïopia
sotto 'l piú ardente sol, com'io sfavillo,   10
perdendo tanto amata cosa propia.
    Cercate dunque fonte piú tranquillo,
ché 'l mio d'ogni liquor sostene inopia,
salvo di quel che lagrimando stillo.

25
    Amor piangeva, et io con lui talvolta,
dal qual miei passi non fur mai lontani,
mirando per gli effecti acerbi et strani
l'anima vostra de' suoi nodi sciolta.
    Or ch'al dritto camin l'à Dio rivolta,   5
col cor levando al cielo ambe le mani,
ringratio lui che' giusti preghi humani

While down on her the sun burned, ardently.
Because no other sight contented me,
I paused to gaze on her, and she, ashamed,
Whether in vengeance or to hide herself,
With her hands splashed the water in my face.   155
The truth I'll tell (though it may falsehood seem):
I felt myself drawn forth from my own shape,
And to a stag, alone and wandering
From wood to wood, I swiftly was transformed,
And still I flee the baying of my hounds.°   160
    O song, I never was that cloud of gold
Which in a priceless rain came falling once—
The one in which Jove's fire, in part, was spent—°
But, lit by one sweet look, I've been a flame,°
Yes, and that bird which shears the upper air,°   165
Bearing her high whom my words celebrate;
Nor could I for a new form learn to part
From that first laurel whose sweet shade yet sweeps
Every delight less lovely from my heart.

24

    Had not those honored leaves that tame the wrath
Of heaven when high Jove thunders, not denied°
To me that crown which customarily
Adorns one who, while shaping verses, writes,°
    I'd be a friend to these your goddesses,°   5
The ones this age abandons wretchedly;
But far that wrong already drives me off
From the inventress of the olive tree.°
    Indeed, no Ethiopic dust boils up
Beneath the hottest sun the way I blush   10
At losing such a treasured gift of mine.
    Search out, therefore, a fountain more serene,
For mine of every cordial stands in need,
Save only that which I well forth in tears.

25

    Love wept, and sometimes I wept with him too
(From him my steps were never far away)
Observing by those strange and grievous signs
That your soul from its shackles was released.
    That God's now set it back on its right road,   5
Within my heart, both hands upraised to heaven,
I thank Him who in tender mercy hears

benignamente, sua mercede, ascolta.
Et se tornando a l'amorosa vita,
per farvi al bel desio volger le spalle,   10
trovaste per la via fossati o poggi,
   fu per mostrar quanto è spinoso calle,
et quanto alpestra et dura la salita,
onde al vero valor conven ch'uom poggi.

26

Piú di me lieta non si vede a terra
nave da l'onde combattuta et vinta,
quando la gente di pietà depinta
su per la riva a ringratiar s'atterra;
   né lieto piú del carcer si diserra   5
chi 'ntorno al collo ebbe la corda avinta,
di me, veggendo quella spada scinta
che fece al segnor mio sí lunga guerra.
   Et tutti voi ch'Amor laudate in rima,
al buon testor degli amorosi detti   10
rendete honor, ch'era smarrito in prima:
   ché piú gloria è nel regno degli electi
d'un spirito converso, et piú s'estima,
che di novantanove altri perfecti.

27

Il successor di Karlo, che la chioma
co la corona del suo antiquo adorna,
prese à già l'arme per fiacchar le corna
a Babilonia, et chi da lei si noma;
   e 'l vicario de Cristo colla soma   5
de le chiavi et del manto al nido torna,
sí che s'altro accidente nol distorna,
verdà Bologna, et poi la nobil Roma.
   La mansüeta vostra et gentil agna
abbatte i fieri lupi: et cosí vada   10
chïunque amor legitimo scompagna.
   Consolate lei dunque ch'anchor bada,
et Roma che del suo sposo si lagna,
et per Iesú cingete omai la spada.

28

O aspectata in ciel beata et bella
anima che di nostra humanitade
vestita vai, non come l'altre carca:

Benignly the just prayers of humankind.
  And if returning to the amorous life,
To make you turn away from fair desire,   10
You've found steep hills or gullies in your path,
  It was to show how thorny grows the way,
How mountainous, how rugged is the climb
Man must endure who seeks for merit true.

26

  More happy than I am you'll never see
A vessel from the waves, tossed, buffetted,
Make land, when people wan with piety
Fall down upon the shore to offer thanks.
  None happier from prison issues forth   5
Who had the rope bound tight around his throat
Than I, who see ungirded now that sword
Which made upon my lord so long a war.
  And all of you who sing Love's praise in rhyme,
To that good weaver of words amorous   10
Who once had gone astray, pay honor due.
  The realm of the elect has for a soul
Converted more esteem, and glory more
Than for the nine-and-ninety blameless ones.°

27

  Charles' successor who now adorns his head°
With his forefather's crown has seized, indeed,
Weapons to crush the horns of Babylon°
And all of those who take their name from her.
  Christ's vicar, laden with his keys and cloak°   5
Returns to his own seat; and so, unless
Some misadventure hinders him, he'll view
Bologna first, and then see noble Rome.
  Your mild and gentle lamb has beaten down°
The savage wolves; and thus will meet their end   10
Whoever puts asunder lawful loves.
  Console her, therefore—she who yet stands guard—
And comfort Rome who for her spouse laments;°
Gird on the sword at last for Jesus now.

28

  O fair and blessed soul whom Heaven awaits,°
You go arrayed in our humanity
Not cumbered by the flesh as others are;

perché ti sian men dure omai le strade,
a Dio dilecta, obedïente ancella,   5
onde al suo regno di qua giú si varca,
ecco novellamente a la tua barca,
ch'al cieco mondo à già volte le spalle
per gir al miglior porto,
d'un vento occidental dolce conforto;   10
lo qual per mezzo questa oscura valle,
ove piangiamo il nostro et l'altrui torto,
la condurrà de' lacci antichi sciolta,
per dritissimo calle,
al verace orïente ov'ella è volta.   15

    Forse i devoti et gli amorosi preghi
et le lagrime sancte de' mortali
son giunte inanzi a la pietà superna;
et forse non fur mai tante né tali
che per merito lor punto si pieghi   20
fuor de suo corso la giustitia eterna;
ma quel benigno re che 'l ciel governa
al sacro loco ove fo posto in croce
gli occhi per gratia gira,
onde nel petto al novo Karlo spira   25
la vendetta ch'a noi tardata nòce,
sí che molt'anni Europa ne sospira:
cosí soccorre a la sua amata sposa
tal che sol de la voce
fa tremar Babilonia, et star pensosa.   30

    Chïunque alberga tra Garona e 'l monte
e 'ntra 'l Rodano e 'l Reno et l'onde salse
le 'nsegne cristianissime accompagna;
et a cui mai di vero pregio calse,
dal Pireneo a l'ultimo orizonte,   35
con Aragon lassarà vòta Hispagna;
Inghilterra con l'isole che bagna
l'Occeano intra 'l Carro et le Colonne,
infin là dove sona
doctrina del sanctissimo Elicona,   40
varie di lingue et d'arme, et de le gonne,
a l'alta impresa caritate sprona.
Deh qual amor sí licito o sí degno,
qua' figli mai, qua' donne
furon materia a sí giusto disdegno?   45

    Una parte del mondo è che si giace
mai sempre in ghiaccio et in gelate nevi

Henceforth those roads will seem less hard to you
By which you pass to His realm from below—   5
God's chosen one, handmaid obedient:
Behold afresh your vessel that has now
Already put behind it this blind world
To steer for the best harbor,
Solaced by a sweet wind from the west.   10
That breeze, amidst this dark and shadowy vale
Where we lament our own and others' woes
Will pilot you, freed from your ancient bonds,
Along the straightest course
To that true orient, where she is bound.   15
    Perhaps the loving and devoted prayers
Of mortal beings, and their sacred tears,
Have gone before supernal mercy's throne;
But maybe they were not enough, nor such
That by their merit, one jot they might turn   20
Aside eternal justice from its course.
But in His grace that kindly King who rules
In Heaven looks toward that sacred place
Where he hung on the cross;
Hence in the breast of this new Charlemagne°   25
That vengeance breathes which, tardy, saps our strength—
Because through long years Europe sighed for it.
Thus Christ brings succor to His cherished spouse
So that his voice alone
Makes Babylon stand quaking and afraid.   30
    All dwellers from the mountains to Garonne,
Between the Rhone, and Rhine, and salty waves,
To those most Christian banners rally now;
And all who ever prized true valor, from
The far horizon to the Pyrenees   35
Will empty Spain to follow Aragon;
From England, with the isles that ocean bathes
Between the Oxcart and the Pillars—from,°
In short, wherever sounds
The teaching of most sacred Helicon—°   40
All varied in their tongues and arms and dress,
Divine love spurs them to high enterprise.
Indeed, what love so lawful, of such worth?
What sons, what women ever
Have been the grounds for such a righteous wrath?   45
    There is a region of the world that lies
In ice forever, under freezing snow

tutta lontana dal camin del sole:
là sotto i giorni nubilosi et brevi,
nemica natural-mente di pace,   50
nasce una gente a cui il morir non dole.
Questa se, piú devota che non sòle,
col tedesco furor la spada cigne,
turchi, arabi et caldei,
con tutti quei che speran nelli dèi   55
di qua dal mar che fa l'onde sanguigne,
quanto sian da prezzar, conoscer dèi:
popolo ignudo paventoso et lento,
che ferro mai non strigne,
ma tutti colpi suoi commette al vento.   60
    Dunque ora è 'l tempo da ritrare il collo
dal giogo antico, et da squarciare il velo
ch'è stato avolto intorno agli occhi nostri,
et che 'l nobile ingegno che dal cielo
per gratia tien' de l'immortale Apollo,   65
et l'eloquentia sua vertú qui mostri
or con la lingua, or co' laudati incostri:
perché d'Orpheo leggendo et d'Amphïone
se non ti meravigli,
assai men fia ch'Italia co' suoi figli   70
si desti al suon del tuo chiaro sermone,
tanto che per Iesú la lancia pigli;
che s'al ver mira questa anticha madre,
in nulla sua tentione
fur mai cagion' sí belle o sí leggiadre.   75
    Tu ch'ài, per arricchir d'un bel thesauro,
volte l'antiche et le moderne carte,
volando al ciel colla terrena soma,
sai da l'imperio del figliuol de Marte
al grande Augusto che di verde lauro   80
tre volte trïumphando ornò la chioma,
ne l'altrui ingiurie del suo sangue Roma
spesse fïate quanto fu cortese:
et or perché non fia
cortese no, ma conoscente et pia   85
a vendicar le dispietate offese,
col figliuol glorïoso di Maria?
Che dunque la nemica parte spera
ne l'umane difese,
se Cristo sta da la contraria schiera?   90
    Pon' mente al temerario ardir di Xerse,

Far distant from the pathway of the sun.
There, subject to days overcast and short,
There teems a folk by nature foes of peace, 50
A people that is not bereaved by death.°
Should these prove more devout than usual
And with Teutonic rage take up the sword,
Then without doubt you'll learn
How much to prize Chaldeans, Arabs, Turks, 55
And all who place their hopes in pagan gods
From here to that sea red with bloody waves—
An unclothed, frightened, backward people who
Never close with swords; instead
They trust the wind to guide their every shot. 60
     The time has therefore come to draw our necks
From out the ancient yoke, to tear away
The veil that has been wound around our eyes.
Show noble genius, which, by Heaven's grace
From Apollo, the immortal one, is yours; 65
And here let eloquence display its power,
Now with the tongue, now celebrated script;
For if you do not wonder, reading of
Orpheus and Amphion,°
Then marvel not when Italy, with all 70
Her sons, by your clear sermon's note is so
Aroused that she takes up the lance for Christ.
For if this ancient matriarch sees truth,
She'll find no cause of hers
Was ever so appropriate or fair. 75
     To profit from rich treasures you have turned
The ancient pages and the modern too,
And flown to Heaven, though in earthly form;
You know how, from the reign of Mars' own son°
To great Augustus, who—thrice triumphing—° 80
Three times adorned his locks with laurel green,
Rome oftentimes, because of others' wounds,
Gave liberally so much of its own blood.
Then why is Rome not now—
Not "liberal"—but thankful and devout 85
In taking vengeance for these cruel affronts
In company with Mary's glorious Son?
How in defences human can the foe
Repose his hope, when Christ
Stands firm in the opposing company? 90
     Consider Xerxes' reckless impudence;°

che fece per calcare i nostri liti
di novi ponti oltraggio a la marina;
et vedrai ne la morte de' mariti
tutte vestite a brun le donne perse,   95
et tinto in rosso il mar di Salamina.
Et non pur questa misera rüína
del popolo infelice d'orïente
victoria t'empromette,
ma Marathona, et le mortali strette   100
che difese il leon con poca gente,
et altre mille ch'ài ascoltate et lette:
perché inchinare a Dio molto convene
le ginocchia et la mente,
che gli anni tuoi riserva a tanto bene.   105
    Tu vedrai Italia et l'onorata riva,
canzon, ch'agli occhi miei cela et contende
non mar, non poggio o fiume,
ma solo Amor che del suo altero lume
piú m'invaghisce dove piú m'incende: 110
né Natura può star contra 'l costume.
Or movi, non smarrir l'altre compagne,
ché non pur sotto bende
alberga Amor, per cui si ride et piagne.

29

    Verdi panni, sanguigni, oscuri o persi
non vestí donna unquancho
né d'òr capelli in bionda treccia attorse,
sí bella com'è questa che mi spoglia
d'arbitrio, et dal camin de libertade   5
seco mi tira, sí ch'io non sostegno
alcun giogo men grave.
    Et se pur s'arma talor a dolersi
l'anima a cui vien mancho
consiglio, ove 'l martir l'adduce in forse,   10
rappella lei da la sfrenata voglia
súbita vista, ché del cor mi rade
ogni delira impresa, et ogni sdegno
fa 'l veder lei soave.
    Di quanto per Amor già mai soffersi,   15
et aggio a soffrir ancho,
fin che mi sani 'l cor colei che 'l morse,
rubella di mercé, che pur l'envoglia,
vendetta fia, sol che contra Humiltade

When with ingenious bridges, he outraged
The sea so he could trample on our shores;
And you will see those Persian women who
Were draped in brown to mourn their husbands' deaths,   95
The sea of Salamis all red with blood.
Not only does the miserable ruin
Of that unhappy people of the East
Foretell your victory;
But Marathon, that deadly pass as well°   100
The Lion held with such a tiny band,°
And countless frays of which you've heard and read.
Most meet it is, therefore, that you subject
Both knee and mind to God
Who now preserves your life for such great good.   105
   Song, Italy you'll see, and see the shore
Revered, which neither stream nor sea nor hill
Can keep from me nor from my eyes conceal,
But only Love who, with his lofty lamp,
Attracts me more, the more that I catch fire—   110
To habit Nature cannot stand opposed;
Now, Song, go forth; lag not behind your fellows,
Not just under kerchiefs°
Does Love reside, who makes us laugh and weep.

29

   Green fabrics, blood-red, dark or violet,
You never gowned a lady
Nor ever in a blond tress wound gold hair
As fair as this that strips free will from me;
It draws me in such fashion from the path   5
Of liberty that no less heavy yoke
Can I endure to bear.
   Yet if the soul to which ill counsel comes
Still sometimes takes up arms
To grieve when suffering leads it to doubt,   10
The sudden sight of her will call it back
From its unchecked desire, will rid my heart
Of frenzied schemes, since seeing her makes sweet
All my indignity.
   For all my former sufferings for Love,   15
For those I still must bear
Till she who gnaws my heart shall make it whole—
She rebel 'gainst the mercy it still craves—
Let vengeance come; save only that against

Orgoglio et Ira il bel passo ond'io vengo   20
non chiuda, et non inchiave.
        Ma l'ora e 'l giorno ch'io le luci apersi
nel bel nero et nel biancho
che mi scacciâr di là dove Amor corse,
novella d'esta vita che m'addoglia   25
furon radice, et quella in cui l'etade
nostra si mira, la qual piombo o legno
vedendo è chi non pave.
        Lagrima dunque che dagli occhi versi
per quelle, che nel mancho   30
lato mi bagna chi primier s'accorse,
quadrella, dal voler mio non mi svoglia,
ché 'n giusta parte la sententia cade:
per lei sospira l'alma, et ella è degno
che le sue piaghe lave.   35
        Da me son fatti i miei pensier' diversi:
tal già, qual io mi stancho,
l'amata spada in se stessa contorse;
né quella prego che però mi scioglia,
ché men son dritte al ciel tutt'altre strade,   40
et non s'aspira al glorïoso regno
certo in piú salda nave.
        Benigne stelle che compagne fersi
al fortunato fiancho
quando 'l bel parto giú nel mondo scórse!   45
ch'è stella in terra, et come in lauro foglia
conserva verde il pregio d'onestade,
ove non spira folgore, né indegno
vento mai che l'aggrave.
        So io ben ch'a voler chiuder in versi   50
suo laudi, fôra stancho
chi piú degna la mano a scriver porse:
qual cella è di memoria in cui s'accoglia
quanta vede vertú, quanta beltade,
chi gli occhi mira d'ogni valor segno,   55
dolce del mio cor chiave?
        Quanto il sol gira, Amor piú caro pegno,
donna, di voi non ave.

30

Giovene donna sotto un verde lauro
vidi piú biancha et piú fredda che neve
non percossa dal sol molti et molt'anni;

Humility, let pride and wrath not block   20
Nor bar my passage fair.
    The day and hour I gazed upon the lights
In that fair black and white°
Which drove me from the place where love rushed in—
Of this new grievous life, that time was root,   25
And she in whom our age admires itself;
Whoever looks upon her unafraid
Is surely lead or wood.
    No teardrop, then, caused by *her* eyes yet spills
From mine to bathe my heart,   30
Which felt that arrow first on my left side;
None causes me to shun my own desire,
For on the proper part this sentence falls;
For her, my soul sighs, and how meet it is
That she should wash my wounds.   35
    My thoughts to me contrary have become:
Once one, like me exhausted,°
Turned the beloved sword upon herself;
I don't ask this one, though, to set me free
For every other road to heaven's less straight;   40
Yes, to that glorious realm one can't aspire
In a more steady ship.
    O stars benign that were companions of
That blessed womb when its
Fair issue slipped into this world below: 45
An earthly star is she; as laurel leaf
Its green, so she the prize of chastity
Preserves; there strikes no lightning, never blows
Base wind to bend her low.
    I know well that my wish to catch in verse   50
Her praises would exhaust
Whoever, worthiest, set his hand to write.
What cell of memory is there to hold
Such virtue, such great beauty as one sees
Who gazes in those eyes—mark of all worth   55
And sweet key of my heart.
    While the sun wheels, Love will not have a pledge
Lady, more dear than you.

30

A youthful lady under a green laurel
I saw once, whiter and more cold than snow
Untouched by sun for many, many years;

e ’l suo parlare, e ’l bel viso, et le chiome
mi piacquen sí ch’i’ l’ò dinanzi agli occhi,   5
ed avrò sempre, ov’io sia, in poggio o ’n riva.
    Allor saranno i miei pensieri a riva
che foglia verde non si trovi in lauro;
quando avrò queto il core, asciutti gli occhi,
vedrem ghiacciare il foco, arder la neve: 10
non ò tanti capelli in queste chiome
quanti vorrei quel giorno attender anni.
    Ma perché vola il tempo, et fuggon gli anni,
sí ch’a la morte in un punto s’arriva,
o colle brune o colle bianche chiome,   15
seguirò l’ombra di quel dolce lauro
per lo piú ardente sole et per la neve,
fin che l’ultimo dí chiuda quest’occhi.
    Non fur già mai veduti sí begli occhi
o ne la nostra etade o ne’ prim’anni,   20
che mi struggon cosí come ’l sol neve;
onde procede lagrimosa riva
ch’Amor conduce a pie’ del duro lauro
ch’à i rami di diamante, et d’òr le chiome.
    I’ temo di cangiar pria volto et chiome   25
che con vera pietà mi mostri gli occhi
l’idolo mio, scolpito in vivo lauro:
che s’al contar non erro, oggi à sett’anni
che sospirando vo di riva in riva
la notte e ’l giorno, al caldo ed a la neve.   30
    Dentro pur foco, et for candida neve,
sol con questi pensier’, con altre chiome,
sempre piangendo andrò per ogni riva,
per far forse pietà venir negli occhi
di tal che nascerà dopo mill’anni,   35
se tanto viver pò ben cólto lauro.
    L’auro e i topacii al sol sopra la neve
vincon le bionde chiome presso agli occhi
che menan gli anni miei sí tosto a riva.

31

    Questa anima gentil che si diparte,
anzi tempo chiamata a l’altra vita,
se lassuso è quanto esser dê gradita,
terrà del ciel la piú beata parte.
    S’ella riman fra ’l terzo lume et Marte,   5
fia la vista del sole scolorita,

I liked her speech, fair features, and her hair
So much that I keep her before my eyes—   5
And ever shall, though I'm on hill or shore.

     And thus my thoughts will stay along the shore,
Where no green leaf is found upon the laurel;
When I have stilled my heart and dried my eyes,
We'll see fire freeze and into flame burst snow;   10
I don't have strands as many in this hair
As, waiting for that day, there would be years.

     Because time flies, however, and since years
Soon flee until one fetches on death's shore—
Whether with locks of brown or with white hair—   15
I'll follow still the shade of that sweet laurel
Through the most parching sun and through the snow
Until the final day shall close these eyes.

     Never before were seen such lovely eyes
Not in our age nor in man's pristine years;   20
They make me melt just as the sun does snow,
From whence a tearful river floods the shore—
Love leads it to the foot of that hard laurel
Whose branches are of diamond, gold its hair.

     I fear the changing of my face and hair   25
Before, with pity true, she shows her eyes—
My idol, sculpted in the living laurel;
For if my count errs not, it's seven years
Today that I have sighed from shore to shore
By night and day, in heat and in the snow.   30

     Still fire within, though outside whitest snow
With these thoughts only, though with altered hair,
Ever in tears, I'll wander every shore,
Perhaps creating pity in the eyes
Of persons born from hence a thousand years—   35
If, tended well, so long can live a laurel.

     In sun, the gold and topaz on the snow
Are conquered by blond hair close by those eyes
That lead my years so swiftly towards the shore.°

                         31
     This noble spirit that now passes on,°
Called to the other life before her time,
If welcomed there above as she should be,
Will dwell in the most blessed part of heaven.

     If she remains twixt Mars and that third light,°   5
The sun's own visage will grow pale and fade;

poi ch'a mirar sua bellezza infinita
l'anime degne intorno a lei fien sparte.

    Se si posasse sotto al quarto nido,
ciascuna de le tre saria men bella,   10
et essa sola avria la fama e 'l grido;

    nel quinto giro non habitrebbe ella;
ma se vola piú alto, assai mi fido
che con Giove sia vinta ogni altra stella.

32

    Quanto piú m'avicino al giorno extremo
· che l'umana miseria suol far breve,
piú veggio il tempo andar veloce et leve,
e 'l mio di lui sperar fallace et scemo.

    I' dico a' miei pensier': Non molto andremo   5
d'amor parlando omai, ché 'l duro et greve
terreno incarco come frescha neve
si va struggendo; onde noi pace avremo:

    perché co·llui cadrà quella speranza
che ne fe' vaneggiar sí lungamente,   10
e 'l riso e 'l pianto, et la paura et l'ira;

    sí vedrem chiaro poi come sovente
per le cose dubbiose altri s'avanza,
et come spesso indarno si sospira.

33

    Già fiammeggiava l'amorosa stella
per l'orïente, et l'altra che Giunone
suol far gelosa nel septentrïone,
rotava i raggi suoi lucente et bella;

    levata era a filar la vecchiarella,   5
discinta et scalza, et desto avea 'l carbone,
et gli amanti pungea quella stagione
che per usanza a lagrimar gli appella:

    quando mia speme già condutta al verde
giunse nel cor, non per l'usata via,   10
che 'l sonno tenea chiusa, e 'l dolor molle;

    quanto cangiata, oimè, da quel di pria!
Et parea dir: Perché tuo valor perde?
Veder quest'occhi anchor non ti si tolle.

34

    Apollo, s'anchor vive il bel desio
che t'infiammava a le thesaliche onde,

To gaze upon her beauty infinite
The other worthy souls will cluster round.
    If she is set beneath the Sun's fourth sphere,°
Each one of its three lights will shine less fair,°   10
And she alone will have renown and fame
    In the fifth sphere of Mars she may not dwell,
But should she higher fly, I'm confident
That she with Jove will dim all other stars.

32

    The closer I approach that final day
Which commonly makes brief man's misery,
The more I see my time speed lightly by,
My hope for it deceptive, on the wane.
    I tell my thoughts: "We shall not wander on   5
Much longer parleying of love, before
This hard and heavy freight of clay consumes
Itself like early snow; then we'll find peace:
    "For with the clay that hope will also fail
Which made us speak so wildly for so long;   10
The smile, the tears, the fear, the wrath will pass.
    "Thus we shall clearly see how oftentimes
Mankind's led on by things illusory,
And how it is one often sighs in vain."

33

    Already in the east the amorous star°
Was flaming forth; another in the north
Whirled lucent, lovely rays about—the one
That long ago caused Juno's jealousy.
    All barefoot and ungirt, arisen to spin,   5
The good old woman had the coals awake,
And stung were lovers also by that hour
Which by old custom summons them to weep,
    When, guttering low already, my hope came
Not by the way most used into my heart,   10
Which sleep held shut and woe kept wet with tears—
    How changed, alas, from what she was before:
She seemed to say: "Why lose your spirit now?
To see these eyes is not denied you yet."

34

    Apollo, if that fair desire still lives
Which once inflamed you by Thessalian waves,

et se non ài l'amate chiome bionde,
volgendo gli anni, già poste in oblio:
    dal pigro gielo et dal tempo aspro et rio,   5
che dura quanto 'l tuo viso s'asconde,
difendi or l'onorata et sacra fronde,
ove tu prima, et poi fu' invescato io;
    et per vertú de l'amorosa speme,
che ti sostenne ne la vita acerba,   10
di queste impressïon' l'aere disgombra;
    sí vedrem poi per meraviglia inseme
seder la donna nostra sopra l'erba,
et far de le sue braccia a se stessa ombra.

35

    Solo et pensoso i piú deserti campi
vo mesurando a passi tardi et lenti,
et gli occhi porto per fuggire intenti
ove vestigio human l'arena stampi.
    Altro schermo non trovo che mi scampi   5
dal manifesto accorger de le genti,
perché negli atti d'alegrezza spenti
di fuor si legge com'io dentro avampi:
    sí ch'io mi credo omai che monti et piagge
et fiumi et selve sappian di che tempre   10
sia la mia vita, ch'è celata altrui.
    Ma pur sí aspre vie né sí selvagge
cercar non so ch'Amor non venga sempre
ragionando con meco, et io co·llui.

36

    S'io credesse per morte essere scarco
del pensiero amoroso che m'atterra,
colle mie mani avrei già posto in terra
queste membra noiose, et quello incarco;
    ma perch'io temo che sarrebbe un varco   5
di pianto in pianto, et d'una in altra guerra,
di qua dal passo anchor che mi si serra
mezzo rimango, lasso, et mezzo il varco.
    Tempo ben fôra omai d'avere spinto
l'ultimo stral la dispietata corda   10
ne l'altrui sangue già bagnato et tinto;
    et io ne prego Amore, et quella sorda
che mi lassò de' suoi color' depinto,
et di chiamarmi a sé non le ricorda.

If to oblivion, with wheeling years
You've not consigned that blonde, beloved hair,
    From sluggard frost, from weather harsh and cruel   5
That lasts as long as you conceal your face,
O, now protect the honored, sacred fronds
Where you first, and then I, were snared with lime;
    And with the power of that amorous hope
Which once sustained you in this bitter life,   10
O clear the air of these obscuring mists;
    Thus you and I will see a wondrous sight:
Our lady sitting down upon the grass
And making, with her arms, shade for herself.

35

    Alone in thought with lagging paces slow,
I wander measuring the barren fields,
My eyes attentive, ready to take flight
Where any human vestige marks the scene.
    I know no other ward to guard myself   5
From clear acknowledgement in every eye,
For with spent cheer I act, and thus reveal
Without—to all who read—the fire within.
    Thus, now I think that even hills and shores,
Rivers and forests know the quality   10
My life must have, though masked from human kind.
    Yet no path can I trace so savage, wild,
But Love comes pressing on; he follows still
Debating with me ever, and I with him.

36

    If I believed through death I'd gain release
From all the amorous thought that crushes me,
With my own hands I'd long since have interred
These cloying limbs, and that oppressive care;
    But as I fear that, dying, I may pass   5
From woe to woe, from one strife to the next,
Here by that passageway still closed to me,
I, weary, half remain and half pass on.
    High time for that compassionless bowstring
To loose its final dart, with mankind's blood   10
Already soaked and reddened; and for death
    I pray to Love, and that unhearing one°
Who left me here in her own colors dyed,
And then forgets to call me to herself.

Sí è debile il filo a cui s'attene
la gravosa mia vita
che, s'altri non l'aita,
ella fia tosto di suo corso a riva;
però che dopo l'empia dipartita   5
che dal dolce mio bene
feci, sol una spene
è stato infin a qui cagion ch'io viva,
dicendo: Perché priva
sia de l'amata vista,   10
mantienti, anima trista;
che sai s'a miglior tempo ancho ritorni
et a piú lieti giorni,
o se 'l perduto ben mai si racquista?
Questa speranza mi sostenne un tempo: 15
or vien mancando, et troppo in lei m'attempo.

Il tempo passa, et l'ore son sí pronte
a fornire il vïaggio,
ch'assai spacio non aggio
pur a pensar com'io corro a la morte: 20
a pena spunta in orïente un raggio
di sol, ch'a l'altro monte
de l'adverso orizonte
giunto il vedrai per vie lunghe et distorte.
Le vite son sí corte,   25
sí gravi i corpi et frali
degli uomini mortali,
che quando io mi ritrovo dal bel viso
cotanto esser diviso,
col desio non possendo mover l'ali,   30
poco m'avanza del conforto usato,
né so quant'io mi viva in questo stato.

Ogni loco m'atrista ov'io non veggio
quei begli occhi soavi
che portaron le chiavi   35
de' miei dolci pensier', mentre a Dio piacque;
et perché 'l duro exilio piú m'aggravi,
s'io dormo o vado o seggio
altro già mai non cheggio,
et ciò ch'i' vidi dopo lor mi spiacque.   40
Quante montagne et acque,
quanto mar, quanti fiumi
m'ascondon que' duo lumi,

37

So feeble is the thread by which is held
This grievous life of mine,
That if no other helps
Then to its journey's end it soon will come;
For after the unpitying farewell   5
I bade my comfort sweet,
One hope alone remained
That till now gave me reason to live on;
It said: "Though you're cut off
From your beloved's sight,   10
Preserve your life, grieved soul;
Who knows if still to better times you may
Return—more joyful days—
Or if lost comfort may not be regained?"
This expectation bore me up a while;   15
Now it serves not; too old in it I've grown.

Time passes and so eager are the hours
Their circuit to complete,
That I have hardly time
To think at all, as I run on toward death.   20
No sooner in the east a sunbeam shows
Than you will see it reach
By paths oblique and long
The other hill's horizon opposite.
So brief, then, are our lives,   25
So heavy and so frail
The flesh of mortal men,
That when I find myself again cut off
From her fair face, and with
Desire quite powerless to move its wings   30
My wonted solace does me little good;
How long I'll live in this plight I know not.

Each place I fail to see those lovely eyes
So gentle, I grow sad;
They bore with them the keys   35
Of all my sweetest thoughts, while it pleased God.
And since hard exile grieves me much, though I
May sleep, or pace, or sit,
I'll not beg other eyes;
Since hers, all eyes I've looked upon displease.   40
So many waters, hills,
So many seas and streams
Hide those two lights from me—

che quasi un bel sereno a mezzo 'l die
fer le tenebre mie,   45
a ciò che 'l rimembrar piú mi consumi,
et quanto era mia vita allor gioiosa
m'insegni la presente aspra et noiosa!
    Lasso, se ragionando si rinfresca
quel'ardente desio   50
che nacque il giorno ch'io
lassai di me la miglior parte a dietro,
et s'Amor se ne va per lungo oblio,
chi mi conduce a l'ésca,
onde 'l mio dolor cresca?   55
Et perché pria tacendo non m'impetro?
Certo cristallo o vetro
non mostrò mai di fore
nascosto altro colore,
che l'alma sconsolata assai non mostri   60
piú chiari i pensier' nostri,
et la fera dolcezza ch'è nel core,
per gli occhi che di sempre pianger vaghi
cercan dí et nocte pur chi glien'appaghi.
    Novo piacer che negli umani ingegni   65
spesse volte si trova,
d'amar qual cosa nova
piú folta schiera di sospiri accoglia!
Et io son un di quei che 'l pianger giova;
et par ben ch'io m'ingegni   70
che di lagrime pregni
sien gli occhi miei sí come 'l cor di doglia;
et perché a·cciò m'invoglia
ragionar de' begli occhi,
né cosa è che mi tocchi   75
o sentir mi si faccia cosí a dentro,
corro spesso, et rïentro,
colà donde piú largo il duol trabocchi,
et sien col cor punite ambe le luci,
ch'a la strada d'Amor mi furon duci.   80
    Le treccie d'òr che devrien fare il sole
d'invidia molta ir pieno,
e 'l bel guardo sereno,
ove i raggi d'Amor sí caldi sono
che mi fanno anzi tempo venir meno,   85
et l'accorte parole,
rade nel mondo o sole,

Those lights that from my darkness almost made
A fair and noonday sky—   45
So that recalling can consume me more,
So that this present harsh, vexatious time
Can teach me how my life was joyful then.
    Alas, if speaking out replenishes
That fiery longing which   50
Was born the day that I
Abandoned quite the best part of myself,
And if through long neglect Love goes away,
Who'll lead me to that bait
Which makes my sorrow grow?   55
Why am I, mute before, not turned to stone?
Yes, on the outside, glass
Or crystal never shows
Its other hidden hues
More clearly than the soul, disconsolate,   60
Reveals our thoughts—shows that
Wild sweetness which is hidden in my heart,
Through eyes that always long to be in tears,
That day and night still seek her who contents them.
    A strange delight that one encounters oft   65
Within the human mind:
In loving some new thing
To welcome yet more thronging troops of sighs:
And I am one whom weeping benefits;
Indeed it seems I strive   70
To breed as many tears
Within my eyes as sorrows in my heart.
Since treating of fair eyes
Incites that state in me,
Since naught else touches me,   75
Nor in me makes itself so deeply felt,
I often flee, go back
There where a vaster sorrow overflows,
And, with my heart, those lights are punished both
That were my guides upon the road of love.   80
    Those golden tresses that must make the sun
Pass by with envy filled,
And that fair, cloudless gaze
From which the rays of Love so hotly shine,
They wither me before my time has come;   85
And words sagacious, rare,
Or peerless in this world

che mi fer già di sé cortese dono,
mi son tolte; et perdono
piú lieve ogni altra offesa,   90
che l'essermi contesa
quella benigna angelica salute
che 'l mio cor a vertute
destar solea con una voglia accesa:
tal ch'io non penso udir cosa già mai   95
che mi conforte ad altro ch'a trar guai.

Et per pianger anchor con piú diletto,
le man'bianche sottili,
et le braccia gentili,
et gli atti suoi soavemente alteri,   100
e i dolci sdegni alteramente humili,
e 'l bel giovenil petto,
torre d'alto intellecto,
mi celan questi luoghi alpestri et feri;
et non so s'io mi speri   105
vederla anzi ch'io mora:
però ch'ad ora ad ora
s'erge la speme, et poi non sa star ferma,
ma ricadendo afferma
di mai non veder lei che 'l ciel honora,   110
ov'alberga Honestate et Cortesia,
et dov'io prego che 'l mio albergo sia.

Canzon, s'al dolce loco
la donna nostra vedi,
credo ben che tu credi   115
ch'ella ti porgerà la bella mano,
ond'io son sí lontano.
Non la tocchar; ma reverente ai piedi
le di' ch'io sarò là tosto ch'io possa,
o spirto ignudo od uom di carne et d'ossa.   120

38
Orso, e' non furon mai fiumi né stagni,
né mare, ov'ogni rivo si disgombra,
né di muro o di poggio o di ramo ombra,
né nebbia che 'l ciel copra e 'l mondo bagni,
né altro impedimento, ond'io mi lagni,   5
qualunque piú l'umana vista ingombra,
quanto d'un vel che due begli occhi adombra,
et par che dica: Or ti consuma et piagni.

Et quel lor inchinar ch'ogni mia gioia

That made themselves to me a courteous gift
Are reft from me, and I
Forgive more lightly all   90
Affronts except one that
Prevents the mild, angelic greeting that
Was wont to rouse my heart
To virtue with a brightly kindled will;
Thus I think I shall never hear a thing   95
Encouraging, unless to bring me woe.
    And still to make me weep with more delight,
Those white and slender hands
And noble, tender arms,
And all those looks of hers, so gently proud,   100
And sweet disdain, so arrogantly meek,
Her fair and youthful breast,
A tower of lofty thoughts,
These savage, alpine places hide from me.
I don't know if before   105
I die I can expect
To see her, since from hour
To hour hope rises, then cannot hold firm,
And, sinking, makes it clear;
One whom Heaven honors I shall see no more.   110
There Chastity and Courtesy reside
And there I pray my dwelling too will be.
    Song, if in some sweet place
Our lady you should see,
I know that you must know   115
That she'll stretch forth to you her lovely hand
From which I am so far.
Don't touch it, but in reverence at her feet,
Tell her I'll come as quickly as I can,
Though naked soul, or man of flesh and bone.   120

38

    Orso, there never was a stream nor pond,°
Nor sea where every rivulet spills forth,
Nor shade of wall or hill or leafy branch,
Nor cloud that covers heaven, bathes the world,
    Nor other hindrance I complained about   5
(No matter what obscures the human view)
More than one veil that shades two lovely eyes—
That seems to say: "Now waste away and weep."
    That lowered gaze that quenches all my joy

spegne o per humiltate o per argoglio,   10
cagion sarà che 'nanzi tempo i' moia.

Et d'una bianca mano ancho mi doglio,
ch'è stata sempre accorta a farmi noia,
et contra gli occhi miei s'è fatta scoglio.

39

Io temo sí de' begli occhi l'assalto
ne' quali Amore et la mia morte alberga,
ch'i' fuggo lor come fanciul la verga,
et gran tempo è ch'i' presi il primier salto.

Da ora inanzi faticoso od alto   5
loco non fia, dove 'l voler non s'erga
per no scontrar chî miei sensi disperga
lassando come suol me freddo smalto.

Dunque s'a veder voi tardo mi volsi
per non ravvicinarmi a chi mi strugge,   10
fallir forse non fu di scusa indegno.

Piú dico, che 'l tornare a quel ch'uom fugge,
e 'l cor che di paura tanta sciolsi,
fur de la fede mia non leggier pegno.

40

S'Amore o Morte non dà qualche stroppio
a la tela novella ch'ora ordisco,
et s'io mi svolvo dal tenace visco,
mentre che l'un coll'altro vero accoppio,

i' farò forse un mio lavor sì doppio   5
tra lo stil de' moderni e 'l sermon prisco,
che, paventosamente a dirlo ardisco,
infin a Roma n'udirai lo scoppio.

Ma però che mi mancha a fornir l'opra
alquanto de le fila benedette   10
ch'avanzaro a quel mio dilecto padre,

perché tien' verso me le man' sí strette,
contra tua usanza? I' prego che tu l'opra,
et vedrai rïuscir cose leggiadre.

41

Quando dal proprio sito si rimove
l'arbor ch'amò già Phebo in corpo humano,
sospira et suda a l'opera Vulcano,
per rinfrescar l'aspre saette a Giove:

il qual or tona, or nevicha et or piove,   5

(Whether with pride or with humility)   10
Will be the cause of my untimely death.
    Then too I still am grieved by one white hand
That always has been quick to frustrate me—
Has made itself a barrier to my eyes.

39

    I fear so the assault of those fair eyes
In which love and my death as well abides,
I flee them as a young child flees the switch—
Long it has been since first I flinched from it.
    Henceforth, no place can be too wearying   5
Or lofty for my will to overtop
In shunning her who makes my senses flee,
While leaving me, as always, stony cold.
    Though I'm late coming back to see you, then,
So I'll avoid that one who lays me waste,   10
The fault perhaps may fitly be excused.
    Yet more I say: to turn toward what man flees,
And liberate one's heart from such great fear
Are no slight tokens of my constancy.

40

    If Love or Death does not create some flaw
Or rend this fabric new whose warp I lay,
If from the limed snare I can free myself,
Till this one with that other truth I wed,
    Perhaps so doubly my one work I'll shape   5
Between the moderns' style and ancient tongue
That (and I dare to say this fearfully)
At length you'll hear it noised abroad in Rome.
    But since I lack to carry out this task
A number of those blessed threads that are   10
Left over from my cherished father's work,°
    Why are you thus close-fisted with me now?
That's not your way; be open-handed, please,
And you will see distinguished things result.

41

    When from its rightful place that tree is gone°
Which in a human form once Phoebus loved,
Then Vulcan at his labor sweats and sighs,
Replenishing the cruel bolts of Jove;°
    Great Jove now thunders, snows now, now rains down,

senza honorar piú Cesare che Giano;
la terra piange, e 'l sol ci sta lontano
che la sua cara amica ved'altrove.
    Allor riprende ardir Saturno et Marte,
crudeli stelle; et Orïone armato
spezza a' tristi nocchier' governi et sarte;
    Eolo a Neptuno et a Giunon turbato
fa sentire, et a noi, come si parte
il bel viso dagli angeli aspectato.

10

42

    Ma poi che 'l dolce riso humile et piano
piú non asconde sue bellezze nove,
le braccia a la fucina indarno move
l'antiquissimo fabbro ciciliano,
    ch'a Giove tolte son l'arme di mano
temprate in Mongibello a tutte prove,
et sua sorella par che si rinove
nel bel guardo d'Apollo a mano a mano.
    Del lito occidental si move un fiato,
che fa securo il navigar senza arte,
et desta i fior' tra l'erba in ciascun prato.
    Stelle noiose fuggon d'ogni parte,
disperse dal bel viso inamorato,
per cui lagrime molte son già sparte.

5

10

43

    Il figliuol di Latona avea già nove
volte guardato dal balcon sovrano,
per quella ch'alcun tempo mosse invano
i suoi sospiri, et or gli altrui commove.
    Poi che cercando stanco non seppe ove
s'albergasse, da presso o di lontano,
mostrossi a noi qual huom per doglia insano,
che molto amata cosa non ritrove.
    Et cosí tristo standosi in disparte,
tornar non vide il viso, che laudato
sarà s'io vivo in piú di mille carte;
    et pietà lui medesmo avea cangiato,
sí che' begli occhi lagrimavan parte:
però l'aere ritenne il primo stato.

5

10

Not Caesar more than Janus honoring;°
The earth sheds tears, and far off stays the sun,
Who sees that his dear love has elsewhere gone.
    Then Saturn's courage reappears, and Mars'—
Those cruel stars; and then Orion armed°   10
Breaks wretched pilots' helms and tatters shrouds,
    And Aeolus, perturbed, lets Juno hear,°
Lets Neptune know, and us, that that fair face°
Awaited by the angels, now is gone.

<h2 style="text-align:center">42</h2>

    But once the modest, sweet and humble smile
No longer hides away its beauties rare,
Then that most venerable Sicilian smith°
Uselessly at his forge exerts his strength.
    For from Jove's hand the weapons are removed—   5
Tempered in Mongibello for all trials—°
And bit by bit Jove's sister reawakes,°
It seems, beneath Apollo's shining gaze.
    Now from the western shore a light breeze stirs
That makes the sailor safe—no need of skill—   10
Wakes flowers in each meadow 'midst the grass.
    The harmful stars take flight on every side,
All scattered by that fair face filled with love
On whose account so many tears were shed.

<h2 style="text-align:center">43</h2>

    Nine times already had Latona's son°
Looked from his princely balcony for her
Who at one time had stirred his sighs in vain,
And now gives rise to those of someone else.
    When after weary search he could not learn   5
Where she might be, near by or far away,
He seemed to us like one insane with grief,
One who can't find again a thing much loved.
    Thus gloomy, standing far away, he failed
To see that face return that, if I live,   10
In pages by the thousand shall be praised.
    And pity so had changed her countenance
That meanwhile those fair eyes were shedding tears;
And thus the air retained its former state.

44

Que' che 'n Tesaglia ebbe le man' sí pronte
a farla del civil sangue vermiglia,
pianse morto il marito di sua figlia,
raffigurato a le fatezze conte;
    e 'l pastor ch'a Golia ruppe la fronte,   5
pianse la ribellante sua famiglia,
et sopra 'l buon Saúl cangiò le ciglia,
ond'assai può dolersi il fiero monte.
    Ma voi che mai pietà non discolora,
et ch'avete gli schermi sempre accorti   10
contra l'arco d'Amor che 'ndarno tira,
    mi vedete straziare a mille morti:
né lagrima però discese anchora
da' be' vostr'occhi, ma disdegno et ira.

45

Il mio adversario in cui veder solete
gli occhi vostri ch'Amore e 'l ciel honora,
colle non sue bellezze v'innamora
piú che 'n guisa mortal soavi et liete.
    Per consiglio di lui, donna, m'avete   5
scacciato del mio dolce albergo fora:
misero exilio, avegna ch'i' non fôra
d'abitar degno ove voi sola siete.
    Ma s'io v'era con saldi chiovi fisso,
non devea specchio farvi per mio danno,   10
a voi stessa piacendo, aspra et superba.
    Certo, se vi rimembra di Narcisso,
questo et quel corso ad un termino vanno,
benché di sí bel fior sia indegna l'erba.

46

L'oro et le perle e i fior' vermigli e i bianchi,
che 'l verno devria far languidi et secchi,
son per me acerbi et velenosi stecchi,
ch'io provo per lo petto et per li fianchi.
    Però i dí miei fien lagrimosi et manchi,   5
ché gran duol rade volte aven che 'nvecchi:
ma piú ne colpo i micidiali specchi,
che 'n vagheggiar voi stessa avete stanchi.
    Questi poser silentio al signor mio,
che per me vi pregava, ond'ei si tacque,   10
veggendo in voi finir vostro desio;

44

That man who with such eagerness prepared°
To redden Thessaly with civil blood,
Shed tears to mourn his daughter's husband's death
When he familiar features recognized;
    The shepherd who Goliath's forehead smote°   5
Wept for the rebel in his family,
And knit his brows above the worthy Saul—
For this the savage mount can much lament;
    But you who never pale for pity's sake,
Who always at the ready have your shields   10
Against Love's bow, which he so vainly draws,
    You see me tortured with a thousand deaths,
No teardrop, nonetheless, spills forth as yet
From your fair eyes, but scorn and wrath instead.

45

My Enemy—the one in whom you see°
Those eyes that Love and Heaven do honor to—
Enamours you with beauties not his own,
Though sweet and joyful past all mortal form.
    On his advice, my Lady, from my sweet   5
Abode you drove me forth, sent me away
A wretched exile, since I was unfit
To sojourn where you now abide alone.
    But if there I were fixed with massive nails,
You'd need no glass to make you haughty, stern   10
To my undoing while you please yourself.
    Yet surely, if Narcissus you'll recall,°
Your course and his both lead to one vain end—
Though grass does not deserve so fair a flower.

46

The gold, the pearls, the crimson blooms and white
That winter must make wither and turn sere
Are poisonous and bitter thorns to me;
I feel them through my breast and in my sides.
    And thus my days are full of tears and few;   5
For seldom does so great a grief grow old.
Yet I blame homicidal mirrors more,
For with fond gazing you exhaust yourself.
    These mirrors force a silence on my lord
Who importuned you for me; he was stilled   10
By seeing your desire end in yourself.

questi fuor fabbricati sopra l'acque
d'abisso, et tinti ne l'eterno oblio,
onde 'l principio de mia morte nacque.

47

Io sentia dentr'al cor già venir meno
gli spirti che da voi ricevon vita;
et perché natural-mente s'aita
contra la morte ogni animal terreno,
 largai 'l desio, ch'i' teng'or molto a freno,   5
et misil per la via quasi smarrita:
però che dí et notte indi m'invita,
et io contra sua voglia altronde 'l meno.
 Et mi condusse, vergognoso et tardo,
a riveder gli occhi leggiadri, ond'io   10
per non esser lor grave assai mi guardo.
 Vivrommi un tempo omai, ch'al viver mio
tanta virtute à sol un vostro sguardo;
et poi morrò, s'io non credo al desio.

48

Se mai foco per foco non si spense,
né fiume fu già mai secco per pioggia,
ma sempre l'un per l'altro simil poggia,
et spesso l'un contrario l'altro accense,
 Amor, tu che' pensier' nostri dispense,   5
al qual un'alma in duo corpi s'appoggia,
perché fai in lei con disusata foggia
men per molto voler le voglie intense?
 Forse sí come 'l Nil d'alto caggendo
col gran suono i vicin' d'intorno assorda,   10
e 'l sole abbaglia chi ben fiso 'l guarda,
 cosí 'l desio che seco non s'accorda,
ne lo sfrenato obiecto vien perdendo,
et per troppo spronar la fuga è tarda.

49

Perch'io t'abbia guardato di menzogna
a mio podere et honorato assai,
ingrata lingua, già però non m'ài
renduto honor, ma facto ira et vergogna:
 ché quando piú 'l tuo aiuto mi bisogna   5
per dimandar mercede, allor ti stai
sempre piú fredda, et se parole fai,

These, shaped beside the streams of the abyss,
Are silvered with eternal disregard;
From them was born the first cause of my death.

47

Already I felt weakening in my heart
Those spirits that receive their life from you,
And since by nature every animal
On earth from death will guard itself, I gave
Desire, which I curb tightly now, free rein   5
And set him, almost lost, upon the way.
From it, by day and night he urges me
While I lead him along against his will.
He has conducted me, ashamed and slow,
To see again delightful eyes, from which   10
I keep away so I don't cause them grief.
I'll live a while yet, for one glance of yours
Has such great power in my life; and then
If to desire I pay no heed, I'll die.

48

If no fire ever was put out with fire,
No river ever dried by falling rain,
But if one always makes its fellow grow,
And oft flame's opposite will kindle it,
Love, you who dominate our thoughts, by whom   5
In our two bodies, one soul is sustained,
Why lessen in this curious way the soul's
Intense desire by making longing fierce?
Perhaps, just as the Nile falls from on high
And deafens with its roar its neighbors round,   10
And as the sun blinds one who on it stares,
Just so, in discord with itself, desire
In uncurbed opposition to itself,
Gets lost and, spurred too much, balks in its flight.

49

Though I have shielded you, ungrateful Tongue,
From lying and within my power have done
You honor great, no honor you've repaid,
But brought both wrath and shame to me, indeed.
For when I most require your aid to beg   5
For mercy, at your coldest you remain;
Or, if you do form words, those words are flawed,

son imperfecte, et quasi d'uom che sogna.
   Lagrime triste, et voi tutte le notti
m'accompagnate, ov'io vorrei star solo,   10
poi fuggite dinanzi a la mia pace;
   et voi sí pronti a darmi angoscia et duolo,
sospiri, allor traete lenti et rotti:
sola la vista mia del cor non tace.

50

   Ne la stagion che 'l ciel rapido inchina
verso occidente, et che 'l dí nostro vola
a gente che di là forse l'aspetta,
veggendosi in lontan paese sola,
la stancha vecchiarella pellegrina   5
raddoppia i passi, et piú et piú s'affretta;
et poi cosí soletta
al fin di sua giornata
talora è consolata
d'alcun breve riposo, ov'ella oblia   10
la noia e 'l mal de la passata via.
Ma, lasso, ogni dolor che 'l dí m'adduce
cresce qualor s'invia
per partirsi da noi l'eterna luce.
   Come 'l sol volge le 'nfiammate rote   15
per dar luogo a la notte, onde discende
dagli altissimi monti maggior l'ombra,
l'avaro zappador l'arme riprende,
et con parole et con alpestri note
ogni gravezza del suo petto sgombra;   20
et poi la mensa ingombra
di povere vivande,
simili a quelle ghiande,
le qua' fuggendo tutto 'l mondo honora.
Ma chi vuol si rallegri ad ora ad ora,   25
ch'i' pur non ebbi anchor, non dirò lieta,
ma riposata un'hora,
né per volger di ciel né di pianeta.
   Quando vede 'l pastor calare i raggi
del gran pianeta al nido ov'egli alberga,   30
e 'nbrunir le contrade d'oriente,
drizzasi in piedi, et co l'usata verga
lassando l'erba et le fontane e i faggi,
move la schiera sua soavemente;
poi lontan da la gente   35

And almost seem those of a man who dreams.
      And mournful Tears, you keep me company
Each night when I would rather be alone,   10
And then you flee, confronted by my Peace;
      And you, so quick to bring me fear and grief,
O Sighs, you heave forth slowly, brokenly;
My countenance alone hides not my heart.

                    50
      In that hour when the heavens quickly wheel,
When toward the west our day flies on to folk
Who may perhaps be waiting for it there,
The good old woman, weary, finds herself
Alone in a far land; fast, faster now   5
Her steps redouble on her pilgrimage,
And then at her day's end
Though by herself, she is
Consoled from time to time
When any brief repose lets her forget   10
The tedium and grief of her hard road.
But every sorrow that day yields to me,
Alas, grows greater, when
Eternal light prepares to part from us.
      And when the sun revolves its flaming wheels   15
To give way to the night, when moving down
From highest peaks, the greatest shadow spreads,
The thrifty tiller of the field collects
His implements; with rustic melodies
And talk he rids his heart of every grief,   20
And lays his table, then,
With scant and humble fare
Much like those acorns that
The whole world celebrates while shunning them.
Let those who will rejoice, though, while they can,   25
For I've not even had—say not a "glad,"
But say a "restful" hour—
Not for the planets' wheeling or the sky's.
      Then when the shepherd sees the rays decline
Of that great planet toward its sheltering nest,   30
Sees dusk engulf the regions of the east,
He rises up, and with his trusty crook,
Leaving behind the grassland, beechtrees, springs,
With gentleness he guides his flock along.
Then, far from everyone,   35

o casetta o spelunca
di verdi frondi ingiuncha:
ivi senza pensier' s'adagia et dorme.
Ahi crudo Amor, ma tu allor piú mi 'nforme
a seguir d'una fera che mi strugge,   40
la voce e i passi et l'orme,
et lei non stringi che s'appiatta et fugge.

    E i naviganti in qualche chiusa valle
gettan le membra, poi che 'l sol s'asconde,
sul duro legno et sotto a l'aspre gonne.   45
Ma io, perché s'attuffi in mezzo l'onde,
et lasci Hispagna dietro a le sue spalle,
et Granata et Marroccho et le Colonne,
et gli uomini et le donne
e 'l mondo et gli animali   50
aquetino i lor mali,
fine non pongo al mio obstinato affanno;
et duolmi ch'ogni giorno arroge al danno,
ch'i' son già pur crescendo in questa voglia
ben presso al decim'anno,   55
né poss'indovinar chi me ne scioglia.

    Et perché un poco nel parlar mi sfogo,
veggio la sera i buoi tornare sciolti
da le campagne et da' solcati colli:
i miei sospiri a me perché non tolti   60
quando che sia? perché no 'l grave giogo?
perché dí et notte gli occhi miei son molli?
Misero me, che volli
quando primier sí fiso
gli tenni nel bel viso   65
per iscolpirlo imaginando in parte
onde mai né per forza né per arte
mosso sarà, fin ch'i' sia dato in perda
a chi tutto diparte!
Né so ben ancho che di lei mi creda.   70

    Canzon, se l'esser meco
dal matino a la sera
t'à fatto di mia schiera,
tu non vorrai mostrarti in ciascun loco;
et d'altrui loda curerai sí poco,   75
ch'assai ti fia pensar di poggio in poggio
come m'à concio 'l foco
di questa viva petra, ov'io m'appoggio.

A cottage or a cave
He strews with verdant fronds;
There, free of care, he lays him down to sleep.
But, ah, harsh Love, it's then you press me most
To track that feral one who lays me waste—   40
Her voice, steps, vestiges—
But bind not her who crouches low, then flees.
    And mariners in some closed inlet safe
After the sun is hid, fling down their limbs,
Upon hard decking, under covers rough;   45
But though the sun plunge deep into the waves
And leave behind his back Granada, Spain,
Hercules' pillars, and Morocco too,
Though men and women too,
The world, the animals   50
May find peace for their ills,
I do not cease from my unyielding grief;
I mourn that every day augments my woe,
For in this longing I am growing still—
Its tenth year is at hand;   55
Who'll free me from it, I cannot divine.
    And since my speaking eases me a bit:
At dusk I see the oxen from the fields
And from the furrowed hills return unyoked;
Why, when it might be so, am I not freed   60
From sighs and why not from my heavy yoke?
And why both night and day are my eyes wet?
Ah, woe! What I desired
When first I fixed my eyes
Upon that lovely face   65
Was by imagining to sculpt it where
No power nor art could ever move it thence
Until I was consigned as prey to one
Who carries all things off;
I'm not sure that I credit that in her.   70
    If being with me, Song,
From morning until eve
Has made you my ally,
Not everywhere you'll want to show yourself;
You'll pay but little heed to others' praise;   75
From hill to hill you'll ponder deeply how
I'm left in such a state
By fire from this live stone on which I lean.

51

Poco era ad appressarsi agli occhi miei
la luce che da lunge gli abbarbaglia,
che, come, vide lei cangiar Thesaglia,
cosí cangiato ogni mia forma avrei.

Et s'io non posso transformarmi in lei   5
piú ch'i' mi sia (non ch'a mercé mi vaglia),
di qual petra piú rigida si 'ntaglia
pensoso ne la vista oggi sarei,

o di diamante, o d'un bel marmo biancho,
per la paura forse, o d'un dïaspro,   10
pregiato poi dal vulgo avaro et sciocco;

et sarei furor del grave giogo et aspro,
per cui i' ò invidia di quel vecchio stancho
che fa co le sue spalle ombra a Marroccho.

52

Non al suo amante piú Dïana piacque,
quando per tal ventura tutta ignuda
la vide in mezzo de le gelide acque,

ch'a me la pastorella alpestra et cruda
posta a bagnar un leggiadretto velo,   5
ch'a l'aura il vago et biondo capel chiuda,

tal che mi fece, or quand'egli arde 'l cielo,
tutto tremar d'un amoroso gielo.

53

Spirto gentil, che quelle membra reggi
dentro a le qua' peregrinando alberga
un signor valoroso, accorto et saggio,
poi che se' giunto a l'onorata verga
colla qual Roma et suoi erranti correggi,   5
et la richiami al suo antiquo vïaggio,
io parlo a te, però ch'altrove un raggio
non veggio di vertú, ch'al mondo è spenta,
né trovo chi di mal far si vergogni.
Che s'aspetti non so, né che s'agogni,   10
Italia, che suoi guai non par che senta:
vecchia, otïosa et lenta,
dormirà sempre, et non fia chi la svegli?
Le man' l'avess'io avolto entro' capegli.

Non spero che già mai dal pigro sonno   15

51

If but a little nearer to my eyes
That light had drawn which, far-off, dazzled them,
Then, just as Thessaly saw her transformed,°
Just so would I have wholly changed my shape.

But if I cannot, more than I have done,   5
Change into her (not that it gains me grace),
Then of the hardest stone one carves would I
Be made today, with thoughtful visage grave,

From diamond, or from marble fine and white
(With fear perhaps), or jasper, and be prized   10
Thenceforth by rabble—stupid, greedy folk.

I would cast off my cruel and heavy yoke
That makes me envy that old, weary one
Who shades Morocco with his shoulders' span.

52

Diana did not please her lover more°
When by like happenstance he looked on her,
Entirely naked 'midst the waters cold,

Than did the rustic, Alpine shepherdess
Please me—she poised to wash a charming veil   5
That shields blond, straying hair from gentle breeze—

So although heaven's burning now, she sets
Me all atremble with an amorous chill.

53

Noble spirit, who rules those limbs wherein,°
Upon their pilgrimage, there dwells a lord
Most valorous, intelligent, and wise,
Since you have grasped the venerable rods
With which you chastise Rome, her erring folk   5
Reprove, and call her to her ancient ways,
I speak to you because, elsewhere, I see
No ray of virtue, in the world quite spent,
Nor find I anyone whom ill deeds shame.
What she awaits and longs for—Italy—   10
I do not know; nor does she sense her woes,
It seems. Old, lazy, slow,
Will no one wake her? Will she ever sleep?
Would that I had my hand wound in her hair.

No hope have I that from her slothful sleep,   15

mova la testa per chiamar ch'uom faccia,
sí gravemente è oppressa et di tal soma;
ma non senza destino a le tue braccia,
che scuoter forte et sollevarla ponno,
è or commesso il nostro capo Roma.   20
Pon' man in quella venerabil chioma
securamente, et ne le treccie sparte,
sí che la neghittosa esca del fango.
I' che dí et notte del suo strazio piango,
di mia speranza ò in te la maggior parte: 25
che se 'l popol di Marte
devesse al proprio honore alzar mai gli occhi,
parmi pur ch'a' tuoi dí la gratia tocchi.

   L'antiche mura ch'anchor teme et ama
et trema 'l mondo, quando si rimembra   30
del tempo andato e 'ndietro si rivolve,
e i sassi dove fur chiuse le membra
di ta' che non saranno senza fama,
se l'universo pria non si dissolve,
et tutto quel ch'una ruina involve,   35
per te spera saldar ogni suo vitio.
O grandi Scipïoni, o fedel Bruto,
quanto v'aggrada, s'egli è anchor venuto
romor là giú del ben locato officio!
Come cre' che Fabritio   40
si faccia lieto, udendo la novella!
Et dice: Roma mia sarà anchor bella.

   Et se cosa di qua nel ciel si cura,
l'anime che lassú son citadine,
et ànno i corpi abandonati in terra,   45
del lungo odio civil ti pregan fine,
per cui la gente ben non s'assecura,
onde 'l camin a' lor tecti si serra:
che fur già sí devoti, et ora in guerra
quasi spelunca di ladron' son fatti,   50
tal ch'a' buon' solamente uscio si chiude,
et tra gli altari et tra le statue ignude
ogni impresa crudel par che se tratti.
Deh quanto diversi atti!
Né senza squille s'incommincia assalto,   55
che per Dio ringraciar fur poste in alto.

   Le donne lagrimose, e 'l vulgo inerme
de la tenera etate, e i vecchi stanchi
ch'ànno sé in odio et la soverchia vita,

Despite men's cries, she'll ever raise her head,
So heavy laden and oppressed is she;
But Rome, our head, and not without fate's help,
At this time is committed to your arms,
Which can with strength arouse her, lift her up.   20
Amidst those venerable locks, and those
Dishevelled tresses firmly thrust your hand
To make that slothful one rise from the mire.
I, who mourn her ruin day and night,
Repose the best part of my hopes in you,   25
For if the Race of Mars°
Can ever raise their eyes to their own worth,
That grace, I think, in your day must befall.

     That ancient rampart which the world still dreads
And loves and quakes before, when it recalls   30
Times now passed by, and turns to look behind;
Those stones where were sealed up the limbs of men
Who will not be without renown unless
The universe first melt away, and in
One ruin everything be swallowed up—   35
These hope to mend their every breach through you.
O, faithful Brutus, O great Scipios,
How it would please you if word came below
How suitably your office has been filled
How joyful I believe   40
Fabritius would be to hear that news:
He'd say: "My Rome will once again be fair."

     If heaven is concerned with earthly things,
Those souls who are the citizens above
And who have left their bodies in the earth   45
Pray you to end this drawn-out civil quarrel
That will not let the people rest secure,
Since to their shrines, the pathway is closed off.
What formerly were sacred places now
Almost the caves of thieves in war become.   50
Thus to the good alone the doors are closed;
Among stripped altars, and 'midst statues bare
It seems that every cruel trade is plied.
Oh, what inhuman acts!
Nor does the onslaught start without those bells   55
That once were hung aloft to give God thanks.

     The weeping women, and the unarmed crowd
Of tender youths and old and worn-out men
Who hate themselves and their superfluous life;

e i neri fraticelli e i bigi e i bianchi, 60
coll'altre schiere travagliate e 'nferme,
gridan: O signor nostro, aita, aita.
Et la povera gente sbigottita
ti scopre le sue piaghe a mille a mille,
ch'Anibale, non ch'altri, farian pio. 65
Et se ben guardi a la magion di Dio
ch'arde oggi tutta, assai poche faville
spegnendo, fien tranquille
le voglie, che si mostran sí 'nfiammate,
onde fien l'opre tue nel ciel laudate. 70

Orsi, lupi leoni, aquile et serpi
ad una gran marmorea colomna
fanno noia sovente, et a sé danno.
Di costor piange quella gentil donna
che t'à chiamato a ciò che di lei sterpi 75
le male piante, che fiorir non sanno.
Passato è già piú che 'l millesimo anno
che 'n lei mancâr quell'anime leggiadre
che locata l'avean là dov'ell'era.
Ahi nova gente oltra misura altera, 80
irreverente a tanta et a tal madre!
Tu marito, tu padre:
ogni soccorso di tua man s'attende,
ché maggior padre ad altr'opera intende.

Rade volte adiven ch'a l'alte imprese 85
fortuna ingiurïosa non contrasti,
ch'agli animosi fatti mal s'accorda.
Ora sgombrando 'l passo onde tu intrasti,
famisi perdonar molt'altre offese,
ch'almen qui da se stessa si discorda: 90
però che, quanto 'l mondo si ricorda,
ad huom mortal non fu aperta la via
per farsi, come a te, di fama eterno,
che puoi drizzar, s'i' non falso discerno,
in stato la piú nobil monarchia. 95
Quanta gloria ti fia
dir: Gli altri l'aitâr giovene et forte;
questi in vecchiezza la scampò da morte.

Sopra 'l monte Tarpeio, canzon, vedrai
un cavalier, ch'Italia tutta honora, 100
pensoso piú d'altrui che di se stesso.
Digli: Un che non ti vide anchor da presso,
se non come per fama huom s'innamora,

The black friars, and the grey friars, and the white°   60
With ranks of other sick, tormented ones
Cry out: "O our dear lord, give aid, give aid,"
The destitute, disheartened people show
To you their thousand, thousand wounds, which would
Make even Hannibal compassionate.°   65
If you examine well the church of God
That's all in flames today, by quenching some
Few sparks, you'll pacify
Those wills that, so inflamed, display themselves,
And thus your works in heaven will be praised.   70

For often bears, wolves, lions, eagles, snakes°
Prove vexing to one marble column great,
And also to themselves do injury.
On their account that noble lady weeps,°
She who called you that you might root out   75
Those noxious weeds that know no flowering.
Indeed, more than a thousand years passed by
Since the departure of those spirits rare
Who in that place had thus established her.
Alas, newcomers, past all measure proud,   80
Irreverent to such a mother great.
You, husband; Father, you:
All succor is expected from your hand;
Our greater Father's bent on other works.°

How seldom does injurious Fortune not   85
Oppose herself to noble enterprise,
For with courageous deeds she ill accords.
Now, sweeping clear the way by which you come,
She makes me pardon many an offence,
As here, at least, she contradicts herself;   90
Because, within the memory of the world
No way was clear, as it is clear for you,
For mortal man to earn eternal fame,
Since you, unless I falsely judge, can set
In order this most noble monarchy.   95
What glory for you when
They say: "Those helped her in her youth and strength;
He rescued her from death in her old age."

Above the Tarpeian mount, Song, you will see°
A knight, one by all Italy revered,°   100
One who considers others more than self.
Tell him: "One who has yet to see you close
At hand, except as fame enamours men,

dice che Roma ognora
con gli occhi di dolor bagnati et molli
ti chier mercé da tutti sette i colli.

54
Perch'al viso d'Amor portava insegna,
mosse una pellegrina il mio cor vano,
ch'ogni altra mi parea d'onor men degna.

Et lei seguendo su per l'erbe verdi,
udí' dir alta voce di lontano:
Ahi, quanti passi per la selva perdi!

Allor mi strinsi a l'ombra d'un bel faggio,
tutto pensoso; et rimirando intorno,
vidi assai periglioso il mio vïaggio;

et tornai indietro quasi a mezzo 'l giorno.

55
Quel foco ch'i' pensai che fosse spento
dal freddo tempo et da l'età men fresca,
fiamma et martir ne l'anima rinfresca.

Non fur mai tutte spente, a quel ch'i' veggio,
ma ricoperte alquanto le faville,
et temo no 'l secondo error sia peggio.
Per lagrime ch'i' spargo a mille a mille,
conven che 'l duol per gli occhi si distille
dal cor, ch'à seco le faville et l'ésca:
non pur qual fu, ma pare a me che cresca.

Qual foco non avrian già spento et morto
l'onde che gli occhi tristi versan sempre?
Amor, avegna mi sia tardi accorto,
vòl che tra duo contrari mi distempre;
et tende lacci in sí diverse tempre,
che quand'ò piú speranza che 'l cor n'esca,
allor piú nel bel viso mi rinvesca.

56
Se col cieco desir che 'l cor distrugge
contando l'ore no m'inganno io stesso,
ora mentre ch'io parlo il tempo fugge
ch'a me fu inseme et a mercé promesso.

Qual ombra è sí crudel che 'l seme adugge,
ch'al disïato frutto era sí presso?
et dentro dal mio ovil qual fera rugge?

105

5

10

5

10

15

5

Says Rome forever will,
Her eyes in sorrow bathed and wet with tears,   105
Beg you for help from all her seven hills."

54

Because she bore Love's emblem in her face,
A pilgrim stirred my empty heart, for all
The rest less fit for honor seemed to me.
    Yet as I followed her through fields of green,
I heard a lofty voice speak from afar: 5
"Ah, in that wood you waste so many steps!"
    At once I pressed myself deep in the shade
Of a fine beech; all pensive, gazing round,
I knew my journey very perilous;
    And it was almost noon when I turned back.°   10

55

That fire which, as I thought, had quite died out,
Quenched by cold time and by my waning youth,
Flares up with flame and torment in my soul.
    It never was all spent, as I now see;
Its sparks, instead, were partly covered up,   5
My second fault, I fear, may be still worse.
From tears that by the thousands I have shed,
It follows that my eyes distill my woe
Within my heart, where sparks and tinder bide,
A fire not as before, but fiercer grown.   10
    What fire would these waves not have quenched
            and drowned
That flow forever from my sorrowing eyes?
Love, though this insight may occur too late,
Wants me stretched then between two opposites,
And in such diverse fashion sets out snares   15
That when I most expect my heart's escape,
Then by that lovely face I'm trapped the more.

56

If, with the blind desire that wrings my heart
While counting hours, I don't delude myself,
Now, as I speak, the time flees fast away,
Time promised both to pity and to me.
    What shade is so malign it blights the seed   5
That was so near to bearing yearned-for fruit?
What wild beast howls within my fold? Between

tra la spiga et la man qual muro è messo?

    Lasso, nol so; ma sí conosco io bene
che per far piú dogliosa la mia vita   10
amor m'addusse in sí gioiosa spene.

    Et or di quel ch'i' ò lecto mi sovene,
che 'nanzi al dí de l'ultima partita
huom beato chiamar non si convene.

57

    Mie venture al venir son tarde et pigre,
la speme incerta, e 'l desir monta et cresce,
onde e 'l lassare et l'aspectar m'incresce;
et poi al partir son piú levi che tigre.

    Lasso, le nevi fien tepide et nigre,   5
e 'l mar senz'onda, et per l'alpe ogni pesce,
et corcherassi il sol là oltre ond'esce
d'un medesimo fonte Eufrate et Tigre,

    prima ch'i' trovi in ciò pace né triegua,
o Amore o madonna altr'uso impari,   10
che m'ànno congiurato a torto incontra.

    Et s'i' ò alcun dolce, è dopo tanti amari,
che per disdegno il gusto si dilegua:
altro mai di lor gratie non m'incontra.

58

    La guancia che fu già piangendo stancha
riposate su l'un, signor mio caro,
et siate ormai di voi stesso piú avaro
a quel crudel che' suoi seguaci imbiancha.

    Coll'altro richiudete da man mancha   5
la strada a' messi suoi ch'indi passaro,
mostrandovi un d'agosto et di genaro,
perch'a la lunga via tempo ne mancha.

    Et col terzo bevete un suco d'erba
che purghe ogni pensier che 'l cor afflige,   10
dolce a la fine, et nel principio acerba.

    Me riponete ove 'l piacer si serba,
tal ch'i' non tema del nocchier di Stige,
se la preghiera mia non è superba.

59

    Perché quel che mi trasse ad amar prima,
altrui colpa mi toglia,
del mio fermo voler già non mi svoglia.

The ripe ear and my hand, what wall is raised?
    Ah, wretched, I know not; but well I know
How Love, to make my life more dolorous,   10
Has urged me forward to such joyous hope.
    And now, what I have read returns to me:
Before his day of final parting comes,
No man should be enrolled among the blest.

57

    My fortunes take shape slowly and too late,
Unsure is hope, and yearning mounts and grows;
It vexes me to quit them, or to wait,
Yet then, more swift than tigers, they depart.
    Ah weary! Warm and black the snows will be,   5
And waveless be the sea, and every fish
Swim through the Alps; the sun will set beyond
Where Tigris and Euphrates share one source,
    Before I find peace, or find truce in this,
Let Love or lady learn some other way,   10
For they conspired against me wrongfully;
    And if I find some sweetness, it succeeds
Such bitterness, that scorn dispels its taste;
No other grace from them do I enjoy.

58

    Ah, rest that cheek, already worn with tears,
Upon this gift, my precious lord; henceforth°
Be much more sparing of yourself with that
Cruel one who makes his retinue turn white.°
    And with the next, seal off the left hand road   5
To messengers of his who pass that way;
In August or in January prove
The same, for time on that long path grows short.
    And from the third, drink herbal nectar that
Will purge your heart of every grievous thought,   10
Sweet at the end, though bitter at the start.
    Tuck me away where pleasure is saved up°
So I won't dread the boatman of the Styx—°
If this request of mine is not too proud.

59

    Because another's guilt deprives me of
What first drew me to love,
I've certainly not lost steadfast desire.

Tra le chiome de l'òr nascose il laccio,
al qual mi strinse, Amore;   5
et da' begli occhi mosse il freddo ghiaccio,
che mi passò nel core,
con la vertú d'un súbito splendore,
che d'ogni altra sua voglia
sol rimembrando anchor l'anima spoglia.   10
    Tolta m'è poi di que' biondi capelli,
lasso, la dolce vista;
e 'l volger de' duo lumi honesti et belli
col suo fuggir m'atrista;
ma perché ben morendo honor s'acquista,   15
per morte né per doglia
non vo' che da tal nodo Amor mi scioglia.

60

L'arbor gentil che forte amai molt'anni,
mentre i bei rami non m'ebber a sdegno
fiorir faceva il mio debile ingegno
a la sua ombra, et crescer negli affanni.
    Poi che, securo me di tali inganni,   5
fece di dolce sé spietato legno,
i' rivolsi i pensier' tutti ad un segno,
che parlan sempre de' lor tristi danni.
    Che porà dir chi per amor sospira,
s'altra speranza le mie rime nove   10
gli avessir data, et per costei la perde?
    Né poeta ne colga mai, né Giove
la privilegi, et al Sol venga in ira,
tal che si secchi ogni sua foglia verde.

61

Benedetto sia 'l giorno, e 'l mese, et l'anno,
et la stagione, e 'l tempo, et l'ora, e 'l punto,
e 'l bel paese, e 'l loco ov'io fui giunto
da' duo begli occhi che legato m'ànno;
    et benedetto il primo dolce affanno   5
ch'i' ebbi ad esser con Amor congiunto,
et l'arco, et le saette ond'i' fui punto,
et le piaghe che 'nfin al cor mi vanno.
    Benedette le voci tante ch'io
chiamando il nome de mia donna ò sparte,   10
e i sospiri, et le lagrime, e 'l desio;
    et benedette sian tutte le carte

Among those golden locks Love hid the springe
In which I was ensnared;   5
And from those lovely eyes came that cold ice
Which pierced into my heart,
And with such force of sudden brightness that,
Still, just remembering
Despoils my soul of every other wish.   10
    And then I was bereft of that blond hair—
Alas, the lovely sight!
The glance of those two chaste and lovely lights,
By its flight saddens me;
But since by dying well one honor gains,   15
Not death nor grief can make
Me wish that Love would free me from that snare.

60

That noble tree, which I so dearly loved
For many years, while its fair limbs have scorned
Me not, has caused my feeble skill to bloom
Within its shade, and grow 'midst suffering.
    Then—just as I felt safe from all such guile—   5
Its wood it changed from sweet to obdurate;
And on one goal I fastened all my thoughts,
Which speak forever of their woeful wrongs.
    What can one utter—one who sighs for love—
If, when my early rhymes had given him   10
Another hope, through her he loses it?
    "Then let no poet ever pluck its fruit,
Nor Jove grant privilege; and may it feel
The Sun's full wrath, so each green leaf may sear."

61

Ah, blessed be the day, the month, the year,
The season, time, the hour, the very stroke,
Fair countryside, and place where I was caught
By those two lovely eyes that bound me fast;
    And blessed be that first sweet breathlessness   5
That caught at me as I was bound to Love;
The bow, the darts that pierced me, be they blest,
And wounds so deep they struck me to the heart;
    And blest the many words I scattered forth
As I invoked my lady's name, and blest   10
My sighs, my passion, and the tears I shed.
    And all those pages, blessed be they too,

ov'io fama l'acquisto, e 'l pensier mio,
ch'è sol di lei, sí ch'altra non v'à parte.

62

Padre del ciel, dopo i perduti giorni,
dopo le notti vaneggiando spese,
con quel fero desio ch'al cor s'accese,
mirando gli atti per mio mal sí adorni,
    piacciati omai col Tuo lume ch'io torni   5
ad altra vita et a piú belle imprese,
sí ch'avendo le reti indarno tese,
il mio duro adversario se ne scorni.
    Or volge, Signor mio, l'undecimo anno
ch'i' fui sommesso al dispietato giogo   10
che sopra i piú soggetti è piú feroce.
    Miserere del mio non degno affanno;
reduci i pensier' vaghi a miglior luogo;
ramenta lor come oggi fusti in croce.

63

Volgendo gli occhi al mio novo colore
che fa di morte rimembrar la gente,
pietà vi mosse; onde, benignamente
salutando, teneste in vita il core.
    La fraile vita ch'ancor meco alberga,   5
fu de' begli occhi vostri aperto dono,
et de la voce angelica soave.
Da lor conosco l'esser ov'io sono:
    ché, come suol pigro animal per verga,
cosí destaro in me l'anima grave.   10
Del mio cor, donna, l'una et l'altra chiave
    avere in mano; et di ciò son contento,
presto di navigare a ciascun vento,
ch'ogni cosa da voi m'è dolce honore.

64

Se voi poteste per turbati segni,
per chinar gli occhi, o per pieghar la testa,
o per esser piú d'altra al fuggir presta,
torcendo 'l viso a' preghi honesti et degni,
    uscir già mai, over per altri ingegni,   5
del petto ove dal primo lauro innesta
Amor piú rami, i' direi ben che questa
fosse giusta cagione a' vostri sdegni:

That purchased fame for her, and blest my thoughts°
Of her alone in which no other shares.

62

Father of heaven, after wasted days,
After those nights spent tossing uselessly
With wild desire that kindled in my heart
From watching deeds so graceful, to my ill:
    Henceforth be pleased, I pray, that by your light,   5
Another life I turn toward, fairer deeds;
So, having woven nets to no effect,
My bitter enemy is put to shame.
    Now the eleventh year, my Lord, rolls round
When I've been subject to that ruthless yoke   10
Which is most savage to the meekest thrall.
    Miserere; pity my worthless woe;
My straying thoughts, lead to a better place;
Remind them: this day You were on the cross.

63

Turning your eyes upon my pallor new,
Which causes everyone to think on death,
Compassion moved you, and so, graciously
You greeted me and kept my heart alive.
    The fragile life that shelters still in me   5
Was openly the gift of your fair eyes
And of your gentle, sweet, angelic voice;
I know that what I am I owe to them,
    For as one with a switch prods lazy beasts
You goad awake the burdened soul in me: 10
Both this and that key, lady, of my heart
    Rest in your hand; with that I am content,
Eager to sail with any wind, because
From you, all things are honor sweet to me.

64

Had you been able by those troubled signs,
By eyes cast down, averting of your head,
Or being quicker than another one
To flee in frowns at chaste and worthy prayers,
    Or ever, by some other tricks to leave   5
My breast where, from the primal laurel, Love
More limbs grafts, I admit that this had been
Just cause for all your outbursts of disdain;

ché gentil pianta in arido terreno
par che si disconvenga, et però lieta   10
naturalmente quindi si diparte;
    ma poi vostro destino a voi pur vieta
l'esser altrove, provedete almeno
di non star sempre in odïosa parte.

65

    Lasso, che mal accorto fui da prima
nel giorno ch'a ferir mi venne Amore,
ch'a passo a passo è poi fatto signore
de la mia vita, et posto in su la cima.
    Io non credea per forza di sua lima   5
che punto di fermezza o di valore
mancasse mai ne l'indurato core;
ma cosí va, chi sopra 'l ver s'estima.
    Da ora inanzi ogni difesa è tarda,
altra che di provar s'assai o poco   10
questi preghi mortali Amore sguarda.
    Non prego già, né puote aver piú loco,
che mesuratamente il mio cor arda,
ma che sua parte abbi costei del foco.

66

    L'aere gravato, et l'importuna nebbia
compressa intorno da rabbiosi vènti
tosto conven che si converta in pioggia;
et già son quasi di cristallo i fiumi,
e 'n vece de l'erbetta per le valli   5
non se ved'altro che pruine et ghiaccio.
    Et io nel cor via piú freddo che ghiaccio
ò di gravi pensier' tal una nebbia,
qual si leva talor di queste valli,
serrate incontra agli amorosi vènti,   10
et circundate di stagnanti fiumi,
quando cade dal ciel piú lenta pioggia.
    In picciol tempo passa ogni gran pioggia,
e 'l caldo fa sparir le nevi e 'l ghiaccio,
di che vanno superbi in vista i fiumi;   15
né mai nascose il ciel sí folta nebbia
che sopragiunta dal furor d'i vènti
non fugisse dai poggi et da le valli.
    Ma, lasso, a me non val fiorir de valli,
anzi piango al sereno et a la pioggia   20

Because for arid soil a noble plant
Ill suited seems, it therefore naturally   10
Is pleased to get away from such a place;
    But since your destiny forbids that you
Live elsewhere, at the least take measures lest
In loathsome regions you forever stay.

65

    Ah, woe, that I was off guard from the first
Upon the day Love came to injure me,
For, step by step, of my life he's become
The lord, and he has occupied its heights.
    I did not think one joy of steadfastness   5
Or worth, by his rasp's power could ever be
Filed down in stubborn heart, yet thus it goes
With one who rates himself above the truth.
    Every defence henceforward is too late,
Except for trying whether Love regards   10
As great or very small these mortals' prayers.
    I'll pray no more—for it can never be—
That with a measured love my heart will burn,
But that she'll bear her portion of the fire.

66

    This heavy air and this persistent fog
Compressed on every side by furious winds,
Must very soon be altered into rain;
Already almost crystal are the streams;
Instead of tender grasses in the vales,   5
Now nothing can be seen but frost and ice.
    And I, in my heart colder far than ice—
I have of heavy troubles such a fog
As that which sometimes rises from these vales,
All tightly sealed against the amorous winds,   10
And circled all about with stagnant streams,
When from the heavens falls the softest rain.
    In a short time will pass each drenching rain,
And heat will melt away the snow and ice—
Before our eyes, these swell with pride the streams;   15
For never was sky hid by such dense fog
That, when it met the fury of the winds,
It did not flee from hillsides and from vales.
    But, oh, no use to me the flowering vales—
I weep beneath clear skies and in the rain   20

et a' gelati et a' soavi vènti:
ch'allor fia un dí madonna senza 'l ghiaccio
dentro, et di for senza l'usata nebbia,
ch'i' vedrò secco il mare, e' laghi, e i fiumi.

Mentre ch'al mar descenderanno i fiumi   25
et le fiere ameranno ombrose valli,
fia dinanzi a' begli occhi quella nebbia
che fa nascer d'i miei continua pioggia,
et nel bel petto l'indurato ghiaccio
che trâ del mio sí dolorosi vènti.   30

Ben debbo io perdonare a tutti vènti,
per amor d'un che 'n mezzo di duo fiumi
mi chiuse tra 'l bel verde e 'l dolce ghiaccio,
tal ch'i' depinsi poi per mille valli
l'ombra ov'io fui, ché né calor né pioggia   35
né suon curava di spezzata nebbia.

Ma non fuggío già mai nebbia per vènti,
come quel dí, né mai fiumi per pioggia,
né ghiaccio quando 'l sole apre le valli.

67

Del mar Tirreno a la sinistra riva,
dove rotte dal vento piangon l'onde,
súbito vidi quella altera fronde,
di cui conven che 'n tante carte scriva.

Amor, che dentro a l'anima bolliva,   5
per rimembranza de le treccie bionde
mi spinse, onde in un rio che l'erba asconde
caddi, non già come persona viva.

Solo ov'io era tra boschetti et colli
vergogna ebbi di me, ch'al cor gentile   10
basta ben tanto, et altro spron non volli.

Piacemi almen d'aver cangiato stile
dagli occhi a' pie', se del lor esser molli
gli altri asciugasse un piú cortese aprile.

68

L'aspetto sacro de la terra vostra
mi fa del mal passato tragger guai,
gridando: Sta' su, misero, che fai?;
et la via de salir al ciel mi mostra.

Ma con questo pensier un altro giostra,   5
et dice a me: Perché fuggendo vai?
se ti rimembra, il tempo passa omai

And in the freezing and the gentle winds;
For on that day my lady's without ice
Inside, has outside no accustomed fog,
I'll see run dry the oceans, lakes, and streams.

As long as to the sea flow down the streams,   25
And savage beasts prefer the shadowed vales,
Before her lovely eyes will stay that fog
Which makes my eyes bring forth continuous rain,
And in her lovely bosom hardened ice
Remain, that draws from mine such woeful winds.   30

Yes, I must offer pardon to all winds
For love of one who, in between two streams,
Shuts me between fair greenery and sweet ice,
So that I pictured in a thousand vales
The shadow where I stood; not heat nor rain   35
I heeded, nor the sound of splitting fog.°

But never have fogs fled before the winds
As on that day, nor ever streams from rain,
Nor ice when sunlight penetrates the vales.

67

By the Tyrrhenian, on the left hand shore,
Where weeping waves are broken by the wind,
There all at once I saw that lofty bough
Of which, on many pages, I must write.

Love, who had been seething in my soul,   5
With recollection of those tresses blond
Impelled me, so that in a brook concealed
By grass I tumbled, scarce a living man.

Alone there, 'midst the woods and hills, I felt
Ashamed within, for to the noble heart   10
Much is enough; I wished no other spur.

At least I'm pleased at having changed my style
From eyes to feet, if by their being wet
A kinder April dry the others' tears.

68

The sacred prospect of your land makes me
Heave sighs for past misdeeds, while I cry out,
"Rise up, you wretched one, what do you do?"
And thus I'm shown the way to climb to heaven.

But with this thought another jousts, and says   5
To me, "Why are you fleeing so? If you
But think of it, the time is nearly past

di tornar a veder la donna nostra.
I' che 'l suo ragionar intendo, allora
m'agghiaccio dentro, in guisa d'uom ch'ascolta   10
novella che di súbito l'accora.
    Poi torna il primo, et questo dà la volta:
qual vincerà, non so; ma 'nfino ad ora
combattuto ànno, et non pur una volta.

69

    Ben sapeva io che natural consiglio,
Amor, contra di te già mai non valse,
tanti lacciuol', tante impromesse false,
tanto provato avea 'l tuo fiero artiglio.
    Ma novamente, ond'io mi meraviglio   5
(diròl, come persona a cui ne calse,
et che 'l notai là sopra l'acque salse,
tra la riva toscana et l'Elba et Giglio),
    i' fuggia le tue mani, et per camino,
agitandom' i vènti e 'l ciel et l'onde,   10
m'andava sconosciuto et pellegrino:
    quando ecco i tuoi ministri, i' non so donde,
per darmi a diveder ch'al suo destino
mal chi contrasta, et mal chi si nasconde.

70

    Lasso me, ch'i' non so in qual parte pieghi
la speme, ch'è tradita omai piú volte:
che se non è chi con pietà m'ascolte,
perché sparger al ciel sí spessi preghi?
Ma s'egli aven ch'anchor non mi si nieghi   5
finir anzi 'l mio fine
queste voci meschine,
non gravi al mio signor perch'io il ripreghi
di dir libero un dí tra l'erba e i fiori:
Drez et rayson es qu'ieu ciant e· m demori.   10
    Ragion è ben ch'alcuna volta io canti,
però ch'ò sospirato sí gran tempo
che mai non incomincio assai per tempo
per adequar col riso i dolor' tanti.
Et s'io potesse far ch'agli occhi santi   15
porgesse alcun dilecto
qualche dolce mio detto,
o me beato sopra gli altri amanti!
Ma piú, quand'io dirò senza mentire:

For turning back to see our lady now."
Then I, who understand his argument,
Am turned to ice inside like one who hears   10
Such tidings that, at once, they pierce his heart.

The first turns then, and puts this one to flight;
I don't know which will win, but up till now
They've been at war, and not for the first time.

69

I surely knew that natural advice
Was never any use against you, Love.
So many little traps and specious vows—
So many times you've fleshed your talons fierce.

But lately—and at this I marvel so—   5
(As one it mattered to I'll speak of it,
And that I marked it on the briny sea,
Off Giglio, Elba, and the Tuscan shore):°

From your hands I escaped, and on my way
I went, whirled round by winds and skies and waves,   10
Unrecognized, a pilgrim stranger, when

Here came your ministers, I knew not whence,
To show me he fares ill who strives against
His fate, and ill fares he who hides from it.

70

Ah wretched me, for I know not on what
To pin my hope, so many times deceived,
If with compassion no one lends me ear,
Why scatter prayers to heaven so frequently?
But if it comes to pass that death does not   5
Prevent my finishing
These paltry songs, let my
Lord not be grieved because I crave once more
Freely, one day, 'midst grass and flowers to say:
"That I rejoice and sing is just and right."°   10
Indeed it's right that I should sometimes sing,
Because I have been sighing for so long
That I cannot begin in ample time
With laughter to make up for such great grief.
If to those blessed eyes with some sweet verse   15
Of mine I could arrange
To offer some delight,
O happy me! Above all lovers else!
Yet more, when I can say without a lie:

Donna mi priegha, per ch'io voglio dire.   20
    Vaghi pensier' che cosí passo passo
scorto m'avete a ragionar tant'alto,
vedete che madonna à 'l cor di smalto,
sí forte, ch'io per me dentro nol passo.
Ella non degna di mirar sí basso   25
che di nostre parole
curi, ché 'l ciel non vòle
al qual pur contrastando i' son già lasso:
onde, come nel cor m'induro e 'naspro,
cosí nel mio parlar voglio esser aspro.   30
    Che parlo? o dove sono? e chi m'inganna,
altri ch'io stesso e 'l desïar soverchio?
Già s'i' trascorro il cie di cerchio in cherchio,
nessun pianeta a pianger mi condanna.
Se mortal velo il mio veder appanna,   35
che colpa è de le stelle,
o de le cose belle?
Meco si sta chi dí et notte m'affanna,
poi che del suo piacer mi fe' gir grave
la dolce vista e 'l bel guardo soave.   40
    Tutte le cose di che 'l mondo è adorno
uscîr buone de man del mastro eterno;
ma me, che cosí adentro non discerno,
abbaglia il bel che mi si mostra intorno;
et s'al vero splendor già mai ritorno,   45
l'occhio non pò star fermo,
cosí l'à fatto infermo
pur la sua propria colpa, et non quel giorno
ch'i' volsi inver' l'angelica beltade
nel dolce tempo de la prima etade.   50

                            71
    Perché la vita è breve,
et l'ingegno paventa a l'alta impresa,
né di lui né di lei molto mi fido;
ma spero che sia intesa
là dov'io bramo, et là dove esser deve,   5
la doglia mia la qual tacendo i' grido.
Occhi leggiadri dove Amor fa nido,
a voi rivolgo il mio debile stile,
pigro da sé, ma 'l gran piacer lo sprona;
et chi di voi ragiona   10
tien dal soggetto un habito gentile,

"A lady entreats me, thus I wish to speak."   20
    Delightful thoughts that have thus, step by step,
In such high fashion guided me to speak,
You see my lady has a heart that's glazed
So hard, that on my own I can't pass in.
And she disdains to glance so low that she   25
Can heed our words; for Heaven—
Opposing which has worn
Me out already—does not wish it so.
As I grow hard and bitter in my heart,
"So in my speech I want to be severe."   30
    What do I say? Where am I? Who tricks me
Except myself and my extreme desire?
Yes, if I scan the heavens from sphere to sphere,
I find no planet damning me to weep.
And if a mortal veil obscures my sight,   35
What fault's that of the stars?
What fault of lovely things?
One stays with me who grieves me day and night
Since by her charm I was afflicted with
"Her features sweet and her fair, gentle glance."   40
    All things with which the world's graced, issue forth
In goodness from the eternal Shaper's hand;
But I, since inner things I don't discern
Am dazzled by the beauty all around,
And if to splendor real I don't return,   45
My eye cannot stay true,
So feeble it has grown
Through its own guilt, and not because that day
I turned to face angelic loveliness,
"In the sweet season of my early youth."   50

71

    Because life is so brief
And my gift quails at this high enterprise,
I do not place much trust in either one;
It will, I hope, be known
Where I would wish it to, and where it must—   5
This woe of mine that, silent, I cry forth.
Fair, graceful eyes, in which Love makes his nest,
To you I turn again my feeble style;
Dull in itself, it's spurred by great delight,
For one who treats of you   10
Draws from his subject usage courteous

che con l'ale amorose
levando il parte d'ogni pensier vile.
Con queste alzato vengo a dire or cose
ch'ò portate nel cor gran tempo ascose.   15
    Non perch'io non m'aveggia
quanto mia laude è 'ngiurïosa a voi:
ma contrastar non posso al gran desio,
lo quale è 'n me da poi
ch'i' vidi quel che pensier non pareggia,   20
non che l'avagli altrui parlar o mio.
Principio del mio dolce stato rio,
altri che voi so ben che non m'intende.
Quando agli ardenti rai neve divegno,
vostro gentile sdegno   25
forse ch'allor mia indignitate offende.
· Oh, se questa temenza
non temprasse l'arsura che m'incende,
beato venir men! ché 'n lor presenza
m'è piú caro il morir che 'l viver senza.   30
    Dunque ch'i' non mi sfaccia,
sí frale obgetto a sí possente foco,
non è proprio valor che me ne scampi;
ma la paura un poco,
che 'l sangue vago per le vene agghiaccia,   35
risalda 'l cor, perché piú tempo avampi.
O poggi, o valli, o fiumi, o selve, o campi,
o testimon' de la mia grave vita,
quante volte m'udiste chiamar morte!
Ahi dolorosa sorte,   40
lo star mi strugge, e 'l fuggir non m'aita
Ma se maggior paura
non m'affrenasse, via corta et spedita
trarrebbe a fin questa aspra pena et dura;
et la colpa è di tal che non à cura.   45
    Dolor, perché mi meni
fuor di camin a dir quel ch'i' non voglio?
Sostien' ch'io vada ove 'l piacer mi spigne.
Già di voi non mi doglio,
occhi sopra 'l mortal corso sereni,   50
né di lui ch'a tal nodo mi distrigne.
Vedete ben quanti color' depigne
Amor sovente in mezzo del mio volto,
et potrete pensar qual dentro fammi,
là 've dí et notte stammi   55

So, rising on the wings
Of Love, he sheds each thought contemptible.
On these wings mounted high I come to say
Now, things I long bore hidden in my heart.   15
    Not that I do not see
How much my praise does injury to you;
Instead, I can't withstand the grand desire
That ever dwells in me
Since I beheld what thought cannot approach,   20
Nor can my words nor others' equal them.
First cause of my sweet, guilty state,
You only comprehend me, I know well.
When, at your ardent rays I turn to snow,
Your noble scorn, perhaps,   25
Will take offense at my effrontery.
Oh, if this bashfulness
Did not abate my raging, burning thirst,
To fail were blessed! In their presence death
Is dearer to me than is life without.   30
Thus, that I do not melt,
So frail an object in so fierce a flame,
Arises in no saving worth of mine
But from a little fear
That ices in my veins the cringing blood,   35
And, so it may blaze longer, heals my heart.
O hills, O vales, O streams, O woods, O fields,
O witnesses of my afflicted life,
How often you have heard me call for death!
Ah, woeful destiny,   40
Enduring you destroys me, and to flee
Affords no help. If no
Fear greater held me back, a short, quick way
Would end this punishment so harsh, so hard;
The fault is of someone who doesn't care.   45
    Why guide me, sorrow, from
My path, to say what I don't want to say?
Where I'm urged on by pleasure let me go.
O eyes, I don't complain
Of you, serene beyond the mortal course,   50
Nor him who in such knots has bound me fast.
You surely see how many colors Love
Oft paints upon my countenance, and can
Imagine how he works at me within
Where, day and night, he's at   55

adosso, col poder ch'à in voi raccolto,
luci beate et liete
se non che 'l veder voi stesse v'è tolto;
ma quante volte a me vi rivolgete,
conoscete in altrui quel che voi siete. 60
    S'a voi fosse sí nota
la divina incredibile bellezza
di ch'io ragiono, come a chi la mira,
misurata allegrezza
non avria 'l cor: però forse è remota 65
dal vigor natural che v'apre et gira.
Felice l'alma che per voi sospira,
lumi del ciel, per li quali io ringratio
la vita che per altro non m'è a grado!
Oimè, perché sí rado 70
mi date quel dond'io mai non son satio?
Perché non piú sovente
mirate qual amor di me fa stracio?
E perché mi spogliate immantanente
del ben ch'ad ora ad or l'anima sente? 75
    Dico ch'ad ora ad ora,
vostra mercede, i' sento in mezzo l'alma
una dolcezza inusitata et nova,
la qual ogni altra salma
di noiosi pensier' disgombra allora, 80
sí che di mille un sol vi si ritrova:
quel tanto a me, non piú, del viver giova.
Et se questo mio ben durasse alquanto,
nullo stato aguagliarse al mio porrebbe;
ma forse altrui farrebbe 85
invido, et me superbo l'onor tanto:
però, lasso, convensi
che l'extremo del riso assaglia il pianto,
e 'nterrompendo quelli spirti accensi
a me ritorni, et di me stesso pensi. 90
    L'amoroso pensero
ch'alberga dentro, in voi mi si discopre
tal che mi trâ del cor ogni altra gioia;
onde parole et opre
escon di me sí fatte allor ch'i' spero 95
farmi immortal, perché la carne moia.
Fugge al vostro apparire angoscia et noia,
et nel vostro partir tornano insieme.
Ma perché la memoria innamorata

My back, with all the power that he's amassed
In you, lights—joyful, blest,
If looking at yourselves were not denied—
But everytime you turn yourselves on me,
You see there in another what you are.   60
    If you had known as well
That beauty, goddesslike, incredible
Of which I tell, as one who'd gazed on it,
Your heart no limit to
Its joy would know; yet from that natural strength,   65
Which stirs and opens you, it may be far.
Happy the soul that breathes its sighs for you,
Celestial lights, for which I thank this life
Where nothing else affords me any joy.
Ah, why so seldom am   70
I given that which never satisfies?
Why not, more often, watch
And see how love is tearing me apart?
And why do you despoil me all at once
Of that good which my spirit sometimes feels?   75
    I say that by your grace,
From time to time, deep in my spirit I
Perceive an unaccustomed sweetness rare,
One that unburdens me
Of each vexatious thought's oppressive weight.   80
So, of their thousands, only one remains:
For me that much—no more—of life brings joy.
If this, my happiness, could just endure
A while, no other state could equal mine;
But such great honor might   85
Make others grow resentful, make me proud.
Woe, therefore; it must be
That weeping will assail mirth's boundaries,
And cutting short roused feelings, I come to
Myself, and of myself think once again.   90
    That loving thought which dwells
Within has been disclosed to me in you,
So from my heart all other joy's withdrawn;
Hence, words and works come forth
From me so shaped that with their aid I hope   95
To make myself immortal, though flesh die.
When you appear, then grief and torment flee;
Together, at your parting, they return.
However, since enamoured memory

chiude lor poi l'entrata,   100
di là non vanno da le parti extreme;
onde s'alcun bel frutto
nasce di me, da voi vien prima il seme:
io per me son quasi un terreno asciutto,
cólto da voi, e 'l pregio è vostro in tutto.   105
    Canzon, tu non m'acqueti, anzi m'infiammi
a dir di quel ch'a me stesso m'invola:
però sia certa de non esser sola.

72

    Gentil mia donna, i' veggio
nel mover de' vostr'occhi un dolce lume
che mi mostra la via ch'al ciel conduce;
et per lungo costume,
dentro là dove sol con Amor seggio,   5
quasi visibilmente il cor traluce.
Questa è la vista ch'a ben far m'induce,
et che mi scorge al glorïoso fine;
questa sola dal vulgo m'allontana:
né già mai lingua humana   10
contar poria quel che le due divine
luci sentir mi fanno,
e quando 'l verno sparge le pruine,
et quando poi ringiovenisce l'anno
qual era al tempo del mio primo affanno.   15
    Io penso: se là suso,
onde 'l motor eterno de le stelle
degnò mostrar del suo lavoro in terra,
son l'altr'opre sí belle,
aprasi la pregione, ov'io son chiuso,   20
et che 'l camino a tal vita mi serra.
Poi mi rivolgo a la mia usata guerra,
ringratiando Natura e 'l dí ch'io nacqui,
che reservato m'ànno a tanto bene,
et lei ch'a tanta spene   25
alzò il mio cor: ché 'nsin allor io giacqui
a me noioso et grave,
da quel dí inanzi a me medesmo piacqui,
empiendo d'un pensier alto et soave
quel core ond'ànno i begli occhi la chiave.   30
    Né mai stato gioioso
Amor o la volubile Fortuna

Then bars their entering,   100
Past my mind's outer parts they cannot come;
So, if some lovely fruit
Is born in me, from you first springs its seed;
I, by myself, am almost dried-out land;
By you I'm tilled, and all the praise is yours.   105
    Song, you quench me not, but kindle me
To tell about what steals me from myself;
And thus ensure that you won't be alone.°

72

    Noble lady mine, I see
A sweet light in the motion of your eyes
That points me toward the path that leads to heaven;
And there within where, by
Long custom, I sit down alone with Love,   5
The heart is shining almost visibly.
This vision is what leads me to do good,
And it will guide me to a glorious end;
From rabble this alone sets me apart.
Nor can a human tongue   10
Ever recount how those two lights divine
Cause me to feel; both when
The winter scatters hoar frost round, and when
The year dons youth again, just so it was
At that time, when I first endured my woe.   15
    I think: "If there on high,
Whence the eternal mover of the stars
Vouchsafes to show his labor to the earth,
Are other works as fair,
Unlock this prison that encloses me   20
And that seals off the pathway to such life."
Then to my wonted warfare I return,
Give thanks to Nature and my day of birth,
Which have preserved me for such blessing great,
Thank her who to such hope   25
Awoke my heart; till then I idle lay,
Tedious and irksome to
Myself; from that day forth I pleased myself
Indeed, filling with one sweet, lofty thought
That heart whose key those lovely eyes possess.   30
    Never in this world
Did Love or wheeling Fortune give a state

dieder a chi piú fur nel mondo amici,
ch'i' nol cangiassi ad una
rivolta d'occhi, ond'ogni mio riposo   35
vien come ogni arbor vien da sue radici.
Vaghe faville, angeliche, beatrici
de la mia vita, ove 'l piacer s'accende
che dolcemente mi consuma et strugge:
come sparisce et fugge   40
ogni altro lume dove 'l vostro splende,
cosí de lo mio core,
quando tanta dolcezza in lui discende,
ogni altra cosa, ogni penser va fore,
et solo ivi con voi rimanse Amore.   45
    Quanta dolcezza unquancho
fu in cor d'aventurosi amanti, accolta
tutta in un loco, a quel ch'i' sento è nulla,
quando voi alcuna volta
soavemente tra 'l bel nero e 'l biancho   50
volgete il lume in cui Amor si trastulla;
et credo da le fasce et da la culla
al mio imperfecto, a la Fortuna adversa
questo rimedio provedesse il cielo.
Torto mi face il velo   55
et la man che sí spesso s'atraversa
fra 'l mio sommo dilecto
et gli occhi, onde dí et notte si rinversa
il gran desio per isfogare il petto,
che forma tien dal varïato aspetto.   60
    Perch'io veggio, et mi spiace,
che natural mia dote a me non vale
né mi fa degno d'un sí caro sguardo,
sforzomi d'esser tale
qual a l'alta speranza si conface,   65
et al foco gentil ond'io tutto ardo.
S'al ben veloce, et al contrario tardo,
dispregiator di quanto 'l mondo brama,
per solicito studio posso farme,
porrebbe forse aitarme   70
nel benigno iudicio una tal fama:
certo il fin de' miei pianti,
che non altronde il cor doglioso chiama,
vèn da' begli occhi alfin dolce tremanti,
ultima speme de' cortesi amanti.   75
    Canzon, l'una sorella è poco inanzi,

So joyous to their best friends, I'd not change
For just one look from eyes
From which my every respite issues forth, 35
Just as, from its own roots, springs every tree.
Bright sparks angelic, how
You bless my life, where pleasure kindles that
Both swallows me and melts me quite away.
As every other light 40
Entirely fades and flees when yours shines clear,
So when such sweetness great
Flows down into my heart, all else from him
Departs, and every care of mine makes way,
And there alone with you Love still remains. 45
    No matter how much sweetness,
All stored up in one place, was in the hearts
Of lovers fortunate, that's nothing to
What I sense when sometimes
So gently you, from that fair black and white, 50
Shed forth the light where Love disports himself.
I think that from my cradle and from birth,
Against contrary Fortune and my faults
This remedy has been prescribed by heaven.
Your veil, then, injures me 55
As does your hand, so often placed between
My unsurpassed delight
And your fair eyes, and thus by day and night
To ease my breast, my great desire spills forth
And takes shape from your changing countenance. 60
    Because, displeased, I see
That Nature's gift to me avails me not,
Nor makes me worthy of one glance so dear,
I force myself to be
One fit for lofty hope, and suited for 65
The noble fire with which I wholly burn.
Thus if with careful pains I mold myself—
Quick to do good, to good's contrary slow—
And hating all the world is greedy for,
Perhaps a certain fame 70
Might, in a clement judgment, lend me aid.
The goal of all my tears
Which elsewhere my sad heart does not invoke
Will come forth sweetly quaking at the last
From gracious lovers' final hope, fair eyes. 75
    O song, one sister is a bit ahead,

et l'altra sento in quel medesmo albergo
apparechiarsi; ond'io piú carta vergo.

73

Poi che per mio destino
a dir mi sforza quell'accesa voglia
che m'à sforzato a sospirar mai sempre,
Amor, ch'a ciò m'invoglia,
sia la mia scorta, e 'nsignimi 'l camino,   5
et col desio le mie rime contempre:
ma non in guisa che lo cor si stempre
di soverchia dolcezza, com'io temo,
per quel ch'i' sento ov'occhio altrui non giugne;
ché 'l dir m'infiamma et pugne,   10
né per mi' 'ngegno, ond'io pavento et tremo,
sí come talor sòle
trovo 'l gran foco de la mente scemo,
anzi mi struggo al suon de le parole,
pur com'io fusse un huom di ghiaccio al sole.   15
Nel cominciar credia
trovar parlando al mio ardente desire
qualche breve riposo et qualche triegua.
Questa speranza ardire
mi porse a ragionar quel ch'i' sentia: 20
or m'abbandona al tempo, et si dilegua.
Ma pur conven che l'alta impresa segua
continüando l'amorose note,
sí possente è 'l voler che mi trasporta;
et la ragione è morta,   25
che tenea 'l freno, et contrastar nol pote.
Mostrimi almen ch'io dica
Amor in guisa che, se mai percote
gli orecchi de la dolce mia nemica,
non mia, ma di pietà la faccia amica.   30
Dico: se 'n quella etate
ch'al vero honor fur gli animi sí accesi,
l'industria d'alquanti huomini s'avolse
per diversi paesi,
poggi et onde passando, et l'onorate   35
cose cercando, e 'l piú bel fior ne colse,
poi che Dio et Natura et Amor volse
locar compitamente ogni virtute
in quei be' lumi, ond'io gioioso vivo,
questo et quell'altro rivo   40

The other I sense readying herself
In that same lodging; hence I rule more leaves.

73

  Since, by my destiny,
I am compelled to sing that ardent wish
Which everlastingly has made me sigh,
Love, who lures me to it,
Must be my escort, must point out the path,   5
And harmonize my rhymes with my desire.
But not in such a way that my heart melts
With too much sweetness—as I fear it may—
Through what I feel where others' eyes can't peer;
For singing goads, inflames me,   10
Nor do I find as once I did, that skill
Diminishes the great
Fire in my mind (at that I fear and quake)
But at the cadence of the words I melt
As if I were a man of ice in sun.   15
  At first I thought I'd find
In uttering my passionate desire
Some brief repose, an armistice of sorts.
This hope emboldened me
To discourse of my feelings, but it now   20
Abandons me in time of need, and fades.
But still I must pursue the venture high,
Continuing my amorous melody,
So mighty's the desire that bears me off;
And dead is reason, which   25
Once held the reins, and can't keep him in check.
At least, Love, show me how
To sing in such a way that if it strikes
The ear some day of my sweet foe, it will
Make her befriend compassion, if not me.   30
  I say, "Though in that time
When minds were burning high for honor true,
A few choice men engaged their energies
In crossing hills and waves
And different lands, and seeking honored things,   35
And gathering the fairest blooms from them,
I need not pass from one shore to the next,
Nor change my homeland, because God and Love
And Nature all desired to situate
Each virtue wholly in   40

non conven ch'i' trapasse, et terra mute.
A°llor sempre ricorro
come a fontana d'ogni mia salute,
et quando a morte disïando corro,
sol di lor vista al mio stato soccorro.   45
     Come a forza di vènti
stanco nocchier di notte alza la testa
a' duo lumi ch'à sempre il nostro polo,
cosí ne la tempesta
ch'i' sostengo d'Amor, gli occhi lucenti   50
sono il mio segno e 'l mio conforto solo.
Lasso, ma troppo è piú quel ch'io ne 'nvolo
or quinci or quindi, come Amor m'informa,
che quel che vèn da gratïoso dono;
et quel poco ch'i' sono   55
mi fa di loro una perpetua norma.
Poi ch'io li vidi in prima,
senza lor a ben far non mossi un'orma:
cosí gli ò di me posti in su la cima,
che 'l mio valor per sé falso s'estima.   60
     I' non poria già mai
imaginar, nonché narrar, gli effecti
che nel mio cor gli occhi soavi fanno:
tutti gli altri diletti
di questa vita ò per minori assai,   65
et tutte altre bellezze indietro vanno.
Pace tranquilla senza alcuno affanno,
simile a quella ch'è nel ciel eterna,
move da lor inamorato riso.
Cosí vedess'io fiso   70
come Amor dolcemente gli governa,
sol un giorno da presso
senza volger già mai rota superna,
né pensasse d'altrui né di me stesso,
e 'l batter gli occhi miei non fosse spesso.   75
     Lasso, che disïando
vo quel ch'esser non puote in alcun modo,
et vivo del desir fuor di speranza:
solamente quel nodo
ch'Amor cerconda a la mia lingua quando   80
l'umana vista il troppo lume avanza,
fosse disciolto, i' prenderei baldanza
di dir parole in quel punto sí nove
che farian lagrimar chi le 'ntendesse;

Those beauteous lights that make me live in joy.
I always run to them
As to the fountainhead of all my health,
And when so longingly I rush toward death,
Their sight alone brings succor in my plight."   45
    As in the windy blast
A weary pilot lifts his head at night
To those two lights that ever are our pole,
So in Love's tempest which
I suffer still, those shining lights become   50
My only consolation and fixed mark.
Ah, woe! But there is so much more, first here,
Then there, I filch as Love instructs,
Than what comes as a gracious gift from them;
What little that I am   55
Makes them eternal patterns for my life.
Since I first saw them I've
Not gone without them one step toward the good.
Thus I have set them highest in me, for
Alone, my merit misesteems itself.   60
    I never could conceive,
Much less recount, all the effects that those
Soft eyes produced within this heart of mine.
Beside these I account
All other pleasures in this life far less,   65
And every other beauty trails behind.
A tranquil peace, one free from any pain,
Like that which in eternal Heaven exists,
From their enamoring laughter issues forth.
If I could steadily   70
Observe from close at hand for just a day
The way Love sweetly governs them
With not one turn of a supernal sphere,
And never think of others, or my self,
I would not have to close my eyes so much.   75
    I go on yearning for
That which, alas, can't be by any means,
And so I live by longing hopelessly.
If that knot could but be
Untied, with which Love bound my tongue when such   80
Excessive light subdued my human sight,
I would take courage at that moment and
I'd speak words so extraordinary, they
Would make whoever understood them weep.

ma le ferite impresse   85
volgon per forza il cor piagato altrove,
ond'io divento smorto,
e 'l sangue si nasconde, i' non so dove,
né rimango qual era; et sonmi accorto
che questo è 'l colpo di che Amor m'à morto.   90
    Canzone, i' sento già stancar la penna
del lungo et dolce ragionar co°llei,
ma non di parlar meco i pensier' mei.

74

    Io son già stanco di pensar sí come
i miei pensier' in voi stanchi non sono,
et come vita anchor non abbandono
per fuggir de sospir' sí gravi some;
    et come a dir del viso et de le chiome   5
et de' begli occhi, ond'io sempre ragiono,
non è mancata omai la lingua e 'l suono
dí et notte chiamando il vostro nome;
    et che' pie' miei non son fiaccati et lassi
a seguir l'orme vostre in ogni parte   10
perdendo inutilmente tanti passi;
    et onde vien l'enchiostro, onde le carte
ch'i' vo empiendo di voi: se 'n ciò fallassi,
colpa d'Amor, non già defecto d'arte.

75

    I begli occhi ond'i' fui percosso in guisa
ch'e' medesmi porian saldar la piaga,
et non già vertú d'erbe, o d'arte maga,
o di pietra dal mar nostro divisa,
    m'ànno la via sí d'altro amor precisa,   5
ch'un sol dolce penser l'anima appaga;
et se la lingua di seguirlo è vaga,
la scorta pò, non ella, esser derisa.
    Questi son que' begli occhi che l'imprese
del mio signor victorïose fanno   10
in ogni parte, et piú sovra 'l mio fianco;
    questi son que' begli occhi che mi stanno
sempre nel cor colle faville accese,
per ch'io di lor parlando non mi stanco.

But my deep injuries   85
Perforce direct my wounded heart elsewhere.
So I grow pale, and my
Blood hides itself, I know not where; I've ceased
To be the man I was; and I suspect
That with this blow I have been killed by Love.   90
    Song, I feel my pen already weary
Of this discourse, so long and sweet, with her,
But my thoughts don't grow tired of talk with me.

74

    I am already worn with thinking how
My thoughts about you are unwearied, and
How, still, I do not leave my life behind
By fleeing such a grievous load of sighs;
    With how in telling of your face, your hair   5
Of your fine eyes, on which I ever dwell,
My tongue has never left off, nor my voice,
Calling your name aloud by day and night;
    And thinking how my feet aren't weakened, worn
By following your footprints everywhere,   10
And squandering fruitlessly so many steps;
    With thinking whence the ink and paper come
That I fill up with you; if I offend
In this, blame Love, not any flaw in art.

75

    Those lovely eyes so beautiful have wounded me
So only they can close the wound, and not
Herb's potency nor witch's charm, indeed,
Nor healing stone from far beyond our sea,
    To other love they've so debarred my way   5
That one sweet thought alone contents my soul;
And if my tongue is fond of its pursuit
Its escort should be scoffed at, not itself.
    These are those beauteous eyes that made my lord's
Exploits victorious on every hand—   10
A victor over my flank most of all;
    These are those fair eyes with their burning sparks
That rest forever in my heart and so
My speaking of them does not weary me.

76

Amor con sue promesse lusingando
mi ricondusse a la prigione antica,
et die' le chiavi a quella mia nemica
ch'anchor me di me stesso tene in bando.

Non me n'avidi, lasso, se non quando   5
fui in lor forza; et or con gran fatica
(chi 'l crederà perché giurando i' 'l dica?)
in libertà ritorno sospirando.

Et come vero pregioniero afflicto
de le catene mie gran parte porto,   10
e 'l cor negli occhi et ne la fronte ò scritto.

Quando sarai del mio colore accorto,
dirai: S'i' guardo et giudico ben dritto,
questi avea poco andare ad esser morto.

77

Per mirar Policleto a prova fiso
con gli altri ch'ebber fama di quell'arte
mill'anni, non vedrian la minor parte
de la beltà che m'ave il cor conquiso.

Ma certo il mio Simon fu in paradiso   5
(onde questa gentil donna si parte),
ivi la vide, et la ritrasse in carte
per far fede qua giú del suo bel viso.

L'opra fu ben di quelle che nel cielo
si ponno imaginar, non qui tra noi,   10
ove le membra fanno a l'alma velo.

Cortesia fe'; né la potea far poi
che fu disceso a provar caldo et gielo,
et del mortal sentiron gli occhi suoi.

Quando giunse a Simon l'alto concetto
ch'a mio nome gli pose in man lo stile,
s'avesse dato a l'opera gentile
colla figura voce ed intellecto,

di sospir' molti mi sgombrava il petto,   5
che ciò ch'altri à piú caro, a me fan vile:
però che 'n vista ella si mostra humile
promettendomi pace ne l'aspetto.

Ma poi ch'i' vengo a ragionar co·llei,
benignamente assai par che m'ascolte,   10
se risponder savesse a' detti miei.

76

Love, with those flattering promises of his,
To my old prison brought me back once more,
And gave the keys to her, my enemy,
Who keeps me yet in exile from myself.

Ah, woe! I did not notice them, till I   5
Was in their power, and now, with effort great
(Who'll credit it unless I give my oath?)
To liberty with sighing I return.

And like a very prisoner, cast down,
I bear the greater portion of my chains;   10
My heart is written in my eyes and brow.

When you perceive my pallor, you will say:
"If I see clearly, if I rightly judge,
This one is but a little way from death."

77

If for a thousand years he closely watched
In contest with the rest famed in his art,
Not the least portion of that loveliness
Which won my heart would Policlitus see.°

But, surely, my Simone was in Heaven°   5
(From whence this noble lady comes); there he
Saw her, and on some paper traced her out,
With her fair visage faith on earth to spread.

This work, assuredly, was one of those
Conceivable in Heaven, but not here   10
Among us, where the body veils the soul.

A courteous deed, but he could do no more
Once he'd come down to try the heat and ice,
And once his eyes perceived as mortals' do.

78

Simone, when he found that high conceit,
Took pencil in his hand on my behalf;
But had he given to that noble work,
Along with shape, both voice and intellect,

My breast would be relieved of many sighs   5
That make whatever others hold most dear
Seem base to me; for in her picture she
Seems meek, and her face promises me peace.

But when I come to hold discourse with her,
She heeds me with great kindness, so it seems,   10
If only she could answer to my words.

Pigmalion, quanto lodar ti dêi
de l'imagine tua, se mille volte
n'avesti quel ch'i' sol una vorrei.

79
S'al principio risponde il fine e 'l mezzo
del quartodecimo anno ch'io sospiro,
piú non mi pò scampar l'aura né 'l rezzo,
sí crescer sento 'l mio ardente desiro.
Amor, con cui pensier mai non amezzo,   5
sotto 'l cui giogo già mai non respiro,
tal mi governa, ch'i' non son già mezzo,
per gli occhi ch'al mio mal sí spesso giro.
Cosí mancando vo di giorno in giorno,
sí chiusamente, ch'i' sol me n'accorgo   10
et quella che guardando il cor mi strugge.
A pena infin a qui l'anima scorgo
né so quanto fia meco il suo soggiorno,
ché la morte s'appressa, e 'l viver fugge.

80
Chi è fermato di menar sua vita
su per l'onde fallaci et per li scogli
scevro da morte con un picciol legno,
non pò molto lontan esser dal fine:
però sarrebbe da ritrarsi in porto   5
mentre al governo anchor crede la vela.
L'aura soave a cui governo et vela
commisi entrando a l'amorosa vita
et sperando venire a miglior porto,
poi mi condusse in piú di mille scogli;   10
et le cagion' del mio doglioso fine
non pur d'intorno avea, ma dentro al legno.
Chiuso gran tempo in questo cieco legno
errai, senza levar occhio a la vela
ch'anzi al mio dí mi trasportava al fine;   15
poi piacque a lui che mi produsse in vita
chiamarme tanto indietro da li scogli
ch'almen da lunge m'apparisse il porto.
Come lume di notte in alcun porto
vide mai d'alto mar nave né legno   20
se non gliel tolse o tempestate o scogli,
cosí di su da la gomfiata vela
vid'io le 'nsegne di quell'altra vita,

Pygmalion, how you ought to give yourself
Praise for your image, if you had from it
A thousand times what I desire just once.

79

If the beginning of this fourteenth year
Of sighs sorts with its middle and its end,
No breeze nor shade can bring me rescue, since
So much I feel my burning passion grow.
    Love, with whom I never share my thoughts,   5
Under whose yoke I hardly ever breathe,
So rules me that I'm less than half myself
Since my eyes turn so often toward my bane.
    Thus I go weakening from day to day
So privately that I alone can see,   10
And she whose look and looking melts my heart.
    I scarcely could direct my soul this far,
Nor know I how much longer it can stay,
For death is pressing near, and this life flees.

80

Whoever has resolved to lead his life
Upon deceitful waves, among the shoals,
From death divided just by a small craft,
Cannot be very distant from his end.
And thus he should withdraw into a port   5
While to the rudder still responds the sail.
    That gentle breeze to which both helm and sail
I trusted, entering the amorous life
And hoping that I'd reach a better port,
Then steered me on at least a thousand shoals,   10
Thus were the reasons for my doleful end
Not merely round about, but in the craft.
    I drifted long enclosed in this blind craft
And never raised my eye up to the sail
That prematurely took me to my end.   15
Then He was pleased, who brought me into life
To call me back a great way from the shoals
So that far off, at least, appeared the port.
    Just as by night a beacon in some port
Is from the high seas seen by ship or craft,   20
If it's not snatched from view by storm or shoals,
Exactly so, beyond the billowing sail
I saw the banners of that other life,

et allor sospirai verso 'l mio fine.

Non perch'io sia securo anchor del fine: 25
ché volendo col giorno esser a porto
è gran vïaggio in cosí poca vita;
poi temo, ché mi veggio in fraile legno,
et piú che non vorrei piena la vela
del vento che mi pinse in questi scogli.   30

S'io esca vivo de' dubbiosi scogli,
et arrive il mio exilio ad un bel fine,
ch'i' sarei vago di voltar la vela,
et l'anchore gittar in qualche porto!
Se non ch'i' ardo come acceso legno,   35
sí m'è duro a lassar l'usata vita.

Signor de la mia fine et de la vita,
prima ch'i' fiacchi il legno tra li scogli
drizza a buon porto l'affannata vela.

81

Io son sí stanco sotto 'l fascio antico
de le mie colpe et de l'usanza ria
ch'i' temo forte di mancar tra via,
et di cader in man del mio nemico.

Ben venne a dilivrarmi un grande amico   5
per somma et ineffabil cortesia;
poi volò fuor de la veduta mia,
sí ch'a mirarlo indarno m'affatico.

Ma la sua voce anchor qua giú rimbomba:
O voi che travagliate, ecco 'l camino;   10
venite a me, se 'l passo altri non serra.

Qual gratia, qual amore, o qual destino
mi darà penne in guisa di colomba,
ch'i' mi riposi, et levimi da terra?

82

Io non fu' d'amar voi lassato unquancho,
madonna, né sarò mentre ch'io viva;
ma d'odiar me medesmo giunto a riva,
et del continuo lagrimar so' stancho;

et voglio anzi un sepolcro bello et biancho,   5
che 'l vostro nome a mio danno si scriva
in alcun marmo, ove di spirto priva
sia la mia carne che pò star seco ancho.

Però, s'un cor pien d'amorosa fede
può contentarve senza farne stracio,   10

And at that moment yearned for my own end.
But not because I'm sure yet of that end,   25
For, wanting with the dawn to be in port
Means a long voyage in so brief a life;
I fear, then, for I see what a frail craft
I'm in; more than I wish it would, the sail
Fills with the wind that pushed me on these shoals.   30
If, living, I escape those doubtful shoals,
And if my exile comes to a fair end,
How happy I should be to furl the sail
And then let down my anchor in some port!
Unless I burn as does a flaming craft,   35
I find it hard to leave my wonted life.
Lord of my end and also of my life,
Before I wreck my craft among the shoals
Direct to a good port my troubled sail.

81

So tired am I beneath my ancient load
Of sins, and of my wicked way of life
That I fear greatly I shall miss my path,
And fall into the power of my foe.
Indeed a great friend came to set me free°   5
With highest courtesy, ineffable,
And then He flew forth from my sight; thus I
In looking vainly for him, tire myself.
But still his voice reverberates below:
"O ye who labor, here the pathway is;   10
Come to me, if no other bar the way."
What love, compassion, or what destiny
Will give me dove-like pinions so that I
May have repose, and raise myself from earth?

82

I was not ever wearied loving you,
My lady, nor while life lasts, shall I be;
But at self-hatred's verge I have arrived,
And I am tired of weeping evermore.
I'd rather wish a fair and unmarked tomb   5
Than that your name be written, to my harm,
Upon some marble, when my spirit shall
Be stripped of flesh (they hold together still).
Thus, if a heart so filled with loving faith
Can gladden you without your rending it,   10

piacciavi omai di questo aver mercede.
　　Se 'n altro modo cerca d'esser sacio,
vostro sdegno erra, et non fia quel che crede:
di che Amor et me stesso assai ringracio.

83

　　Se bianche non son prima ambe le tempie
ch'a poco a poco par che 'l tempo mischi,
securo non sarò, bench'io m'arrischi
talor ov'Amor l'arco tira et empie.
　　Non temo già che piú mi strazi o scempie,　　　　　5
né mi ritenga perch'anchor m'invischi,
né m'apra il cor perché di fuor l'incischi
con sue saette velenose et empie.
　　Lagrime omai dagli occhi uscir non ponno,
ma di gire infin là sanno il vïaggio,　　　　　10
sí ch'a pena fia mai ch'i' 'l passo chiuda.
　　Ben mi pò riscaldare il fiero raggio,
non sí ch'i' arda; et può turbarmi il sonno,
ma romper no, l'imagine aspra et cruda.

84

　　—Occhi, piangete: accompagnate il core
che di vostro fallir morte sostene.
—Cosí sempre facciamo; et ne convene
lamentar piú l'altrui, che 'l nostro errore.
　　—Già prima ebbe per voi l'entrata Amore,　　　　　5
là onde anchor come in suo albergo vène.
—Noi gli aprimmo la via per quella spene
che mosse d'entro da colui che more.
　　—Non son, come a voi par, le ragion' pari:
ché pur voi foste ne la prima vista　　　　　10
del vostro et del suo mal cotanto avari.
　　—Or questo è quel che piú ch'altro n'atrista,
che' perfetti giudicii son sí rari,
et d'altrui colpa altrui biasmo s'acquista.

85

　　Io amai sempre, et amo forte anchora,
et son per amar piú di giorno in giorno
quel dolce loco, ove piangendo torno
spesse fiate, quando Amor m'accora.
　　Et son fermo d'amare il tempo et l'ora　　　　　5
ch'ogni vil cura mi levâr d'intorno;

O please, at last, have mercy on this one.
    If your disdain seeks surfeit otherwise,
It errs, and what it thinks to have, cannot—
For that, to Love I'm grateful, and myself.

83

    If both my temples aren't soon all white hair,
Which bit by bit it seems that time blends in,
I shall not rest secure, though I at times
Take risks where Love draws back and arms his bow.
    Indeed, I do not fear that he can hurt   5
Me more, destroy, nor capture me because
I still am snared, nor split my heart since it's
Still pierced with his darts, wicked, poisonous.
    No tears henceforth can issue from my eyes,
Though having gone that far, the path they know,   10
Thus it is hard to bar their way at all.
    Indeed, the cruel ray can make me hot
Yet not burn me; that image harsh and hard
Can trouble sleep, but cannot break it off.

84°

    —"O weep, my eyes; accompany my heart
That now, through your transgression, suffers death."
    —"So we forever do, and must lament
Another's error more than one we made."
    —"Indeed, through you Love made his entry first,   5
There where he still, as to his dwelling, comes."
    —"The way we opened to him with the hope
That moved within that one who now expires."
    —"Though these facts seem of equal weight to you,
They aren't, for at that first sight you were far   10
Too avid, to his detriment and yours."
    —"Now, more than anything, this saddens us:
That perfect justice is so rare, and that
For someone's crime, another takes the blame."

85

    I always loved, and I love strongly still,
And I shall go on loving more each day
That sweet place where, with weeping, I return
So frequently when Love aggrieves my heart.
    The time I love steadfastly, and the hour,   5
Which took all my base cares away from me;

et piú colei, lo cui bel viso adorno
di ben far co' suoi exempli m'innamora.

Ma chi pensò veder mai tutti insieme
per assalirmi il core, or quindi or quinci,   10
questi dolci nemici, ch'i' tant'amo?

Amor, con quanto sforzo oggi mi vinci!
Et se non ch'al desio cresce la speme,
i' cadrei morto, ove piú viver bramo.

86

Io avrò sempre in odio la fenestra
onde Amor m'aventò già mille strali,
perch'alquanti di lor non fur mortali:
ch'è bel morir, mentre la vita è dextra.

Ma 'l sovrastar ne la pregion terrestra   5
cagion m'è, lasso, d'infiniti mali;
et piú mi duol che fien meco immortali,
poi che l'alma dal cor non si scapestra.

Misera, che devrebbe esser accorta
per lunga experïentia omai che 'l tempo   10
non è chi 'ndietro volga, o chi l'affreni.

Piú volte l'ò con ta' parole scorta:
Vattene, trista, ché non va per tempo
chi dopo lassa i suoi dí piú sereni.

87

Sí tosto come aven che l'arco scocchi,
buon sagittario di lontan discerne
qual colpo è da sprezzare, et qual d'averne
fede ch'al destinato segno tocchi

similemente il colpo de' vostr'occhi,   5
donna, sentiste a le mie parti interne
dritto passare, onde conven ch'eterne
lagrime per la piaga il cor trabocchi.

Et certo son che voi diceste allora:
Misero amante, a che vaghezza il mena?   10
Ecco lo strale onde Amor vòl che mora.

Ora veggendo come 'l duol m'affrena,
quel che mi fanno i miei nemici anchora
non è per morte, ma per piú mia pena.

88

Poi che mia speme è lunga a venir troppo,
et de la vita il trappassar sí corto,

I most love her whose comely face by its
Example makes me love to do good works.

But who had ever thought to see all these
Joined to besiege my heart, first here, then there—   10
All these sweet enemies I love so much?

With what force, Love, you conquer me today!
And if desiring did not make hope grow,
I should fall dead where I most yearn to live.

86

I'll always hold that window in contempt
Whence Love has surely shot a thousand darts,
Because they were not mortal—none of them—
For it is sweet to die when life is right.

But too long staying in earth's prison-house   5
Occasions boundless ills for me, alas!
I sorrow, too, that with me these will be
Immortal; from the heart no soul is loosed.

Ah, wretched one! who should have realized
Through long experience by now, that none   10
Can turn time back, and none can check his course.

Oftimes with words like these I cautioned her:
"Depart, sad soul! Who does not die in time
Is one who leaves his fairest days behind."

87

The moment that he lets his arrow fly,
A worthy archer from afar can see
Which shot he may shrug off, and which he may
Feel confident will hit its destined mark.

Just so, my lady, you sensed from your eyes   5
That bolt shot forth directly into my
Internal parts, thus everlastingly
From my heart's injury must tears well up.

And I am certain that you then observed:
"Ah, wretched lover, where will yearning lead?   10
Behold the dart with which love seeks to kill."

Now, seeing how my sorrow reins me in,
Whatever else my foes may do to me
Is not so they can kill, but hurt me more.

88

Because my hope takes so long to fulfill,
And since through life one's passage is so short,

vorreimi a miglior tempo esser accorto,
per fuggir dietro piú che di galoppo;
    et fuggo anchor cosí debile et zoppo   5
da l'un de'lati, ove 'l desio m'à storto:
securo omai, ma pur nel viso porto
segni ch'i' ò presi a l'amoroso intoppo.
    Ond'io consiglio: Voi che siete in via,
volgete i passi; et voi ch'Amore avampa,   10
non v'indugiate su l'extremo ardore;
    ché perch'io viva de mille un no scampa;
era ben forte la nemica mia,
et lei vid'io ferita in mezzo 'l core.

89

    Fuggendo la pregione ove Amor m'ebbe
molt'anni a far di me quel ch'a lui parve,
donne mie, lungo fôra a ricontarve
quanto la nova libertà m'increbbe.
    Diceami il cor che per sé non saprebbe   5
viver un giorno; et poi tra via m'apparve
quel traditore in sí mentite larve
che piú saggio di me inganato avrebbe.
    Onde piú volte sospirando indietro
dissi: Oimè, il giogo et le catene e i ceppi   10
eran piú dolci che l'andare sciolto.
    Misero me, che tardo il mio mal seppi;
et con quanta faticha oggi mi spetro
de l'errore, ov'io stesso m'era involto!

90

    Erano i capei d'oro a l'aura sparsi
che 'n mille dolci nodi gli avolgea,
e 'l vago lume oltra misura ardea
di quei begli occhi, ch'or ne son sí scarsi;
    e 'l viso di pietosi color' farsi,   5
non so se vero o falso, mi parea:
i' che l'ésca amorosa al petto avea,
qual meraviglia se di súbito arsi?
    Non era l'andar suo cosa mortale,
ma d'angelica forma; et le parole   10
sonavan altro, che pur voce humana.
    Uno spirto celeste, un vivo sole
fu quel ch'i' vidi: et se non fosse or tale,
piagha per allentar d'arco non sana.

I wish that sooner I had been aware
And faster than a gallop, had fled back.
    And still I flee, so weak and staggering 5
Upon that side where passion wrenches me;
Secure at last, I yet bear on my face
Signs that I tripped upon Love's stumbling block.
    So I advise: All you who take that way,
Retrace your steps; and you whom Love inflames, 10
O do not linger in those fires extreme;
    For though I live, of thousands not a one
Escapes; indeed, my foe was strong, and yet
I saw her wounded deep within her heart.

89

    I fled that prison where Love held me for
So many years, on me to work his will,
And long, my ladies, it would take to tell
How I regretted my new liberty.
    My heart told me that, by itself, it could 5
Not live a day; and then along the way
I saw that traitor in such false disguise
That wiser men than I would have been tricked.
    And thus so often sighing for the past
I say: "Oh woe! My shackles, yoke, and chains 10
Were sweeter far than being free of them."
    Ah, wretched me, who knew my woe too late!
I extricate myself, and with what pains,
From error in which I had snared myself.

90

    Her golden hair was scattered on the breeze
That tossed it in a thousand tangles sweet;
Enchanting light beyond all measure burned
In those fair eyes, so sparing with it now.
    It seemed to me—although I do not know 5
If true or false—her face took pity's hue;
And I—who bore love's tinder in my breast—
What marvel if I blazed up all at once?
    Her pace was not a mortal being's, but
Was some angelic sort, and her words, too, 10
Did not sound like a merely human voice.
    A heavenly spirit and a living sun
Was what I saw; if she were not so now,
No wound is healed by slackening the bow.

91

La bella donna che cotanto amavi
subitamente s'è da noi partita,
et per quel ch'io ne speri al ciel salita,
sí furon gli atti suoi dolci soavi.

Tempo è da ricovrare ambe le chiavi   5
del tuo cor, ch'ella possedeva in vita,
et seguir lei per via dritta expedita:
peso terren non sia piú che t'aggravi.

Poi che se' sgombro de la maggior salma,
l'altre puoi giuso agevolmente porre,   10
sallendo quasi un pellegrino scarco.

Ben vedi omai sí come a morte corre
ogni cosa creata, et quanto all'alma
bisogna ir lieve al periglioso varco.

92

Piangete, donne, et con voi pianga Amore;
piangete, amanti, per ciascun paese,
poi ch'è morto collui che tutto intese
in farvi, mentre visse, al mondo honore.

Io per me prego il mio acerbo dolore,   5
non sian da lui le lagrime contese,
et mi sia di sospir' tanto cortese,
quanto bisogna a disfogare il core.

Piangan le rime anchor, piangano i versi,
perché 'l nostro amoroso messer Cino   10
novellamente s'è da noi partito.

Pianga Pistoia, e i citadin perversi
che perduto ànno sí dolce vicino;
et rallegresi il cielo, ov'ello è gito.

93

Piú volte Amor m'avea già detto: Scrivi,
scrivi quel che vedesti in lettre d'oro,
sí come i miei seguaci discoloro,
e 'n un momento gli fo morti et vivi.

Un tempo fu che 'n te stesso 'l sentivi,   5
volgare exemplo a l'amoroso choro;
poi di man mi ti tolse altro lavoro;
ma già ti raggiuns'io mentre fuggivi.

E se' begli occhi, ond'io me ti mostrai
et là dove era il mio dolce ridutto   10
quando ti ruppi al cor tanta durezza,

91

That beauteous lady whom you loved so much°
Has all at once departed from our midst,
And as I hope, has risen up to Heaven,
So gentle were her actions and so sweet.
    The time has come to take back both the keys   5
Of your own heart—keys she possessed in life,
And by a swift, straight way to follow her.
May earthly weight no longer cumber you.
    Once you're unburdened of your heaviest weight
The rest with more ease you will put aside,   10
And like a pilgrim now unladen, climb.
    Now you can see how each created thing
Runs on toward death, and see how light the soul
Must travel to that pass so dangerous.

92

O ladies weep, and may Love weep with you,
Through every land; O lovers weep, for he
Is dead who wholly set his mind to pay
You honor in this world while he yet lived.°
    For me, I beg my bitter sorrow that   5
It won't impede my tears, and that through its
Great courtesy, by sighing I can give
As much ease to my heart as it may need.
    Let rhymes still weep, and verses weep as well,
Because our amorous Master Cino has   10
So recently departed from our midst.
    Pistoia weep—you citizens perverse—
That you have such a genial townsman lost;
Let Heaven, where he's gone, be filled with joy.

93

Indeed, how often has Love said to me:
"Write! Write in golden letters what you saw,
Just how my followers grow pale, and in
One moment how I make them die and live,
    "There was a time you felt it in yourself—   5
A noted instance for the amorous choir;
Then other labors took you from my hand,
But all the same I caught you while you fled.
    "And if those lovely eyes where I showed you
Myself, and where I had my sweet redoubt,   10
That time I breached your unrelenting heart,

mi rendon l'arco ch'ogni cosa spezza,
forse non avrai sempre il viso asciutto:
ch'i' mi pasco di lagrime, et tu 'l sai.

94

Quando giugne per gli occhi al cor profondo
l'imagin donna, ogni altra indi si parte,
et le vertú che l'anima comparte
lascian le membra, quasi immobil pondo.

Et del primo miracolo il secondo   5
nasce talor, che la scacciata parte
da se stessa fuggendo arriva in parte
che fa vendetta e 'l suo exilio giocondo.

Quinci in duo volti un color morto appare,
perché 'l vigor che vivi gli mostrava   10
da nessun lato è piú là dove stava.

Et di questo in quel dí mi ricordava,
ch'i' vidi duo amanti trasformare,
et far qual io mi soglio in vista fare.

95

Cosí potess'io ben chiudere in versi
i miei pensier', come nel cor gli chiudo
ch'animo al mondo non fu mai sí crudo
ch'i' non facessi per pietà dolersi.

Ma voi, occhi beati, ond'io soffersi   5
quel colpo, ove non valse elmo né scudo,
di for et dentro mi vedete ignudo,
benché 'n lamenti il duol non si riversi.

Poi che vostro vedere in me risplende,
come raggio di sol traluce in vetro,   10
basti dunque il desio senza ch'io dica.

Lasso, non a Maria, non nocque a Pietro
la fede, ch'a me sol tanto è nemica;
et so ch'altri che voi nessun m'intende.

96

Io son de l'aspectar omai sí vinto,
et de la lunga guerra de' sospiri,
ch'i' aggio in odio la speme e i desiri,
ed ogni laccio ond'è 'l mio core avinto.

Ma 'l bel viso leggiadro che depinto   5
porto nel petto, et veggio ove ch'io miri,
mi sforza; onde ne' primi empii martiri

"Restore to me the bow that sunders all,
Perhaps your face won't be forever dry—
I feed myself on tears as you well know."

94

When through my eyes into my inmost heart
There comes that ruling image, all else thence
Departs, and so those powers the soul bestows
Desert the limbs, as if they were fixed weights;
  And then from that first miracle, sometimes   5
The next is born, because the banished power,
In fleeing from itself, comes to a place
That takes revenge, and makes its exile blithe.
  Thus in two faces one dead hue appears
Because the strength that proved they were alive   10
In neither one remains where once it was.
  And this I was recalling on that day
When I observed two lovers' faces change
And grow to look as mine does usually.°

95

Could I confine my thoughts in verse as well
As I encompass them within my heart,
In all this world no nature is so crude
But, for compassion, I could make it grieve.
  But you, O blessed eyes from whom I bore   5
That stroke which took no heed of helm nor shield,
You see me naked outside and within,
Although in plaints no woe of mine pours forth.
  Because your sight shines in me as a ray
Of sunlight passes through the glass, then let   10
My passion be enough without my speech.
  Woe, not to Mary, nor to Peter was
Harm done by faith, which is my foe alone;
Save you, none understands me as I know.

96

With waiting now, and this long war of sighs
I am so overcome, that I abhor
My hope and my desires and every snare
By which my heart was so securely tied.
  But that enchanting face, which pictured in   5
My heart I bear, and see no matter where
I glance, compels me; and thus into those

pur son contra mia voglia risospinto.
    Allor errai quando l'antica strada
di libertà mi fu precisa et tolta,   10
ché mal si segue ciò ch'agli occhi agrada;
    allor corse al suo mal libera et sciolta:
ora a posta d'altrui conven che vada
l'anima che peccò sol una volta.

97

    Ahi bella libertà, come tu m'ài,
partendoti da me, mostrato quale
era 'l mio stato, quando il primo strale
fece la piagha ond'io non guerrò mai!
    Gli occhi invaghiro allor sí de' lor guai,   5
che 'l fren de la ragione ivi non vale,
perch'ànno a schifo ogni opera mortale:
lasso, cosí da prima gli avezzai!
    Né mi lece ascoltar chi non ragiona
de la mia morte; et solo del suo nome   10
vo empiendo l'aere, che sí dolce sona.
    Amor in altra parte non mi sprona,
né i pie' sanno altra via, né le man' come
lodar si possa in carte altra persona.

98

    Orso, al vostro destrier si pò ben porre
un fren, che di suo corso indietro il volga;
ma 'l cor chi legherà, che non si sciolga,
se brama honore, e 'l suo contrario abhorre?
    Non sospirate: a lui non si pò tôrre   5
suo pregio, perch'a voi l'andar si tolga;
ché, come fama publica divolga,
egli è già là, ché null'altro il precorre.
    Basti che si ritrove in mezzo 'l campo
al destinato dí, sotto quell'arme   10
che gli dà il tempo, amor, vertute e 'l sangue,
    gridando: D'un gentil desire avampo
col signor mio, che non pò seguitarme,
et del non esser qui si strugge et langue.

99

    Poi che voi et io piú volte abbiam provato
come 'l nostro sperar torna fallace,
dietro a quel sommo ben che mai non spiace

First torments wicked I am still forced back.
    I lost my way, then, when that ancient road
Of liberty was cut and seized from me;   10
One ill pursues what gratifies his eyes.
    Then toward its woe my soul rushed—loosed, set free;
Now, at another's bidding it must serve,
That soul which one time only ever sinned.

97

    Fair liberty—ah, how your leaving me
Has shown me what my situation was,
When that first arrow caused the injury
From whose effect I never shall be healed.
    My eyes, then, were so captivated by   5
Their woe, that reason's curb there has no force,
For they abhor all mortal works, since I
Alas, from the beginning trained them so!
    None I'm allowed to hear who do not speak
About my death; and with her name alone   10
I fill the air, because it sounds so sweet.
    Love spurs me nowhere else; no other way
Do my feet know, nor my hands how they can
On paper give another person praise.

98

    Upon your charger, Orso, one can place°
A curb that turns it from its course, but who
Will tie the heart so he cannot get free,
If he for honor yearns, hates the reverse?
    Sigh not; his merit can't be seized from him   5
Because you cannot make that journey now,
For popular report reveals he is
Already there, and none takes precedence.
    Enough that in the middle of the field
We'll find him on the destined day, beneath   10
Arms given him by time, love, strength and blood.
    He'll cry out, "With one noble wish my lord
And I blaze forth, though he can't follow me;
His absence makes him pine and waste away."

99

    Since you and I so frequently have proved
How all our hopes turn to deceit, to find
That highest good which never causes grief,

levate il core a piú felice stato.

Questa vita terrena è quasi un prato, 5
che 'l serpente tra' fiori et l'erba giace;
et s'alcuna sua vista agli occhi piace,
è per lassar piú l'animo invescato.

Voi dunque, se cercate aver la mente
anzi l'extremo dí queta già mai, 10
seguite i pochi, et non la volgar gente.

Ben si può dire a me: Frate, tu vai
mostrando altrui la via, dove sovente
fosti smarrito, et or se' piú che mai.

100

Quella fenestra ove l'un sol si vede,
quando a lui piace, et l'altro in su la nona;
et quella dove l'aere freddo suona
ne' brevi giorni, quando borrea 'l fiede;

e 'l sasso, ove a' gran dí pensosa siede 5
madonna, et sola seco si ragiona,
con quanti luoghi sua bella persona
corpí mai d'ombra, o disegnò col piede;

e 'l fiero passo ove m'angiunse Amore;
e lla nova stagion che d'anno in anno 10
mi rinfresca in quel dí l'antiche piaghe;

e 'l volto, et le parole che mi stanno
altamente confitte in mezzo 'l core,
fanno le luci mie di pianger vaghe.

101

Lasso, ben so che dolorose prede
di noi fa quella ch'a nullo huom perdona,
et che rapidamente n'abandona
il mondo, et picciol tempo ne tien fede;

veggio a molto languir poca mercede, 5
et già l'ultimo dí nel cor mi tuona:
per tutto questo Amor non mi spregiona,
che l'usato tributo agli occhi chiede.

So come i dí, come i momenti et l'ore
ne portan gli anni, et non ricevo inganno, 10
ma forza assai maggior che d'arti maghe.

La voglia et la ragion combattuto ànno
sette et sette anni; et vincerà il migliore,
s'anime son qua giú del ben presaghe.

Lift up your hearts to a more happy state.
    Most like a meadow is this earthly life,   5
Where 'midst the grass and flowers the serpent lurks;
If his appearance pleases someone's eyes,
It is to let the mind be more ensnared.
    You, therefore, if you ever seek to have
A tranquil mind before your final day,   10
Keep with the few, not with the vulgar folk.
    Well you may say to me: "Brother, you point
That way to others upon which you were
So often lost—and more than ever now."

100

    That window from which, when it pleases her,
One sun is seen, the other at high noon,
And that one where the cold air whistles shrill
On short days, when the north wind rattles it;
    That stone where on long days my lady sits   5
Alone and thoughtful, speaking with herself;
The many places that with her fair form
She's ever shadowed, patterned with her foot;
    The savage pass where Love accosted me
And the fresh season that, year in year out,   10
Reopens on that day my ancient wounds,
    And that face, and those words of hers, which stay
So firmly fastened deep within my heart—
These cause my eyes to be in love with tears.

101

    Alas, I know too well that she who spares
No human being makes us wretched prey,
That speedily the world abandons us,
And such a little time with us keeps faith.
    In so much longing little grace I see;   5
Indeed, the last day thunders in my heart.
Love will not set me free despite all this,
But asks accustomed tribute from my eyes.
    I know how moments, days and hours bear off
Our years, and I'm not fooled; but I endure   10
A power stronger far than magic arts.
    My Will and Reason have contended for
Seven plus seven years; the better one
Will win, if souls down here can good foretell.

Cesare, poi che 'l traditor d'Egitto
li fece il don de l'onorata testa,
celando l'allegrezza manifesta,
pianse per gli occhi fuor sí come è scritto;
 et Hanibàl, quando a l'imperio afflitto   5
vide farsi Fortuna sí molesta,
rise fra gente lagrimosa et mesta
per isfogare il suo acerbo despitto.
 Et cosí aven che l'animo ciascuna
sua passïon sotto 'l contrario manto   10
ricopre co la vista or chiara or bruna:
 però, s'alcuna volta io rido o canto,
facciol, perch'i' non ò se non quest'una
via da celare il mio angoscioso pianto.

Vinse Hanibàl, et non seppe usar poi
ben la vittorïosa sua ventura:
però, signor mio caro, aggiate cura,
che similmente non avegna a voi.
 L'orsa, rabbiosa per gli orsacchi suoi,   5
che trovaron di maggio aspra pastura,
rode sé dentro, e i denti et l'unghie endura
per vendicar suoi danni sopra noi.
 Mentre 'l novo dolor dunque l'accora,
non riponete l'onorata spada   10
anzi seguite là dove vi chiama
 vostra fortuna dritto per la strada
che vi può dar, dopo la morte anchora
mille et mille anni, al mondo honor et fama.

L'aspectata vertú che 'n voi fioriva
quando Amor cominciò darvi bataglia,
produce or frutto, che quel fiore aguaglia,
et che mia speme fa venire a riva.
 Però mi dice il cor ch'io in carte scriva   5
cosa, onde 'l vostro nome in pergio saglia,
ché 'n nulla parte sí saldo s'intaglia
per far di marmo una persona viva.
 Credete voi che Cesare o Marcello
o Paolo od Affrican fossin cotali   10
per incude già mai né per martello?

102

Caesar, when the Egyptian traitor made°
A gift to him of that much honored head,
As it is written, outwardly shed tears
To keep his manifest delight concealed.

And Hannibal, when he saw Fortune vex°   5
His troubled realm so greatly, laughed among
His people, tearful and distraught, to ease
The bitter outrage deep within his heart.

And so it happens that each mind will mask
And cloak its passions with its opposite,   10
Its face now clear and open, now obscure.

And if, on that account, I laugh sometimes
Or sing, I do so since I have no means
But this to hide away my anguished tears.

103

Hannibal won, but knew not how to put
Victorious success to proper use;
On that account, be careful, my dear lord,
Lest you encounter a like circumstance.

That she-bear, rabid for her cubs, who found°   5
Harsh pasture in the month of May, consumes
Herself within, and hardens teeth and claws
To take revenge upon us for her loss.

So, while new sorrow pierces through her heart,
Do not again put up your honored sword,   10
But where your fortune calls you, follow on

Directly by that road which after death
Can give you fame and honor in the world
Although a thousand, thousand years have passed.

104

That virtue, much desired, which bloomed in you°
When Love began to battle with you, now
Produces fruit in keeping with its flower—
Fruit that insures my hope comes safe to shore.

My heart thus tells me, that on paper I   5
Must something write that lifts your name in praise;
In no way can one sculpt so solidly
From marble as to make a living being.

Were Caesar or Marcellus, do you think,
Or Africanus, Paulus what they were   10
Because of anvil's or of hammer's work?°

Pandolfo mio, quest'opere son frali
a·llungo andar, ma 'l nostro studio è quello
che fa per fama gli uomini immortali.

105

Mai non vo' piú cantar com'io soleva,
ch'altri no m'intendeva, ond'ebbi scorno;
et puossi in bel soggiorno esser molesto.
Il sempre sospirar nulla releva;
già su per l'Alpi neva d'ogni 'ntorno;   5
et è già presso al giorno: ond'io son desto.
Un acto dolce honesto è gentil cosa;
et in donna amorosa anchor m'aggrada,
che 'n vista vada altera et disdegnosa,
non superba et ritrosa: 10
Amor regge suo imperio senza spada.
Chi smarrita à la strada, torni indietro;
chi non à albergo, posisi in sul verde;
chi non à l'auro, o 'l perde,
spenga la sete sua con un bel vetro.   15
I' die' in guarda a san Pietro; or non piú, no:
intendami chi pò, ch'i' m'intend'io.
Grave soma è un mal fio a mantenerlo:
quando posso mi spetro, et sol mi sto.
Fetonte odo che 'n Po cadde, et morío;   20
et già di là dal rio passato è 'l merlo:
deh, venite a vederlo. Or i' non voglio:
non è gioco uno scoglio in mezzo l'onde,
e'ntra le fronde il visco. Assai mi doglio
quando un soverchio orgoglio   25
molte vertuti in bella donna asconde.
Alcun è che risponde a chi nol chiama;
altri, chi 'l prega, si delegua et fugge;
altri al ghiaccio si strugge;
altri dí et notte la sua morte brama.   30
Proverbio «ama chi t'ama» è fatto antico.
I' so ben quel ch'io dico: or lass'andare,
ché conven ch'altri impare a le sue spese.
Un'humil donna grama un dolce amico.
Mal si conosce il fico. A me pur pare   35
senno a non cominciar tropp'alte imprese;
et per ogni paese è bona stanza.
L'infinita speranza occide altrui;
et anch'io fui alcuna volta in danza.

Pandolfo mine, such works are far too frail
To last for long, but our pursuit is one°
That makes men grow immortal through renown.

105

I never want to sing as once I did,°
For since she did not heed me, I was scorned;
On pleasant sojourns one can come to grief.
This constant sighing brings me no surcease—
Already in the Alps it snows all round,   5
And day already dawns, so I'm alert.
A chaste, sweet action is a noble thing,
And in a loving lady still I'm pleased
When hauteur and disdain show in her face,
Not pride and bashfulness.   10
And Love his empire rules without the sword.
Who's lost upon the road may turn around;
Who has no home may rest upon the grass;
Who's lost his gold or who
Has none, may slake thirst from a lovely glass.   15
    Saint Peter I put trust in; no more, now;
(Judge this who can; I understand myself).
Ill tribute is so burdensome to bear;
I pull free—as I can—stand by myself.
Phaeton, I hear, fell in the Po and died.   20
Already has the blackbird crossed the stream—
Ah, come and see! I do not wish to now.
A shoal amidst the waves is not a jest,
Nor birdlime in the branches. Much I grieve
When overweening pride   25
Hides many virtues in a lady fair.
A few will answer when nobody calls.
And others, whom one begs, disperse and flee;
Others are turned to ice,
And others, day and night, yearn for their deaths.   30
    That proverb: "Love who loves you"—ancient truth!
I know well what I say. Now let it go,
For everyone must learn at his own cost.
A humble lady saddens a sweet friend;
Assessing figs is hard. Not to begin   35
Too high an enterprise seems wise to me;
In every land exists a pleasant home.
A hope unlimited can kill someone,
And I was sometime also in that dance.

Quel poco che m'avanza   40
fia chi nol schifi, s'i' 'l vo', dare a lui.
I' mi fido in Colui che 'l mondo regge,
et che' seguaci Suoi nel boscho alberga,
che con pietosa verga
mi meni a passo omai tra le Sue gregge.   45
 Forse ch'ogni uom che legge non s'intende;
et la rete tal tende che non piglia;
et chi troppo assotiglia si scavezza.
Non fia zoppa la legge ov'altri attende.
Per bene star si scende molte miglia.   50
Tal par gran meraviglia, et poi si sprezza,
Una chiusa bellezza è piú soave.
Benedetta la chiave che s'avvolse
al cor, et sciolse l'alma, et scossa l'ave
di catena sí grave,   55
e 'nfiniti sospir' del mio sen tolse!
Là dove piú mi dolse, altri si dole,
et dolendo adolcisse il mio dolore:
ond'io ringratio Amore
che piú nol sento, et è non men che suole.   60
 In silentio parole accorte et sagge,
e 'l suon che mi sottragge ogni altra cura,
et la pregione oscura ov'è 'l bel lume;
le nocturne vïole per le piagge,
et le fere selvagge entr'a le mura,   65
et la dolce paura, e 'l bel costume,
et di duo fonti un fiume in pace vòlto
dov'io bramo, et raccolto ove che sia:
Amor et Gelosia m'ànno il cor tolto,
e i segni del bel volto   70
che mi conducon per piú piana via
a la speranza mia, al fin degli affanni.
O riposto mio bene, et quel che segue,
or pace or guerra or triegue,
mai non m'abbandonate in questi panni.   75
 De' passati miei danni piango et rido,
perché molto mi fido in quel ch'i' odo.
Del presente mi godo, et meglio aspetto,
et vo contando gli anni, et taccio et grido.
E 'n bel ramo m'annido, et in tal modo   80
ch'i' ne ringratio et lodo il gran disdetto
che l'indurato affecto alfine à vinto,
et ne l'alma depinto «I' sare' udito,

[*150*]

What little I have left   40
He won't shun If I wish to yield it up.
I trust myself to Him who rules the world
And cares for his disciples in the woods,
For with His loving crook
He guides my steps at last among His flock.   45
       Perhaps not all who read will understand,
Who sets the net may not bring in the catch;
Who sharpens wits too fine will break his neck.
While people wait, let not the law go lame.
For one's good health, one many miles descends.   50
What seems a marvel great is soon disdained.
A beauty that's reserved is gentlest.
Ah, blessed be the key that turned within
My heart, unbound my soul and freed it from
Such heavy chains, and that   55
Unshackled from my breast sighs infinite!
There where I sorrowed most, another mourns,
And by that mourning makes my sorrow sweet.
So I thank Love that I
Feel it no more; yet it's not any less.   60
       And in the silence, words adroit and sage
Form sounds that save me from all other care,
From this dark prison where a fair light shines.
The nighttime violets along the bank
And savage animals within the walls,   65
And that sweet fear, and manners beautiful,
And from two founts, where now I yearn, there wound
In peace one stream, and where it stood made pools.
Both Love and Jealousy have seized my heart
As have the lodestars of   70
Her fair face, which along more level paths
Led to my hope, the end of all my pains.
O secret love of mine, and come what may—
Now peace, now war, now armistice—you won't
Desert me ever in this earthly garb.   75
       For my past injuries I weep and laugh,
Because I trust so much in what I hear.
The present pleases me; the best I wait.
I wander counting years, fall silent, shout,
And on a fair branch I so build my nest   80
I'm grateful, and I praise that great denial
Which overcame engrafted love at last,
And painted in my soul: "I would be known

et mostratone a dito», et ànne extinto
(tanto inanzi son pinto,   85
ch'i' 'l pur dirò) «Non fostú tant'ardito»:
chi m'à 'l fianco ferito, et chi 'l risalda,
per cui nel cor via piú che 'n carta scrivo;
chi mi fa morto et vivo,
chi 'n un punto m'agghiaccia et mi riscalda.   90

106

Nova angeletta sovra l'ale accorta
scese dal cielo in su la fresca riva,
là 'nd'io passava sol per mio destino.
      Poi che senza compagna et senza scorta
mi vide, un laccio che di seta ordiva   5
tese fra l'erba, ond'è verde il camino.
      Allor fui preso; et non mi spiacque poi,
sí dolce lume uscia degli occhi suoi.

107

Non veggio ove scampar mi possa omai:
sí lunga guerra i begli occhi mi fanno,
ch'i' temo, lasso, no 'l soverchio affanno
distruga 'l cor che triegua non à mai.
      Fuggir vorei: ma gli amorosi rai,   5
che dí et notte ne la mente stanno,
risplendon sí, ch'al quintodecimo anno
m'abbaglian piú che 'l primo giorno assai;
      et l'imagine lor son sí cosparte
che volver non mi posso, ov'io non veggia   10
o quella o simil indi accesa luce.
      Solo d'un lauro tal selva verdeggia
che 'l mio adversario con mirabil arte
vago fra i rami ovunque vuol m'adduce.

108

Aventuroso piú daltro terreno,
ov'Amor vidi già fermar le piante
ver' me volgendo quelle luci sante
che fanno intorno a sé l'aere sereno,
      prima poria per tempo venir meno   5
un'imagine salda di diamante
che l'atto dolce non mi stia davante
del qual ò la memoria e 'l cor sí pieno:
      né tante volte ti vedrò già mai

And pointed at for that;" next was crossed out
(I'll even say it, since   85
I'm deeply moved) "You were not very bold":
She pierced my side, she makes it whole; for her
I write more in my heart than on a page;
She makes me die and live;
She in one moment burns and freezes me.   90

106

A wondrous angel small, on quick bright wings
Came down from heaven to that springtime shore
Where led by destiny I walked alone.
Since there she saw me with no friend or guide,
She spread the snare she wove from silk amidst   5
The grass, by which the pathway is made green.
Caught then, I was not sorry afterwards,
When such a sweet light issued from her eyes.

107

Henceforth I see no way I can be saved;
So long her lovely eyes make war on me
That now I fear, ah woe, lest pain too great
Lay waste my heart, which never has a truce.
I'd like to flee; yet still the amorous rays   5
That, day and night, stay in my memory
Blaze so that in this fifteenth year much more
They dazzle me than that first day they did.
Their images are scattered so about
That nowhere can I turn that I don't see   10
That light, or else its likeness, kindled thence.
From just one laurel, such a forest thrives
That with amazing art my foe leads me
Astray amidst the branches, where he will.

108

Land, more than any other fortunate,
Where once I saw Love stay a lady's step,
Saw turned toward me those sacred lights that made
The air around her grow serene and bright.
An image made of solid diamond   5
Could time erode, before that deed so sweet
Deserts my mind, that deed with which I have
So filled my heart and memory as well.
A time will never come when, seeing you,

ch'i' non m'inchini a ricercar de l'orme   10
che 'l bel pie' fece in quel cortese giro.

    Ma se 'n cor valoroso Amor non dorme,
prega, Sennuccio mio, quando 'l vedrai,
di qualche lagrimetta, o d'un sospiro.

109

    Lasso, quante fiate Amor m'assale,
che fra la notte e 'l dí son piú di mille,
torno dov'arder vidi le faville
che 'l foco del mio cor fanno immortale.

    Ivi m'acqueto; et son condotto a tale,   5
ch'a nona, a vespro, a l'alba et a le squille
le trovo nel pensier tanto tranquille
che di null'altro mi rimembra o cale.

    L'aura soave che dal chiaro viso
move col suon de le parole accorte   10
per far dolce sereno ovunque spira,

    quasi un spirto gentil di paradiso
sempre in quell'aere par che mi conforte,
si che 'l cor lasso altrove non respira.

110

    Persequendomi Amor al luogo usato,
ristretto in guisa d'uom ch'aspetta guerra,
che si provede, e i passi intorno serra,
de' miei antichi pensier' mi stava armato.

    Volsimi, et vidi un'ombra che da lato   5
stampava il sole, et riconobbi in terra
quella che, se 'l giudicio mio non erra,
era piú degna d'immortale stato.

    I' dicea fra mio cor: Perché paventi?
Ma non fu prima dentro il penser giunto   10
che i raggi, ov'io mi struggo, eran presenti.

    Come col balenar tona in un punto,
cosí fu' io de' begli occhi lucenti
et d'un dolce saluto inseme aggiunto.

111

    La donna che 'l mio cor nel viso porta,
là dove sol fra bei pensier' d'amore
sedea, m'apparve; et io per farle honore
mossi con fronte reverente et smorta.

    Tosto che del mio stato fussi accorta,   5

I do not bend down low to seek the marks   10
Her fair feet made when courteously she turned.
    But as Love never sleeps in valorous hearts,
Ask my Sennuccio, when you see him next,°
For just a little tear or for a sigh.

109
    Alas, so often Love assails me still—
More than a thousand times both night and day—
That I return where those sparks I saw blaze
That make the fire immortal in my heart.
    There I grow quiet, am so guided that—   5
At nones and vespers, dawn and angelus—
In thoughts of them I find such peacefulness,
There's nothing else I care for or recall.
    The gentle breeze that from her candid face
Moves with the sound of measured words to make   10
The clear sky sweet wherever it breathes forth,
    Seems like a noble spirit heavenly,
Forever in that air which comforts me,
So that my wretched heart breathes nowhere else.

110
    Driven by Love to that accustomed place,
I—girded like a man who waits for war,
Who is prepared, who seals approaches round
On every side—stood armed with my old thoughts.
    I turned and, nearby, saw a shadow that   5
The sun was tracing, and I recognized
On earth one who if judgment does not stray,
For an immortal state was worthier.
    And in my heart I said: "Why do you fear?"
And yet before that thought arrived within,   10
Those rays were manifest that lay me waste.
    As, instantly with lightning, thunder sounds,
So was I by those brilliant, lovely eyes
And by a greeting sweet at once caught up.

111
    That lady whom my heart bears on his face
Appeared to me where by myself I sat
Amidst fair thoughts of love, and I to pay
Her honor, rose with wan and reverent brow.
    As soon as she took notice of my state   5

[155]

a me si volse in sí novo colore
ch'avrebbe a Giove nel maggior furore
tolto l'arme di mano, et l'ira morta.
　　I' mi riscossi; et ella oltra, parlando,
passò, che la parola i' non soffersi,　　　　　　　　　10
né 'l dolce sfavillar degli occhi suoi.
　　Or mi ritrovo pien di sí diversi
piaceri, in quel saluto ripensando,
che duol non sento, né sentí' ma' poi.

112

　　Sennuccio i' vo' che sapi in qual manera
tractato sono, et qual vita è la mia:
ardomi et struggo anchor com'io solia;
l'aura mi volve, et son pur quel ch'i' m'era.
　　Qui tutta humile, et qui la vidi altera,　　　　　5
or aspra, or piana, or dispietata, or pia;
or vestirsi honestate, or leggiadria,
or mansüeta, or disdegnosa et fera.
　　Qui cantò dolcemente, et qui s'assise;
qui si rivolse, et qui rattenne il passo;　　　　　　10
qui co' begli occhi mi trafisse il core;
　　qui disse una parola, et qui sorrise;
qui cangiò 'l viso. In questi pensier', lasso,
nocte et dí tiemmi il signor nostro Amore.

113

　　Qui dove mezzo son, Sennuccio mio
(cosí ci foss'io intero, et voi contento),
venni fuggendo la tempesta e 'l vento
ch'ànno súbito fatto il tempo rio.
　　Qui son securo: et vo'vi dir perch'io　　　　　　5
non come soglio il folgorar pavento,
et perché mitigato, nonché spento,
né-micha trovo il mio ardente desio.
　　Tosto che giunto a l'amorosa reggia
vidi onde nacque l'aura dolce et pura　　　　　　　10
ch'acqueta l'aere, et mette i tuoni in bando,
　　Amor ne l'alma, ov'ella signoreggia,
raccese 'l foco, et spense la paura:
che farei dunque gli occhi suoi guardando?

She turned to me with such a color fresh,
It would have plucked Jove's weapons from his hand,
Though in his wildest rage, and killed his ire.
　　I roused myself and she, in discourse, passed
Along, for I could neither bear her speech　　　　　10
Nor stand the gentle brilliance of her eyes.
　　And now with such strange pleasures am I filled
When I think on that greeting once again
That no grief do I feel, nor since have felt.

112

　　Sennuccio, I desire that you should know°
How I am treated, and what life is mine:
I burn still, and I melt as was my wont;
I'm still swayed by the breeze, still what I was.
　　All meek I saw her here, and haughty there,　　　5
Now harsh, now mild, now cruel, now merciful;
Now chastely garbed, now elegantly gay,
Now gentle, now contemptuous and wild.
　　Here she so sweetly sang, was seated there;
Here she turned back, and there restrained her step;　　10
Here through my heart she pierced with lovely eyes;
　　There just one word she spoke, and here she smiled,
Here knit her brows; and to these thoughts, ah woe,
Our master, Love, confines me night and day.

113

　　Here where I half exist, Sennuccio mine,
(Ah, would I were all whole, and you content)
I came to flee the tempest and the wind,
Which suddenly have made the weather harsh.
　　Here I'm secure and wish to tell you why　　　5
The lightning fails to fright me as before,
Why not the least abated, or much less
Burnt out, I find my passionate desire.
　　As soon as to this amorous realm I came,
I saw from whence was sprung that sweet, pure breeze　　10
That calms the air, outlaws the thunder's roar.
　　Now Love, within my soul where she holds sway
Has lit the fire again and quenched my fear:
What would I do, then, looking in her eyes?

114

De l'empia Babilonia, ond'è fuggita
ogni vergogna, ond'ogni bene è fori,
albergo di dolor, madre d'errori,
son fuggito io per allungar la vita.

Qui mi sto solo; et come Amor m'invita,   5
or rime et versi, or colgo herbette et fiori,
seco parlando, et a tempi migliori
sempre pensando: et questo sol m'aita.

Né del vulgo mi cal, né di Fortuna,
né di me molto, né di cosa vile,   10
né dentro sento né di fuor gran caldo.

Sol due persone cheggio: et vorrei l'una
col cor ver' me pacificato humile,
l'altro col pie', sí come mai fu, saldo.

115

In mezzo di duo amanti honesta altera
vidi una donna, et quel signor co lei
che fra gli uomini regna et fra li dèi;
et da l'un lato il Sole, io da l'altro era.

Poi che s'accorse chiusa da la spera   5
de l'amico piú bello, agli occhi miei
tutta lieta si volse, et ben vorrei
che mai non fosse inver' di me piú fera.

Súbito in allegrezza si converse
la gelosia che 'n su la prima vista   10
per sí alto adversario al cor mi nacque.

A lui la faccia lagrimosa et trista
un nuviletto intorno ricoverse:
cotanto l'esser vinto li dispiacque.

116

Pien di quella ineffabile dolcezza
che del bel viso trassen gli occhi miei
nel dí che volentier chiusi gli avrei
per non mirar già mai minor bellezza,

lassai quel ch'i' piú bramo; et ò sí avezza   5
la mente a contemplar sola costei,
ch'altro non vede, et ciò che non è lei
già per antica usanza odia et disprezza.

In una valle chiusa d'ogni 'ntorno,
ch'è refrigerio de' sospir' miei lassi,   10
giunsi sol cum Amor, pensoso et tardo.

Ivi non donne, ma fontane et sassi,

114

From impious Babylon, whence every sense°
Of shame has fled, and every good's withdrawn—
Mother of error and Woe's dwelling place—
Have I fled forth to live a longer life.

Alone I stay here, and as Love invites°   5
I pluck now rhymes and verse, now herbs and flowers,
Conversing just with him, and thinking on
Much better times; my only solace, this.

Not for the crowd nor Fortune do I care,
Nor for myself, much, nor for lowly things,   10
Nor do I feel great heat inside or out.

I beg for just two persons: And I'd wish
Her heart were humble, reconciled to me,
And wish him with his foot once more all healed.°

115

A lady, chaste and proud, I once beheld
Between two lovers, saw with her that lord
Who rules among men and among the gods;
On one side was the sun, the other I.

When from the sphere of that more comely friend   5
She found herself cut off, all full of joy
To my eyes she repaired; indeed, I wish
That she might never be more cruel to me.

For all at once to joyfulness was turned
The jealousy that on first sight was born   10
Within my heart at such a rival high.

With one small cloud his sad and tearful face
Was overcast once more, so much did he
Feel sorrow at his being conquered thus.

116

Filled with that sweetness inexpressible
That from her lovely face my eyes drew forth,
That day when I'd have closed them willingly
To gaze no more on lesser loveliness,

I left what most I yearn for, and have schooled   5
My mind to contemplate her only, so
It sees no other, and what is not she,
Indeed by custom old it loathes and scorns.

Into a valley closed on every side
Where there is solace for my weary sighs,   10
Pensive and slow I went alone with Love.

No ladies there, but rather founts and stones

et l'imagine trovo di quel giorno
che 'l pensier mio figura, ovunque io sguardo.

117

   Se 'l sasso, ond'è piú chiusa questa valle,
di che 'l suo proprio nome si deriva,
tenesse vòlto per natura schiva
a Roma il viso et a Babel le spalle,
   i miei sospiri piú benigno calle   5
avrian per gire ove lor spene è viva:
or vanno sparsi, et pur ciascuno arriva
là dov'io il mando, che sol un non falle.
   Et son di là sí dolcemente accolti,
com'io m'accorgo, che nessun mai torna: 10
con tal diletto in quelle parti stanno.
   Degli occhi è 'l duol, che, tosto che s'aggiorna,
per gran desio de' be' luoghi a lor tolti,
dànno a me pianto, et a' pie' lassi affanno.

118

   Rimansi a dietro il sestodecimo anno
de' miei sospiri, et io trapasso inanzi
verso l'extremo; et parmi che pur dianzi
fosse 'l principio di cotanto affanno.
   L'amar m'è dolce, et util il mio danno,   5
e 'l viver grave; et prego ch'egli avanzi
l'empia Fortuna, et temo no chiuda anzi
Morte i begli occhi che parlar mi fanno.
   Or qui son, lasso, et voglio esser altrove;
et vorrei piú volere, et piú non voglio;   10
et per piú non poter fo quant'io posso;
   et d'antichi desir' lagrime nove
provan com'io son pur quel ch'i' mi soglio,
né per mille rivolte anchor son mosso.

119

   Una donna piú bella assai che 'l sole,
et piú lucente, et d'altrettanta etade,
con famosa beltade
acerbo anchor mi trasse a la sua schiera.
Questa in penseri, in opre et in parole   5
(però ch'è de le cose al mondo rade),
questa per mille strade
sempre inanzi mi fu leggiadra altera.

I find, and find in every place I look
The likeness of that day which shapes my thoughts.

117

If the steep rock that nearly closes off
This vale—and whence it takes its proper name—
Fastidious in nature, turned its face
Toward Rome and showed its back to Babylon,
    My sighs would have a more propitious path   5
To travel where their hope still lives, for now
They wander scattered, yet each one arrives
Where I have sent it; not a one falls short.
    And there they are received so sweetly that
Not one of them, it seems to me, returns   10
From regions where they stay with such delight.
    My eyes are grieved; for at the dawn, through great
Desire for places fair denied them now,
They bring me tears, bring toil for weary feet.

118

My sixteenth year of sighs has come and gone,
And I, before my time, pass toward my end,
And yet it seems to me the start of such
Great pain was but a little while ago.
    The bitter's sweet to me, of use my woe,   5
Life heavy grows, I pray it may escape
My wicked Fortune, and I fear lest Death
Too soon close those fair eyes that give me speech.
    Alas, I'm here, and elsewhere wish to be;
More I would want to wish, yet more wish not—   10
And, since I can't do more, do what I can.
    And these new tears shed for old yearning prove
How I am still that which I used to be;
Through thousands of reverses I've not changed.

119

A lady much more lovely than the sun—°
More radiant, and of the selfsame age—
With beauty far renowned
Drew me, still immature, into her train.
This lady in my thoughts, my works, and words   5
(For she ranks with the rare things in this world)
Along a thousand roads
Before me ever went in stately grace.

Solo per lei tornai da quel ch'i' era,
poi ch'i' soffersi gli occhi suoi da presso;   10
per suo amor m'er'io messo
a faticosa impresa assai per tempo:
tal che, s'i' arrivo al disïato porto,
spero per lei gran tempo
viver, quand'altri mi terrà per morto.   15
    Questa mia donna mi menò molt'anni
pien di vaghezza giovenile ardendo,
sí come ora io comprendo,
sol per aver di me piú certa prova,
mostrandomi pur l'ombra o 'l velo o' panni   20
talor di sé, ma 'l viso nascondendo;
et io, lasso, credendo
vederne assai, tutta l'età mia nova
passai contento, e 'l rimembrar mi giova,
poi ch'alquanto di lei veggi' or piú inanzi.   25
I' dico che pur dianzi
qual io non l'avea vista infin allora,
mi si scoverse: onde mi nacque un ghiaccio
nel core, et èvvi anchora,
et sarà sempre fin ch'i' le sia in braccio.   30
    Ma non me 'l tolse la paura o 'l gielo
che pur tanta baldanza al mio cor diedi
ch'i' le mi strinsi a' piedi
per piú dolcezza trar degli occhi suoi;
et ella, che remosso avea già il velo   35
dinanzi a' miei, mi disse:—Amico, or vedi
com'io son bella, et chiedi
quanto par si convenga agli anni tuoi.—
—Madonna—dissi—già gran tempo in voi
posi 'l mio amor, ch'i' sento or sí infiammato,   40
ond'a me in questo stato
altro volere o disvoler m'è tolto.—
Con voce allor di sí mirabil' tempre
rispose, et con un volto
che temer et sperar mi farà sempre: 45
    —Rado fu al mondo fra cosí gran turba
ch'udendo ragionar del mio valore
non si sentisse al core
per breve tempo almen qualche favilla;
ma l'adversaria mia che 'l ben perturba   50
tosto la spegne, ond'ogni vertú more
et regna altro signore

Through her alone I turned from what I was,
Once I'd withstood her eyes from near at hand;   10
For her love, early on
I set myself to tiring enterprise
So that, if I achieve that wished-for port,
I hope through her to live
A long time after others think me dead.   15
   This lady mine for many years led me—
All filled with burning, youthful urgency,
As I now comprehend—
Only to make of me a surer test
And showed me just her shadow, veil or robes—   20
Sometimes herself, but with her face concealed;
And I, ah woe, believing
I saw much more of her, passed all my youth
Content, and to recall it pleases me
Since I see more in her now than before.   25
A short time past, I say,
Since I had never seen her until then,
She showed herself to me: whence in my heart
Ice formed, it still remains
And always shall till I am in her arms.   30
   But neither fear nor chill could hinder me
From bearing such great boldness in my heart
That I pressed near her feet,
To draw a greater sweetness from her eyes:
And she, who had already taken off   35
The veil from mine, to me said: "Friend, now see
How fair I am, and ask
As much as to your age seems suitable."
"My lady," said I, "long ago in you
I fixed my love, which I feel kindled so   40
That in this plight, to wish
For other things—or not—is reft from me."
She, in a voice of wondrous timbre, then
Replied, and with a face
That will forever make me fear and hope: 45
   "Rare in this world amidst the mob so great
Was one who, hearing my worth talked about,
Did not feel in his heart
For some brief time, at least, a certain spark.
But my opponent who confounds that good,   50
So quickly quenches it, each virtue dies;
Then reigns another lord

che promette una vita piú tranquilla.
De la tua mente Amor, che prima aprilla,
mi dice cose veramente ond'io   55
veggio che 'l gran desio
pur d'onorato fin ti farà degno;
et come già se' de' miei rari amici,
donna vedrai per segno
che farà gli occhi tuoi via piú felici.—   60
    I' volea dir:—Quest'è impossibil cosa—;
quand'ella:—Or mira—et leva' gli occhi un poco
in piú riposto loco—
donna ch'a pochi si mostrò già mai.—
Ratto inchinai la fronte vergognosa,   65
sentendo novo dentro maggior foco;
et ella il prese in gioco,
dicendo:—I' veggio ben dove tu stai.
Sí come 'l sol con suoi possenti rai
fa súbito sparire ogni altra stella,   70
cosí par or men bella
la vista mia cui maggior luce preme.
Ma io però da' miei non ti diparto,
ché questa et me d'un seme,
lei davanti et me poi, produsse un parto.—   75
    Ruppesi intanto di vergogna il nodo
ch'a la mia lingua era distretto intorno
su nel primiero scorno,
allor quand'io del suo accorger m'accorsi;
e 'ncominciai:—S'egli è ver quel ch'i' odo,   80
beato il padre, et benedetto il giorno
ch'à di voi il mondo adorno,
et tutto 'l tempo ch'a vedervi io corsi;
et se mai da la via dritta mi torsi,
duolmene forte, assai piú ch'i' non mostro;   85
ma se de l'esser vostro
fossi degno udir piú, del desir ardo.—
Pensosa mi rispose, et cosí fiso
tenne il suo dolce sguardo,
ch'al cor mandò co le parole il viso: 90
    —Sí come piacque al nostro eterno padre,
ciascuna di noi due nacque immortale.
Miseri, a voi che vale?
Me' v'era che da noi fosse il defecto.
Amate, belle, gioveni et leggiadre   95
fummo alcun tempo: et or siam giunte a tale

Who promises a life more filled with ease.
Love, who at first unsealed your intellect,
Tells me things truly, and from them I see   55
That your great yearning will
Yet make you worthy of an honored end;
Since you indeed are one of my few friends,
For a sign you'll see
A lady who'll make your eyes happier far."°   60
     I meant to say: "This is not possible!"
When she: "Now slightly raise your eyes to a
More secret place; Behold
A lady who never appears but to a few."
Abashed, I bowed my head immediately,   65
And felt a new and greater fire within;
And she took that in jest,
Saying: "Well do I know your plight; just as
The sun with his rays powerful, at once
Makes vanish every other star, thus now   70
Less lovely seems my face
That is diminished by a greater light.
But I on that account won't part from you,
For one birth has produced
Us both from the same seed—her first, then me."   75
     At once that knot of shame was severed which
So tightly had been bound about my tongue
Upon my first disgrace;
At this, I saw that she had noticed me,
And started out: "If what I hear is true,   80
Blest be the Father, blest the day that has
With you adorned the world,
Blest all that time I rushed to look on you;
If ever from the path direct I strayed,
It grieves me deeply, much more than I show;   85
But if I'm fit to hear
More of your nature, with that wish I burn."
She, thoughtful, answered me, and her sweet glance
So steady held, that she
Sent to my heart her visage, with these words: 90
     "Since our eternal Father so was pleased,
Immortal each of us was born, we two;
What use to you, poor folk?
If your defect were ours, better for you!
Beloved, beauteous, young, and charming we   95
For some time were: and now we have arrived

                                                          [165]

che costei batte l'ale
per tornar a l'anticho suo ricetto;
i' per me sono un'ombra. Et or t'ò detto
quanto per te sí breve intender puossi.—   100
Poi che i pie' suoi fur mossi,
dicendo:—Non temer ch'i' m'allontani—,
di verde lauro una ghirlanda colse,
la qual co le sue mani
intorno intorno a le mie tempie avolse.   105

    Canzon, chi tua ragion chiamasse obscura,
di':—Non ò cura, perché tosto spero
ch'altro messaggio il vero
farà in piú chiara voce manifesto.
I' venni sol per isvegliare altrui,   110
se chi m'impose questo
non m'inganò, quand'io partí' da lui.—

120

    Quelle pietose rime in ch'io m'accorsi
di vostro ingegno et del cortese affecto,
ebben tanto vigor nel mio conspetto
che ratto a questa penna la man porsi
    per far voi certo che gli extremi morsi   5
di quella ch'io con tutto 'l mondo aspetto
mai non sentí', ma pur senza sospetto
infin a l'uscio del suo albergo corsi;
    poi tornai indietro, perch'io vidi scripto
di sopra 'l limitar che 'l tempo anchora   10
non era giunto al mio viver prescritto,
    bench'io non vi legessi il dí né l'ora.
Dunque s'acqueti omai 'l cor vostro afflitto,
et cerchi huom degno, quando sí l'onora.

121

    Or vedi, Amor, che giovenetta donna
tuo regno sprezza, et del mio mal non cura,
et tra duo ta' nemici è sí secura.
    Tu se' armato, et ella in treccie e 'n gonna
si siede, et scalza, in mezzo i fiori et l'erba,   5
ver' me spietata, e 'ncontra te superba.
    I' son pregion; ma se pietà anchor serba
l'arco tuo saldo, et qualchuna saetta,
fa' di te et di me, signor, vendetta.

At such a state she beats
Her wings to fly back to her old refuge;
For me, I'm but a shade. Now I have told
You all that you can grasp in such brief time." 100
Then as she stepped away
She said: "Be not afraid that I'll go far;"
She plucked a garland of green laurel leaves,
Which with her hands she wreathed
About my temples, round and round again. 105
    Song, to whoever calls your discourse dark,
Say this: "I do not care, for soon I hope
Another messenger will make the truth
More evident, in a much clearer voice.
Just to awaken people did I come 110
If he who posed this task°
Deceived me not when I set forth from him."

120

    In these lamenting rhymes in which I saw
Your talent and your courteous sentiments°
There was so much strength, as it seemed to me,
That swiftly to this pen I set my hand,
    To reassure you I have not yet felt 5
The final stings of her whom I await
With all the world, although without a doubt
I reached the very doorway of her home;
    Then I turned back because I saw inscribed
Above the lintel that the time ordained 10
For my life had not been fulfilled as yet,
    Though there I could not read the day or hour.
Then let your troubled mind grow quiet now
And seek a worthy man to honor so.

121

    See now, Love, how a youthful lady slights
Your reign, and for my malady cares not;
Twixt two such enemies, how safe she stands.
    You go in armor; she in braids and gown
Sits down, and barefoot 'midst the grass and flowers 5
Is cruel to me and arrogant toward you.
    A prisoner am I; but if your bow
Pity yet keeps intact—some arrows too—
For you, my Lord, and for me, take revenge.

122

Dicesetta anni à già rivolto il cielo
poi che 'mprima arsi, et già mai non mi spensi;
ma quando aven ch'al mio stato ripensi,
sento nel mezzo de le fiamme un gielo.

Vero è 'l proverbio, ch'altri cangia il pelo   5
anzi che 'l vezzo, et per lentar i sensi
gli umani affecti non son meno intensi:
ciò ne fa l'ombra ria del grave velo.

Oïmè lasso, e quando fia quel giorno
che, mirando il fuggir degli anni miei,   10
esca del foco, et di sí lunghe pene?

Vedrò mai il dí che pur quant'io vorrei
quel'aria dolce del bel viso adorno
piaccia a quest'occhi, et quanto si convene?

123

Quel vago impallidir che 'l dolce riso
d'un'amorosa nebbia ricoperse,
con tanta maiestade al cor s'offerse
che li si fece incontr' a mezzo 'l viso.

Conobbi allor sí come in paradiso   5
vede l'un l'altro, in tal guisa s'aperse
quel pietoso penser ch'altri non scerse:
ma vidil'io, ch'altrove non m'affiso.

Ogni angelica vista, ogni atto humile
che già mai in donna ov'amor fosse apparve,   10
fôra uno sdegno a lato a quel ch'i' dico.

Chinava a terra il bel guardo gentile,
et tacendo dicea, come a me parve:
Chi m'allontana il mio fedele amico?

124

Amor, Fortuna et la mia mente, schiva
di quel che vede e nel passato volta,
m'affligon sí ch'io porto alcuna volta
invidia a quei che son su l'altra riva.

Amor mi strugge 'l cor, Fortuna il priva   5
d'ogni conforto, onde la mente stolta
s'adira et piange: et cosí in pena molta
sempre conven che combattendo viva.

Né spero i dolci dí tornino indietro,
ma pur di male in peggio quel ch'avanza;   10
et di mio corso ò già passato 'l mezzo.

122

Seventeen years by now the heavens have rolled
Since first I burned, and never am I quenched;
But when it happens that I contemplate
My plight, amidst my flames I sense a chill.

The proverb's true that hair will change before   5
One's habits do; with slowing sense, no less
Intense do human feelings grow. In us
The dread shade of the heavy veil does that.

Ah weary me, and when will that day come
When, looking on the flight of all my years,   10
From fire I issue, and from torture long?

Ah, shall I ever see that day when as
I'd wish, and as it's meet—adorned by her
Fair face, that air so sweet will please these eyes?

123

That charming loss of color that concealed
In amorous mist her sweet smile, to my heart
Was profered with such majesty that he
Came forth to greet it in my countenance.

I knew then how in paradise one sees   5
Another; thus revealed itself that thought
Compassionate, which no one else discerned,
But I could see, since nowhere else I gaze.

Each sight angelic, every modest act
Seen always in a lady where Love dwelt   10
Would seem disdain beside what I recount.

Her noble gaze was bent upon the earth,
And, keeping silent, said, or so it seemed:
"Who sends my faithful friend away from me?"

124

Love, Fortune, and my mind—which shuns all it
Now looks upon, and turns to time gone by—
Distress me so that I feel envious,
Sometimes, of those upon the other shore.°

My heart's laid waste by Love; and Fortune steals   5
Its every solace, so my foolish mind
Becomes enraged and weeps; and so I must
Forever live at war and in much pain.

Nor hope I sweet days will return, but think
That what remain will go from bad to worse,   10
For I've now passed the midpoint of my race.

Lasso, non di diamante, ma d'un vetro
veggio di man cadermi ogni speranza,
et tutti miei pensier' romper nel mezzo.

125

Se 'l pensier che mi strugge,
com'è pungente et saldo,
così vestisse d'un color conforme,
forse tal m'arde et fugge,
ch'avria parte del caldo,   5
et desteriasi Amor là dov'or dorme;
men solitarie l'orme
fôran de' miei pie' lassi
per campagne et per colli,
men gli occhi ad ognor molli,   10
ardendo lei che come un ghiaccio stassi,
et non lascia in me dramma
che non sia foco et fiamma.
    Però ch'Amor mi sforza
et di saver mi spoglia,   15
parlo in rime aspre, et di dolcezza ignude:
ma non sempre a la scorza
ramo, né in fior, né 'n foglia
mostra di for sua natural vertude.
Miri ciò che 'l cor chiude   20
Amor et que' begli occhi,
ove si siede a l'ombra.
Se 'l dolor che si sgombra
aven che 'n pianto o in lamentar trabocchi,
l'un a me nòce et l'altro   25
altrui, ch'io non lo scaltro.
    Dolci rime leggiadre
che nel primiero assalto
d'Amor usai, quand'io non ebbi altr'arme,
chi verrà mai che squadre   30
questo mio cor di smalto
ch'almen com'io solea possa sfogarme?
Ch'aver dentro a lui parme
un che madonna sempre
depinge et de lei parla: 35
a voler poi ritrarla
per me non basto, et par ch'io me ne stempre.
Lasso, così m'è scorso
lo mio dolce soccorso.

Not diamond, ah woe, but like a glass
I see fall from my hand my every hope,
And in two halves are broken all my thoughts.

125

If that thought melting me
As strong and poignant as
It is, were clothed in colors fit, one who
First burns me and then flees
Perhaps would share its heat,   5
And Love would rouse himself, where now he sleeps;
Less lonely'd be the trace
Of these my weary feet
In meadows and on hills,
Less tearful every hour   10
My eyes; if she who stands like ice burned too,
She leaves no scrap in me
That's neither flame nor fire.
    Because Love weakens me,
And steals my eloquence,   15
I speak in rugged rhymes of sweetness bare;
Not always in its bark,
Though, will a branch display
Its native strength, nor in its flower nor leaf.
Let Love—where in the shade   20
He sits—let those fair eyes,
See what my heart enfolds.
If woe that gushes forth
Should overflow in weeping or lament,
Me this one harms, that her,   25
Unless I smooth what's rough.
    You sweet, delightful rhymes
That in Love's first assault
I used when I had no arms else, will no
One ever come to break   30
The glaze from my heart so
I can at least vent feelings as I did?
For one's in my heart who
It seems forever draws
My lady—speaks of her.   35
Then, when I wish to sketch
Her, I'm not skilled enough alone, and that
Unstrings me. Woe! thus my
Sweet succor slips away.

Come fanciul ch'a pena   40
volge la lingua et snoda,
che dir non sa, ma 'l piú tacer gli è noia,
cosí 'l desir mi mena
a dire, et vo' che m'oda
la dolce mia nemica anzi ch'io moia.   45
Se forse ogni sua gioia
nel suo bel viso è solo,
et di tutt'altro è schiva,
odil tu, verde riva,
e presta a' miei sospir' sí largo volo,   50
che sempre si ridica
come tu m'eri amica.
 Ben sai che sí bel piede
non tocchò terra unquancho
come quel di che già segnata fosti;   55
onde 'l cor lasso riede
col tormentoso fiancho
a partir teco i lor pensier' nascosti.
Cosí avestú riposti
de' be' vestigi sparsi   60
anchor tra' fiori et l'erba
che la mia vita acerba,
lagrimando, trovasse ove acquetarsi!
Ma come pò s'appaga
l'alma dubbiosa et vaga.   65
 Ovunque gli occhi volgo
trovo un dolce sereno
pensando: Qui percosse il vago lume.
Qualunque herba o fior colgo
credo che nel terreno   70
aggia radice, ov'ella ebbe in costume
gir fra le piagge e 'l fiume,
et talor farsi un seggio
fresco, fiorito et verde.
Cosí nulla se 'n perde,   75
et piú certezza averne fôra il peggio.
Spirto beato, quale
se', quando altrui fai tale?
 O poverella mia, come se' rozza!
Credo che tel conoschi: 80
rimanti in questi boschi.

A child who scarcely can   40
His tongue unloose or rule,
Who cannot speak, but tires of keeping still,
So I'm led by desire,
To speak, and my sweet foe
I want to lend me ear before I die.   45
If she finds all her joy
In her fair face alone
And if she shuns all else,
Then hear you this, green bank,
And such wide-ranging flight give my sighs that   50
It always will be told
How you were friends with me.
    You know, indeed, no foot
So fair has ever touched
The earth as on that day hers left its sign;   55
So both my wretched heart
And my vexatious side
Return to share with you their secret cares.
If you had but concealed
Some scattered vestiges   60
Still 'midst the flowers and grass
So that my bitter life,
In tears, could find some place to soothe itself!
My doubtful, straying soul
Though, as may be, is eased.   65
    Each place I cast my eyes
I find a radiance sweet
And I reflect: "Here fell that lovely light."
Each herb or flower I pick
Takes root, I think, in earth   70
Where she took her accustomed walk along
The slopes and by the stream,
And made sometimes a seat,
One flowery, green and cool.
Thus none of that is lost;   75
And it were worse to be more sure of it.
What are you, Spirit blest,
When you shape someone thus?
    O, my poor little song, how rough you are!
You know it, I believe,   80
Keep then within these woods.

Chiare, fresche et dolci acque,
ove le belle membra
pose colei che sola a me par donna;
gentil ramo ove piacque
(con sospir' mi rimembra)   5
a lei di fare al bel fiancho colonna;
herba et fior' che la gonna
leggiadra ricoverse
co l'angelico seno;
aere sacro, sereno,   10
ove Amor co' begli occhi il cor m'aperse:
date udïenzia insieme
a le dolenti mie parole extreme.

    S'egli è pur mio destino,
e 'l cielo in ciò s'adopra,   15
ch'Amor quest'occhi lagrimando chiuda,
qualche gratia il meschino
corpo fra voi ricopra,
e torni l'alma al proprio albergo ignuda.
La morte fia men cruda   20
se questa spene porto
a quel dubbioso passo:
ché lo spirito lasso
non poria mai in piú riposato porto
né in piú tranquilla fossa   25
fuggir la carne travagliata et l'ossa.

    Tempo verrà anchor forse
ch'a l'usato soggiorno
torni la fera bella et mansüeta,
et là 'v'ella mi scorse   30
nel benedetto giorno,
volga la vista disïosa et lieta,
cercandomi: et, o pieta!,
già terra in fra le pietre
vedendo, Amor l'inspiri   35
in guisa che sospiri
sí dolcemente che mercé m'impetre,
et faccia forza al cielo,
asciugandosi gli occhi col bel velo.

    Da' be' rami scendea   40
(dolce ne la memoria)
una pioggia di fior' sovra 'l suo grembo;
et ella si sedea

Waters clear and cool and sweet,
Beside which she reposed
Fair limbs, the only lady, as I think;
Courteous branch she liked
(With sighing I recall)   5
To make a pillar for her comely form;
Herbs and flowers that her
Light, graceful gown concealed
And that angelic breast;
Skies holy, tranquil, bright   10
Where Love with those fair eyes unlocked my heart;
Together pay close heed
To my lamenting, to my final words.
    If it is still my fate
And heaven so decrees   15
That Love should close these weeping eyes of mine,
Here in your midst some grace
My wretched corpse may cover,
Send back my naked soul to its own home.
Less cruel my death may be   20
If I sustain this hope
Till that last doubtful step,
Because my weary soul
To a more restful port could never flee,
Nor fly tormented flesh   25
And troubled bones for a more peaceful grave.
    The time may yet arrive
When to her usual haunts
That fair, untamed and gentle one returns,
And in that place where she   30
First saw me that blest day,
May turn in search of me her yearning gaze
So filled with joy, and—oh how pitiful!—
See me already earth
Amidst the stones. And thus   35
Love inspire her so
That sweetly sighing, she will win me grace,
And heaven take by force,
Drying her eyes upon her lovely veil.
    From those fair boughs a rain   40
(Sweet in my memory)
Of flowers floated down upon her lap;
She, modest in such glory

humile in tanta gloria,
coverta già de l'amoroso nembo.   45
Qual fior cadea sul lembo,
qual su le treccie bionde,
ch'oro forbito et perle
eran quel dí a vederle;
qual si posava in terra, et qual su l'onde;   50
qual con un vago errore
girando parea dir: Qui regna Amore.
    Quante volte diss'io
allor pien di spavento:
Costei per fermo nacque in paradiso.   55
Cosí carco d'oblio
il divin portamento
e 'l volto e le parole e 'l dolce riso
m'aveano, et sí diviso
da l'imagine vera,   60
ch'i' dicea sospirando:
Qui come venn'io, o quando?;
credendo esser in ciel, non là dov'era.
Da indi in qua mi piace
questa herba sí, ch'altrove non ò pace.   65
    Se tu avessi ornamenti quant'ài voglia,
poresti arditamente
uscir del boscho, et gir in fra la gente.

127

    In quella parte dove Amor mi sprona
conven ch'io volga le dogliose rime,
che son seguaci de la mente afflicta.
Quai fien ultime, lasso, et qua' fien prime?
Collui che del mio mal meco ragiona   5
mi lascia in dubbio, sí confuso ditta.
Ma pur quanto l'istoria trovo scripta
in mezzo 'l cor (che sí spesso rincorro)
co la sua propria man de' miei martiri,
dirò, perché i sospiri   10
parlando àn triegua, et al dolor soccorro.
Dico che, perch'io miri
mille cose diverse attento et fiso,
sol una donna veggio, e 'l suo bel viso.
    Poi che la dispietata mia ventura   15
m'à dilungato dal maggior mio bene,

Was seated there, bedecked
Indeed by all that amorous shower.   45
Some flowers fell on her skirt
Some on her tresses blond
That to one seeing her
That day, seemed polished gold
And pearl; some dropped to earth, on water some,   50
Some wafting prettily
While swirling, seemed to say: "Ah, Love reigns here."
    How often then I said
While trembling with fear,
"In paradise she certainly was born!"   55
Thus with oblivion
Her carriage heavenly,
Her face, her speech, and her sweet laugh have weighed
Me down, have cut me off
From her true image so,   60
With sighing I must ask:
"How came I here or when?"—
Thinking myself in heaven, not where I was.
From that time forth I've liked
This green place so, elsewhere I have no peace.   65
    Had you as much grace as you have desire,
With daring you could leave
This glade, and pass about among the folk.

127

    Wherever I am spurred by Love I must
Urge on these doleful rhymes, which are
The rag-tag creatures of my troubled mind.
Which should be last, ah me! and which come first?
He who discourses with me of my pain   5
Leaves me in doubt with his confused advice.
But since I find inscribed with his own hand
Within my heart the history of all
My martyrdom (which often I consult),
I'll speak, because sighs uttered   10
Declare an armistice and ease my pain.
I'll say, though raptly gazing
Upon a thousand varied things, I saw
One lady only—and her lovely face.
    Since that remorseless one, my destiny—   15
Vexatious, ineluctable and proud—

noiosa, inexorabile et superba,
Amor col rimembrar sol mi mantene:
onde s'io veggio in giovenil figura
incominciarsi il mondo a vestir d'erba,   20
parmi vedere in quella etate acerba
la bella giovenetta, ch'ora è donna;
poi che sormonta riscaldando il sole,
parmi qual esser sòle
fiamma d'amor che 'n cor alto s'endonna;   25
ma quando il dí si dole
di lui che passo passo a dietro torni,
veggio lei giunta a' suoi perfecti giorni.

   In ramo fronde, over vïole in terra,
mirando a la stagion che 'l freddo perde,   30
et le stelle miglior' acquistan forza,
negli occhi ò pur le vïolette e 'l verde
di ch'era nel principio de mia guerra
Amor armato, sí ch'anchor mi sforza,
et quella dolce leggiadretta scorza   35
che ricopria le pargolette membra
dove oggi alberga l'anima gentile
ch'ogni altro piacer vile
sembiar mi fa: sí forte mi rimembra
del portamento humile   40
ch'allor fioriva, et poi crebbe anzi agli anni,
cagion sola et riposo de' miei affanni.

   Qualor tenera neve per li colli
dal sol percossa veggio di lontano,
come 'l sol neve, mi governa Amore,   45
pensando nel bel viso piú che humano
che pò da lunge gli occhi miei far molli,
ma da presso gli abbaglia, et vince il core:
ove fra 'l biancho et l'aurëo colore
sempre si mostra quel che mai non vide   50
occhio mortal, ch'io creda, altro che 'l mio;
et del caldo desio
che, quando sospirando ella sorride,
m'infiamma sí che oblio
nïente aprezza, ma diventa eterno,   55
né state il cangia, né lo spegne il verno.

   Non vidi mai dopo nocturna pioggia
gir per l'aere sereno stelle erranti,
et fiammeggiar fra la rugiada e 'l gielo,
ch'i' non avesse i begli occhi davanti   60

Has come between me and my greatest good,
Love shores me up with memory alone.
Therein I see the world in youthful form
Beginning to array itself in green;   20
In that unripened time I seem to see
The lovely girl who is a lady now.
Then later when the warming sun mounts high,
I see in it Love's flame
That kindles womanhood in noble heart;   25
But when day sorrows for
The sun who step by step turns back, I see
Her brought to the perfection of her years.

    When I gaze on a leafy bough, look where
The earth bears violets, in springtime when   30
Cold wanes and stars benign wax strong, I still
See violet and green before my eyes,
In which hues at the onset of my war
Love armed himself; garbed thus he drives me still;
So does the sweet delightful shape that once   35
Enclosed those maiden limbs, and where today
Her gentle spirit dwells, that spirit which
Makes every pleasure else
Seem vile to me. So clearly I recall
Her modest person that   40
Then budding, early grew into full flower,
Sole reason for, yet respite from, my griefs.

    Each time I see from far away fresh snow
Upon the hills struck by the sun, as sun
Strikes light from snow Love deals with me: when I   45
Reflect upon that more than human face
So fair, far off it blurs my eyes with tears,
But, nearby, dazzles them and wins my heart;
There always 'midst the white and gold appear
Those hues that, as I think, no mortal eye   50
Besides my own has ever looked upon;
As for that hot desire
Which when she, sighing, smiles inflames me so,
Oblivion sets all
At naught, indeed forever it endures;   55
No summer changes it, nor winter kills.

    After a nighttime rain I never saw
The errant stars spin through the lambent air
And flame amidst the dew and chill, that I
Had not her beauteous eyes before me, eyes   60

ove la stancha mia vita s'appoggia,
quali io gli vidi a l'ombra d'un bel velo;
et sí come di lor bellezze il cielo
splendea quel dí, cosí bagnati anchora
il veggio sfavillare, ond'io sempre ardo.   65
Se 'l sol levarsi sguardo,
sento il lume apparir che m'innamora;
se tramontarsi al tardo,
parmel veder quando si volge altrove
lassando tenebroso onde si move.   70

   Se mai candide rose con vermiglie
in vasel d'oro vider gli occhi miei
allor allor da vergine man colte,
veder pensaro il viso di colei
ch'avanza tutte l'altre meraviglie   75
con tre belle excellentie in lui raccolte:
le bionde treccie sopra 'l collo sciolte,
ov'ogni lacte perderia sua prova,
e le guancie ch'adorna un dolce foco.
Ma pur che l'òra un poco   80
fior' bianchi et gialli per le piaggie mova,
torna a la mente il loco
e 'l primo dí ch'i' vidi a l'aura sparsi
i capei d'oro, ond'io sí súbito arsi.

   Ad una ad una annoverar le stelle,   85
e 'n picciol vetro chiuder tutte l'acque,
forse credea, quando in sí poca carta
novo penser di ricontar mi nacque
in quante parti il fior de l'altre belle,
stando in se stessa, à la sua luce sparta   90
a ciò che mai da lei non mi diparta:
né farò io; et se pur talor fuggo,
in cielo e 'n terra m'à rachiuso i passi,
perch'agli occhi miei lassi
sempre è presente, ond'io tutto mi struggo.   95
Et cosí meco stassi,
ch'altra non veggio mai, né veder bramo,
né 'l nome d'altra ne' sospir' miei chiamo.

   Ben sai, canzon, che quant'io parlo è nulla
al celato amoroso mio pensero,   100
che dí et nocte ne la mente porto,
solo per cui conforto
in cosí lunga guerra ancho non pèro:
ché ben m'avria già morto

On which this weary life of mine depends
Just as I saw a fair veil shade them once
And as I saw the heavens blaze forth that day
So, bathed in radiance I see them still,
Whence still I burn. If I glance upward at   65
The rising sun, I see
The light that yet enamours me appear;
If at the setting sun,
I seem to see it when it turns away,
Leaving in gloom the place from which it came.   70
    If on white roses my eyes ever gazed
Or on vermilion, in a vase of gold,
Plucked at that instant by a virgin hand,
They hoped to see the face of that one who
Surpasses everything that's marvelous,   75
For in her, three perfections fair combine:
Her tresses blonde, set free about her throat
Where any milk will fail comparison;
And then her cheeks, which a sweet fire adorns;
And if the breeze but lightly   80
Stirs white and yellow flowers on the slopes
I think about the place
And day I saw dishevelled by the wind
That golden hair, and suddenly I burned.
    Perhaps I thought that one by one I'd count   85
The stars, and in a little glass contain
The seas; and then I had the new idea
In these few pages to recount how this
Flower 'midst these other flowers fair,
Herself unique, has shed her light all round.   90
So never was I distant from her, nor
Shall I be ever; and if still sometimes
I flee, she closes off my way to heaven
And earth, for always she
Is present to my wretched eyes; by her   95
I am consumed, and thus it stands with me;
I'll never see, nor long to see, another,
Nor in my sighs invoke another's name.
    Song, well you know that anything I say
Is nothing to my secret loving thoughts,   100
For day and night I bear those in my mind,
And only by their solace
In this long war I have not perished yet.
Indeed, so distant from

la lontananza del mio cor piangendo,   105
ma quinci da la morte indugio prendo.

128

Italia mia, benché 'l parlar sia indarno
a le piaghe mortali
che nel bel corpo tuo sí spesse veggio,
piacemi almen che' miei sospir' sian quali
spera 'l Tevero et l'Arno,   5
e 'l Po, dove doglioso et grave or seggio.
Rettor del cielo, io cheggio
che la pietà che Ti condusse in terra
Ti volga al Tuo dilecto almo paese.
Vedi, Segnor cortese,   10
di che lievi cagion' che crudel guerra;
e i cor', che 'ndura et serra
Marte superbo et fero,
apri Tu, Padre, e 'ntenerisci et snoda;
ivi fa' che 'l Tuo vero,   15
qual io mi sia, per la mia lingua s'oda.

Voi cui Fortuna à posto in mano il freno
de le belle contrade,
di che nulla pietà par che vi stringa,
che fan qui tante pellegrine spade?   20
perché 'l verde terreno
del barbarico sangue si depinga?
Vano error vi lusinga:
poco vedete, et parvi veder molto,
ché 'n cor venale amor cercate o fede.   25
Qual piú gente possede,
colui è piú da' suoi nemici avolto.
O diluvio raccolto
di che deserti strani,
per inondar i nostri dolci campi!   30
Se da le proprie mani
questo n'avene, or chi fia che ne scampi?

Ben provide Natura al nostro stato,
quando de l'Alpi schermo
pose fra noi et la tedesca rabbia;   35
ma 'l desir cieco, e 'ncontra 'l suo ben fermo,
s'è poi tanto ingegnato,
ch'al corpo sano à procurato scabbia.
Or dentro ad una gabbia
fiere selvagge et mansüete gregge   40

My weeping heart I might have died, but I   105
By virtue of them am reprieved from death.

128

My Italy, though speech may not avail°
Against those deadly wounds
I see so often in your body fair,
Allow at least my sighs to bring some hope
To Tiber, to the Arno,   5
And to Po's banks where sad and grave I sit.
Ruler of heaven, I pray,
Now turn that mercy which led you to earth
Upon your chosen, sacred, fruitful land.
Regard, O gracious Lord: 10
From such slight causes, such a cruel war:
And hearts that proud, ferocious Mars makes hard
And locks tight; Father, may
You open them; them soften; set them free.
Though I be what I am,   15
Ordain that through my voice your truth be heard.
All you into whose hands Fortune has placed
The reins of these fair lands,
For which no pity stirs you, as it seems:
So many roaming swords, why are they here?   20
Why is this verdant earth
All painted over with barbaric blood?
You're fooled by error vain:
You see so little, think you see so much,
For you seek love and faith in hireling hearts.   25
Who most retainers owns
Is most encircled by his enemies.
O deluge channelled from
What wild and foreign wastes
To inundate our lovely countryside!   30
And if by our own hands
This comes to pass, who'll save us from it then?
Nature made good provision for our state,
To set an Alpine shield
Between us and the Germans' ravening.   35
But blind desire stands firm 'gainst his own good;
Much has he exercised his wits
And to this healthy body brought the pox:
Now in one pen bed down
With tame herds, savage beasts   40

s'annidan sí, che sempre il miglior geme;
et è questo del seme,
per piú dolor, del popol senza legge,
al qual, come si legge,
Mario aperse sí 'l fianco,   45
che memoria de l'opra ancho non langue,
quando assetato et stanco
non piú bevve del fiume acqua che sangue.

    Cesare taccio che per ogni piaggia
fece l'erbe sanguigne   50
di lor vene, ove 'l nostro ferro mise.
Or par, non so per che stelle maligne,
che 'l cielo in odio n'aggia:
vostra mercé, cui tanto si commise
Vostre voglie divise   55
guastan del mondo la piú bella parte.
Qual colpa, qual giudicio o qual destino
fastidire il vicino
povero, et le fortune afflicte et sparte
perseguire, e 'n disparte   60
cercar gente et gradire,
che sparga 'l sangue et venda l'alma a prezzo?
Io parlo per ver dire,
non per odio d'altrui, né per disprezzo.

    Né v'accorgete anchor per tante prove   65
del bavarico inganno
ch'alzando il dito colla morte scherza?
Peggio è lo strazio, al mio parer, che 'l danno;
ma 'l vostro sangue piove
piú largamente, ch'altr'ira vi sferza.   70
Da la matina a terza
di voi pensate, et vederete come
tien caro altrui che tien sé cosí vile.
Latin sangue gentile,
sgombra da te queste dannose some;   75
non far idolo un nome
vano senza soggetto:
ché 'l furor de lassú, gente ritrosa,
vincerne d'intellecto,
peccato è nostro, et non natural cosa.   80

    Non è questo 'l terren ch'i' tocchai pria?
Non è questo il mio nido
ove nudrito fui sí dolcemente?
Non è questa la patria in ch'io mi fido,

And wild, so that the worthier ever mourn.
More grief, this seed is sown
By that barbaric lawless people, they
Whose side, one reads, was so
Pierced through by Marius°   45
That still the memory dims not of his work
When he athirst and tired,
No more drank water from the stream but blood.
    Of Caesar I speak not; in every field
He bloodied all the grass   50
From their own veins where he thrust home our steel.
Now, by what stars malign I do not know,
Heaven hates us as it seems,
Thanks to you who bear so great a charge;
Your sundered wills lay waste   55
That part of all the world which is most fair:
What stroke, what judgment, or what destiny
Impels you to disdain
A neighbor poor, and ruined, scattered fortunes
To persecute; to seek afar   60
And happily receive a crew
Who, for a price, shed blood and sell their souls?
I speak to make truth plain,
And not from hate of others or contempt.
    Do you not notice yet, from many proofs,   65
Bavarian deceit,
That raising high the finger, jokes with death?
Worse than the loss derision seems to me;
But more profusely pours
Your blood, for other anger scourges you.   70
From matins until tierce°
Think on yourselves, and you will see how dear
Others hold one who holds himself so vile.
Noble Latin blood,
Cast off these hurtful burdens from yourself: 75
No idol make of names,
Insubstantial, void;
And if that furious, backward race up there
Prevail with intellect,
The sin is ours, and nothing natural.   80
    Is this soil not the earth that I first touched?
This not the nest where I
Have been so sweetly nursed?
And is this not my homeland that I trust?

madre benigna et pia, 85
che copre l'un et l'altro mio parente?
Perdio, questo la mente
talor vi mova, et con pietà guardate
le lagrime del popol doloroso,
che sol da voi riposo 90
dopo Dio spera; et pur che voi mostriate
segno alcun di pietate,
vertú contra furore
prenderà l'arme, et fia 'l combatter corto:
ché l'antiquo valore 95
ne l'italici cor' non è anchor morto.

    Signor', mirate come 'l tempo vola,
et sí come la vita
fugge, et la morte n'è sovra le spalle.
Voi siete or qui; pensate a la partita: 100
ché l'alma ignuda et sola
conven ch'arrive a quel dubbioso calle.
Al passar questa valle
piacciavi porre giú l'odio et lo sdegno
vénti contrari a la vita serena; 105
et quel che 'n altrui pena
tempo si spende, in qualche acto piú degno
o di mano o d'ingegno,
in qualche bella lode,
in qualche honesto studio si converta: 110
cosí qua giú si gode,
et la strada del ciel si trova aperta.

    Canzone, io t'ammonisco
che tua ragion cortesemente dica,
perché fra gente altera ir ti convene, 115
et le voglie son piene
già de l'usanza pessima et antica,
del ver sempre nemica.
Proverai tua ventura
fra' magnanimi pochi a chi 'l ben piace. 120
Di' lor:—Chi m'assicura?
I' vo gridando: Pace, pace, pace.—

129

    Di pensier in pensier, di monte in monte
mi guida Amor, ch'ogni segnato calle
provo contrario a la tranquilla vita.
Se 'n solitaria piaggia, rivo o fonte,

A mother, pious, kind,   85
Who shelters both my parents in her soil?
By God, may this sometimes
Arouse your minds, and may you look with ruth
Upon the tears of this grief-stricken folk,
Who, save from God, may hope   90
For no relief unless from you: but if
You'll show some trace of mercy,
Then Virtue will seize arms
'Gainst madness, and the battle will be brief,
For ancient valor is   95
Not dead, as yet, within Italian hearts.
    My lords, regard the way time flies and how,
Just so, life quickly flees,
And ever at our backs, death follows on.
Now you are here, but of that parting think: 100
For naked and alone
Must be the soul that treads that doubtful path.
In passing through this vale,
Consent to put aside disdain and hate—
Those gales contrary to a life serene—   105
The time you use to grieve
Those others, spend on some more fitting work
Of hand or else of wit:
Some commendation fine,
Some edifying study undertake: 110
Thus, down here one rejoices
And finds the road to heaven open wide.
    Song, I admonish you:
You should present your case with courtesy,
For 'midst smug, haughty people you must go   115
Whose wills are surely full
Of habit infamous and deep ingrained,
Ever the foe of truth.
You'll cast your lot among
That magnanimous few who joy in good.   120
Ask them: "Who'll shelter me?
I wander crying: 'Peace, Peace, Peace.'"

129

    From thought to thought, from mount to mount, Love leads
Me on, for each well-beaten path I prove
Contrary to the peaceful way of life.
If by a lonely heath or shore or fount

se 'nfra duo poggi siede ombrosa valle,   5
ivi s'acqueta l'alma sbigottita;
et come Amor l'envita,
or ride, or piange, or teme, or s'assecura;
e 'l volto che lei segue ov'ella il mena
si turba et rasserena,   10
et in un esser picciol tempo dura;
onde a la vista huom di tal vita experto
diria: Questo arde, et di suo stato è incerto.

    Per alti monti et per selve aspre trovo
qualche riposo: ogni habitato loco   15
è nemico mortal degli occhi miei.
A ciascun passo nasce un penser novo
de la mia donna, che sovente in gioco
gira 'l tormento ch'i' porto per lei;
et a pena vorrei   20
cangiar questo mio viver dolce amaro,
ch'i' dico: Forse anchor ti serva Amore
ad un tempo migliore;
forse, a te stesso vile, altrui se' caro.
Et in questa trapasso sospirando: 25
Or porrebbe esser vero? or come? or quando?

    Ove porge ombra un pino alto od un colle
talor m'arresto, et pur nel primo sasso
disegno co la mente il suo bel viso.
Poi ch'a me torno, trovo il petto molle   30
de la pietate; et alor dico: Ahi lasso,
dove se' giunto! et onde se' diviso!
Ma mentre tener fiso
posso al primo pensier la mente vaga,
et mirar lei, et oblïar me stesso,   35
sento Amor sí da presso,
che del suo proprio error l'alma s'appaga:
in tante parti et sí bella la veggio,
che se l'error durasse, altro non cheggio.

    I' l'ò piú volte (or chi fia che mi 'l creda?)   40
ne l'acqua chiara et sopra l'erba verde
veduto viva, et nel tronchon d'un faggio
e 'n bianca nube, sí fatta che Leda
avria ben detto che sua figlia perde,
come stella che 'l sol copre col raggio;   45
et quanto in piú selvaggio
loco mi trovo e 'n piú deserto lido,
tanto piú bella il mio pensier l'adombra.

Or if between two lofty hills there lies   5
A shadowed vale, there my soul terrified
Grows calm; as Love invites
It laughs, now weeps, now fears, stands now assured.
And then my face, which follows where she leads,
Is stormy then serene;   10
And in the same guise stays but little time.
Thus seeing it, one expert in such life
Would say, "Uncertain of his state, he burns."
    Amidst high mountains and in rugged woods
I find some peace; each spot that's tenanted   15
Of my eyes is a deadly enemy.
At every stride springs up a fresh thought of
My lady, and it often turns to joy
The suffering I bear on her account;
And scarcely would I want   20
To change this life so bittersweet of mine,
For I say: "Love preserves you still perhaps
Until a better time;
Though worthless to yourself, perhaps you're dear
To someone;" to this thought I turn in sighs: 25
"Now could this be the truth? But how? Or when?"
    Where some tall pine tree or a hill gives shade
Sometimes I pause and, on the very first
Stone with my mind trace her fair countenance.
Then, coming to myself, I feel my breast   30
Wet through with pity; then I say: "Ah, woe!
Where have you come? From what are you cut off?"
But while I can hold firm
On that first thought my straying intellect,
Can gaze upon her and forget myself,   35
So near is Love, I feel
The soul with its own error is content.
So many places I see her so fair
That if illusion lasts, naught else I'll ask.
    Alive I've seen her many times (now who   40
Is there to credit me?), in water clear
And on green grass, and in a beech's trunk;
In white cloud, formed so Leda might indeed°
Have said her daughter vanished like a star,
One that the sun with its bright ray obscures.   45
Whenever I discover
Myself in some most savage place, or on
Some utterly forsaken shore, then my

Poi quando il vero sgombra
quel dolce error, pur lí medesmo assido   50
me freddo, pietra morta in pietra viva,
in guisa d'uom che pensi et pianga et scriva.

Ove d'altra montagna ombra non tocchi,
verso 'l maggiore e 'l piú expedito giogo
tirar mi suol un desiderio intenso;   55
indi i miei danni a misurar con gli occhi
comincio, e 'ntanto lagrimando sfogo
di dolorosa nebbia il cor condenso,
alor ch'i' miro et penso
quanta aria dal bel viso mi diparte   60
che sempre m'è sí presso et sí lontano.
Poscia fra me pian piano:
Che sai tu, lasso? forse in quella parte
or di tua lontananza si sospira.
Et in questo penser l'alma respira.   65

Canzone, oltra quell'alpe
là dove il ciel è piú sereno et lieto
mi rivedrai sovr'un ruscel corrente,
ove l'aura si sente
d'un fresco et odorifero laureto.   70
Ivi è 'l mio cor, et quella che 'l m'invola;
qui veder pôi l'imagine mia sola.

130

Poi che 'l camin m'è chiuso di Mercede,
per desperata via son dilungato
dagli occhi ov'era, i' non so per qual fato,
riposto il guidardon d'ogni mia fede.

Pasco 'l cor di sospir', ch'altro non chiede,   5
e di lagrime vivo a pianger nato:
né di ciò duolmi, perché in tale stato
è dolce il pianto piú ch'altri non crede.

Et sol ad una imagine m'attegno,
che fe' non Zeusi, o Prasitele, o Fidia,   10
ma miglior mastro, et di piú alto ingegno.

Qual Scithia m'assicura, o qual Numidia,
s'anchor non satia del mio exilio indegno,
cosí nascosto mi ritrova Invidia?

131

Io canterei d'amor sí novamente
ch'al duro fiancho il dí mille sospiri

Thought sketches her more fair.
When truth sweeps sweet illusion out, there I   50
Sit down, cold through, dead stone on living stone,
Shaped like a man who thinks and weeps and writes.
    Up where no other mountain casts its shade
And toward the greatest, least obstructed height
I'm often drawn by an intense desire;   55
From there I start surveying with my eyes
My injuries; meanwhile, with tears I vent
The mist of woe condensed within my heart,
Then as I gaze and think
What distance cuts me off from her fair face,   60
So near me always, yet so far away.
Within me softly, then:
"What do you know, unhappy one? Perhaps
Now one sighs there because you're far away."
And with this thought my soul can breathe again.   65
    O song, across those Alps,
There where the heavens are joyful, more serene,
Once more you'll see me near a running brook;
There, of a laurel tree,
One fresh, sweet-smelling, you can feel the breeze.   70
My heart is there, and she who steals it too;
Here, only on my image can you look.

130

    Since Mercy's path is barred to me, along
A desperate road I've wandered, far from eyes
In which, I know not by what destiny,
Was stored up the reward of all my faith.
    On sighs I feed my heart, it asks naught else;   5
On tears I live, and am to weeping born;
Nor do I grieve at that; in such a plight
Complaint is sweeter than one might believe.
    To just one image I pay heed, not made
By Zeuxis, Phidias, or Praxiteles,°   10
But by a master greater, with more skill.
    What Scythia or what Numidia
Can save me if, not sated yet with my
Base exile, Envy finds me hidden so?

131

    In such new fashion would I sing of love
That from her hard side I would draw by force

trarrei per forza, et mille alti desiri
raccenderei ne la gelata mente;
   e 'l bel viso vedrei cangiar sovente,   5
et bagnar gli occhi, et piú pietosi giri
far, come suol che degli altrui martiri
et del suo error quando non val si pente;
   et le rose vermiglie infra la neve
mover da l'òra, et discovrir l'avorio   10
che fa di marmo chi da presso 'l guarda;
   e tutto quel per che nel viver breve
non rincresco a me stesso, anzi mi glorio
d'esser servato a la stagion piú tarda.

132

   S'amor non è, che dunque è quel ch'io sento?
Ma s'egli è amor, perdio, che cosa et quale?
Se bona, onde l'effecto aspro mortale?
Se ria, onde sí dolce ogni tormento?
   S'a mia voglia ardo, onde 'l pianto e lamento?   5
S'a mal mio grado, il lamentar che vale?
O viva morte, o dilectoso male,
come puoi tanto in me, s'io nol consento?
   Et s'io 'l consento, a gran torto mi doglio.
Fra sí contrari vènti in frale barca   10
mi trovo in alto mar senza governo,
   sí lieve di saver, d'error sí carca
ch'i' medesmo non so quel ch'io mi voglio,
e tremo a mezza state, ardendo il verno.

133

   Amor m'à posto come segno a strale,
come al sol neve, come cera al foco,
et come nebbia al vento; et son già roco,
donna, mercé chiamando, et voi non cale.
   Dagli occhi vostri uscío 'l colpo mortale,   5
contra cui non mi val tempo né loco;
da voi sola procede, et parvi un gioco,
il sole e 'l foco e 'l vento ond'io son tale.
   I pensier' son saette, e 'l viso un sole,
e 'l desir foco: e 'nseme con quest'arme   10
mi punge Amor, m'abbaglia et mi distrugge;
   et l'angelico canto et le parole,
col dolce spirto ond'io non posso aitarme,
son l'aura inanzi a cui mia vita fugge.

A thousand sighs a day, and light again
In her cold mind a thousand high desires;
    And I would often see that fair face change,   5
And weep, and cast looks more compassionate,
As is the case when idly one repents
Of others' torments and one's own mistakes;
    'Midst snows I'd see vermilion roses blown
Upon the breeze, and find the ivory that turns   10
To marble one who sees it close at hand.
    All that I'd do since I don't sorrow for
Myself in this brief life, but glory that
I am preserved until some later age.

132
    If not love, then what is this that I feel?
If love it is, by God, which sort? What kind?
If good, whence comes its deadly, harsh effect?
If wicked, whence its every torment sweet?
    If willingly I burn, why weep and grieve?   5
Unwillingly, what can lamenting do?
O, living death; O, pleasurable pain,
Can you hold sway in me if I refuse?
    Yet if I do consent, how wrong to grieve!
Between winds so opposed, in this frail craft   10
On high seas, rudderless, I find myself
    Of wisdom empty and so error filled
That for myself I don't know what I wish;
In summer's heat I shake, in winter burn.

133
    Love set me as a target for his darts,
As snow to sun, as wax to fire, and as
The fog to wind; already I am hoarse
From calling "mercy," lady; you care not.
    From your eyes issued forth that deadly shot   5
Against which neither time nor place availed;
From you alone proceeds (a game, you think)
The sun and fire and wind that shaped me thus.
    These thoughts are arrows, and your face a sun,
Desire a flame; with these assembled arms   10
Love pierces me and blinds me, melts me down.
    That song angelic and those words, with that
Sweet wit from which I can't defend myself,
They are the breeze before which my life flies.

134

Pace non trovo, et non ò da far guerra;
e temo, et spero; et ardo, et son un ghiaccio;
et volo sopra 'l cielo, et giaccio in terra;
et nulla stringo, et tutto 'l mondo abbraccio.

    Tal m'à in pregion, che non m'apre né serra,   5
né per suo mi riten né scioglie il laccio;
et non m'ancide Amore, et non mi sferra,
né mi vuol vivo, né mi trae d'impaccio.

    Veggio senza occhi, et non ò lingua et grido;
et bramo di perir, et cheggio aita;   10
et ò in odio me stesso, et amo altrui.

    Pascomi di dolor, piangendo rido;
egualmente mi spiace morte et vita:
in questo stato son, donna, per voi.

135

    Qual piú diversa et nova
cosa fu mai in qual che stranio clima,
quella, se ben s'estima,
piú mi rasembra: a tal son giunto, Amore.
Là onde il dí vèn fore,   5
vola un augel che sol senza consorte
di volontaria morte
rinasce, et tutto a viver si rinova.
Cosí sol si ritrova
lo mio voler, et cosí in su la cima   10
de' suoi alti pensieri al sol si volve,
et cosí si risolve,
et cosí torna al suo stato di prima:
arde, et more, et riprende i nervi suoi,
et vive poi con la fenice a prova.   15
    Una petra è sí ardita
là per l'indico mar, che da natura
tragge a sé il ferro e 'l fura
dal legno, in guisa che' navigi affonde.
Questo prov'io fra l'onde   20
d'amaro pianto, ché quel bello scoglio
à col suo duro argoglio
condutta ove affondar conven mia vita:
cosí l'alm'à sfornita
(furando 'l cor che fu già cosa dura,   25
et me tenne un, ch'or son diviso et sparso)
un sasso a trar piú scarso

134

No peace I find, and no means to make war;
I fear and hope; I burn and turn to ice;
I fly above the skies, fall to the earth
I nothing clasp, yet all the world embrace.
    And one who neither locks nor unlocks holds   5
Me prisoner, yet won't account me his,
Love won't unchain me, kill me, strike my bonds,
Nor want me free from death's snare, nor alive.
    I see without eyes, have no tongue, yet shout;
I yearn to perish, and I beg for aid,   10
Myself I hate, and someone else I love.
    I feed myself on woe; in tears I laugh;
Both death and life displease me equally;
For you, my lady, I am in this plight.

135

    The strangest, rarest thing
That ever was in some exotic clime,
If one esteems aright,
Seems most like me; Love, such have I become:
There, where the day springs forth   5
A bird flies that, unique and consortless,
From voluntary death
Is born again, restores itself to life.
Like it, my own desire
Is peerless, thus upon the highest point   10
Of its high thoughts, it turns to face the sun,
Annihilates itself,
And thus to its first state of being returns.
It burns, it dies, its sinews it resumes,
And lives then with the Phoenix as its match.   15
There's in the Indian sea
A stone of such audacious nature that
It draws iron to itself,
Steals it from wood so as to make ships sink.
This I test out 'midst waves   20
Of bitter tears, since that alluring reef
With her unyielding pride
Has brought me where my life must be engulfed.
A stone's thus reft my soul
(Stealing my heart that was a solid thing,   25
And kept me whole, who now am split and strewn)—
A stone more avid to

carne che ferro. O cruda mia ventura,
che 'n carne essendo, veggio trarmi a riva
ad una viva dolce calamita!   30
    Ne l'extremo occidente
una fera è soave et queta tanto
che nulla piú, ma pianto
et doglia et morte dentro agli occhi porta:
molto convene accorta   35
esser qual vista mai ver' lei si giri;
pur che gli occhi non miri,
l'altro puossi veder securamente.
Ma io incauto, dolente,
corro sempre al mio male, et so ben quanto   40
n'ò sofferto, et n'aspetto; ma l'engordo
voler ch'è cieco et sordo
sí mi trasporta, che 'l bel viso santo
et gli occhi vaghi fien cagion ch'io pèra,
di questa fera angelica innocente.   45
    Surge nel mezzo giorno
una fontana, e tien nome dal sole,
che per natura sòle
bollir le notti, e 'n sul giorno esser fredda;
e tanto si raffredda   50
quanto 'l sol monta, et quanto è piú da presso.
Cosí aven a me stesso,
che son fonte di lagrime et soggiorno:
quanto 'l bel lume adorno
ch'è 'l mio sol s'allontana, et triste et sole   55
son le mie luci, et notte oscura è loro,
ardo allor; ma se l'oro
e i rai veggio apparir del vivo sole,
tutto dentro et di for sento cangiarme,
et ghiaccio farme, cosí freddo torno.   60
    Un'altra fonte à Epiro,
di cui si scrive ch'essendo fredda ella,
ogni spenta facella
accende, et spegne qual trovasse accesa.
L'anima mia, ch'offesa   65
anchor non era d'amoroso foco,
appressandosi un poco
a quella fredda, ch'io sempre sospiro,
arse tutta: et martiro
simil già mai né sol vide né stella,   70
ch'un cor di marmo a pietà mosso avrebbe;

Draw flesh than iron. O my cruel fortune! for,
Existing in the flesh, I see myself
By one sweet, living lodestone drawn aground.   30
    Far in the distant west
Exists a gentle beast, and one more calm
Than all the rest, but she
Bears woe and plaint and death within her eyes.
Most cautious sight must be   35
If it in her direction turns; if it
Looks not into her eyes,
The rest of her, then, it can safely see.
But heedless, mournful, I
Run ever toward my ill, and well I know   40
How I have suffered for it, and still yearn.
But gluttonous, my wish—
Both blind and deaf—transports me so that her
Fair, sacred face and eyes that charm will make
Me die—this innocent, angelic beast.   45
    A fountain gushes in
The south (and from the sun it takes its name),
Which boils by nature just
At night and in the day stays cold; and it
Grows colder even as   50
The sun mounts high and as it nearer draws;
To me the same occurs,
For I'm a fount, and dwelling-place of tears;
When that light beautiful
Departs—that sun of mine—my eyes are sad,   55
Alone, and theirs the dark night is; it's then
I burn, but if the gold
And rays of that live sun I see appear,
Within me and without I feel a change
And turn to ice, so cold do I become.   60
    Epirus has a fount
About which it is written that, while cold,
Each burnt-out torch it can
Ignite, and put out those it finds alight.
My soul, which still had not   65
Yet suffered damage from the amorous fire,
Drawing a little near
That icy one for whom I always sigh,
Caught all on fire; and no
Like pain was ever seen by sun or star;   70
A marble heart to pity would it move;

poi che 'nfiammata l'ebbe,
rispensela vertú gelata et bella.
Cosí piú volte à 'l cor racceso et spento:
i' 'l so che 'l sento, et spesso me n'adiro.   75
    Fuor tutti nostri lidi,
ne l'isole famose di Fortuna,
due fontí à: chi de l'una
bee, mor ridendo; et chi de l'altra, scampa.
Simil fortuna stampa   80
mia vita, che morir poria ridendo,
del gran piacer ch'io prendo,
se nol temprassen dolorosi stridi.
Amor, ch'anchor mi guidi
pur a l'ombra di fama occulta et bruna,   85
tacerem questa fonte, ch'ognor piena,
ma con piú larga vena
veggiam, quando col Tauro il sol s'aduna:
cosí gli occhi miei piangon d'ogni tempo,
ma piú nel tempo che madonna vidi.   90
    Chi spïasse, canzone,
quel ch'i' fo, tu pôi dir: Sotto un gran sasso
in una chiusa valle, ond'esce Sorga,
si sta; né chi lo scorga
v'è se no Amor, che mai nol lascia un passo,   95
et l'imagine d'una che lo strugge,
ché per sé fugge tutt'altre persone.

136

    Fiamma dal ciel su le tue treccie piova,
malvagia, che dal fiume et da le ghiande
per l'altrui impoverir se' ricca et grande,
poi che di mal oprar tanto ti giova;
    nido di tradimenti, in cui si cova   5
quanto mal per lo mondo oggi si spande,
de vin serva, di lecti et di vivande,
in cui Luxuria fa l'ultima prova.
    Per le camere tue fanciulle et vecchi
vanno trescando, et Belzebub in mezzo   10
co' mantici et col foco et co li specchi.
    Già non fostú nudrita in piume al rezzo,
ma nuda al vento, et scalza fra gli stecchi:
or vivi sí ch'a Dio ne venga il lezzo.

Once she had kindled it,
Then virtue, frozen, lovely, snuffed it out.
How often has she lit and quenched my heart.
Ah, I who feel it know; oft I am vexed.   75
    Far past these shores of ours
In fortune's famous islands rise two founts.
Whoever takes a drink from one of them
Dies laughing, from the other one survives.
So Fortune moulds my life,   80
For, laughing I could die from that great joy
I feel, were it not mixed with doleful shrieks.
Ah Love, who guides me yet,
Even to the shade of Fame, occult and dark,
About this fount let us keep still; we see   85
It ever full, but with
Its greatest flow when Taurus joins the sun;
And thus at every season my eyes weep—
That time I saw my lady—most of all.   90
    To someone who inquires,
Song, what I do, say this: "By a great stone,
Within a closed vale where Sorgue springs, he bides;
Of him none there takes note
But Love, who never strays one step away,   95
And that one's image who is wasting him;
As for himself, he flees all persons else."

136

    Let flame from heaven upon your tresses rain,
Malign one; you ate nuts and drank from brooks,°
But now from others' ruin grow rich and grand,
For doing evil deeds so profits you.
    You nest of treason, where there incubates   5
That evil spreading through the world today,
You slave of wine, of beds, of victuals,
In which Excess tries all that she can do;
    Throughout your rooms young girls and old men play,
Lust wantonly, Beelzebub in their midst   10
With bellows and with fire and mirrors too.
    Indeed, you were not reared in shady ease
But naked to the wind, barefoot 'midst thorns.
Now you live so, the stench must rise to God!

137

L'avara Babilonia à colmo il sacco
d'ira di Dio, e di vitii empii et rei,
tanto che scoppia, ed à fatti suoi dèi
non Giove et Palla, ma Venere et Bacco.

Aspectando ragion mi struggo et fiacco;   5
ma pur novo soldan veggio per lei,
lo qual farà, non già quand'io vorrei,
sol una sede, et quella fia in Baldacco.

Gl'idoli suoi sarranno in terra sparsi,
et le torre superbe, al ciel nemiche,   10
e i suoi torrer' di for come dentro arsi.

Anime belle et di virtute amiche
terranno il mondo; et poi vedrem lui farsi
aurëo tutto, et pien de l'opre antiche.

138

Fontana di dolore, albergo d'ira,
scola d'errori et templo d'eresia,
già Roma, or Babilonia falsa et ria,
per cui tanto si piange et si sospira;

o fucina d'inganni, o pregion dira,   5
ove 'l ben more, e 'l mal si nutre et cria,
di vivi inferno, un gran miracol fia
se Cristo teco alfine non s'adira.

Fondata in casta et humil povertate,
contra' tuoi fondatori alzi le corna,   10
putta sfacciata: et dove ài posto spene?

negli adúlteri tuoi? ne le mal nate
richezze tante? Or Constantin non torna;
ma tolga il mondo tristo che 'l sostene.

139

Quanto piú disïose l'ali spando
verso di voi, o dolce schiera amica,
tanto Fortuna con piú visco intrica
il mio volare, et gir mi face errando.

Il cor che mal suo grado a torno mando,   5
è con voi sempre in quella valle aprica,
ove 'l mar nostro piú la terra implica;
l'altrier da lui partimmi lagrimando.

I' da man manca, e' tenne il camin dritto;
i' tratto a forza, et e' d'Amore scorto;   10
egli in Ierusalem, et io in Egipto.

137

Rapacious Babylon has stuffed her sack
With God's wrath and with guilty, impious vice
Until it bursts; Venus and Bacchus she
Has made her gods, but Pallas not, nor Jove.°

Awaiting reason I'm consumed and worn;   5
Yet I foresee a Sultan new for her,
One who'll set up a single throne (and none
Too soon for me); in Baghdad it will be.

Her idols will be strewn upon the earth,
And burnt her haughty towers, the foes of heaven,   10
Their warders too, from outside, and within.

Then worthy souls and friends of virtue shall
Inherit earth; then shall we see it made
All golden, filled with honest deeds of old.

138

You fount of woe and dwelling-place of wrath,
You school of wrongs and shrine of heresy,
Once Rome, now false and guilty Babylon
For whom one weeps so much, and so much sighs;

Forge of deception; O you prison dire,   5
Where goodness dies and evil feeds and forms,
Hell for the quick, how great the miracle
If Christ does not at last grow wroth with you.

Begun in chaste and lowly poverty,
Against your authors do you raise the horn,   10
You cheeky whore? Where do you rest your hope?

In your adulterers? In evil born
From riches great? Now comes no Constantine;°
Let that sad world that keeps him take you too!°

139

Filled with desire, the more I spread my wings
Toward you, O my sweet company of friends,
The more with birdlime Fortune then impedes
My flight, and causes me to miss my way.

My heart, whom I send out against his will   5
Is with you always in that sunny vale,
Where our sea most encompasses the land;°
In tears, I left him there the other day.

I took the left-hand, he the straight road held,
I, dragged by force, and he led forth by Love;   10
He to Jerusalem; to Egypt I.°

Ma sofferenza è nel dolor conforto,
ché per lungo uso già fra noi prescripto
il nostro esser insieme è raro et corto.

140

Amor, che nel penser mio vive et regna
e 'l suo seggio maggior nel mio cor tene,
talor armato ne la fronte vène,
ivi si loca, et ivi pon sua insegna.
 Quella ch'amare et sofferir ne 'nsegna   5
e vòl che 'l gran desio, l'accesa spene,
ragion, vergogna et reverenza affrene,
di nostro ardir fra se stessa si sdegna.
 Onde Amor paventoso fugge al core,
lasciando ogni sua impresa, et piange, et trema;   10
ivi s'asconde, et non appar piú fore.
 Che poss'io far, temendo il mio signore,
se non star seco infin a l'ora extrema?
Ché bel fin fa chi ben amando more.

141

Come talora al caldo tempo sòle
semplicetta farfalla al lume avezza
volar negli occhi altrui per sua vaghezza,
onde aven ch'ella more, altri si dole:
 cosí sempre io corro al fatal mio sole   5
degli occhi onde mi vèn tanta dolcezza
che 'l fren de la ragion Amor non prezza,
e chi discerne è vinto da chi vòle.
 E veggio ben quant'elli a schivo m'ànno,
e so ch'i' ne morrò veracemente,   10
ché mia vertú non pò contra l'affanno;
 ma sí m'abbaglia Amor soavemente,
ch'i' piango l'altrui noia, et no 'l mio danno;
et cieca al suo morir l'alma consente.

142

A la dolce ombra de le belle frondi
corsi fuggendo un dispietato lume
che 'nfin qua giú m'ardea dal terzo cielo;
et disgombrava già di neve i poggi
l'aura amorosa che rinova il tempo,   5
et fiorian per le piagge l'erbe e i rami.
 Non vide il mondo sí leggiadri rami,

Endurance, though, brings comfort in my woe,
For by long custom once between us fixed,
Our meetings are infrequent, and are brief.

140

Love, who in my thought both lives and reigns
And holds his greatest court within my heart
Sometimes comes armed into my brow, and there
He takes his place, and there his ensign plants.

That one who teaches us to love, endure,   5
Who wishes great desire and ardent hope
By reason, shame and reverence were curbed,
Within grows wrathful at our impudence.

At this Love, timorous, to my heart flees;
Leaving his every task he weeps and quakes,   10
And hides there and appears no more without.

What can I do when my lord fears, if not
Bide with him till the final hour, for one
A fair end makes, who dies while loving well.

141

Just as the artless butterfly sometimes,
Lured by the light, will fly in someone's eyes,
In the hot season, drawn by its desire,
And chancing thus to die, hurts someone else,

So ever I run toward my fatal sun,   5
Toward eyes from which such sweetness comes to me,
That reason's curb Love does not prize, and one
Who judges is o'erthrown by one who wills.

I see, indeed, how they're avoiding me;
In truth, I know that I shall die from it,   10
Because my strength cannot withstand the pain;

But Love so sweetly blinds my eyes that I
Lament another's ill and not my loss,
And, sightless, to its death my soul consents.

142

Toward the sweet shadow of those lovely fronds
I rushed, while fleeing a relentless light
That burned me, even here, from the third heaven;°
Already sweeping snow from off the hills
The amorous breeze blew, which revives the season,   5
And all along the slopes bloomed grass and boughs.

The world had never seen such graceful boughs,

né mosse il vento mai sí verdi frondi
come a me si mostrâr quel primo tempo:
tal che, temendo de l'ardente lume,   10
non volsi al mio refugio ombra di poggi,
ma de la pianta piú gradita in cielo.

    Un lauro mi difese allor dal cielo,
onde piú volte vago de' bei rami
da po' son gito per selve et per poggi;   15
né già mai ritrovai tronco né frondi
tanto honorate dal superno lume
che non mutasser qualitate a tempo.

    Però piú fermo ognor di tempo in tempo,
seguendo ove chiamar m'udia dal cielo   20
e scorto d'un soave et chiaro lume,
tornai sempre devoto ai primi rami
et quando a terra son sparte le frondi
et quando il sol fa verdeggiar i poggi.

    Selve, sassi, campagne, fiumi et poggi,   25
quanto è creato, vince et cangia il tempo:
ond'io cheggio perdono a queste frondi,
se rivolgendo poi molt'anni il cielo
fuggir disposi gl'invescati rami
tosto ch'incominciai di veder lume.   30

    Tanto mi piacque prima il dolce lume
ch'i' passai con diletto assai gran poggi
per poter appressar gli amati rami:
ora la vita breve e 'l loco e 'l tempo
mostranmi altro sentier di gire al cielo   35
et di far frutto, non pur fior' et frondi.

    Altr'amor, altre frondi et altro lume,
altro salir al ciel per altri poggi
cerco, ché n'è ben tempo, et altri rami.

143

    Quand'io v'odo parlar sí dolcemente
com'Amor proprio a' suoi seguaci instilla,
l'acceso mio desir tutto sfavilla,
tal che 'nfiammar devria l'anime spente.

    Trovo la bella donna allor presente   5
ovunque mi fu mai dolce o tranquilla
ne l'habito ch'al suon non d'altra squilla
ma' di sospir' mi fa destar sovente.

    Le chiome a l'aura sparse, et lei conversa
indietro veggio; et cosí bella riede   10

Nor had the wind blown through more verdant fronds
Than those revealed to me in that first season,
So that, in terror of the burning light, 10
I sought my safety, not in shade from hills,
But from that plant most pleasing to high heaven.

    A laurel, then, protected me from heaven,
Whence, often longing for those lovely boughs,
Since then I've wandered through the woods and hills; 15
Again I never found a trunk or fronds
So venerated by supernal light
But they would change condition at their season.

    More steadfast ever, thus, through every season,
Where I heard one who called to me from heaven 20
I followed, led by clear and gentle light,
I came back always, pledged to those first boughs,
Both when on earth lay scattered all their fronds
And when the sun to green turns all the hills.

    The woodlands, rocks and meadows, streams and hills,
And what's created, changes with the season,
Is overcome, and thus I from those fronds
Ask pardon if, when many years the heavens
Had rolled, I vowed to flee those bird-limed boughs
As soon as I began to see the light. 30

    At first, I was so pleased by that sweet light
That with delight I crossed enormous hills
Just to be nearer those beloved boughs,
But now my brief life, and the place and season
Direct me to another path to heaven, 35
To bring forth fruit, not merely flowers and fronds.

    Some other love, new fronds, another light,
Another stair to heaven through other hills
I seek (the season's right), and other boughs.

143

    When I hear you discourse so sweetly, just
As Love instructs his own disciples, then,
Inflamed, my passion strikes such glowing sparks
That it must kindle lifeless souls to flame.

    That lovely lady present then I find 5
Wherever her behavior to me was
So sweet and soothing that I often wake
Not to the sound of bells, but that of sighs.

    I see her turn, her hair all scattered by
The breeze, and, beautiful, come back again 10

nel cor, come colei che tien la chiave.
    Ma 'l soverchio piacer, che s'atraversa
a la mia lingua, qual dentro ella siede,
di mostrarla in palese ardir non ave.

144
    Né cosí bello il sol già mai levarsi
quando 'l ciel fosse piú de nebbia scarco,
né dopo pioggia vidi 'l celeste arco
per l'aere in color' tanti varïarsi,
    in quanti fiammeggiando trasformarsi,   5
nel dí ch'io presi l'amoroso incarco,
quel viso al quale, et son del mio dir parco,
nulla cosa mortal pote aguagliarsi.
    I' vidi Amor che' begli occhi volgea
soave sí, ch'ogni altra vista oscura   10
da indi in qua m'incominciò apparere.
    Sennuccio, i' 'l vidi, et l'arco che tendea,
tal che mia vita poi non fu secura,
et è sí vaga anchor del rivedere.

145
    Ponmi ove 'l sole occide i fiori et l'erba,
o dove vince lui il ghiaccio et la neve;
ponmi ov'è 'l carro suo temprato et leve,
et ov'è chi ce 'l rende, o chi ce 'l serba;
    ponmi in humil fortuna, od in superba,   5
al dolce aere sereno, al fosco et greve;
ponmi a la notte, al dí lungo ed al breve,
a la matura etate od a l'acerba;
    ponmi in cielo, od in terra, od in abisso,
in alto poggio, in valle ima et palustre,   10
libero spirto, od a' suoi membri affisso;
    ponmi con fama oscura, o con ilustre:
sarò qual fui, vivrò com'io son visso,
continüando il mio sospir trilustre.

146
    O d'ardente vertute ornata et calda
alma gentil chui tante carte vergo;
o sol già d'onestate intero albergo,
torre in alto valor fondata et salda;
    o fiamma, o rose sparse in dolce falda   5
di viva neve, in ch'io mi specchio et tergo;

Into my heart; with her she keeps its key;
  But my surpassing joy (which checks my tongue)
Has not the hardihood to show her forth
In public as she reigns within my thoughts.

144

  I never saw the sunrise lovelier
When skies were cloudless and most clear of mist
Nor, after rain, saw the celestial bow
In colors so much vary through the air,
  As that day I assumed my amorous task   5
I saw that face in such a blaze of light
Transform itself—I'm chary with my speech—
That nothing mortal can compare with it.
  I looked on Love, who turned her lovely eyes
So tenderly that every other sight   10
From that time started seeming dark to me.
  I looked on him, Sennuccio, saw the bow
He drew, thus safe no longer was my life,
Yet still it longs to look on him again.

145

  Ah, set me where the sun kills flowers and grass,
Or where he's vanquished by the ice and snow;
Or set me where his car is gentle, mild,°
Where he's restored to us, or for us kept;
  In humble fortune set me or in proud,   5
In sweet serene air, or in dull and dense;
Set me in night, or long days, or in short,
Or in the ripened or unripened state;
  Set me in heaven, in earth, or the abyss,
On lofty hills or in low, marshy vales,   10
A spirit free, or held fast to its limbs;
  Give me repute obscure, or great renown,
I shall be what I was, live as I have,
While I continue my trilustral sighs.

146

  O noble soul with ardent virtue graced
And flushed, how many leaves I rule for you,
O sole abode of spotless chastity,
O tower founded firm on merit high.
  O flame, O roses strewn in a sweet fold   5
Of living snow, where mirrored, I'm made pure;

o piacer onde l'ali al bel viso ergo,
che luce sovra quanti il sol ne scalda:
del vostro nome, se mie rime intese
fossin sí lunge, avrei pien Tyle et Battro,
la Tana e 'l Nilo, Athlante, Olimpo et Calpe.
Poi che portar nol posso in tutte et quattro
parti del mondo, udrallo il bel paese
ch'Appennin parte, e 'l mar circonda et l'Alpe.

147

Quando 'l voler che con duo sproni ardenti,
et con un duro fren, mi mena et regge
trapassa ad or ad or l'usata legge
per far in parte i miei spirti contenti,
trova chi le paure et gli ardimenti
del cor profondo ne la fronte legge,
et vede Amor che sue imprese corregge
folgorar ne' turbati occhi pungenti.
Onde, come collui che 'l colpo teme
di Giove irato, si ritragge indietro:
ché gran temenza gran desire affrena.
Ma freddo foco et paventosa speme
de l'alma che traluce come un vetro
talor sua dolce vista rasserena.

148

Non Tesin, Po, Varo, Arno, Adige et Tebro,
Eufrate, Tigre, Nilo, Hermo, Indo et Gange,
Tana, Histro, Alpheo, Garona, e 'l mar che frange,
Rodano, Hibero, Ren, Sena, Albia, Era, Hebro;
non edra, abete, pin, faggio o genebro
poria 'l foco allentar che 'l cor tristo ange,
quant'un bel rio ch'ad ognor meco piange,
co l'arboscel che 'n rime orno et celebro.
Questo un soccorso trovo tra gli assalti
d'Amore, ove conven ch'armato viva
la vita che trapassa a sí gran salti.
Cosí cresca il bel lauro in fresca riva,
et chi 'l piantò pensier' leggiadri et alti
ne la dolce ombra al suon de l'acque scriva.

149

Di tempo in tempo mi si fa men dura
l'angelica figura e 'l dolce riso,

O pleasure, when I raise my wings toward that
Fair face whose light the sun warms past all else.
    Thule, Bactria, the Don, the Nile would be
Filled with your names—Olympus, Calpe too,°   10
And Atlas—if my rhymes were heard that far.
    Since I can't take them to the world's four parts,
That lovely land shall hear them that the sea
And Alps enclose, and Appenines divide.°

147

    When with two flaming spurs, and with cruel reins
I'm goaded and directed by my Will
To break, from time to time, accustomed law
And make my spirits rest, in part, content,
    He finds one who can read temerity°   5
And fear deep in my heart and on my brow,
And Love, who checks his enterprise, he sees
Flash lightning from her troubled, piercing eyes.
    So, like a man who's frightened of the bolt
Of irate Jove, he once again withdraws;   10
For terror great restrains a great desire.
    But that cold fire and timid hopefulness
Which shine through from my soul as through a glass,
Will sometimes brighten her sweet face again.

148

    Not Tesin, Tiber, Arno, Adige,
Po, Varo, Tigris, Hermus, Indus, Nile,
Euphrates, Ganges, Danube, Don, Garonne,
Alpheus, cleaving sea; no Ebro, Rhone,
    Rhine, Elbe, Seine, nor Hebrus, not the Loire,°   5
Nor ivy, fir, pine, beech, nor juniper
Can ease the fire tormenting my sad heart
Like that fair stream which sometimes weeps with me,°
    Like that small tree I praise, adorn in rhyme.
Against Love's onslaughts this an aid I find   10
Where I must live in arms while life strides on.
    May that fair laurel grow on this cool bank,
And in its sweet shade he who planted it
Where waters sound write down high, graceful thoughts.

149

    From time to time less obdurate to me
Her face angelic grows, and her sweet smile,

et l'aria del bel viso
e degli occhi leggiadri meno oscura.
    Che fanno meco omai questi sospiri   5
che nascean di dolore,
et mostravan di fore
la mia angosciosa et desperata vita?
S'aven che 'l volto in quella parte giri
per acquetare il core,   10
parmi vedere Amore
mantener mia ragion, et darmi aita:
né però trovo anchor guerra finita,
né tranquillo ogni stato del cor mio,
ché più m'arde 'l desio,   15
quanto più la speranza m'assicura.

150

—Che fai, alma? che pensi? avrem mai pace?
avrem mai tregua? od avrem guerra eterna?
—Che fia di noi, non so; ma, in quel ch'io scerna,
a' suoi begli occhi il mal nostro non piace.
—Che pro, se con quelli occhi ella ne face   5
di state un ghiaccio, un foco quando iverna?
—Ella non, ma colui che gli governa.
Questo ch'è a noi, s'ella sel vede, et tace?
—Talor tace la lingua, e 'l cor si lagna
ad alta voce, e 'n vista asciutta et lieta,   10
piange dove mirando altri nol vede.
—Per tutto ciò la mente non s'acqueta,
rompendo il duol che 'n lei s'accoglie et stagna,
ch'a gran speranza huom misero non crede.

151

    Non d'atra et tempestosa onda marina
fuggío in porto già mai stanco nocchiero,
com'io dal fosco et torbido pensero
fuggo ove 'l gran desio mi sprona e 'nchina.
    Né mortal vista mai luce divina   5
vinse, come la mia quel raggio altero
del bel dolce soave bianco et nero,
in che i suoi strali Amor dora et affina.
    Cieco non già, ma pharetrato il veggo;
nudo, se non quanto vergogna il vela;   10

And the expression of
Her lovely face and charming eyes less dark.
 Henceforward, what will these sighs do with me,   5
These sighs from sorrow born
That once displayed abroad
This stricken and despairing life of mine?
And if in her direction I should turn
My face to ease my heart,   10
It seems I see Love lend
His aid to me, see him maintain my right.
Yet neither do I find war at an end
Nor find peace anywhere within my heart,
For passion burns me more,   15
The more I'm reassured by hopefulness.

150°

—"What do you, Soul? What think you? Will we
   have
Peace, ever? Ever truce? Forever war?"
—"What we may have in store, I do not know,
But in my view, no joy her fair eyes take
 In our ill." —"What good, then, if summers she
Makes ice of us, and fire in wintertime?"
—"She? No, but *he* who governs them." —"But what's
This to us if she sees it and keeps still?"
—"Sometimes the tongue keeps silent, yet the heart
Complains aloud; a glad, and tearless face   10
Will weep where others, peering, cannot see."
—"By none of that my mind is reassured:
The gathered woe bursts forth that stagnates there,
For one who's wretched credits not great hope."

151

 Ah, never from the sea's dark, stormy waves
To harbor has some weary helmsman fled,
As I flee from that dark and troubled thought
Towards which I'm bent and spurred by my desire.
 Nor ever overcome by light divine   5
Was mortal vision, as was mine by that
Proud beam from her fair, sweet, soft white and black
Where Love engilds his darts, and sharpens them.
 I see him quiver-armed; not blind, indeed,
And nude but what for modesty is veiled;   10

garzon con ali: non pinto, ma vivo.
    Indi mi mostra quel ch'a molti cela,
ch'a parte a parte entro a' begli occhi leggo
quant'io parlo d'Amore, et quant'io scrivo.

152

    Questa humil fera, un cor di tigre o d'orsa,
che 'n vista humana e 'n forma d'angel vène,
in riso e 'n pianto, fra paura et spene
mi rota sí ch'ogni mio stato inforsa.
    Se 'n breve non m'accoglie o non mi smorsa,   5
ma pur come suol far tra due mi tene,
per quel ch'io sento al cor gir fra le vene
dolce veneno, Amor, mia vita è corsa.
    Non pò piú la vertú fragile et stanca
tante varïetati omai soffrire,   10
che 'n un punto arde, agghiaccia, arrossa e 'nbianca.
    Fuggendo spera i suoi dolor' finire,
come colei che d'ora in hora manca:
ché ben pò nulla chi non pò morire.

153

    Ite, caldi sospiri, al freddo core,
rompete il ghiaccio che Pietà contende,
et se prego mortale al ciel s'intende,
morte o mercé sia fine al mio dolore.
    Ite, dolci penser', parlando fore   5
di quello ove 'l bel guardo non s'estende:
se pur sua asprezza o mia stella n'offende,
sarem fuor di speranza et fuor d'errore.
    Dir se pò ben per voi, non forse a pieno,
che 'l nostro stato è inquïeto et fosco,   10
sí com'è 'l suo pacifico et sereno.
    Gite securi omai, ch'Amor vèn vosco;
et ria fortuna pò ben venir meno,
s'ai segni del mio sol l'aere conosco.

154

    Le stelle, il cielo et gli elementi a prova
tutte lor arti et ogni extrema cura
poser nel vivo lume, in cui Natura
si specchia, e 'l sol ch'altrove par non trova.
    L'opra è sí altera, sí leggiadra et nova   5
che mortal guardo in lei non s'assecura:

A boy with wings; not painted but alive.
What he conceals from many, there he shows
To me, for bit by bit in her fair eyes
I read all that I say and write of Love.

152

This meek wild thing, this tiger's heart or bear's,
Who comes with human face and angel's form,
So whirls me round between my fear and hope
My tears and laughter, every state's in doubt.
Love, my life's past if she won't welcome me,   5
Or soon release me; but between those two
She keeps me as she has, and thus I feel
Sweet venom through my veins spread to my heart.
Nor can my frail and worn-out virtue stand
Henceforth, so much variety; at once   10
It burns and ices; reddens and grows pale.
By flight it hopes to end its woes, as one
Who weakens from one hour to the next;
He surely can do nothing who can't die.

153

Go forth you ardent sighs, to that cold heart;
That ice contending with compassion, break,
And if a mortal's prayer is heard in heaven,
My woe then death or pity will conclude.
Go, you sweet thoughts, bear open witness to   5
What dwells where her fair glance can't penetrate.
If yet her harshness or my stars assail
Us, past both hope and error shall we be.
You certainly can say, though not in full,
Perhaps that our state's troubled and as dark   10
As her condition's peaceful and serene.
Go now assured, accompanied by Love,
And wicked fortune may well lessen if
From my sun's signs the weather I can tell.

154

The stars, the heavens, and the elements
In contest set their utmost care, each art
In living light, where Nature's mirrored, and
The sun that elsewhere finds no parallel.
So lofty is that work, so striking, rare,   5
That mortal gaze can't safely rest on her.

tanta negli occhi bei for di misura
par ch'Amore et dolcezza et gratia piova.
    L'aere percosso da' lor dolci rai
s'infiamma d'onestate, et tal diventa,   10
che 'l dir nostro e 'l penser vince d'assai.
    Basso desir non è ch'ivi si senta,
ma d'onor, di vertute: or quando mai
fu per somma beltà vil voglia spenta?

155

    Non fur ma' Giove et Cesare sí mossi
a folminar collui, questo a ferire,
che Pietà non avesse spente l'ire,
e lor de l'usate arme ambeduo scossi.
    Piangea madonna, e 'l mio signor ch'i' fossi   5
volse a vederla, et suoi lamenti a udire,
per colmarmi di doglia et di desire,
et ricercarmi le medolle et gli ossi.
    Quel dolce pianto mi depinse Amore,
anzi scolpío, et que' detti soavi   10
mi scrisse entro un diamante in mezzo 'l core;
    ove con salde ed ingegnose chiavi
ancor torna sovente a trarne fore
lagrime rare et sospir' lunghi et gravi.

156

    I' vidi in terra angelici costumi
et celesti bellezze al mondo sole,
tal che di rimembrar mi giova et dole,
ché quant'io miro par sogni, ombre et fumi;
    et vidi lagrimar que' duo bei lumi,   5
ch'àn fatto mille volte invidia al sole;
et udí' sospirando dir parole
che farian gire i monti e stare i fiumi.
    Amor, Senno, Valor, Pietate et Doglia
facean piangendo un piú dolce concento   10
d'ogni altro che nel mondo udir si soglia;
    ed era il cielo a l'armonia sí intento
che non se vedea in ramo mover foglia,
tanta dolcezza avea pien l'aere e 'l vento.

157

    Quel sempre acerbo et honorato giorno
mandò sí al cor l'imagine sua viva

For, past all measure, in her eyes it seems
That Love rains down his sweetness and his grace.
    Struck by their beams so sweet, the atmosphere's
Ablaze with chastity, is so transformed   10
That it quite overcomes our speech and thought.
    In that place no low passion does one feel,
But only honor, virtue; now, when did
Sublimest beauty ever quench base will?

155

    Never were Jove and Caesar so provoked—
That one, to thunder, or this one to wound—
But their compassion would extinguish wrath
And both of them cast down accustomed arms.
    My lady wept, and my lord willed that I   5
Should see her and give ear to her laments
To fill me thus with passion and with woe,
And penetrate my marrow and my bones.
    For me Love has portrayed that sweet complaint,
Rather, he's sculpted it; those soft words he   10
Inscribed upon a diamond in my heart
    Where still with massive and ingenious keys
He comes again, from thence he often draws
Rare tears, and long and heavy sighs as well.

156

    I saw angelic temperament on earth,
Celestial beauties in the world unmatched,
Such that recalling them brings joy and woe;
All else I look on seems smoke, dreams and shades.
    And I saw weeping those two lovely lights   5
That envious made the sun a thousand times,
And, sighing, I heard uttered words that would
Cause mountains to run on, make streams stand still.
    Love, Wisdom, Valor, Piety, and Woe—
These made a sweeter consort when they wept   10
Than any that the world is used to hear.
    And on their harmony was heaven so bent,
No leaf was seen to stir upon the bough,
So great a sweetness filled the air and breeze.

157

    That day forever bitter and revered
Conveyed its living image to my heart

che 'ngegno o stil non fia mai che 'l descriva,
ma spesso a lui co la memoria torno.

L'atto d'ogni gentil pietate adorno,   5
e 'l dolce amaro lamentar ch'i' udiva,
facean dubbiar, se mortal donna o diva
fosse che 'l ciel rasserenava intorno.

La testa òr fino, et calda neve il volto,
hebeno i cigli, et gli occhi eran due stelle,   10
onde Amor l'arco non tendeva in fallo;

perle et rose vermiglie, ove l'accolto
dolor formava ardenti voci et belle;
fiamma i sospir', le lagrime cristallo.

158
Ove ch'i' posi gli occhi lassi o giri
per quetar la vaghezza che gli spinge,
trovo chi bella donna ivi depinge
per far sempre mai verdi i miei desiri.

Con leggiadro dolor par ch'ella spiri   5
alta pietà che gentil core stringe:
oltra la vista, agli orecchi orna e 'nfinge
sue voci vive et suoi sancti sospiri.

Amor e 'l ver fur meco a dir che quelle
ch'i' vidi, eran bellezze al mondo sole,   10
mai non vedute piú sotto le stelle.

Né sí pietose et sí dolci parole
s'udiron mai, né lagrime sí belle
di sí belli occhi uscir mai vide 'l sole.

159
In qual parte del ciel, in quale ydea
era l'exempio, onde Natura tolse
quel bel viso leggiadro, in ch'ella volse
mostrar qua giú quanto lassú potea?

Qual nimpha in fonti, in selve mai qual dea,   5
chiome d'oro sí fino a l'aura sciolse?
quando un cor tante in sé vertuti accolse?
benché la somma è di mia morte rea.

Per divina bellezza indarno mira
chi gli occhi de costei già mai non vide   10
come soavemente ella gli gira;

non sa come Amor sana, et come ancide,
chi non sa come dolce ella sospira,
et come dolce parla, et dolce ride.

So that no skill or style can write it down;
I often turn to it in memory.
    Her manner, with all noble mercy graced   5
And bitter-sweet laments I listened to,
Made me unsure if mortal lady she
Or goddess were, who brightened heaven all round.
    Her head was purest gold, her face warm snow,
Her eyebrows ebony, her eyes two stars   10
In which Love did not aim his bow amiss;
    Pearls and vermillion roses, where that woe
Was gathered, shaped those ardent, lovely words;
Her sighs were flame, and crystalline her tears.

158

    No matter where I rest my weary eyes
Or turn to still desire that drives them on,
I find one paints a lovely lady there
To keep my passions ever green in me.
    With comely woe she breathes forth, as it seems,   5
A lofty pity that wrings gentle hearts;
Not just my sight, my hearing she adorns
Likewise with heartfelt words and sacred sighs.
    With me were Love and Truth, to say that what
I saw were beauties in the world unmatched   10
And never seen before beneath the stars.
    No words so sweet or so compassionate
Were ever heard, nor tears so lovely did
The sun see issue from such lovely eyes.

159

    In which of heaven's parts, in what idea
Was that original whence Nature took
The lovely, graceful face, by which she wished
To show, down here, what could be done above?
    What fountain-nymph or goddess in the woods,   5
Lets hair of such pure gold stray in the breeze?
When did one heart store up such virtues in
Itself (though their sum's guilty of my death)?
    For godlike beauty one will look in vain,
If he has never gazed upon her eyes   10
As she so gently casts them all about;
    Nor knows he how Love cures, nor how he kills,
If he knows not the way she sweetly sighs,
The way she sweetly speaks and sweetly laughs.

160

Amor et io sí pien' di meraviglia
come chi mai cosa incredibil vide,
miriam costei quand'ella parla o ride
che sol se stessa, et nulla altra, simiglia.

Dal bel seren de le tranquille ciglia   5
sfavillan sí le mie due stelle fide,
ch'altro lume non è ch'infiammi et guide
chi d'amar altamente si consiglia.

Qual miracolo è quel, quando tra l'erba
quasi un fior siede, over quand'ella preme   10
col suo candido seno un verde cespo!

Qual dolcezza è ne la stagione acerba
vederla ir sola coi pensier' suoi inseme,
tessendo un cerchio a l'oro terso et crespo!

161

O passi sparsi, o pensier' vaghi et pronti,
o tenace memoria, o fero ardore,
o possente desire, o debil core,
oi occhi miei, occhi non già, ma fonti!

O fronde, honor de le famose fronti,   5
o sola insegna al gemino valore!
O faticosa vita, o dolce errore,
che mi fate ir cercando piagge et monti!

O bel viso ove Amor inseme pose
gli sproni e 'l fren ond'el mi punge et volve,   10
come a lui piace, et calcitrar non vale!

O anime gentili et amorose,
s'alcuna à 'l mondo, et voi nude ombre et polve,
deh ristate a veder quale è 'l mio male.

162

Lieti fiori et felici, et ben nate herbe
che madonna pensando premer sòle;
piaggia ch'ascolti sue dolci parole,
et del bel piede alcun vestigio serbe;

schietti arboscelli et verdi frondi acerbe,   5
amorosette et pallide vïole;
ombrose selve, ove percote il sole
che vi fa co' suoi raggi alte et superbe;

o soave contrada, o puro fiume,
che bagni il suo bel viso et gli occhi chiari   10
et prendi qualità dal vivo lume;

160

Full of amazement are both Love and I,
Like one who's never seen a prodigy;
We stare at her when she speaks out or laughs,
For she is like herself and no one else.
    From the fair brightness of her brow serene,   5
Such sparks do both my trusted stars send forth
That no light else exists to set aflame
And guide one who resolves on lofty love.
    Ah, what a miracle occurs when she
Almost a flower herself, sits on the grass   10
Or presses with her white breast some green plant!
    What sweetness in the budding time it is,
To see her walk alone with just her thoughts,
And weave a wreath for burnished, curling gold.

161

O scattered steps, O longing thoughts alert,
O constant memory, O ardor wild,
O mighty passion, O my weakening heart,
O eyes of mine—not eyes indeed but founts!
    O fronds, you glory of those brows renowned,   5
O single symbol of that double worth!
O life so wearying, O error sweet,
Which make me search out mountains, seek the coasts.
    O beauteous face, where Love together set
His spurs and reins, with which he goads and checks   10
Me as he wills—and no curvetting helps!
    O noble souls and amorous (if, still
The world holds some), you dust, you naked shades,
Ah pause to see what my misfortune is!

162

You joyous, happy flowers, well-favored grass
That, lost in thought, my lady's used to press;
O slope that listens to her discourse sweet,
And some trace of her lovely feet preserves,
    You saplings innocent, green fronds unripe,   5
You tiny, love-tinged, pallid violets;
You shady forests where the sun beats down,
There where his beams make you grow high and proud;
    O gentle region; O you river pure,
Who bathes her lovely face and brilliant eyes   10
And take your quality from their bright light;

quanto v'invidio gli atti honesti et cari!
Non fia in voi scoglio omai che per costume
d'arder co la mia fiamma non impari.

163

Amor, che vedi ogni pensero aperto
e i duri passi onde tu sol mi scorgi,
nel fondo del mio cor gli occhi tuoi porgi,
a te palese, a tutt'altri coverto.

Sai quel che per seguirte ò già sofferto: 5
et tu pur via di poggio in poggio sorgi,
di giorno in giorno, et di me non t'accorgi
che son sí stanco, e 'l sentier m'è troppo erto.

Ben veggio io di lontano il dolce lume
ove per aspre vie mi sproni et giri,   10
ma non ò come tu da volar piume.

Assai contenti lasci i miei desiri,
pur che ben desïando i' mi consume,
né le dispiaccia che per lei sospiri.

164

Or che 'l ciel et la terra e 'l vento tace
et le fere e gli augelli il sonno affrena,
Notte il carro stellato in giro mena
et nel suo letto il mar senz'onda giace,

vegghio, penso, ardo, piango; et chi mi sface   5
sempre m'è inanzi per mia dolce pena:
guerra è 'l mio stato, d'ira et di duol piena,
et sol di lei pensando ò qualche pace.

Cosí sol d'una chiara fonte viva
move 'l dolce et l'amaro ond'io mi pasco;   10
una man sola mi risana et punge;

e perché 'l mio martir non giunga a riva,
mille volte il dí moro et mille nasco,
tanto da la salute mia son lunge.

165

Come 'l candido pie' per l'erba fresca
i dolci passi honestamente move,
vertú che 'ntorno i fiori apra et rinove,
de le tenere piante sue par ch'esca.

Amor che solo i cor' leggiadri invesca   5
né degna di provar sua forza altrove,
da' begli occhi un piacer sí caldo piove

I envy you those dear chaste actions so!
For now there cannot be a stone in you
But learns through practice with my flames to burn.

163

O Love, who clearly sees my every thought,
Sees those rough pathways where you only lead,
Let your eyes probe the bottom of my heart,
Known well to you, but from all others hid.

You know what I've pursued, pursuing you,　　　5
And still you climb ahead from hill to hill,
And day by day, you take no note that I'm
So tired, and that for me the trail's too steep.

Far off I see indeed that sweet light where
Along harsh paths you goad me, urge me on,　　　10
But wings like yours for flying I have none.

You only leave my passions gratified
If I consume myself desiring good,
So that my sighs for her offend her not.

164

Now while the earth and heaven and wind keep still,
And sleep restrains wild beasts and little birds,
Night guides her starry chariot above,
And in his bed the waveless sea lies down;

I watch, think, burn, and weep; to my sweet pain　　　5
She's ever in my sight who ruins me;
War's my condition, wrath-filled, sorrowful,
Only in thoughts of her have I some peace.

Thus from one single fountain, living, clear,
Do sweet and bitter flow on which I'm fed;　　　10
One single hand restores and pierces me.

And since my torment never terminates,
A thousand times a day I die, am born,
So far from my salvation am I still.

165

As through untrodden grass her white foot takes
Its way so modestly, a virtue that
Unfolds the flowers, renews them all about,
Seems from her soles so delicate to spread.

And Love, who only birdlimes noble hearts,　　　5
Nor elsewhere condescends to test his strength,
From her fair eyes such warm joy rains that I

ch'i' non curo altro ben né bramo altr'ésca.

Et co l'andar et col soave sguardo
s'accordan le dolcissime parole,   10
et l'atto mansüeto, humile et tardo.

Di tai quattro faville, et non già sole,
nasce 'l gran foco, di ch'io vivo et ardo,
che son fatto un augel notturno al sole.

166

S'i' fussi stato fermo a la spelunca
là dove Apollo diventò profeta,
Fiorenza avria forse oggi il suo poeta,
non pur Verona et Mantoa et Arunca;

    ma perché 'l mio terren piú non s'ingiunca   5
de l'humor di quel sasso, altro pianeta
conven ch'i' segua, et del mio campo mieta
lappole et stecchi co la falce adunca.

L'oliva è secca, et è rivolta altrove
l'acqua che di Parnaso si deriva,   10
per cui in alcun tempo ella fioriva.

Cosí sventura over colpa mi priva
d'ogni buon fructo, se l'etterno Giove
de la sua gratia sopra me non piove.

167

Quando Amor i belli occhi a terra inchina
e i vaghi spirti in un sospiro accoglie
co le sue mani, et poi in voce gli scioglie,
chiara, soave, angelica, divina,

    sento far del mio cor dolce rapina,   5
et sí dentro cangiar penseri et voglie,
ch'i' dico: Or fien di me l'ultime spoglie,
se 'l ciel sí honesta morte mi destina.

Ma 'l suon che di dolcezza i sensi lega
col gran desir d'udendo esser beata   10
l'anima al dipartir presta raffrena.

Cosí mi vivo, et cosí avolge et spiega
lo stame de la vita che m'è data,
questa sola fra noi del ciel sirena.

168

Amor mi manda quel dolce pensero
che secretario anticho è fra noi due,
et mi conforta, et dice che non fue

Heed no care else, nor long for other bait.
And with her carriage and her gentle gaze
Her words, surpassing sweetness, well accord,　　　　10
As does her modest aspect, meek and grave.
　　From four such sparks—and not them only—is
The great fire born from which I live and burn,
For I've become a night bird in the sun.

166

　　If staunchly I'd remained within that cave—
There where to prophecy Apollo turned—°
Its bard, perhaps, would Florence have today,
Not just Verona, Mantua, Arunca;
　　But as my soil grows no more rushes from　　　　5
The moisture of that stone, some planet else
Must I pursue, and from my field must mow
The thorns and thistles with my crooked scythe.
　　The olive tree is sere, and elsewhere turned
That water—from Parnassus once drawn off—　　　　10
By which it flourished in a time gone by.°
　　Just so will my bad fortune or my guilt
Strip me of every worthy fruit unless
Eternal Jove rain down his grace on me.

167

　　When Love inclines those beauteous eyes toward earth,
Collects her straying breath into a sigh
With his own hands, then frees them in her song,
So clear, angelic, gentle, and divine,
　　I feel my heart becoming plunder sweet,　　　　5
My thoughts and wishes changing so within
I say; "Their last spoil now they'll make of me,
If heaven destines me to such chaste death."
　　That sound though, which with sweetness binds my sense
Holds back my soul so eager to be gone,　　　　10
With great desire to hear it, and be blest.
　　Thus still I live; thus still she cards and spins
The fine thread of the life she's granted me,
This heavenly siren peerless in our midst.

168

　　To me Love sends that sweet thought which of old
Was confidential clerk between us two
And cheers me, says I never was more near

mai come or presto a quel ch'io bramo et spero.

Io, che talor menzogna et talor vero   5
ò ritrovato le parole sue,
non so s'i' 'l creda, et vivomi intra due,
né sí né no nel cor mi sona intero.

In questa passa 'l tempo, et ne lo specchio
mi veggio andar ver' la stagion contraria   10
a sua impromessa, et a la mia speranza.

Or sia che pò: già sol io non invecchio;
già per etate il mio desir non varia;
ben temo il viver breve che n'avanza.

169

Pien d'un vago penser che me desvia
da tutti gli altri, et fammi al mondo ir solo,
ad or ad ora a me stesso m'involo
pur lei cercando che fuggir devria;

et veggiola passar sí dolce et ria   5
che l'alma trema per levarsi a volo,
tal d'armati sospir' conduce stuolo
questa bella d'Amor nemica, et mia.

Ben s'i' non erro di pietate un raggio
scorgo fra 'l nubiloso, altero ciglio,   10
che 'n parte rasserena il cor doglioso:

allor raccolgo l'alma, et poi ch'i' aggio
di scovrirle il mio mal preso consiglio,
tanto gli ò a dir, che 'ncominciar non oso.

170

Piú volte già dal bel sembiante humano
ò preso ardir co le mie fide scorte
d'assalir con parole honeste accorte
la mia nemica in atto humile et piano.

Fanno poi gli occhi suoi mio penser vano   5
perch'ogni mia fortuna, ogni mia sorte,
mio ben, mio male, et mia vita, et mia morte,
quei che solo il pò far, l'à posto in mano.

Ond'io non poté' mai formar parola
ch'altro che da me stesso fosse intesa: 10
così m'à fatto Amor tremante et fioco.

Et veggi' or ben che caritate accesa
lega la lingua altrui, gli spirti invola:
chi pò dir com'egli arde, è 'n picciol foco.

To what I hope and long for than right now.
　　But I, who sometimes falsehood, sometimes truth,　　5
Have in his words found, am not sure if I
Believe him, and between these two I live:
Not "yes," nor "no," rings quite true in my heart.
　　In this way time goes by, and in my glass
I see myself approaching that age which　　10
Gainsays his promise to me, and my hope.
　　Now, come what may, I'm not the only one
To age, nor will my aging change desire;
I fear the life that's left me will be brief.

169

　　Filled with one longing thought that leads me far
From all else, makes me wander lonely through
This world, I now and then hide from myself,
Still seeking her whom, rather, I should flee;
　　So wicked and so sweet I see her pass　　5
That my soul quakes to lift itself in flight,
Such is the troop of armed sighs she conducts,
This beauteous foe of Love's, and mine as well.
　　Yes, if I do not err, I note a ray
Of pity cross her clouded, haughty brow　　10
That in some measure brightens my sad heart;
　　Then I gird up my soul; yet when I have
Resolved almost to tell her of my ill,
So much have I to say, I dare not start.

170

　　How often from her human aspect fair
Have I, together with my loyal guides
Found courage with astute and honest words
To storm my foe, so plain and meek in deeds.
　　And then my thought's made useless by her eyes　　5
For every fortune, every chance of mine
My weal, harm, life, and death are put into
Her hand by him who only has that power.
　　And thus I cannot ever shape a word
That anyone but I, myself, can grasp,　　10
So trembling has Love made me and so weak.
　　And now how well I see that kindled Love
Can tie one's tongue and take one's breath away.
He burns in not much fire who can say how.

171

Giunto m'à Amor fra belle et crude braccia,
che m'ancidono a torto; et s'io mi doglio,
doppia 'l martir; onde pur, com'io soglio
il meglio è ch'io mi mora amando, et taccia:
    ché poria questa il Ren qualor piú agghiaccia   5
arder con gli occhi, et rompre ogni aspro scoglio;
et à sí egual a le bellezze orgoglio,
che di piacer altrui par che le spiaccia.
    Nulla posso levar io per mi' 'ngegno
del bel diamante, ond'ell'à il cor sí duro;   10
l'altro è d'un marmo che si mova et spiri:
    ned ella a me per tutto 'l suo disdegno
torrà già mai, né per sembiante oscuro,
le mie speranze, e i mei dolci sospiri.

172

O Invidia nimica di vertute,
ch'a' bei principii volentier contrasti,
per qual sentier cosí tacita intrasti
in quel bel petto, et con qual' arti il mute?
    Da radice n'ài svelta mia salute: 5
troppo felice amante mi mostrasti
a quella che' miei preghi humili et casti
gradí alcun tempo, or par ch'odi et refute.
    Né però che con atti acerbi et rei
del mio ben pianga, et del mio pianger rida,   10
poria cangiar sol un de' pensier' mei;
    non, perché mille volte il dí m'ancida,
fia ch'io non l'ami, et ch'i' non speri in lei:
che s'ella mi spaventa, Amor m'affida.

173

Mirando 'l sol de' begli occhi sereno,
ove è chi spesso i miei depinge et bagna,
dal cor l'anima stanca si scompagna
per gir nel paradiso suo terreno.
    Poi trovandol di dolce et d'amar pieno,   5
quant'al mondo si tesse, opra d'aragna
vede: onde seco et con Amor si lagna,
ch'à sí caldi gli spron', sí duro 'l freno.
    Per questi extremi duo contrari et misti,
or con voglie gelate, or con accese   10
stassi cosí fra misera et felice;

171

Love's clasped me in a fair and cruel embrace,
Which kills me wrongfully; if I lament,
My torture doubles; thus, as usual
It's best that I die loving and keep still.

This girl could set the frozen Rhine aflame   5
With her eyes, and demolish each bleak cliff;
So equal to her beauty is her pride
That pleasing others seems her to displease.

None of that diamond beautiful, which makes
Her heart so hard, can wit of mine remove;   10
All else is marble that can move and breathe.

But she, with all her haughtiness, or with
Her frowning looks, will never steal away
These hopes of mine, nor hinder my sweet sighs.

172

O envy, virtue's foe, one who to fair
Beginnings is so eagerly opposed,
Along what ways into that fair breast did
You, silent, steal? Or change it with what arts?

You've torn up my well-being by its root: 5
Too glad a lover you revealed me to
That one by my chaste, humble prayers once pleased.
But who rebuffs and hates them now, it seems.

Though in a harsh and wicked manner she
Weeps at my fortune, at my weeping laughs,   10
No single thought of mine can she transform,

Nor, though she murder me a thousand times
A day, make me not love her, hope in her;
For though she makes me fear, Love gives me faith.

173

Admiring the sun of those eyes fair and clear
Where oft one is who makes mine weep, grow red,
My weary spirit takes leave of my heart
To travel to its earthly paradise.

Then, finding it with sweet and bitter filled,   5
It sees that spider's work is what the world
Is weaving, so laments to her and Love
That he has such hot spurs, so hard a rein.

Through these two opposite and mixed extremes,
With longing frozen first and then aflame,   10
It lives thus, between wretchedness and bliss.

ma pochi lieti, et molti penser' tristi,
e 'l piú si pente de l'ardite imprese:
tal frutto nasce di cotal radice.

174

Fera stella (se 'l cielo à forza in noi
quant'alcun crede) fu sotto ch'io nacqui,
et fera cuna, dove nato giacqui,
et fera terra, ove' pie' mossi poi;

 et fera donna, che con gli occhi suoi,   5
et con l'arco a cui sol per segno piacqui,
fe' la piaga onde, Amor, teco non tacqui,
che con quell'arme risaldar la pôi.

 Ma tu prendi a diletto i dolor' miei:
ella non già, perché non son piú duri,   10
e 'l colpo è di saetta, et non di spiedo.

 Pur mi consola, che languir per lei
meglio è, che gioir d'altra; et tu me 'l giuri
per l'orato tuo strale, et io tel credo.

175

Quando mi vène inanzi il tempo e 'l loco
ov'i' perdei me stesso, e 'l caro nodo
ond'Amor di sua man m'avinse in modo
che l'amar mi fe' dolce, e 'l pianger gioco,

 solfo et ésca son tutto, e 'l cor un foco   5
da quei soavi spirti, in quai sempre odo,
acceso dentro sí ch'ardendo godo,
et di ciò vivo, et d'altro mi cal poco.

 Quel sol, che solo agli occhi mei resplende,
coi vaghi raggi anchor indi mi scalda   10
a vespro tal, qual era oggi per tempo;

 et cosí di lontan m'alluma e 'ncende,
che la memoria ad ognor fresca et salda
pur quel nodo mi mostra e 'l loco e 'l tempo.

176

Per mezz'i boschi inhospiti et selvaggi,
onde vanno a gran rischio uomini et arme,
vo securo io, ché non pò spaventarme
altri che 'l sol ch'à d'amor vivo i raggi;

 et vo cantando (o penser' miei non saggi!)   5
lei che 'l ciel non poria lontana farme,
ch'i' l'ò negli occhi, et veder seco parme

Few are its joyous, many its sad thoughts;
Its daring deeds it most of all repents;
From such a root does fruit like this spring forth.

174
A harsh star I was born beneath (if heaven
Has all that force in us which some believe),
And harsh the crib where, newborn, I was lain,
And earth was harsh, whereon my feet then trod,
    A lady harsh who with her eyes and bow   5
(Which only as a mark did I amuse)
Has made this wound; thus with you, Love, I've not
Kept silent; you can heal it with those arms.
    My sorrows you enjoy; not she, because
They are not harder, and because the blow   10
Is only from an arrow, not a spear.
    Yet I take heart; I'd better pine for her
Than joy in someone else; by your gold dart
You swear it, and from you, that I believe.

175
When I recall the time and place that I
Quite lost myself, recall the precious knot
Love tied me with by his own hand, so it
Makes bitter sweet for me, and weeping joy;
    All sulphur, tinder, I become, my heart   5
A flame from those soft sighs I always hear;
Thus burned so much within, I joy to burn;
I live for that and care for little else.
    That sun, which with inviting rays beams on
My eyes alone, still warms me afterwards   10
At vespers as it early did today.
    From far off it so lights and kindles me
That memory, entire and ever fresh,
Still shows to me the knot, the place, the time.

176
Through forests inhospitable and wild°
Where, at great peril, wander men-at-arms,
I walk secure, for naught can frighten me
Except that sun whose beams are living love.
    And I walk singing (O my foolish thoughts!)   5
Of her whom heaven can't separate from me;
My eyes behold her; ladies and young girls

donne et donzelle, et sono abeti et faggi.

Parme d'udirla, udendo i rami et l'òre
et le frondi, et gli augei lagnarsi, et l'acque
mormorando fuggir per l'erba verde.

Raro un silentio, un solitario horrore
d'ombrosa selva mai tanto mi piacque:
se non che dal mio sol troppo si perde.

177

Mille piagge in un giorno et mille rivi
mostrato m'à per la famosa Ardenna
Amor, ch'a' suoi le piante e i cori impenna
per fargli al terzo ciel volando ir vivi.

Dolce m'è sol senz'arme esser stato ivi,   5
dove armato fier Marte, et non acenna,
quasi senza governo et senza antenna
legno in mar, pien di penser' gravi et schivi.

Pur giunto al fin de la giornata oscura,
rimembrando ond'io vegno, et con quai piume,   10
sento di troppo ardir nascer paura.

Ma 'l bel paese e 'l dilectoso fiume
con serena accoglienza rassecura
il cor già vòlto ov'abita il suo lume.

178

Amor mi sprona in un tempo et affrena,
assecura et spaventa, arde et agghiaccia,
gradisce et sdegna, a sé mi chiama et scaccia,
or mi tene in speranza et or in pena,

or alto or basso il meo cor lasso mena: 5
onde 'l vago desir perde la traccia
e 'l suo sommo piacer par che li spiaccia,
d'error sí novo la mia mente è piena.

Un amico penser le mostra il vado,
non d'acqua che per gli occhi si resolva,   10
da gir tosto ove spera esser contenta;

poi, quasi maggior forza indi la svolva,
conven ch'altra via segua, et mal suo grado
a la sua lunga, et mia, morte consenta.

179

Geri, quando talor meco s'adira
la mia dolce nemica, ch'è sí altera,
un conforto m'è dato ch'i' non pèra,

With her I seem to see (they're beech and fir).
    I seem to hear her, but hear just the boughs
And breezes, fronds, lamenting birds, and hear   10
The waters' murmur, fleeing through green grass.
    But silence rarely, or the lonely dread
Of shadowed forests never pleased me more;
Were I not from my sun so much cut off.

177

    A thousand slopes and banks in just one day
Love in renowned Ardennes has shown to me,
Who wings the heels and hearts of his own folk
To make them fly, alive, to the third heaven.
    There to have stood alone is sweet to me,   5
Unarmed where, armed, Mars wounds and gives no sign—
I, nearly rudderless and with no mast,
Filled with grave, troubled thoughts, a ship at sea.
    At last, the end of that dark day I've reached;
Recalling whence I came, and with what plumes,   10
I feel fear born of too great hardihood.
    But that fair landscape and delightful stream
With cloudless welcome sets at ease my heart,
Who's turned already where his light abides.

178

    At once, Love spurs me on and holds me back,
Assures and frightens, sears and freezes, scorns
And welcomes me; he summons me and drives
Me forth, keeps me now hopeful, now in pain.
    Now high, now low he guides my wretched heart;   5
Thus does my straying passion lose its way;
And it dislikes its greatest joy, it seems—
With such odd wanderings my mind is filled.
    A loving thought then shows to it that ford—
Not one through water flowing from the eyes—   10
To cross where it hopes soon to be content.
    Then, as if greater power diverts it thence,
It must pursue that other way, agree
Against its will to its slow death and mine.

179

    Ah Geri, when sometimes my foe so sweet,°
That haughty one, grows angry with me, then
One comfort's granted me lest I should die,

solo per cui vertú l'alma respira.

    Ovunque ella sdegnando li occhi gira   5
(che di luce privar mia vita spera?)
le mostro i miei pien' d'umiltà sí vera,
ch'a forza ogni suo sdegno indietro tira.

    E·cciò non fusse, andrei non altramente
a veder lei, che 'l volto di Medusa,   10
che facea marmo diventar la gente.

    Cosí dunque fa' tu: ch'i' veggio exclusa
ogni altra aita, e 'l fuggir val nïente
dinanzi a l'ali che 'l signor nostro usa.

180

    Po, ben puo' tu portartene la scorza
di me con tue possenti et rapide onde,
ma lo spirto ch'iv'entro si nasconde
non cura né di tua né d'altrui forza;

    lo qual senz'alternar poggia con orza   5
dritto per l'aure al suo desir seconde,
battendo l'ali verso l'aurea fronde,
l'acqua e 'l vento e la vela e i remi sforza.

    Re degli altri, superbo altero fiume,
che 'ncontri 'l sol quando e' ne mena 'l giorno,   10
e 'n ponente abandoni un piú bel lume,

    tu te ne vai col mio mortal sul corno;
l'altro coverto d'amorose piume
torna volando al suo dolce soggiorno.

181

    Amor fra l'erbe una leggiadra rete
d'oro et di perle tese sott'un ramo
dell'arbor sempre verde ch'i' tant'amo,
benché n'abbia ombre piú triste che liete.

    L'ésca fu 'l seme ch'egli sparge et miete,   5
dolce et acerbo, ch'i' pavento et bramo;
le note non fur mai, dal dí ch'Adamo
aperse gli occhi, sí soavi et quete.

    E 'l chiaro lume che sparir fa 'l sole
folgorava d'intorno; e 'l fune avolto   10
era a la man ch'avorio et neve avanza.

    Cosí caddi a la rete, et qui m'àn colto
gli atti vaghi et l'angeliche parole,
e 'l piacer e 'l desire e la speranza.

And only by its power does my soul breathe.
    Wherever in disdain she casts her eyes   5
(Does she expect to rid my life of light?)
I show her mine, filled with humility
So true that she, perforce, remits all scorn.
    If that were not the case, I'd no more go
To see her than to see Medusa's face   10
Instead, that turned the people into stone.
    So must you do; for every other aid
I see cut off; and naught avails to flee
Before the wings that lord of ours employs.

180

    Po, you can bear my body easily
Upon your waves so powerful and swift;
My spirit, though, which shelters there within
Is not concerned with you, nor with your strength;
    Not on the leeward or the windward tack,   5
Against the wind it follows its desire;
Beating its wings to reach those golden fronds,
It conquers water, wind and sail, and oars.
    O king of other rivers, proud, superb,
You greet the sun when he leads daybreak forth,   10
And in the west desert a fairer light,
    With what is mortal of me on your reach
You flow; the rest arrayed in amorous plumes,
Goes flying to its shelter sweet again.

181

    Love wove amidst the grass a charming snare
Of gold and pearls, beneath a bough of that
Tree, ever green, I love so well—although
I had more woe than gladness from its shade.
    Its bait was seed he scatters and he reaps—   5
That sweet and bitter I both fear and crave—
Such gentle, quiet notes were never heard
Since that day Adam opened first his eyes.
    And all round flashed clear light, which made the sun
Grow dim; the rope was wound about that hand   10
By far surpassing snow and ivory.
    So I fell in the snare, and here am trapped
By charming deeds and by angelic speech,
By pleasure, by my passion, and my hope.

Amor, che 'ncende il cor d'ardente zelo,
di gelata paura il tèn constretto,
et qual sia piú, fa dubbio a l'intellecto,
la speranza o 'l temor, la fiamma o 'l gielo.

    Trem'al piú caldo, ard'al piú freddo cielo,   5
sempre pien di desire et di sospetto,
pur come donna in un vestire schietto
celi un huom vivo, o sotto un picciol velo.

    Di queste pene è mia propia la prima,
arder dí et notte: et quanto è 'l dolce male   10
né 'n penser cape, nonché 'n versi o 'n rima;

    l'altra non già: ché 'l mio bel foco è tale,
ch'ogni uom pareggia; et del suo lume in cima
chi volar pensa, indarno spiega l'ale.

Se 'l dolce sguardo di costei m'ancide,
et le soavi parolette accorte,
et s'Amor sopra me la fa sí forte
sol quando parla, over quando sorride,

    lasso, che fia, se forse ella divide,   5
o per mia colpa o per malvagia sorte,
gli occhi suoi da Mercé, sí che di morte,
là dove or m'assicura, allor mi sfide?

    Però s'i' tremo, et vo col cor gelato,
qualor veggio cangiata sua figura,   10
questo temer d'antiche prove è nato.

    Femina è cosa mobil per natura:
ond'io so ben ch'un amoroso stato
in cor di donna picciol tempo dura.

Amor, Natura, et la bella alma humile
ov'ogn'alta vertute alberga et regna,
contra me son giurati: Amor s'ingegna
ch'i' mora a fatto, e 'n ciò segue suo stile;

    Natura tèn costei d'un sí gentile   5
laccio, che nullo sforzo è che sostegna;
ella è sí schiva, ch'abitar non degna
piú ne la vita faticosa et vile.

    Cosí lo spirto d'or in or vèn meno
a quelle belle care membra honeste   10
che specchio eran di vera leggiadria;

182

With burning zeal Love sets aflame my heart,
Who holds him back, restrained by chilling fear;
He leads my intellect to doubt which one
Counts most, the hope or fear, the flame or ice.

I quake beneath the hottest skies and burn   5
In coldest, always filled with doubt, desire,
As if a lady 'neath her modest gown
Masked some strong man, or under her brief veil.

Of these woes just the first is mine; it burns
Both day and night; how great my illness sweet   10
No thought can tell—much less can verse or rhyme.

Not mine alone, that other; all men are
Alike to such fair fire; who seeks to fly
To her light's highest point spreads wings in vain.

183

If that sweet look of hers, her little words,
So gentle and so wise should murder me,
And over me Love give to her such power
When she but speaks or even when she smiles,

Ah woe, what will I do if she, perhaps,   5
Through fault of mine, or through some wicked fate
Drives mercy from her eyes, where now I'm safe
So that to death, I then shall be betrayed?

Thus, if I shiver, walk with frozen heart
At those times when I see her shape transformed,   10
That terror has been born from ancient trial.

By nature, woman is a fickle thing;
So I know well that any amorous state
Will not endure long in a woman's heart.

184

Love, Nature, and that comely, modest soul
In which each lofty virtue lives and rules,
Have all conspired against me; Love contrives
My utter death and, in that, suits his style.

Nature supports her by so fine a thread   5
That it can bear no strain; no longer does
She deign, so unassuming, to abide
In this fatiguing life, so vile and mean.

So now from hour to hour the spirit wanes
Within those lovely, chaste, and precious limbs   10
That were the glass of true nobility.

et s'a Morte Pietà non stringe 'l freno,
lasso, ben veggio in che stato son queste
vane speranze, ond'io viver solia.

185

Questa fenice de l'aurata piuma
al suo bel collo, candido, gentile,
forma senz'arte un sí caro monile,
ch'ogni cor addolcisce, e 'l mio consuma:
    forma un diadema natural ch'alluma   5
l'aere d'intorno; e 'l tacito focile
d'Amor tragge indi un liquido sottile
foco che m'arde a la piú algente bruma.
    Purpurea vesta d'un ceruleo lembo
sparso di rose i belli homeri vela: 10
novo habito, et bellezza unica et sola.
    Fama ne l'odorato et ricco grembo
d'arabi monti lei ripone et cela,
che per lo nostro ciel sí altera vola.

186

Se Virgilio et Homero avessin visto
quel sole il qual vegg'io con gli occhi miei,
tutte lor forze in dar fama a costei
avrian posto, et l'un stil coll'altro misto:
    di che sarebbe Enea turbato et tristo,   5
Achille, Ulixe et gli altri semidei,
et quel che resse anni cinquantasei
sí bene il mondo, et quel ch'ancise Egisto.
    Quel fiore anticho di vertuti et d'arme
come sembiante stella ebbe con questo   10
novo fior d'onestate et di bellezze!
    Ennio di quel cantò ruvido carme,
di quest'altro io: et oh pur non molesto
gli sia il mio ingegno, e 'l mio lodar non sprezze!

187

Giunto Alexandro a la famosa tomba
del fero Achille, sospirando disse:
O fortunato, che sí chiara tromba
trovasti, et chi di te sí alto scrisse!
    Ma questa pura et candida colomba,   5
a cui non so s'al mondo mai par visse,
nel mio stil frale assai poco rimbomba:

Indeed, if Pity does not curb Death's course,
Alas, I see well in what plight stand these
Vain hopes in which I have grown used to live.

185

This phoenix—with the golden plumage at
Her lovely, noble, pure white throat and with
No artifice—a precious necklace forms
That sweetens every heart and lays mine waste.
   It forms a natural diadem that lights   5
The air about; Love's soundless flintstone draws
From thence a pure and fluid fire that burns
Me in the coldest mists of wintertime.
   A crimson dress, with a cerulean hem
And scattered roses, veils her shoulders fair—   10
A new gown and a peerless beauty too.
   In rich and perfumed vales 'midst Arab hills,
Report locates and hides that one who through
Our skies is flying now so loftily.

186

If Virgil and if Homer had but seen
That sun which, with my eyes I see, they would
Have bent their every power to bring her fame,
And one style with the other have combined.
   For that, Aeneas would be saddened, wroth—   5
Achilles, Ulysses, and such demi-gods,
And he who fifty-six years ruled the world
So well, and him Aegisthus murdered too.°
   That ancient flower of virtue and of arms,
How similar that star of his to this   10
New flower of loveliness and chastity!
   Of that one Ennius sang a rough-hewn hymn,°
I of this other; O, let not my skill°
Be grievous to her or my praise disdained.

187

On reaching fierce Achilles' famous tomb,
Great Alexander with a sigh remarked,
"Happy one! Such a trumpet clear you found,
And one who wrote so loftily of you!"
   Yet this dove, pure and white, whose like has not   5
Lived, to my knowledge, ever in the world,
Echoes but weakly in my feeble style:

così son le sue sorti a ciascun fisse.

    Ché d'Omero dignissima et d'Orpheo,
o del pastor ch'anchor Mantova honora,
ch'andassen sempre lei sola cantando,

    stella difforme et fato sol qui reo
commise a tal che 'l suo bel nome adora,
ma forse scema sue lode parlando.

188

    Almo Sol, quella fronde ch'io sola amo,
tu prima amasti, or sola al bel soggiorno
verdeggia, et senza par poi che l'addorno
suo male et nostro vide in prima Adamo.

    Stiamo a mirarla: i' ti pur prego et chiamo,
o Sole; et tu pur fuggi, et fai d'intorno
ombrare i poggi, et te ne porti il giorno,
et fuggendo mi toi quel ch'i' piú bramo.

    L'ombra che cade da quel' humil colle,
ove favilla il mio soave foco,
ove 'l gran lauro fu picciola verga,

    crescendo mentr'io parlo, agli occhi tolle
la dolce vista del beato loco,
ove 'l mio cor co la sua donna alberga.

189

    Passa la nave mia colma d'oblio
per aspro mare, a mezza notte il verno,
enfra Scilla et Caribdi; et al governo
siede 'l signore, anzi 'l nimico mio.

    A ciascun remo un penser pronto et rio
che la tempesta e 'l fin par ch'abbi a scherno;
la vela rompe un vento humido eterno
di sospir', di speranze et di desio.

    Pioggia di lagrimar, nebbia di sdegni
bagna et rallenta le già stanche sarte,
che son d'error con ignorantia attorto.

    Celansi i duo mei dolci usati segni;
morta fra l'onde è la ragion et l'arte,
tal ch'incomincio a desperar del porto.

190

    Una candida cerva sopra l'erba
verde m'apparve, con duo corna d'oro,
fra due riviere, all'ombra d'un alloro,

Thus are the destinies of each one fixed.
　She worthiest for Homer, Orpheus,°
Or for that shepherd Mantova still lauds—°   10
Of her alone forever should they sing;
　A star deformed, fate wicked just in this,
Chose one who her fair name adores, but who°
Perhaps, when speaking of her, spoils her praise.

188

　O vital Sun, the only tree I love
(You loved her first) now thrives alone in her
Fair bower, and she's unequalled since the time
Adam first saw his lovely woe, and ours.
　"Let's pause and gaze on her," I pray, and call   5
Your name, O Sun; yet darkening the hills
Around, you flee and steal our day from us,
And fleeing, snatch from me my heart's desire.
　The shadow falling from that lowly hill—
There where my gentle fire sends forth her sparks,   10
Where this great laurel was a little branch—
　Grows longer while I speak, steals from my eyes
The lovely prospect of that blessed spot
Where my Heart with his lady now abides.

189

　My vessel, with oblivion awash,
Drives on in winter midnight through rough seas
Twixt Scylla and Charybdis; sitting at°
Its helm, my lord—indeed, my enemy.
　At each oar sits an urgent, wicked thought   5
That seems to sneer both at the tempest and
Its end; a damp, unceasing wind of sighs,
Of hopes and of desires now splits the sail.
　A rain of tears, a thick fog of contempt
Soak through and slacken shrouds already strained—   10
They're formed from error spliced with ignorance.
　My two accustomed lodestars sweet concealed,
And Art and Reason dead amidst the waves,
Whence I begin to lose all hope of port.

190

　A pure white doe with golden horns appeared°
Before me, on the verdant grass between
Two rivers, in a laurel's shade, at break°

levando 'l sole a la stagione acerba.

 Era sua vista sí dolce superba,   5
ch'i' lasciai per seguirla ogni lavoro:
come l'avaro che 'n cercar tesoro
con diletto l'affanno disacerba.

 «Nessun mi tocchi—al bel collo d'intorno
scritto avea di diamanti et di topazi—:   10
libera farmi al mio Cesare parve».

 Et era 'l sol già vòlto al mezzo giorno,
gli occhi miei stanchi di mirar, non sazi,
quand'io caddi ne l'acqua, et ella sparve.

191

 Sí come eterna vita è veder Dio,
né piú si brama, né bramar piú lice,
cosí me, donna, il voi veder, felice
fa in questo breve et fraile viver mio.

 Né voi stessa com'or bella vid'io   5
già mai, se vero al cor l'occhio ridice:
dolce del mio penser hora beatrice,
che vince ogni alta speme, ogni desio.

 Et se non fusse il suo fuggir sí ratto,
piú non demanderei: che s'alcun vive   10
sol d'odore, et tal fama fede acquista,

 alcun d'acqua o di foco, e 'l gusto e 'l tatto
acquetan cose d'ogni dolzor prive,
i' perché non de la vostra alma vista?

192

 Stiamo, Amor, a veder la gloria nostra,
cose sopra natura altere et nove:
vedi ben quanta in lei dolcezza piove,
vedi lume che 'l cielo in terra mostra,

 vedi quant'arte dora e 'mperla e 'nostra   5
l'abito electo, et mai non visto altrove,
che dolcemente i piedi et gli occhi move
per questa di bei colli ombrosa chiostra.

 L'erbetta verde e i fior' di color' mille
sparsi sotto quel'elce antiqua et negra   10
pregan pur che 'l bel pe' li prema o tocchi;

 e 'l ciel di vaghe et lucide faville
s'accende intorno, e 'n vista si rallegra
d'esser fatto seren da sí belli occhi.

Of day, in the unripened time of year.
    So sweetly splendid was her look that I   5
Deserted every task to follow her,
Just like the miser, seeking treasure, who
Dispels the pain of labor with delight.
    "Let no one touch me," round her lovely throat
With diamonds and with topaz was inscribed,   10
"My Caesar has been pleased to make me free."°
    The sun had turned already at midday;
My eyes were worn with gazing, though not filled,
When I fell in the water, and she fled.

191

    Just as eternal life is seeing God,
And for no more one yearns, nor may one yearn,
So, lady, looking on you gives me joy,
Here in my all-too-brief and fragile life.
    I never saw you lovelier than now   5
If, to my heart, my eyes repeat the truth;
Sweet in my thought this blissful hour, for it
Outrivals each high hope and all desire,
    And if its flight were not so rapid, I
Would crave no more; for if some creature lives   10
(And such reports gain credence) just on scents,
    On water, some on fire, if things devoid
Of any sweetness sate their taste and touch,°
Can I not live on your life-giving sight?

192

    Love, on our glory let us pause to look,
See things above all nature lofty, rare.
Indeed, you see what sweetness rains on her,
You see the light revealing heaven to earth.
    You see what art empearls, makes crimson, gilds   5
That chosen flesh, seen nowhere else before;
And with what sweetness feet and eyes she moves
Throughout this shadowed cloister of fair hills.
    The new green grass, the thousand-colored blooms
Scattered beneath that holm-oak ancient, black,   10
Pray her fair feet to touch or tread on them.
    All round with vagrant glowing sparks the sky's
Aflame; before our eyes it fills with joy
At being made serene by eyes so fair.

193

Pasco la mente d'un sí nobil cibo,
ch'ambrosia et nectar non invidio a Giove,
ché, sol mirando, oblio ne l'alma piove
d'ogni altro dolce, et Lethe al fondo bibo.

Talor ch'odo dir cose, e 'n cor describo,   5
per che da sospirar sempre ritrove,
rapto per man d'Amor, né so ben dove,
doppia dolcezza in un volto delibo:

ché quella voce infin al ciel gradita
suona in parole sí leggiadre et care,   10
che pensar nol poria chi non l'à udita.

Allor inseme, in men d'un palmo, appare
visibilmente quanto in questa vita
arte, ingegno et Natura e 'l Ciel pò fare.

194

L'aura gentil, che rasserena i poggi
destando i fior' per questo ombroso bosco,
al soave suo spirto riconosco,
per cui conven che 'n pena e 'n fama poggi.

Per ritrovar ove 'l cor lasso appoggi,   5
fuggo dal mi' natio dolce aere tosco;
per far lume al penser torbido et fosco,
cerco 'l mio sole et spero vederlo oggi.

Nel qual provo dolcezze tante et tali
ch'Amor per forza a lui mi riconduce;   10
poi sí m'abbaglia che 'l fuggir m'è tardo.

I' chiedrei a scampar, non arme, anzi ali;
ma perir mi dà 'l ciel per questa luce,
ché da lunge mi struggo et da presso ardo.

195

Di dí in dí vo cangiando il viso e 'l pelo,
né però smorso i dolce inescati hami,
né sbranco i verdi et invescati rami
de l'arbor che né sol cura né gielo.

Senz'acqua il mare et senza stelle il cielo   5
fia inanzi ch'io non sempre tema et brami
la sua bell'ombra, et ch'i' non odi et ami
l'alta piaga amorosa, che mal celo.

Non spero del mio affanno aver mai posa,
infin ch'i' mi disosso et snervo et spolpo,   10
o la nemica mia pietà n'avesse.

193

I feed my mind upon such lordly fare
No nectar or ambrosia I grudge Jove;
Just looking rains forgetfulness of all
Else sweet in my soul; Lethe to the lees
    I drink. Sometimes I hear things said, and trace   5
Them in my heart so always it finds cause
For sighs; borne off I know not where by Love,
I taste a double sweetness in one face.
    For that voice, welcome clear to heaven, sounds
In words so charming and so precious that   10
One can't imagine them who has not heard.
    Together, then, in less than one hand's breadth
Appears before my eyes all in this life
That art and talent, Nature and Heaven can do.

194

This noble breeze that sweeps hills clear again°
Awakes the flowers throughout this shadowed wood,
And in its gentle breath I know that one
For whom with pains I must mount high in fame.
    Once more to find a place my weary heart   5
Can rest, I flee sweet, native, Tuscan air
To give some light to thoughts disturbed and dark,
My sun I seek, and hope to see today.
    In her I taste so many sweetnesses,
Ones such that Love by force brings me again   10
To her, then blinds me so my flight's too slow.
    No arms I'd beg to save me, rather wings;
But heaven decrees I perish by this light,
It melts me from afar, and nearby burns.

195

My face and hair keep changing day by day,
Yet I don't cease on that account to take
Sweet-baited hooks, nor fly the green, limed boughs
Of that tree which heeds neither sun nor chill.
    The sea will have no water, heaven no stars   5
Before I ever cease to fear and yearn
For her fair shade—to hate and love the deep
And amorous wound that I can scarce conceal.
    I'll never hope for respite from my pains
Till I am boneless, nerveless, stripped of flesh,   10
Or till my foe takes pity on my plight.

Esser pò in prima ogni impossibil cosa,
ch'altri che morte, od ella, sani 'l colpo
ch'Amor co' suoi belli occhi al cor m'impresse.

196

L'aura serena che fra verdi fronde
mormorando a ferir nel volto viemme,
fammi risovenir quand'Amor diemme
le prime piaghe, sí dolci profonde;
    e 'l bel viso veder, ch'altri m'asconde,   5
che sdegno o gelosia celato tiemme;
et le chiome or avolte in perle e 'n gemme,
allora sciolte, et sovra òr terso bionde:
    le quali ella spargea sí dolcemente,
et raccogliea con sí leggiadri modi,   10
che ripensando anchor trema la mente;
    torsele il tempo poi in piú saldi nodi,
et strinse 'l cor d'un laccio sí possente,
che Morte sola fia ch'indi lo snodi.

197

L'aura celeste che 'n quel verde lauro
spira, ov'Amor ferí nel fianco Apollo,
et a me pose un dolce giogo al collo,
tal che mia libertà tardi restauro,
    pò quello in me, che nel gran vecchio mauro   5
Medusa quando in selce transformollo;
né posso dal bel nodo omai dar crollo,
là 've il sol perde, non pur l'ambra o l'auro:
    dico le chiome bionde, e 'l crespo laccio,
che sí soavemente lega et stringe   10
l'alma, che d'umiltate e non d'altr'armo.
    L'ombra sua sola fa 'l mio cor un ghiaccio,
et di bianca paura il viso tinge;
ma li occhi ànno vertú di farne un marmo.

198

L'aura soave al sole spiega et vibra
l'auro ch'Amor di sua man fila et tesse
là da' belli occhi, et de le chiome stesse
lega 'l cor lasso, e i lievi spirti cribra.
    Non ò medolla in osso, o sangue in fibra,   5
ch'i' non senta tremar, pur ch'i' m'apresse
dove è chi morte et vita inseme, spesse

All things impossible can come to pass
Ere anyone but death or she can heal
The thrust Love gave my heart with her fair eyes.

196

The tranquil breeze that, 'midst the verdant fronds,
Comes murmuring softly to caress my face,
Calls to my mind again the time when Love
Gave to me my first wounds, so deep and sweet;
It makes me see the fair face she conceals,   5
Which scorn and jealousy still keep from me,
And see her hair—now bound with pearls and gems,
But then unbound, and blond past burnished gold—
Which she let down so sweetly and, in such
Attractive fashion, gathered up again,   10
So that recalling still makes my heart quake;
Time later twisted it in knots more firm,
And bound my heart with cord so powerful
That only death can loose me from its toils.

197

The heavenly breeze sighs in that laurel green
Where Love once struck Apollo in his side
And placed about my neck so sweet a yoke
That too late I regain my liberty.
In me, she can do what Medusa did°   5
To that old giant Moor when she changed him
To stone; I can't shrug off that fair knot which
Dims not just gold and amber, but the sun.
I speak of that blond hair, that twining net
Which gently binds my soul, holds it so fast   10
That it's armed only with humility.
Though her mere shadow turns my heart to ice,
And makes my face grow pale with blanching fear,
Made marble by the power of her eyes.

198

The soft breeze strews and ruffles in the sun
Gold that, near her fair eyes, Love spins and weaves
With his hand, and with that same hair he binds
My flagging heart, and sifts light spirits out.
In fiber, blood, in bone no pith have I   5
That does not shiver if I but come near
Where she is, who ofttimes suspends and weighs

volte, in frale bilancia appende et libra,
vedendo ardere i lumi ond'io m'accendo,
et folgorare i nodi ond'io son preso,
or su l'omero dextro et or sul manco.

I' nol posso ridir, ché nol comprendo:
da ta' due luci è l'intellecto offeso,
et di tanta dolcezza oppresso et stanco.

199

O bella man, che mi destringi 'l core,
e 'n poco spatio la mia vita chiudi;
man ov'ogni arte et tutti loro studi
poser Natura e 'l Ciel per farsi honore;

di cinque perle oriental' colore,
et sol ne le mie piaghe acerbi et crudi,
diti schietti soavi, a tempo ignudi
consente or voi, per arricchirme, Amore.

Candido leggiadretto et caro guanto,
che copria netto avorio et fresche rose,
chi vide al mondo mai sí dolci spoglie?

Cosí avess'io del bel velo altrettanto!
O inconstantia de l'umane cose!
Pur questo è furto, et vien chi me ne spoglie.

200

Non pur quell'una bella ignuda mano,
che con grave mio danno si riveste,
ma l'altra et le duo braccia accorte et preste
son a stringere il cor timido et piano.

Lacci Amor mille, et nesun tende invano,
fra quelle vaghe nove forme honeste
ch'adornan sí l'alto habito celeste,
ch'agiunger nol pò stil né 'ngegno humano:

li occhi sereni et le stellanti ciglia,
la bella bocca angelica, di perle
piena et di rose et di dolci parole,

che fanno altrui tremar di meraviglia,
et la fronte, et le chiome, ch'a vederle
di state, a mezzo dí, vincono il sole.

201

Mia ventura et Amor m'avean sí adorno
d'un bello aurato et serico trapunto,
ch'al sommo del mio ben quasi era aggiunto,

In fragile balance death and life at once;
    I see those lights ablaze that kindle me
And see those braids that bind me flashing so,   10
Now on the right-hand shoulder, now the left,
    I can't recount what I don't understand;
My intellect is dazed by two such lights
And by such sweetness wearied and weighed down.

199

    O lovely hand, you clasp my heart so fast
And in a little span enfold my life;
O hand, where Nature and Heaven bend every art
And all their pains to glorify themselves.
    Colored like five pearls from the orient,   5
Pure gentle fingers, only harsh and sharp
When in my wounds—Love just in time consents
That you be bare so he can make me rich.
    White, graceful, charming, precious little glove
That covered flawless ivory, roses fresh,   10
Who's seen in all this world such plunder sweet?
    I wish I had the like from that fair veil!
Oh, the inconstancy of mortal things!
But this is theft; one comes to rob me too.

200

    Not only that one bare and lovely hand
That now, to my grave harm, reclothes itself,
That other too, and both arms eagerly
Prepare to wring my simple, timorous heart.
    Love spreads a thousand nets, and none in vain,   5
Among those rare, chaste, lovely forms that so
Adorn her lofty and celestial garb
That human style or skill can add no more.
    Her tranquil eyes, her eyebrow radiant
Her beautiful, angelic mouth all filled   10
With pearls and roses and with soft, sweet words
    That make a person tremble, marvelling,
And her fair forehead and her tresses—they
When seen at summer noontime, dim the sun.

201

    My Fortune, and Love too, had graced me so
With a fair gold and silk embroidery
I'd almost reached the summit of my peace

pensando meco: A chi fu quest'intorno?

Né mi riede a la mente mai quel giorno 5
che mi fe' ricco et povero in un punto,
ch'i' non sia d'ira et di dolor compunto,
pien di vergogna et d'amoroso scorno,

che la mia nobil preda non piú stretta
tenni al bisogno, et non fui piú constante 10
contra lo sforzo sol d'un'angioletta;

o, fugendo, ale non giunsi a le piante,
per far almen di quella man vendetta
che de li occhi mi trahe lagrime tante.

202

D'un bel chiaro polito et vivo ghiaccio
move la fiamma che m'incende et strugge,
et sí le vene e 'l cor m'asciuga et sugge
che 'nvisibilemente i' mi disfaccio.

Morte, già per ferire alzato 'l braccio, 5
come irato ciel tona o leon rugge,
va perseguendo mia vita che fugge;
et io, pien di paura, tremo et taccio.

Ben poria anchor Pietà con Amor mista,
per sostegno di me, doppia colonna 10
porsi fra l'alma stancha e 'l mortal colpo;

ma io nol credo, né 'l conosco in vista
di quella dolce mia nemica et donna:
né di ciò lei, ma mia ventura incolpo.

203

Lasso, ch'i' ardo, et altri non me 'l crede;
sí crede ogni uom, se non sola colei
che sovr'ogni altra, et ch'i' sola, vorrei:
ella non par che 'l creda, et sí sel vede.

Infinita bellezza et poca fede, 5
non vedete voi 'l cor nelli occhi mei?
Se non fusse mia stella, i' pur devrei
al fonte di pietà trovar mercede.

Quest'arder mio, di che vi cal sí poco,
e i vostri honori, in mie rime diffusi, 10
ne porian infiammar fors'anchor mille:

ch'i' veggio nel penser, dolce mio foco,
fredda una lingua et duo belli occhi chiusi
rimaner, dopo noi, pien' di faville.

By thinking to myself, "Who wore this once?"
 That day which in one instant made me rich   5
And poor, never returns to mind that I
Do not feel stung by sorrow and by wrath,
Feel full of shame and amorous disdain
 That in necessity I did not hold
My noble prey more fast nor stand more firm   10
Against the strength of just one angel small;
 Or, fleeing, fixed no wings upon my feet
To wreak at least some vengeance on that hand
Which draws forth from my eyes so many tears.

202

 From ice that's living, lovely, clear and smooth
The flame breaks out that melts and kindles me;
It parches so, sucks dry my heart and veins
That I invisibly am done to death.
 Already Death has raised her arm to strike;   5
As thunders wrathful heaven, or as roars
A lion, she pursues my fleeting life,
And, filled with fear, I shudder and grow mute.
 If mercy mixed with love could only raise
For my support a double column twixt   10
My weary spirit and that mortal stroke;
 But I don't credit that, nor see it in
The face of my sweet foe and lady; I
Reproach my fortune for it, but not her.

203

 Woe, for I burn and one believes me not;
Thus all believe save only she, who past
All others I'd wish did so—she alone,
She seems not to believe it, yet she sees.
 O, beauty infinite and little faith,   5
Do you not see the heart within my eyes?
If not for my star, some compassion I
Should find at pity's fountain, certainly.°
 The flame of mine that you so little prize
And all your merits in my rhymes spread far   10
Can set aflame perhaps more thousands still,
 For in my thought I see, sweet fire of mine,
A tongue grown cold, and closed two lovely eyes,
Remaining after us, and filled with sparks.

204

Anima, che diverse cose tante
vedi, odi et leggi et parli et scrivi et pensi;
occhi miei vaghi, et tu, fra li altri sensi,
che scorgi al cor l'alte parole sante:
    per quanto non vorreste o poscia od ante   5
esser giunti al camin che sí mal tiensi,
per non trovarvi i duo bei lumi accensi,
né l'orme impresse de l'amate piante?
    Or con sí chiara luce, et con tai segni,
errar non dêsi in quel breve vïaggio,   10
che ne pò far d'etterno albergo degni.
    Sfôrzati al cielo, o mio stancho coraggio,
per la nebbia entro de' suoi dolci sdegni,
seguendo i passi honesti e 'l divo raggio.

205

Dolci ire, dolci sdegni et dolci paci,
dolce mal, dolce affanno et dolce peso,
dolce parlare, et dolcemente inteso,
or di dolce òra, or pien di dolci faci:
    alma, non ti lagnar, ma soffra et taci,   5
et tempra il dolce amaro, che n'à offeso,
col dolce honor che d'amar quella ài preso
a cui io dissi: Tu sola mi piaci.
    Forse anchor fia chi sospirando dica,
tinto di dolce invídia: Assai sostenne   10
per bellissimo amor quest'al suo tempo.
    Altri: O Fortuna agli occhi miei nemica,
perché non la vid'io? perché non venne
ella piú tardi, over io piú per tempo?

206

S'i' 'l dissi mai, ch'i' vegna in odio a quella
del cui amor vivo, et senza 'l qual morrei;
s'i' 'l dissi, che miei dí sian pochi et rei,
et di vil signoria l'anima ancella;
    s'i' 'l dissi, contra me s'arme ogni stella,   5
et dal mio lato sia
Paura et Gelosia,
et la nemica mia
piú feroce ver' me sempre et piú bella.

204

Soul, you who see so many varied things,
Who hear, speak, write, and think; my yearning eyes
And you among my other senses who
To my heart lead those lofty, sacred words,
    How strongly would you wish you had not reached— 5
Not soon, not late—this path you hold so ill,
If you'd not found there two, fair, glowing lights,
Nor footprints left by those beloved soles?
    Now, having such bright light, such vestiges,
We must not stray in this our journey brief. 10
Which for eternal shelter makes us fit.
    Press on to heaven, O my weary heart,
Press through the inner mist of her sweet scorn,
And follow her chaste steps and ray divine.

205

Sweet rages, sweet contempt, and sweet accords,
Sweet ill, sweet breathlessness, and burden sweet,
Sweet conversation, sweetly understood,
Now filled with breezes sweet, now with sweet fire.
    Do not lament, soul; suffer and keep still 5
And mix sweet bitterness that hurt us so
With honor sweet you gain in loving her
To whom I uttered: "Only you please me."
    Perhaps, yet someone sighing will remark
(Tinged with sweet jealousy): "In his time this 10
One's borne much for a love most beautiful."
    Some other one: "O Fortune, my eyes' foe,
Why did I see her not? Why did she not
Come later on, or I in better time?"

206

If ever I said that, may she hate me
Whose love I live for, and would die without;
If I said that, be my days few and sad,
My soul the handmaid of dominion vile;
If I said that, may every star against 5
Me arm, and at my side
Be Jealousy and Fear
My enemy as well,
More fierce against me ever, and more fair.

S'i' 'l dissi, Amor l'aurate sue quadrella   10
spenda in me tutte, et l'impiombate in lei;
s'i' 'l dissi, cielo et terra, uomini et dèi
mi sian contrari, et essa ognor piú fella;
s'i' 'l dissi, chi con sua cieca facella
dritto a morte m'invia,   15
pur come suol si stia,
né mai piú dolce a pia
ver' me si mostri, in atto od in favella.
    S'i' 'l dissi mai, di quel ch'i' men vorrei
piena trovi quest'aspra et breve via;   20
s'i' 'l dissi, il fero ardor che mi desvia
cresca in me quanto il fier ghiaccio in costei;
s'i' 'l dissi, unqua non veggian li occhi mei
sol chiaro, o sua sorella,
né donna né donzella   25
ma terribil procella,
qual Pharaone in perseguir li hebrei.
    S'i' 'l dissi, coi sospir', quant'io mai fei,
sia Pietà per me morta, et Cortesia;
s'i' 'l dissi, il dir s'innaspri, che s'udia   30
sí dolce allor che vinto mi rendei;
s'i' 'l dissi, io spiaccia a quella ch'i' torrei
sol, chiuso in fosca cella,
dal dí che la mamella
lasciai, finché si svella   35
da me l'alma, adorar: forse e 'l farei.
    Ma s'io nol dissi, chi sí dolce apria
meo cor a speme ne l'età novella,
regg'anchor questa stanca navicella
col governo di sua pietà natia,   40
né diventi altra, ma pur qual solia
quando piú non potei,
che me stesso perdei
(né piú perder devrei).
Mal fa chi tanta fe' sí tosto oblia.   45
    I' nol dissi già mai, né dir poria
per oro o per cittadi o per castella.
Vinca 'l ver dunque, et si rimanga in sella,
et vinta a terra caggia la bugia.
Tu sai in me il tutto, Amor: s'ella ne spia,   50
dinne quel che dir dêi.
I' beato direi,
tre volte et quattro et sei,

If I said that, may Love spend all his darts   10
Of gold on me, and those of lead on her;
If I said that, may heaven and earth, may men
And gods oppose me, she e'er be more cruel.
If I said that, to death straight may she guide
Me with her lightless torch,   15
Stay as she's ever wont,
Now show herself more sweet
Or kind toward me in discourse or in deed.
    If ever I said that, this path may I
Find rough and short, filled with what I'd least wish   20
If I said that, may fierce, deceptive flame
Grow great in me as cruel ice in her;
If I said that, may my eyes never see
The bright sun nor his sister,
No lady nor no maiden,   25
But see an awful storm
As Pharoh did in following the Jews.°
    If I said that, with every sigh I've heaved,
May Pity die for me, and Courtesy;
If I said that, may her speech bitter grow,   30
Speech sweetly heard when, conquered, I succumbed.
If I said that, may I displease her whom
Alone I'd steal to adore
Though closed in a dark cell
From that day I was weaned   35
Till my soul's plucked from me (I might do that!)
    But if I said that not, may one who in
My youth unsealed my heart so sweetly to
Its hope still guide this small tired vessel with
The rudder of her native clemency.   40
May she not change, but still be as she was
When more I could not do,
For I had lost myself
(And I must lose no more)
One does harm who so soon forgets great faith.   45
    I said that never, not for gold could I,
For cities nor for castles utter it.
Then let truth win, and in its saddle stay,
And falsehood, overcome, be cast to earth;°
What's in me, Love, you know; should she inquire,   50
Tell about me what you ought
To say. I would say "blessed,
Three times and four and six,

chi, devendo languir, si morí pria.

Per Rachel ò servito, et non per Lia; 55
né con altra saprei
viver, et sosterrei,
quando 'l ciel ne rappella,
girmen con ella in sul carro de Helia.

207

Ben mi credea passar mio tempo omai
come passato avea quest'anni a dietro,
senz'altro studio et senza novi ingegni:
or poi che da madonna i' non impetro
l'usata aita, a che condutto m'ài, 5
tu 'l vedi, Amor, che tal arte m'insegni.
Non so s'i' me ne sdegni,
che 'n questa età mi fai divenir ladro
del bel lume leggiadro,
senza 'l qual non vivrei in tanti affanni. 10
Cosí avess'io i primi anni
preso lo stil ch'or prender mi bisogna,
ché 'n giovenil fallir è men vergogna.

Li occhi soavi ond'io soglio aver vita,
de le divine lor alte bellezze 15
furmi in sul cominciar tanto cortesi,
che 'n guisa d'uom cui non proprie ricchezze,
ma celato di for soccorso aita,
vissimi, che né lor né altri offesi.
Or, bench'a me ne pesi, 20
divento ingiurïoso et importuno:
ché 'l poverel digiuno
vèn ad atto talor che 'n miglior stato
avria in altrui biasmato.
Se le man' di Pietà Invidia m'à chiuse, 25
fame amorosa, e 'l non poter, mi scuse.

Ch'i ò cercate già vie piú di mille
per provar senza lor se mortal cosa
mi potesse tener in vita un giorno.
L'anima, poi ch'altrove non à posa, 30
corre pur a l'angeliche faville;
et io, che son di cera, al foco torno;
et pongo mente intorno
ove si fa men guardia a quel ch'i' bramo;
et come augel in ramo, 35
ove men teme, ivi piú tosto è colto,

Is one, obliged to languish, who first dies."
For Rachel, not for Leah, have I served,°   55
With no other could I live;
I would keep on—I'd ride up,
when heaven called us back,
In Elijah's chariot with her.°

207

I thought that I could surely spend my time
Henceforth as I had passed these latter years
Without more study, new contrivances;
But now, since from my lady I do not
Receive accustomed aid, you see where you   5
Have brought me, Love, by teaching me such art.
I don't know at this age
If I should be upset that you make me
Steal that fair, charming light
Without which, in such pain, I could not live.   10
Would I had mastered in
My early years the style that, now, I must
Employ, for in youth's faults is less disgrace.
    Those soft eyes whence I used to draw my life
Were, with their beauties lofty and divine,   15
So courteous at first to me that I
Was like a man who lived on wealth not his,
But secret aid, aid from without; for I
Offended neither them nor anyone.
Now, though it weighs on me,   20
I've grown abusive, importune because,
A starveling beggar does
Deeds sometimes in another he would blame
Were he in better state.
If Envy has to me closed Mercy's hand   25
Love's hunger and my weakness pardon me.
    For I have traced a thousand paths and more
To try if, lacking them, some mortal thing
Could even for one day sustain my life.
My soul, since elsewhere it can have no rest,   30
Still hurries after those angelic sparks,
And made of wax, I to the fire return.
And closely I take note
Of each place she guards least what I desire.
And, like a bird upon   35
The bough, where least it fears is soonest caught,

così dal suo bel volto
l'involo or uno et or un altro sguardo;
et di ciò inseme mi nutrico et ardo.
    Di mia morte mi pasco, et vivo in fiamme: 40
stranio cibo, et mirabil salamandra;
ma miracol non è, da tal si vòle.
Felice agnello a la penosa mandra
mi giacqui un tempo; or a l'extremo famme
et Fortuna et Amor pur come sòle: 45
così rose et vïole
à primavera, e 'l verno à neve et ghiaccio.
Però, s'i' mi procaccio
quinci et quindi alimenti al viver curto,
se vòl dir che sia furto,   50
sí ricca donna deve esser contenta,
s'altri vive del suo, ch'ella nol senta.
    Chi nol sa di ch'io vivo, et vissi sempre,
dal dí che 'n prima que' belli occhi vidi,
che mi fecer cangiar vita et costume?   55
Per cercar terra et mar da tutti lidi,
chi pò saver tutte l'umane tempre?
L'un vive, ecco, d'odor, là sul gran fiume;
io qui di foco et lume
queto i frali et famelici miei spirti.   60
Amor, et vo' ben dirti,
disconvensi a signor l'esser sí parco.
Tu ài li strali et l'arco:
fa' di tua man, non pur bramand'io mora,
ch'un bel morir tutta la vita honora.   65
    Chiusa fiamma è piú ardente; et se pur cresce,
in alcun modo piú non pò celarsi:
Amor, i' 'l so, che 'l provo a le tue mani.
Vedesti ben, quando sí tacito arsi;
or de' miei gridi a me medesmo incresce,   70
che vo noiando et proximi et lontani.
O mondo, o penser' vani;
o mia forte ventura a che m'adduce!
O di che vaga luce
al cor mi nacque la tenace speme,   75
onde l'annoda et preme
quella che con tua forza al fin mi mena!
La colpa è vostra, et mio 'l danno et la pena.
    Cosí di ben amar porto tormento,
et del peccato altrui cheggio perdono: 80

So from her lovely face,
I filch now one and now another glimpse,
And thereby I am fed and burned at once.
    Upon my death I feed and dwell in flame: 40
Strange fare, and salamander marvellous!
But that's no miracle; a certain one
So wills! A happy lamb in that sad flock
I once lay down; now in extremity
Both Love and Fortune use me as they're wont.   45
So spring has roses and
Its violets, and winter snow and ice.
Thus if I take for my
Brief life some viands here and there; if she
Should want to call it theft,   50
So rich a lady ought to be content
If some live on what's hers, and she knows not.
    Who knows not what I live on, ever have,
Since that day I first saw those beauteous eyes
That made me alter habits, change my life?   55
By searching land and sea and every shore,
Who can learn all the qualities of men?
Lo, there by that great stream, one lives on scent;
Here I with fire and light
My weak and famished spirits satisfy.   60
Love—I must tell you this—
It ill becomes a lord to be so mean;
You have your darts, your bow;
By your hand, not from longing, may I die;
For fitly dying honors all one's life.   65
    Flame closed within's more ardent; if it still
Increases, there's no way to keep it hid.
I know this, Love, I prove it at your hand;
You saw it sure, when I so silent, blazed.
My own cries make me suffer now, so that   70
I wander vexing those both near and far.
O world, O idle thoughts;
O my hard fortune, what you lead me to!
From what bewitching light
Was born that constant hope within my heart   75
With which she binds and crushes it,
For with your strength she leads me to my end!
The guilt is yours; the harm and pain are mine.
    From loving rightly thus, I suffer woe,
And beg forgiveness for another's sin—   80

anzi del mio, che devea torcer li occhi
dal troppo lume, et di sirene al suono
chiuder li orecchi; et anchor non me 'n pento,
che di dolce veleno il cor trabocchi.
Aspett'io pur che scocchi   85
l'ultimo colpo chi mi diede 'l primo;
et fia, s'i' dritto extimo,
un modo di pietate occider tosto,
non essendo ei disposto
a far altro di me che quel che soglia: 90
ché ben muor chi morendo esce di doglia.
    Canzon mia, fermo in campo
starò, ch'elli è disnor morir fuggendo;
et me stesso reprendo
di tai lamenti, sí dolce è mia sorte,   95
pianto, sospiri et morte.
Servo d'Amor, che queste rime leggi,
ben non à 'l mondo, che 'l mio mal pareggi.

208

    Rapido fiume che d'alpestra vena
rodendo intorno, onde 'l tuo nome prendi,
notte et dí meco disïoso scendi
ov'Amor me, te sol Natura mena,
    vattene innanzi: il tuo corso non frena   5
né stanchezza né sonno; et pria che rendi
suo dritto al mar, fiso u' si mostri attendi
l'erba piú verde, et l'aria piú serena.
    Ivi è quel nostro vivo et dolce sole,
ch'addorna e 'nfiora la tua riva manca: 10
forse (o che spero?) e 'l mio tardar le dole.
    Basciale 'l piede, o la man bella et bianca;
dille, e 'l basciar sie 'nvece di parole:
Lo spirto è pronto, ma la carne è stanca.

209

    I dolci colli ov'io lasciai me stesso,
partendo onde partir già mai non posso,
mi vanno innanzi, et èmmi ognor adosso
quel caro peso ch'Amor m'à commesso.
    Meco di me mi meraviglio spesso,   5
ch'i' pur vo sempre, et non son anchor mosso
dal bel giogo piú volte indarno scosso,
ma com piú me n'allungo, et piú m'appresso.

For mine, instead—since I ought to have turned
My eyes from too much light, and stopped my ears
Against the sirens' song; yet I do not
Repent of it, for with sweet poison my
Heart brims. I still await   85
The final shaft from him who shot me first;
And if I rightly judge,
To swiftly kill's a form of mercy, for
He is not predisposed
To treat me otherwise than he is wont: 90
One dies well who, by dying, flees his woe.
    My song, upon the field
I'll stand firm, for to die while fleeing is
Inglorious, and I
Reproach myself for such complaints, so sweet   95
My fate, tears, sighs, and death.
Love's servant, you who read these lines, this world
Possesses no good that can match my ill.

208

    Swift stream from Alpine springs, eroding all—
From which you take your name—with me you yearn°
And night and day rush down to where you're led
By Nature only, and I'm led by love,
    Go on ahead; not weariness nor sleep   5
Can check your course; and then before you pay
Your homage to the sea, look closely where
The grass appears most green, the air most clear.
    There dwells that sweet, that living sun of ours,
Adorning with strewn flowers your left bank.   10
Perhaps my lateness grieves her (dare I hope?).
    Then kiss that foot, or that white, comely hand;
Tell her, and let the kiss stand for the words:
"The spirit's eager, but the flesh is faint."

209

    Those sweet hills where I left myself behind
(Thence parting whence I cannot ever part)
Before me rise, and ever on my back
I bear the precious burden Love imposed.
    Within, I marvel often at myself   5
That ever wandering, I've not yet shed
That fair yoke I've oft tried to shake in vain—
As far from it I go, I nearer draw.

Et qual cervo ferito di saetta,
col ferro avelenato dentr'al fianco,
fugge, et piú duolsi quanto piú s'affretta,   10
   tal io, con quello stral dal lato manco,
che mi consuma, et parte mi diletta,
di duol mi struggo, et di fuggir mi stanco.

210

Non da l'hispano Hibero a l'indo Ydaspe
ricercando del mar ogni pendice,
né dal lito vermiglio a l'onde caspe,
né 'n ciel né 'n terra, è piú d'una fenice.
   Qual dextro corvo o qual mancha cornice   5
canti 'l mio fato, o qual Parca l'innaspe?
che sol trovo Pietà sorda com'aspe,
misero, onde sperava esser felice.
   Ch'i' non vo' dir di lei: ma chi la scorge,
tutto 'l cor di dolcezza et d'amor gli empie,   10
tanto n'à seco, et tant'altrui ne porge;
   et per far mie dolcezze amare et empie,
o s'infinge o non cura, o non s'accorge,
del fiorir queste inanzi tempo tempie.

211

Voglia mi sprona, Amor mi guida et scorge,
Piacer mi tira, Usanza mi trasporta,
Speranza mi lusinga et riconforta
et la man destra al cor già stanco porge;
   e 'l misero la prende, et non s'accorge   5
di nostra cieca et disleale scorta:
regnano i sensi, et la ragion è morta;
de l'un vago desio l'altro risorge.
   Vertute, Honor, Bellezza, atto gentile,
dolci parole ai be' rami m'àn giunto   10
ove soavemente il cor s'invesca.
   Mille trecento ventisette, a punto
su l'ora prima, il dí sesto d'aprile,
nel laberinto intrai, né veggio ond'esca.

212

Beato in sogno et di languir contento,
d'abbracciar l'ombre et seguir l'aura estiva,
nuoto per mar che non à fondo o riva,
solco onde, e 'n rena fondo, et scrivo in vento;

And, as an arrow-wounded stag flees on
With iron envenomed in its flank, and as   10
It plunges on the more, endures more pain,
    So I, with that dart, which consumes me and
Delights me equally, in my left side
Am torn by woe and tire myself in flight.

210

    In earth or heaven, from Indic Hydaspes°
To Spanish Ebro; from the Caspian waves
To the Red shore, one Phoenix only lives
Though sought along each hillside by the sea.
    What right-hand crow, or raven on the left°   5
Can croak my lot, or which Fate wind it up?°
For I alone find Pity deaf as asps,
I, wretched where I'd hoped for happiness.
    So I've no wish to talk of her; but love
And sweetness fill his heart who looks on her;   10
She has so much; so much to others gives.
    To make my sweetness harsh and pitiless,
She feigns, or cares not, or she takes no note,
That ere their time these temples bloom with white.

211

    Will spurs me forth, Love guides me and directs,
My Pleasure pulls me, Custom drives me on,
Hope flatters and revives me, stretches forth
Her right hand to my heart, indeed worn out.
    That poor wretch seizes it, and takes no note   5
Of our unseeing and unfaithful guide.
My senses dominate, my reason's dead:
From one misled desire another springs.
    Sweet words and Virtue, Honor, noble deeds,
And beauty in fair branches have set me   10
Where, bird-limed, gently my heart's been ensnared.
    In thirteen hundred twenty-seven, just at
The first hour—April sixth the day—into°
The labyrinth I stepped; I see no gate.

212

    In dream blest and in languishing content,
Embracing shades and chasing summer's breeze,
Through bottomless and shoreless seas I swim,
Plough waves, build on the sand, and write on wind;

e 'l sol vagheggio, sí ch'elli à già spento 5
col suo splendor la mia vertú visiva,
et una cerva errante et fugitiva
caccio con un bue zoppo e 'nfermo et lento.
    Cieco et stanco ad ogni altro ch'al mio danno
il qual dí et notte palpitando cerco, 10
sol Amor et madonna, et Morte, chiamo.
    Cosí venti anni, grave et lungo affanno,
pur lagrime et sospiri et dolor merco:
in tale stella presi l'ésca et l'amo.

213

    Gratie ch'a pochi il ciel largo destina:
rara vertú, non già d'umana gente,
sotto biondi capei canuta mente,
e 'n humil donna alta beltà divina;
    leggiadria singulare et pellegrina, 5
e 'l cantar che ne l'anima si sente,
l'andar celeste, e 'l vago spirto ardente,
ch'ogni dur rompe et ogni altezza inchina;
    et que' belli occhi che i cor' fanno smalti,
possenti a rischiarar abisso et notti, 10
et tôrre l'alme a' corpi, et darle altrui;
    col dir pien d'intellecti dolci et alti,
coi sospiri soave-mente rotti:
da questi magi transformato fui.

214

    Anzi tre dí creata era alma in parte
da por sua cura in cose altere et nove,
et dispregiar di quel ch'a molti è 'n pregio.
Quest'anchor dubbia del fatal suo corso,
sola pensando, pargoletta et sciolta, 5
intrò di primavera in un bel bosco.
    Era un tenero fior nato in quel bosco
il giorno avanti, et la radice in parte
ch'appressar nol poteva anima sciota:
ché v'eran di lacciuo' forme sí nove, 10
et tal piacer precipitava al corso,
che perder libertate ivi era in pregio.
    Caro, dolce, alto et faticoso pregio,
che ratto mi volgesti al verde bosco
usato di sviarne a mezzo 'l corso! 15
Et ò cerco poi 'l mondo a parte a parte,

I fondly gaze upon the sun, and thus   5
His splendor has quite quenched my power of sight,
I hunt a wandering and fleeing doe
Upon an ox that's slow, infirm, and lame.
  I'm tired and blind to all else but my harm,
Which, quaking, I search out both night and day;   10
I cry out only, "Love," "my lady," "Death."
  Thus twenty years, a long and irksome trial,
I still have dealt in tears and sighs and woe.
'Neath such a star I swallowed bait and hook.

213

  Graces that bounteous heaven grants to few,
Rare virtue not the human kind, indeed,
A mind mature beneath those tresses blond,
In modest lady, beauty high, divine;
  Extraordinary charm and singular,   5
A song that one feels in the soul; a walk
Celestial and a spirit lovely, bright,
That breaks all hardness and bows grandeur low,
  And those fair eyes that glaze my heart, have power
To brighten night and the abyss, to steal   10
Souls from their flesh, to give to someone else.
  With conversation full of import sweet
And lofty, and with softly broken sighs
Was I by these same sorcerers transformed.

214

  A soul had been embodied in its parts
Some three days past, devoted to things rare
and lofty, and to scorn what crowds esteem.
This soul, unsure yet of her destined course,
Alone in thought, a youthful spirit free,   5
In springtime entered in a lovely wood.
  A tender bloom was born within that wood
The day before, and rooted in a part
That could not be approached by spirit free;
For springes there were set of shapes most rare,   10
And such great pleasure pressed one on that course,
To lose one's freedom there was much esteemed.
  Dear, lofty, sweet, and wearying esteem,
Which turned me swiftly toward that verdant wood,
Employed to make us wander from our course!   15
And thus I searched the world from part to part

se versi o petre o suco d'erbe nove
mi rendesser un dí la mente sciolta.

  Ma, lasso, or veggio che la carne sciolta
fia di quel nodo ond'è 'l suo maggior pregio   20
prima che medicine, antiche o nove,
saldin le paighe ch'i' presi in quel bosco,
folto di spine, ond'i' ò ben tal parte,
che zoppo n'esco, e 'ntra'vi a sí gran corso.

  Pien di lacci et di stecchi un duro corso   25
aggio a fornire, ove leggera et sciolta
pianta avrebbe uopo, et sana d'ogni parte.
Ma Tu, Signor, ch'ài di pietate il pregio,
porgimi la man dextra in questo bosco:
vinca 'l Tuo sol le mie tenebre nove.   30

  Guarda 'l mio stato, a le vaghezze nove
che 'nterrompendo di mia vita il corso
m'àn fatto habitador d'ombroso bosco;
rendimi, s'esser pò, libera et sciolta
l'errante mia consorte; et fia Tuo 'l pregio,   35
s'anchor Teco la trovo in miglior parte.

  Or ecco in parte le question' mie nove:
s'alcun pregio in me vive, o 'n tutto è corso,
o l'alma sciolta, o ritenuta al bosco.

215

  In nobil sangue vita humile et queta
et in alto intellecto un puro core,
frutto senile in sul giovenil fiore
e 'n aspetto pensoso anima lieta

  raccolto à 'n questa donna il suo pianeta,   5
anzi 'l re de le stelle; e 'l vero honore,
le degne lode, e 'l gran pregio, e 'l valore,
ch'è da stanchar ogni divin poeta.

  Amor s'è in lei con Honestate aggiunto,
con beltà naturale habito adorno,   10
et un atto che parla con silentio,

  et non so che nelli occhi, che 'n un punto
pò far chiara la notte, oscuro il giorno,
e 'l mèl amaro, et adolcir l'assentio.

216

  Tutto 'l dí piango; et poi la notte, quando
prendon riposo i miseri mortali,
trovomi in pianto, et raddopiarsi i mali:

To see if one day, verses, stones, or rare
Herb potions could bring me a mind that's free.
    But, woe, I see now, my flesh will be free
Of that knot whence it gains the most esteem   20
Ere medicines can heal, antique or rare,
The wounds I suffered in that thorn-thick wood;
I came forth lame, of thorns I'd had such part,
Yet there I'd entered by so broad a course.
    All filled with snares and brambles, my hard course   25
I must conclude, and that would take a free
And light foot, one that's sound in every part.
But you, Lord, who hold pity in esteem,
Extend to me Your right hand in the wood;
Let Your sun overcome my darkness rare.   30
    Look on my plight, on those distractions rare
That, interrupting my life on its course,
Made me a dweller in a dusky wood;
Release me, if it can be so; set free
My errant bride, and yours be the esteem   35
If I find her with you in that best part.
    And now behold, in part, my conflict rare;
Survives esteem in me? Or has all coursed
Away? Is my soul free or trapped in woods?

215

    In noble blood, a quiet, modest life,
In lofty intellect, a heart that's pure,
The fruit of old age in a youthful bloom,
And in a thoughtful face, a joyful soul,
    Her planet in this lady has conjoined—   5
In fact the King of stars has—honor true,
Fit praises, great esteem, and that worth which
Is sure to wear out every godlike bard.
    For Love has joined with chastity in her,
And natural loveliness with comely ways   10
And a comportment that, with silence, speaks;
    I don't know what is in her eyes that can
At once illumine night and darken day,
Make honey bitter, oil of wormwood sweet.

216

    I weep all day, and then at night, when all
We wretched mortals take repose, I find
Myself in tears, redoubled all my ills;

così spendo 'l mio tempo lagrimando.

In tristo humor vo li occhi consumando,   5
e 'l cor in doglia; et son fra li animali
l'ultimo, sí che li amorosi strali
mi tengon ad ogni or di pace in bando.

Lasso, che pur da l'un a l'altro sole,
et da l'una ombra a l'altra, ò già 'l piú corso   10
di questa morte, che si chiama vita.

Piú l'altrui fallo che 'l mi' mal mi dole:
ché Pietà viva, e 'l mio fido soccorso,
védem' arder nel foco, et non m'aita.

217

Già desïai con sí giusta querela
e 'n sí fervide rime farmi udire,
ch'un foco di pietà fessi sentire
al duro cor ch'a mezza state gela;

et l'empia nube che 'l rafredda et vela,   5
rompesse a l'aura del mi' ardente dire;
o fessi quell' altrui in odio venire,
che' belli, onde mi strugge, occhi mi cela.

Or non odio per lei, per me pietate
cerco: ché quel non vo', questo non posso   10
(tal fu mia stella, et tal mia cruda sorte);

ma canto la divina sua beltate,
ché, quand'i' sia di questa carne scosso,
sappia 'l mondo che dolce è la mia morte.

218

Tra quantunque leggiadre donne et belle
giunga costei ch'al mondo non à pare,
col suo bel viso suol dell'altre fare
quel che fa 'l dí de le minori stelle.

Amor par ch'a l'orecchie mi favelle,   5
dicendo: Quanto questa in terra appare,
fia 'l viver bello; et poi 'l vedrem turbare,
perir vertuti, e 'l mio regno con elle.

Come Natura al ciel la luna e 'l sole,
a l'aere i vènti, a la terra herbe et fronde,   10
a l'uomo et l'intellecto et le parole,

et al mar ritollesse i pesci et l'onde:
tanto et piú fien le cose oscure et sole,
se Morte li occhi suoi chiude et asconde.

And thus in mourning I employ my time.
  I wander in sad humor wearing out   5
My eyes and heart in woe, and I am least
Among the creatures, so these amorous darts
At every hour exile me from peace.
  Ah woe, that from one sunrise to the next,
One darkness to another I've rushed through,   10
Already, most of this death we call life.
  I rue another's sin more than my ill,
For heartfelt Pity and my loyal aid
Both watch me burn in fire, and help me not.

217

  With such a just complaint I once desired
To make myself heard in such fervid rhymes
That I would make compassion's fire be felt
Within a hard heart, cold in summer's heat;
  Such rhymes, the breeze of my impassioned words,   5
Would rend the wicked cloud that chills and veils
That heart, or make her hateful to mankind;
She hides fair eyes from me, whence I'm destroyed.
  No hate for her I beg now, and for me
No ruth; that I don't wish, this cannot have;   10
My star was such, and such my bitter lot;
  But I shall sing her heavenly beauty, for,
When from this flesh I am set free, the world
Will understand how sweet's this death of mine.

218

  Among however many ladies fair
And charming she may come, unequalled in
This world, with her fair face she does to all
The rest what day does to the minor stars.
  It seems Love in my ear explains, and says: 5
"As long as she appears on earth will life
Be fair, but then, we'll see it overcast,
See virtues perish, and with them my reign.
  "As heaven would be if Nature took the moon
And stars away, the wind from air, and grass   10
And foliage from earth, from man his speech
  "And mind, and from the sea took fish and waves;
So much and more dark, lonely would things be
If Death should close and should conceal her eyes."

Il cantar novo e 'l pianger delli augelli
in sul dí fanno retentir le valli,
e 'l mormorar de' liquidi cristalli
giú per lucidi, freschi rivi et snelli.

Quella ch'à neve il volto, oro i capelli,   5
nel cui amor non fur mai inganni né falli,
destami al suon delli amorosi balli,
pettinando al suo vecchio i bianchi velli.

Cosí mi sveglio a salutar l'aurora,
e 'l sol ch'è seco, et piú l'altro ond'io fui   10
ne' primi anni abagliato, et son anchora.

I' gli ò veduti alcun giorno ambedui
levarsi inseme, e 'n un punto e 'n un'hora
quel far le stelle, et questo sparir lui.

Onde tolse Amor l'oro, et di qual vena,
per far due treccie bionde? e 'n quali spine
colse le rose, e 'n qual piaggia le brine
tenere et fresche, et die' lor polso et lena?

onde le perle, in ch'ei frange et affrena   5
dolci parole, honeste et pellegrine?
onde tante bellezze, et sí divine,
di quella fronte, piú che 'l ciel serena?

Da quali angeli mosse, et di qual spera,
quel celeste cantar che mi disface,   10
sí che m'avanza omai da disfar poco?

Di qual sol nacque l'alma luce altera
di que' belli occhi ond'io ò guerra et pace,
che mi cuocono il cor in ghiaccio e 'n foco?

Qual mio destin, qual forza o qual inganno
mi riconduce disarmato al campo,
là 've sempre son vinto? et s'io ne scampo,
meraviglia n'avrò; s'i' moro, il danno.

Danno non già, ma pro: sí dolci stanno   5
nel mio cor le faville e 'l chiaro lampo
che l'abbaglia e lo strugge, e 'n ch'io m'avampo,
et son già ardendo nel vigesimo anno.

Sento i messi di Morte, ove apparire
veggio i belli occhi, et folgorar da lunge;   10
poi, s'aven ch'appressando a me li gire,

The early song, the weeping of the birds
Makes all the vales resound at break of day,
As do the crystal ripples murmuring
Along the sparkling freshets, swift and cool.

That one with face of snow and golden hair,   5
She in whose love was never guile nor fault,
Awakes me to the strains of amorous dance,
As her old spouse's whitened locks she combs.°

Thus I awake to greet Aurora, and
The sun with her; and more, to greet that sun   10
Who blinded me in youth, and does so still.

Some days, together I have seen them both
Arise, and in that moment, in that hour,
He makes stars vanish; she makes him grow dim.

220

Where did Love steal the gold, and from what lode,
To make two tresses blond; and from what thorns
Plucked roses? On what heath found hoar-frost fresh
And tender, and to them gave pulse and breath?

Whence came the pearls with which he separates   5
And checks sweet, chaste, extraordinary words?
Whence took he for that brow more radiant
Than heaven its many beauties so sublime?

From what sphere, from what angels did he draw
That heavenly song by which I'm torn apart   10
So that but little's left of me to tear?

From what sun sprang the proud, life-giving light
Of those fair eyes whence I have war and peace,
Which vex my heart in ice and in the fire?

221

What fate of mine, what force or ruse again
Leads me, disarmed, upon that field where I'm
Forever vanquished? If I'm saved from it,
I'll wonder at it; if I die, be lost.

No loss, but benefit: so sweetly in   5
My heart remain the sparks and lightning bright
That melt and dazzle me, where I blaze up,
Where after twenty years I'm burning still.

I feel Death's harbingers when those fair eyes
I see appear—flash lightning from afar—   10
And when, if coming near, they fall on me.

Amor con tal dolcezza m'unge et punge,
ch'i' nol so ripensar, nonché ridire:
ché né 'ngegno né lingua al vero agiunge.

222

Liete et pensose, accompagnate et sole,
donne che ragionando ite per via,
ove è la vita, ove la morte mia?
perché non è con voi, com'ella sòle?
—Liete siam per memoria di quel sole; 5
dogliose per sua dolce compagnia,
la qual ne toglie Invidia et Gelosia,
che d'altrui ben, quasi suo mal, si dole.
—Chi pon freno a li amanti, o dà lor legge?
—Nesun a l'alma; al corpo Ira et Asprezza: 10
questo or in lei, talor si prova in noi.
Ma spesso ne la fronte il cor si legge:
sí vedemmo oscurar l'alta bellezza,
et tutti rugiadosi li occhi suoi.

223

Quando 'l sol bagna in mar l'aurato carro,
et l'aere nostro et la mia mente imbruna,
col cielo et co le stelle et co la luna
un'angosciosa et dura notte innarro.
Poi, lasso, a tal che non m'ascolta narro 5
tutte le mie fatiche, ad una ad una,
et col mondo et con mia cieca fortuna,
con Amor, con madonna et meco garro.
Il sonno è 'n bando, et del riposo è nulla;
ma sospiri et lamenti infin a l'alba, 10
et lagrime che l'alma a li occhi invia.
Vien poi l'aurora, et l'aura fosca inalba,
me no: ma 'l sol che 'l cor m'arde et trastulla,
quel pò solo adolcir la doglia mia.

224

S'una fede amorosa, un cor non finto,
un languir dolce, un desïar cortese;
s'oneste voglie in gentil foco accese,
un lungo error in cieco laberinto;
se ne la fronte ogni penser depinto, 5
od in voci interrotte a pena intese,
or da paura, or da vergogna offese;

So sweetly Love both stings me and anoints,
That I cannot recall it, much less tell,
For neither skill nor tongue comes near the truth.

222°

—"Carefree and grave, with others and alone,
You ladies who pass chatting by the way,
Where is my life? Where is that death of mine?
Why is she not as usual with you?"
    —"We're joyful at the memory of that sun,   5
And grieve at missing her sweet company
That Envy plucks from us, and Jealousy,
Still pained by others' good as by its ill."
    —"Who reins in lovers, or who gives them laws?"
—"For souls none do; for flesh, Hardship and Wrath;   10
This now in her, and now in us is proved.
    "But often in the brow one reads the heart;
Thus we saw lofty beauty overcast,
And all bedewed with tears we saw her eyes."

223

When in the sea his golden chariot
The sun dips, makes our air dark and my mind,
I set out on a hard and anguished night.
Together with the stars, the moon, and sky,
    Alas then, to that one who does not hear,   5
One at a time my hardships I recount,
And with the world, blind fortune and my love,
And with my lady and myself dispute.
    Sleep is in exile; there is no repose,
But till the daybreak sighing and lament,   10
And tears my soul sends forth into my eyes.
    Then comes the dawn, to brighten the dark breeze,
But not so me; alone that sun which burns
And trifles with my heart can sweeten woe.

224

If amorous faith, and if a heart sincere,
A languor sweet, a longing courteous,
If chaste desiring, lit in noble fire,
If roaming long a dark, blind labyrinth;
    If every thought depicted on the brow,   5
Now hardly understood in halting words,
Now marred by fear or by embarrassment;

s'un pallor di vïola et d'amor tinto;
s'aver altrui piú caro che se stesso;
se sospirare et lagrimar maisempre,
pascendosi di duol, d'ira et d'affanno;
s'arder da lunge et agghiacciar da presso
son le cagion' ch'amando i' mi distempre,
vostro, donna, 'l peccato, et mio fia 'l danno.

10

225

Dodici donne honestamente lasse,
anzi dodici stelle, e 'n mezzo un sole,
vidi in una barchetta allegre et sole,
qual non so s'altra mai onde solcasse.

Simil non credo che Iason portasse
al vello onde oggi ogni uom vestir si vòle
né 'l pastor di ch'anchor Troia si dole,
de' qua' duo tal romor al mondo fasse.

Poi le vidi in un carro trïumphale,
Laurëa mia con suoi santi atti schifi
sedersi in parte, et cantar dolcemente.

Non cose humane, o visïon mortale:
felice Autumedon, felice Tiphi,
che conduceste sí leggiadra gente!

5
10

226

Passer mai solitario in alcun tetto
non fu quant'io né fera in alcun bosco,
ch'i' non veggio 'l bel viso, et non conosco
altro sol, né quest'occhi ànn'altro obiecto.

Lagrimar sempre è 'l mio sommo diletto,
il rider doglia, il cibo assentio et tòsco,
la notte affanno, e 'l ciel seren m'è fosco,
et duro campo di battaglia il letto.

Il sonno è veramente qual uom dice,
parente de la morte, e 'l cor sottragge
a quel dolce penser che 'n vita il tene.

Solo al mondo paese almo, felice,
verdi rive fiorite, ombrose piagge,
vio possedete, et io piango, il mio bene.

5
10

227

Aura che quelle chiome bionde et crespe
cercondi et movi, et se' mossa da loro,
soavemente, et spargi quel dolce oro,

If pallor like the violet's, tinged with love;
    If holding someone dearer than one's self,
If heaving sighs and weeping evermore,   10
And nourishing on woe and wrath and pain;
    If burning from afar and freezing near
Make up the reasons I'm unstrung by love;
Yours, lady, is the fault, and mine the harm.

225

    Twelve ladies chastely resting at their ease—
Twelve stars, instead, and in their midst a sun—
I saw alone and joyful in a barque
Whose like, I think has never plowed the waves.°
    Nor did its like, I think, bear Jason to   5
That fleece that all men would put on today,
Nor bore the shepherd for whom Troy still grieves—°
About those two the world makes much ado.
    In a triumphal car I saw them next
My Laura with her shy and holy deeds   10
Was seated at one side and sweetly sang:
    No human things, nor yet a mortal sight;
O happy Tiphys, glad Automedon,
For such a graceful crew you piloted!

226

    There never was a sparrow on some roof
Alone as I, no wild beast in some wood;
Her fair face I see not, nor do I know
Another sun; these eyes have no goal else.
    To weep forever is my highest joy;   5
To laugh is woe, my food is poison, gall;
For me the night is sorrow, bright sky dark;
And bed for me a grievous battleground.
    Ah, truly, sleep is what men say it is,
Death's kinsman, and it takes my heart away   10
From that sweet worry which sustains my life.
    You fertile, happy land; green blooming shores
And shady slopes, in this world only you
Possess, and I bewail, my dearest good.

227

    Breeze, you embrace those blond and curling locks,
And stir in them, and by them, gently, you
Are stirred; you strew forth that sweet gold, then pick

et poi 'l raccogli, e 'n bei nodi il rincrespe,
    tu stai nelli occhi ond'amorose vespe   5
mi pungon sí, che 'nfin qua il sento et ploro,
et vacillando cerco il mio thesoro,
come animal che spesso adombre e 'ncespe:
    ch'or me 'l par ritrovar, et or m'accorgo
ch'i' ne son lunge, or mi sollievo or caggio,   10
ch'or quel ch'i' bramo, or quel ch'è vero scorgo.
    Aër felice, col bel vivo raggio
rimanti; et tu corrente et chiaro gorgo,
ché non poss'io cangiar teco vïaggio?

228

    Amor co la man dextra il lato manco
m'aperse, et piantòvi entro in mezzo 'l core
un lauro verde, sí che di colore
ogni smeraldo avria ben vinto et stanco.
    Vomer di pena, con sospir' del fianco,   5
e 'l piover giú dalli occhi un dolce humore
l'addornâr sí, ch'al ciel n'andò l'odore,
qual non so già se d'altre frondi unquanco.
    Fama, Honor et Vertute et Leggiadria,
casta bellezza in habito celeste   10
son le radici de la nobil pianta.
    Tal la mi trovo al petto, ove ch'i' sia,
felice incarco; et con preghiere honeste
l'adoro e 'nchino come cosa santa.

229

    Cantai, or piango, et non men di dolcezza
del pianger prendo che del canto presi,
ch'a la cagion, non a l'effetto, intesi
son i miei sensi vaghi pur d'altezza.
    Indi et mansüetudine et durezza   5
et atti feri, et humili et cortesi,
porto egualmente, né me gravan pesi,
né l'arme mie punta di sdegni spezza.
    Tengan dunque ver' me l'usato stile
Amor, madonna, il mondo et mia fortuna,   10
ch'i' non penso esser mai se non felice.
    Viva o mora o languisca, un piú gentile
stato del mio non è sotto la luna,
sí dolce è del mio amaro la radice.

It up again, and wreathe it in fair knots;
    You're there in eyes whence amorous wasps so sting   5
Me that I feel it even here, and mourn,
And wavering, search for my treasure like
An animal that often trips and shies;
    For now I seem to have her back, see now
I'm far from her, raised up now, now downcast,   10
I see now what I long for, now see truth.
    O blessed air, with that fair living ray
You bide, and you, O water flowing clear,
Why can I not exchange my course for yours?

228

    With his right hand my left side Love unsealed,
And there, amidst my heart, a laurel tree
He planted, one so green that every hue
Of emerald it conquered and made dim.
    With pen for plow, with heartfelt sighs, and with   5
This downpour of sweet humor from my eyes—
So nurtured, then, its fragrance spread to heaven;
If ever other boughs' did, I know not.
    Ah, Honor, Virtue, Gracefulness, and Fame,
Chaste beauty clothed in a celestial garb—   10
Of that illustrious plant these are the roots.
    A burden glad I find it in my breast
No matter where I am; in virtuous prayer
I bow, adore it as a sacred thing.

229

    I sang once, now I weep, but from my tears
Draw no less sweetness than I drew from song;
Since they care for the cause, not the effect,
My senses after loftiness still yearn.
    Since then, both mildness and severity,   5
Deeds fierce, and modest actions courteous,
I equally endure; nor does their weight
Oppress me, nor scorn's point my armor pierce.
    Let Love, my lady, fortune and the world
Their wonted manner, then, toward me maintain;   10
I can't think what to be, except content.
    Alive or dead or languishing, no state
Beneath the moon's more noble than my own,
So sweet the root is of my bitter lot.

I' piansi, or canto, ché 'l celeste lume
quel vivo sole alli occhi mei non cela,
nel qual honesto Amor chiaro revela
sua dolce forza et suo santo costume;
   onde e' suol trar di lagrime tal fiume,   5
per accorciar del mio viver la tela,
che non pur ponte o guado o remi o vela,
ma scampar non potienmi ale né piume.
   Sí profondo era et di sí larga vena
il pianger mio et sí lunge la riva,   10
ch'i' v'aggiungeva col penser a pena.
   Non lauro o palma, ma tranquilla oliva
Pietà mi manda, e 'l tempo rasserena,
e 'l pianto asciuga, et vuol anchor ch'i' viva.

I' mi vivea di mia sorte contento,
senza lagrime et senza invidia alcuna,
ché, s'altro amante à piú destra fortuna,
mille piacer' non vaglion un tormento.
   Or quei belli occhi ond'io mai non mi pento   5
de le mie pene, et men non ne voglio una,
tal nebbia copre, sí gravosa et bruna,
che 'l sol de la mia vita à quasi spento.
   O Natura, pietosa et fera madre,
onde tal possa et sí contrarie voglie   10
di far cose et disfar tanto leggiadre?
   D'un vivo fonte ogni poder s'accoglie:
ma Tu come 'l consenti, o sommo Padre,
che del Tuo caro dono altri ne spoglie?

Vincitore Alexandro l'ira vinse,
et fe' 'l minore in parte che Philippo:
che li val se Pyrgotile et Lysippo
l'intagliâr solo et Appelle il depinse?
   L'ira Tydëo a tal rabbia sospinse,   5
che, morendo ei, si róse Menalippo;
l'ira cieco del tutto, non pur lippo,
fatto avea Silla: a l'ultimo l'extinse.
   Sa 'l Valentinïan, ch'a simil pena
ira conduce: et sa 'l quei che ne more,   10

230

I used to weep but now I sing, since from
My eyes that living sun no longer hides
Her light celestial where chaste love reveals
His gentle might, and sacred practices.

    From my eyes he's accustomed to draw forth   5
Such streams of tears to shorten my life's thread
That not by bridge or ford could I escape,
Nor by oars, sail, or even feathered wings.

    My weeping was so deep, and from so wide
A wellspring, and the shore so far away,   10
That I could scarce arrive at it in thought.

    No laurel Mercy sends me, and no palm,
But peaceful olive, and the weather clears;°
She dries my tears and wills that I still live.°

231

I used to live contented with my lot,
With neither tears nor any envy, for
Though happier fortune other lovers have,
Their thousand joys aren't worth one pang of mine.

    Now those fair eyes on whose account I'll not   5
Repent my pains nor wish them one whit less
Are hidden by so thick and dark a fog
That my life's sun has almost been put out.

    O, Nature, mother fierce, compassionate,
Whence comes such power, and whence such wills opposed,
To fashion, then destroy such graceful things?

    All power from one living fount is drawn,
But how, O highest Father, can you let
Another strip your precious gift from us?

232

Wrath conquered Alexander, conqueror,
And therein made him less than Philip was;
What use if Pyrgoteles and Lysippus
Alone could sculpt him, and Appelles paint?

    Tydeus' wrath kept him so rabid that   5
While dying he chewed Menalippus' head.
And wrath made Sulla wholly blind, did not
Just cloud his sight, but killed him at the last.

    Valentinianus knows wrath leads
To penalties like that—and Ajax knows;   10

Aiace in molti, et poi in se stesso, forte.
Ira è breve furore, et chi nol frena,
è furor lungo, che 'l suo possessore
spesso a vergogna, et talor mena a morte.

233

Qual ventura mi fu, quando da l'uno
de' duo i piú belli occhi che mai furo,
mirandol di dolor turbato et scuro,
mosse vertú che fe' 'l mio infermo et bruno!
Send'io tornato a solver il digiuno   5
di veder lei che sola al mondo curo,
fummi il Ciel et Amor men che mai duro,
se tutte altre mie gratie inseme aduno:
ché dal dextr'occhio, anzi dal dextro sole,
de la mia donna al mio dextr'occhio venne   10
il mal che mi diletta, et non mi dole;
et pur com'intellecto avesse et penne,
passò quasi una stella che 'n ciel vole;
et Natura et Pietate il corso tenne.

234

O cameretta che già fosti un porto
a le gravi tempeste mie dïurne,
fonte se' or di lagrime nocturne,
che 'l dí celate per vergogna porto.
O letticciuol che requie eri et conforto   5
in tanti affanni, di che dogliose urne
ti bagna Amor, con quelle mani eburne,
solo ver' me crudeli a sí gran torto!
Né pur il mio secreto e 'l mio riposo
fuggo, ma piú me stesso e 'l mio pensero,   10
che, seguendol, talor levommi a volo;
e 'l vulgo a me nimico et odïoso
(chi 'l pensò mai?) per mio refugio chero:
tal paura ò di ritrovarmi solo.

235

Lasso, Amor mi trasporta ov'io non voglio,
et ben m'accorgo che 'l dever si varcha,
onde, a chi nel mio cor siede monarcha,
sono importuno assai piú ch'i' non soglio;
né mai saggio nocchier guardò da scoglio   5
nave di merci precïose carcha,

It killed that scourge of many and himself.

Wrath is brief madness, or long madness for
One who restrains it not; it often leads
Its owner to disgrace and sometimes death.°

233

What chance befell me when, from one of two
Of the most beauteous eyes that ever were,
When I perceived them strained and dark with woe,
A power stirred that made mine weak and dim.

To break my fast by seeing her whom I   5
Heed only in this world, I had returned;
And less than ever hard were Heaven and Love
Though all their former grace to me I count.

For from my lady's right eye—rather her
Right sun—there passed into my own right eye   10
This malady that brings me joy, not grief;

As if it had both intellect and wings,
It crossed, almost a star that shoots through heaven;
And Nature and Compassion held their course.

234

O little room, you sometimes were a port
In these oppressive daily storms of mine,
You are the fount, now, of my nightly tears,
Which for the shame I bear, the day conceals.

O little bed, a solace and a rest   5
In many trials, from what a doleful urn
Love bathes you with those hands of ivory,
So cruel to me alone, so wrongfully!

I flee not just seclusion and my rest,
But flee myself more, flee my very thoughts,   10
Which, heeded, in times past bore me aloft.

And for asylum, I seek out the crowd,
My odious foe—who'd ever credit that?
So much I fear to find myself alone.

235

Ah woe, Love bears me where I would not go—
Past reason as I well perceive—and thus
To one who reigns a queen within my heart,
Much more vexatious am I than before.

A wary pilot never kept off shoals   5
A ship with precious tradegoods laden full,

quant'io sempre la debile mia barcha
da le percosse del suo duro orgoglio.
    Ma lagrimosa pioggia et fieri vènti
d'infiniti sospiri or l'ànno spinta,   10
ch'è nel mio mare horribil notte et verno,
    ov'altrui noie, a sé doglie et tormenti
porta, et non altro, già da l'onde vinta,
disarmata di vele et di governo.

236

    Amor, io fallo, et veggio il mio fallire,
ma fo sí com'uom ch'arde e 'l foco à 'n seno,
ché 'l duol pur cresce, et la ragion vèn meno,
et è già quasi vinta dal martire.
    Solea frenare il mio caldo desire,   5
per non turbare il bel viso sereno:
non posso piú; di man m'ài tolto il freno,
et l'alma desperando à preso ardire.
    Però s'oltra suo stile ella s'aventa,
tu 'l fai, che sí l'accendi, et sí la sproni,   10
ch'ogni aspra via per sua salute tenta;
    et piú 'l fanno i celesti et rari doni
ch'à in sé madonna: or fa' almeno ch'ella il senta,
et le mie colpe a se stessa perdoni.

237

    Non à tanti animali il mar fra l'onde,
né lassú sopra 'l cerchio de la luna
vide mai tante stelle alcuna notte,
né tanti augelli albergan per li boschi,
né tant'erbe ebbe mai campo né piaggia,   5
quant'à 'l mio cor pensier' ciascuna sera.
    Di dí in dí spero omai l'ultima sera
che scevri in me dal vivo terren l'onde
et mi lasci dormire in qualche piaggia,
ché tanti affanni uom mai sotto la luna   10
non sofferse quant'io: sannolsi i boschi,
che sol vo ricercando giorno et notte.
    Io non ebbi già mai tranquilla notte,
ma sospirando andai matino et sera,
poi ch'Amor femmi un cittadin de' boschi.   15
Ben fia, prima ch'i' posi, il mar senz'onde,
et la sua luce avrà 'l sol da la luna,
e i fior' d'april morranno in ogni piaggia.

As I keep my frail vessel ever from
The buffets of her harsh, unyielding pride.
　　But tearful rains, and sighs' ferocious gales
That never cease, have now so driven it,　　　　　　10
There's dreadful night and winter on my sea,
　　Where vexing others, only grief and woe
It brings itself, already overwhelmed
By waves, and stripped of rudder and of sails.

236

　　I fail, Love, and I see my failure, but
Behave like one who burns with fire inside
His breast, for pain still grows and reason faints—
Indeed, is nearly vanquished by its woe.
　　My hot desire I used to curb so that　　　　　　5
I would not overcloud her tranquil face;
I can no more; from my hand you have wrenched
The reins and, stripped of hope, my soul's grown bold.
　　Thus, if my soul takes unaccustomed risks,
You cause it; you so spur and kindle her,　　　　　10
To save herself she tries out each hard path;
　　But most, my lady's rare celestial gifts
Account for it; may she at least take note
Of that, and my sins pardon in herself.

237

　　So many fish dwell not in ocean's waves,
Nor up above the circles of the moon
Were ever seen so many stars at night,
Nor live as many birds throughout the woods,
Nor any field has grass, nor any slope,　　　　　　5
As troubles to my heart come every eve.
　　Day in, day out, I hope for that last eve
That shall cut off my sentient clay from waves
And let me find my rest upon some slope;
Nor ever did a man beneath the moon　　　　　　10
Endure such worries as do I; the woods
Know I stray seeking, lonely, day and night.
　　I've never had again a peaceful night
But, sighing, passed the morning and the eve,
Since Love made me a freeman of the woods.　　　15
Before I rest, the sea will lose its waves,
And all his light shall sun take from the moon,
And April's blooms expire on every slope.

Consumando mi vo di piaggia in piaggia
el dí pensoso, poi piango la notte;   20
né stato ò mai, se non quanto la luna.
Ratto come imbrunir veggio la sera,
sospir' del petto, et de li occhi escono onde
da bagnar l'erbe, et da crollare i boschi.

Le città son nemiche, amici i boschi,   25
a' miei pensier', che per quest'alta piaggia
sfogando vo col mormorar de l'onde,
per lo dolce silentio de la notte:
tal ch'io aspetto tutto 'l dí la sera,
che 'l sol si parta et dia luogo a la luna.   30

Deh or foss'io col vago de la luna
adormentato in qua' che verdi boschi,
et questa ch'anzi vespro a me fa sera,
con essa et con Amor in quella piaggia
sola venisse a starsi ivi una notte;   35
e 'l dí si stesse e 'l sol sempre ne l'onde.

Sovra dure onde, al lume de la luna
canzon nata di notte in mezzo i boschi,
ricca piaggia vedrai deman da sera.

238

Real natura, angelico intelletto,
chiara alma, pronta vista, occhio cerviero,
providentia veloce, alto pensero,
et veramente degno di quel petto:

sendo di donne un bel numero eletto   5
per adornar il dí festo et altero,
súbito scorse il buon giudicio intero
fra tanti, et sí bei, volti il piú perfetto.

L'altre maggior' di tempo o di fortuna
trarsi in disparte comandò con mano,   10
et caramente accolse a sé quell'una.

Li occhi et la fronte con sembiante humano
basciolle sí che rallegrò ciascuna:
me empié d'invidia l'atto dolce et strano.

239

Là ver' l'aurora, che sí dolce l'aura
al tempo novo suol movere i fiori,
et li augelletti incominciar lor versi,
sí dolcemente i pensier' dentro a l'alma
mover mi sento a chi li à tutti in forza,   5

Wasting myself, I rove from slope to slope,
Spend all day pensive, weep away the night,   20
Find no more resting place than does the moon.
As quickly as I see grow dark the eve,
Sighs heave forth from my breast, from my eyes waves,
Which inundate the grass, uproot the woods.

Towns are the enemies, but friends the woods   25
To my sad thoughts, which I on this high slope
Go pouring forth with murmuring of the waves
All through the pleasant silence of the night
So that throughout the day I wait the eve
When sun departs and gives place to the moon.   30

Ah, would that by that lover of the moon°
I now lay slumbering in some green woods,
And she who before vespers brings me eve
With Love and with the moon upon that slope
Would come alone, there stay for just one night;   35
Then day and sun stay ever 'neath the waves!

By bitter waves and by the glimmering moon,
O song brought forth by night amidst the woods,
A bounteous slope you'll see tomorrow eve.

238

A nature regal, an angelic mind,
A bright soul, eager look, and lynx's eye,
Swift prescience, and those elevated thoughts
That certainly are fitting for his breast:°

To ornament that high and festive day,   5
A lovely group of ladies being picked,
At once his judgment, sound and good, discerned
The face most perfect 'midst so many fair,

The rest, in fortune greater or in age,
He ordered with his hand to draw aside,   10
And to himself he warmly welcomed her.

With courteous countenance, her eyes and brow
He kissed so each rejoiced; with jealousy
Though, his sweet unexpected deed filled me.

239

When dawn draws near, how sweetly the spring breeze
Is then accustomed to go stirring flowers,
And little birds to make anew their verse;
How sweetly I feel thoughts roused in my soul
By him who over all has such great power,   5

che ritornar convenmi a le mie note.
  Temprar potess'io in sí soavi note
i miei sospiri ch'addolcissen Laura,
faccendo a lei ragion ch'a me fa forza!
Ma pria fia 'l verno la stagion de'fiori,   10
ch'amor fiorisca in quella nobil alma,
che non curò già mai rime né versi.
  Quante lagrime, lasso, et quanti versi
ò già sparti al mio tempo, e 'n quante note
ò riprovato humilïar quell'alma!   15
Ella si sta pur com'aspr'alpe a l'aura
dolce, la qual ben move frondi et fiori,
ma nulla pò se 'ncontra maggior forza.
  Homini et dèi solea vincer per forza
Amor, come si legge in prose e 'n versi: 20
et io 'l provai in sul primo aprir de' fiori.
Ora né 'l mio signor né le sue note
né 'l pianger mio né i preghi pòn far Laura
trarre o di vita o di martir quest'alma.
  A l'ultimo bisogno, o misera alma,   25
accampa ogni tuo ingegno, ogni tua forza,
mentre fra noi di vita alberga l'aura.
Nulla al mondo è che non possano i versi:
et li aspidi incantar sanno in lor note,
nonché 'l gielo adornar di novi fiori.   30
  Ridon or per le piaggie herbette et fiori:
esser non pò che quella angelica alma
non senta il suon de l'amorose note.
Se nostra ria fortuna è di piú forza,
lagrimando et cantando i nostri versi   35
et col bue zoppo andrem cacciando l'aura.
  In rete accolgo l'aura, e 'n ghiaccio i fiori,
e 'n versi tento sorda et rigida alma,
che né forza d'Amor prezza né note.

240

  I' ò pregato Amor, e 'l ne riprego,
che mi scusi appo vio, dolce mia pena,
amaro mio dilecto, se con piena
fede dal dritto mio sentier mi piego.
  I' nol posso negar, donna, et nol nego,   5
che la ragion, ch'ogni bona alma affrena,
non sia dal voler vinta; ond'ei mi mena
talor in parte ov'io per forza il sego.

Who once again makes me resume my notes.
    Would I could temper in such gentle notes
My sighing so it makes more sweet my Breeze—°
Makes reason work in her as, in me, power!
But winter will become the time for flowers   10
Before love blooms within her noble soul
That never cared for poems nor for verse.
    Oh woe! how many tears and how much verse
I've scattered in my time; how many notes
I've tried but vainly, to bring low that soul!   15
She stands like rugged alps in the sweet breeze
That stirs the fronds, of course, and moves the flowers
But can do naught against a greater power.
    Love's used to conquering men and gods with power,
As can be read in prose as well as verse,   20
And this I proved with those first opening flowers.
Now neither can my lord nor can his notes
Nor weeping nor my prayers induce my Breeze
To draw from torture or from life this soul.
    In this last trial of yours, O wretched soul,   25
Your every talent marshal, all your power,
While still there shelters in our midst life's breeze.
In this world, naught exceeds the power of verse,
Which knows how to charm vipers with its notes
Not just how to bedeck frost with fresh flowers.   30
    Along the slopes now laugh spring grass and flowers;
It cannot be that her angelic soul
Hears not the music of those amorous notes;
Yet if our wicked fortune has more power,
We shall go weeping, singing out our verse   35
And with a limping ox go chase the breeze.
    In nets I gather breeze, in ice the flowers,
And tempt in verse a deaf, unyielding soul
Who neither values Love's power nor his notes.

240
    I've prayed to Love, and beg him now again
O my sweet punishment, my bitter joy,
That you'll forgive me in your mind if I
With utter faith stray from my proper path.
    My lady, I cannot—do not—deny   5
That reason, which curbs every worthy soul,
By will is vanquished, whence sometimes I'm led
To regions where perforce I follow him.

Voi, con quel cor, che di sí chiaro ingegno,
di sí alta vertute il cielo alluma,   10
quanto mai piovve da benigna stella,
　devete dir, pietosa et senza sdegno:
Che pò questi altro? il mio volto il consuma:
ei perché ingordo, et io perché sí bella?

241

L'alto signor dinanzi a cui non vale
nasconder né fuggir, né far difesa,
di bel piacer m'avea la mente accesa
con un ardente et amoroso strale;
　et benché 'l primo colpo aspro et mortale   5
fossi da sé, per avanzar sua impresa
una saetta di pietate à presa,
et quinci et quindi il cor punge et assale.
　L'una piaga arde, et versa foco et fiamma;
lagrime l'altra che 'l dolor distilla,   10
per li occhi mei, del vostro stato rio:
　né per duo fonti sol una favilla
rallenta de l'incendio che m'infiamma,
anzi per la pietà cresce 'l desio.

242

Mira quel colle, o stanco mio cor vago:
ivi lasciammo ier lei, ch'alcun tempo ebbe
qualche cura di noi, et le ne 'ncrebbe,
or vorria trar de li occhi nostri un lago.
　Torna tu in là, ch'io d'esser sol m'appago;   5
tenta se forse anchor tempo sarebbe
da scemar nostro duol, che 'nfin qui crebbe,
o del mio mal participe et presago.
　—Or tu ch'ài posto te stesso in oblio
et parli al cor pur come e' fusse or teco,   10
miser, et pien di pensier' vani et sciocchi!
　ch'al dipartir dal tuo sommo desio
tu te n'andasti, e' si rimase seco,
et si nascose dentro a' suoi belli occhi.

243

Fresco, ombroso, fiorito et verde colle,
ov'or pensando et or cantando siede,
et fa qui de' celesti spirti fede,
quella ch'a tutto 'l mondo fama tolle:

You, with that heart which heaven sets alight
With lofty virtue and so bright a mind—   10
As much as ever from a kind star rained—
    Not with disdain, with ruth you ought to say:
"How else can he behave? My face melts him:
He, why so greedy? Why so lovely I?"

241

    That haughty lord before whom it does not
Avail to hide, or flee, or frame defence,
With sweet delight has set my mind afire
With one dart blazing hot and amorous.
    Though that first hit was harsh and deadly by   5
Itself, he seized an arrow of compassion to
Promote his cause; and first with that, then this
He stings my heart and mounts assault on it.
    The first wound burns and spills forth fire and flame;
The other one sheds tears that through my eyes   10
My woe distills at that sad plight of yours.
    But not a single spark is quenched by those
Two fountains, of this fire where I'm aflame,
Instead, through pity passion greater grows.

242°

    "Behold that hill, my weary, straying heart;
There yesterday we left her, who sometimes
Paid us a little heed and pitied us;
Who now would bring a lake forth from our eyes.
    "Go back there—I'm content to stay alone—   5
See if perhaps it's time yet to abate
Our sorrow, which till now has grown apace,
O partner and presager of my ill."
    "Now you have quite forgot yourself; as if
Your heart were with you still to him you speak,   10
Poor wretch, and filled with hollow, silly thoughts!
    "For in departing from your highest joy
You went from him, and he remained with her,
And in her lovely eyes concealed himself."

243

    O flowered, verdant, fresh and shady hill,
Where now she sits in thought and now in song,
And, here, in heavenly spirits gives us faith,
She who has robbed its fame from all the world.

il mio cor che per lei lasciar mi volle   5
(et fe' gran senno, et piú se mai non riede)
va or contando ove da quel bel piede
segnata è l'erba, et da quest'occhi è molle.

Seco si stringe, et dice a ciascun passo:
Deh fusse or qui quel miser pur un poco,   10
ch'è già di pianger et di viver lasso!

Ella sel ride, et non è pari il gioco:
tu paradiso, i' senza cor un sasso,
o sacro, aventuroso et dolce loco.

244

Il mal mi preme, et mi spaventa il peggio,
al qual veggio sí larga et piana via,
ch'i' son intrato in simil frenesia,
et con duro penser teco vaneggio;

né so se guerra o pace a Dio mi cheggio,   5
ché 'l danno è grave, et la vergogna è ria.
Ma perché piú languir? di noi pur fia
quel ch'ordinato è già nel sommo seggio.

Bench'i' non sia di quel grand'onor degno
che tu mi fai, ché te n'inganna Amore,   10
che spesso occhio ben san fa veder torto,

pur d'alzar l'alma a quel celeste regno
è il mio consiglio, et di spronare il core:
perché 'l camin è lungo, e 'l tempo è corto.

245

Due rose fresche, et colte in paradiso
l'altrier, nascendo il dí primo di maggio,
bel dono, et d'un amante antiquo et saggio,
tra duo minori egualmente diviso

con sí dolce parlar et con un riso   5
da far innamorare un huom selvaggio,
di sfavillante et amoroso raggio
et l'un et l'altro fe' cangiare il viso.

—Non vede un simil par d'amanti il sole—
dicea, ridendo et sospirando inseme;   10
et stringendo ambedue, volgeasi a torno.

Cosí partia le rose et le parole,
onde 'l cor lasso anchor s'allegra et teme:
o felice eloquentia, o lieto giorno!

My heart, who wished to leave me for her (and   5
Great sense showed—more if never he returns)
Strays counting places now, where grass is blest
By her fair foot, and watered by my eyes.

He presses near her, and at each step says:
"Ah would that wretch, already weary of   10
Both tears and life, were here for just a while."

At that she smiles, the contest is no match:
You're paradise, and I'm stone with no heart,
O place so sacred, fortunate, and sweet.

244
I'm crushed by ill, appalled, too, by the worst
Toward which I see a way so wide and clear
That like you, into frenzy I have lapsed°
And in my laboring thoughts with you I rave.

And whether to beg peace or war from God   5
I do not know; harm's grave, and shame is wrong.
But why pine longer? In the highest seat
Our future has already been decreed.

Though I don't merit that great honor you
Pay me, for Love deceives you in this now;   10
He often makes a sound eye see askew.

To raise your soul to that celestial realm
Is my advice still, and to spur your heart
Because the journey's long, and time is brief.

245
Two roses fresh were picked in paradise
Just two days past at break of May's first day—
A fine gift by a lover old and sage,
Shared out between two young ones equally

With such sweet speech and with a smile to make   5
A rude and savage person fall in love,
And by its amorous and brilliant beam,
To change first one, and then the other's face.

"No lovers like this pair the sun will see,"
He said, and at the same time smiled and sighed,   10
And, having clasped them both, he turned away.

Thus each he gave his roses and his words;
At that my worn heart gladdens still, and fears.
O happy eloquence, O joyous day!

L'aura che 'l verde lauro et l'aureo crine
soavemente sospirando move,
fa con sue viste leggiadrette et nove
l'anime da' lor corpi pellegrine.

    Candida rosa nata in dure spine,   5
quando fia chi sua pari al mondo trove,
gloria di nostra etate? O vivo Giove,
manda, prego, il mio in prima che 'l suo fine:

    sí ch'io non veggia il gran publico danno,
e 'l mondo remaner senza 'l suo sole,   10
né li occhi miei, che luce altra non ànno;

    né l'alma che pensar d'altro non vòle,
né l'orecchie, ch'udir altro non sanno,
senza l'oneste sue dolci parole.

    Parrà forse ad alcun che 'n lodar quella
ch'i' adoro in terra, errante sia 'l mio stile,
faccendo lei sovr'ogni altra gentile,
santa, saggia, leggiadra, honesta et bella.

    A me par il contrario; et temo ch'ella   5
non abbia a schifo il mio dir troppo humile,
degna d'assai piú alto et piú sottile:
et chi nol crede, venga egli a vedella;

    sí dirà ben: Quello ove questi aspira
è cosa da stancare Athene, Arpino,   10
Mantova et Smirna, et l'una et l'altra lira.

    Lingua mortale al suo stato divino
giunger non pote: Amor la spinge et tira,
non per electïon, ma per destino.

    Chi vuol veder quantunque pò Natura
e 'l Ciel tra noi, venga a mirar costei,
ch'è sola un sol, non pur a li occhi mei,
ma al mondo cieco, che vertú non cura;

    et venga tosto, perché Morte fura   5
prima i migliori, et lascia star i rei:
questa aspettata al regno delli dèi
cosa bella mortal passa, et non dura.

    Vedrà, s'arriva a tempo, ogni vertute,
ogni bellezza, ogni real costume,   10
giunti in un corpo con mirabil' tempre:

246

The breeze that sways the verdant laurel, and
That gently sighing, stirs those golden locks,
With rare, alluring glimpses makes souls go
Out from their bodies, pilgrim wanderers.
    A pure white rose, sprung forth amidst cruel thorns: 5
When will one like it in this world be found,
The glory of our age? O living Jove,
I pray, send me my end before her own;
    Thus I'll not see that great communal loss,°
See left behind the world without its sun,   10
And my eyes too, which have no other light,
    And my soul, which would think of nothing else,
And my ears, which can hear no other thing
Without those sweet and virtuous words of hers.

247

    It will to some, perhaps, seem that my style
In praising her whom I adore on earth,
Is wrong to draw her far above the rest,
Wise, noble, holy, charming, chaste, and fair.
    The case seems opposite to me; I fear   5
That she may scorn my far too modest speech;
She merits what is highest and most fine;
Who thinks not so, to see her let him come.
    Sure he'll speak thus: "To aim where he aspires
Would tire Arpinum, Athens, Mantua,   10
And Smyrna, and the one and other lyre.°
    "Her state divine a mortal tongue cannot
Describe; Love urges it and draws it on,
Not by election, but by destiny."

248

    Who'd see what Nature and what Heaven can frame
Among us, let him come admire her who
Alone a sun is—not just to my eyes—
But to a world gone blind, which heeds not worth;
    And let him come at once, for death first steals   5
The best, and leaves the wicked still behind.
This one, awaited where gods reign, a fair
And mortal thing, will pass and not endure.
    He'll gaze upon—if he arrives in time—
All virtue, beauty, regal manner joined   10
In one flesh with admixture marvellous;

allor dirà che mie rime son mute,
l'ingegno offeso dal soverchio lume;
ma se piú tarda, avrà da pianger sempre.

249

Qual paura ò, quando mi torna a mente
quel giorno ch'i' lasciai grave et pensosa
madonna, e 'l mio cor seco! et non è cosa
che sí volentier pensi, et sí sovente.
I' la riveggio starsi humilemente   5
tra belle donne, a guisa d'una rosa
tra minor' fior', né lieta né dogliosa,
come chi teme, et altro mal non sente.
Deposta avea l'usata leggiadria,
le perle et le ghirlande e i panni allegri,   10
e 'l riso e 'l canto e 'l parlar dolce humano.
Cosí in dubbio lasciai la vita mia:
or tristi auguri, et sogni et penser' negri
mi dànno assalto, et piaccia a Dio che 'nvano.

250

Solea lontana in sonno consolarme
con quella dolce angelica sua vista
madonna; or mi spaventa et mi contrista,
né di duol né di tema posso aitarme:
ché spesso nel suo volto veder parme   5
vera pietà con grave dolor mista,
et udir cose onde 'l cor fede acquista
che di gioia et di speme si disarme.
«Non ti soven di quella ultima sera
—dice ella—ch'i' lasciai li occhi tuoi molli   10
et sforzata dal tempo me n'andai?
I' non tel potei dir, allor, né volli;
or tel dico per cosa experta et vera:
non sperar di vedermi in terra mai».

251

O misera et horribil visïone!
E dunque ver che 'nnanzi tempo spenta
sia l'alma luce che suol far contenta
mia vita in pene et in speranze bone?
Ma come è che sí gran romor non sone   5
per altri messi, et per lei stessa il senta?
Or già Dio et Natura nol consenta,

Then he shall say my poetry is mute,
My wit is addled by that sovereign light;
But if he's late, forever must he weep.

249
How fearful I become when I recall
That day I left my lady, thoughtful, grave,
And left with her my heart! And yet I think
Of nothing else so fondly, or so oft.
    Again I see her standing modestly   5
Among fair ladies, looking like a rose
'Midst lesser flowers, neither gay nor sad,
Like one who fears, but feels no evil else.
    Accustomed elegance she'd laid aside—
Her pearls and garlands and her cheerful clothes,   10
Her laugh, her song and her sweet, gracious speech.
    Thus in uncertainty I left my life;
Now omens sad, sad dreams and darkened thoughts°
Lay siege to me: pray God they are but vain.

250
In sleep, though far away, my lady used
To soothe me with her sweet angelic look,
But now she frightens and she saddens me,
Nor can I help myself in fear or woe;
    For often in her face I seem to see   5
Compassion true with heavy sorrow mixed,
And seem to hear things that convince my heart
It must disarm itself of joy and hope.
    "Don't you remember how, that final night,"
She says, "I left you with your tearful eyes,   10
And pressed by time, I went away from you?
    "I could not tell you then, nor wished I to;
Now as a certainty, I tell you this:
Hope not to see me ever more on earth."

251
O woe! Unhappy vision horrible!
Before her time, is her life-giving light
In truth put out, which always made my life
Content in pain or expectation fair?
    But why is such grave news not cried aloud   5
By other heralds? Why hear it from herself?
Sure God and Nature will not let that be!

et falsa sia mia trista opinïone.
    A me pur giova di sperare anchora
la dolce vista del bel viso adorno,   10
che me mantene, e 'l secol nostro honora.
    Se per salir a l'eterno soggiorno
uscita è pur del bel'albergo fora,
prego non tardi il mio ultimo giorno.

252

    In dubbio di mio stato, or piango or canto,
et temo et spero; et in sospiri e 'n rime
sfogo il mio incarco: Amor tutte sue lime
usa sopra 'l mio core, afflicto tanto.
    Or fia già mai che quel bel viso santo   5
renda a quest'occhi le lor luci prime
(lasso, non so che di me stesso estime)?
o li condanni a sempiterno pianto;
    et per prendere il ciel, debito a lui,
non curi che si sia di loro in terra,   10
di ch'egli è 'l sole, et non veggiono altrui?
    In tal paura e 'n sí perpetua guerra
vivo ch'i' non son piú quel che già fui,
qual chi per via dubbiosa teme et erra.

253

    O dolci sguardi, o parolette accorte,
or fia mai il dí ch'i' vi riveggia et oda?
O chiome bionde di che 'l cor m'annoda
Amor, et cosí preso il mena a morte;
    o bel viso a me dato in dura sorte,   5
di ch'io sempre pur pianga, et mai non goda:
o chiuso inganno et amorosa froda,
darmi un piacer che sol pena m'apporte!
    Et se talor da' belli occhi soavi,
ove mia vita e 'l mio pensero alberga,   10
forse mi vèn qualche dolcezza honesta,
    súbito, a ciò ch'ogni mio ben disperga
et m'allontane, or fa cavalli or navi
Fortuna, ch'al mio mal sempre è sí presta.

254

    I' pur ascolto, et non odo novella
de la dolce et amata mia nemica,
né so ch'i' me ne pensi o ch'i' mi dica,

Now let my sorrowful surmise be false!
    It does me good still to expect to have
The sweet sight of her fair and comely face,
Which nutures me, and honors this our age.
    If to ascend to her eternal home
Indeed she's gone forth from her fair abode,
I pray my final day will not come late.

252

    In doubt about my state, now I shed tears,
Now sing, fear, hope; and my anxiety
I ease with sighs and rhymes; Love uses all
His rasps upon my sore-afflicted heart:
    Nor ever will her holy, sacred face
Restore to these eyes their chief light? (alas!
I know not how to weigh this by myself)
Or will it damn them to eternal tears?
    Will heaven, taking what is owing it
Heed not what may become of those on earth,
For whom she is the sun, who see naught else?
    In such dread, and such war perpetual
I live that I am not what I once was,
But one who on a dark path fears and strays.

253

    O glances sweet, O clever little words,
Will that day ever come when, once more, I
Shall see and hear you? O blonde hair with which
Love snares my heart, that captured thus is led
    To death; O fair face, gift of my hard fate,
For which I ever weep, am never glad:
O secret fraud and amorous deceit
To grant me joy that brings me only pain.
    And if sometimes from soft, fair eyes where dwell
My life and thoughts, some sweetness virtuous
Perhaps should come to me, then Fortune, who
    Is ever eager for my ill, prepares
Now ships, now horses hastily, so all
My good may be dispersed, and I sent far.

254

    Though ever listening, I hear no news
Of my sweet and beloved foe; nor know
I what to think or tell myself of her,

sí 'l cor tema et speranza mi puntella.

 Nocque ad alcuna già l'esser sí bella;   5
questa piú d'altra è bella et piú pudica:
forse vuol Dio tal di vertute amica
tôrre a la terra, e 'n ciel farne una stella;
 anzi un sole: et se questo è, la mia vita,
i miei corti riposi e i lunghi affanni   10
son giunti al fine. O dura dipartita,
 perché lontan m'ài fatto da' miei danni?
La mia favola breve è già compita,
et fornito il mio tempo a mezzo gli anni.

255
 La sera desïare, odiar l'aurora
soglion questi tranquilli et lieti amanti;
a me doppia la sera et doglia et pianti,
la matina è per me piú felice hora:
 ché spesso in un momento apron allora   5
l'un sole et l'altro quasi duo levanti,
di beltate et di lume sí sembianti,
ch'anco il ciel de la terra s'innamora;
 come già fece allor che' primi rami
verdeggiâr, che nel cor radice m'ànno,   10
per cui sempre altrui piú che me stesso ami.
 Cosí di me due contrarie hore fanno;
et chi m'acqueta è ben ragion ch'i' brami,
et tema et odî chi m'adduce affanno.

256
 Far potess'io vendetta di colei
che guardando et parlando mi distrugge,
et per piú doglia poi s'asconde et fugge,
celando li occhi a me sí dolci et rei.
 Cosí li afflicti et stanchi spirti mei   5
a poco a poco consumando sugge,
e 'n sul cor quasi fiero leon rugge
la notte allor quand'io posar devrei.
 L'alma, cui Morte del suo albergo caccia,
da me si parte, et di tal nodo sciolta,   10
vassene pur a lei che la minaccia.
 Meravigliomi ben s'alcuna volta,
mentre le parla et piange et poi l'abbraccia,
non rompe il sonno suo, s'ella l'ascolta.

In hope and fear my heart is so confirmed.
　　To be so lovely harmed someone before; 5
More than that other is she fair and chaste,
And such a friend of virtue, God perhaps
Wants raised from earth to form a star in heaven—
　　A sun instead; and should this be, my life,
My respites brief, my troubles long, are at 10
An end. O separation hard, why have
　　You kept me far from my adversities?
My little fable is already done
And my life ended in my middle years.

255

　　For evening always yearning, hating dawn
Are these untroubled lovers full of joy.
To me, though, nightfall doubles woes and tears,
Most happy is the morning hour for me.
　　Because then, in one moment often shine 5
Both my sun and that other—almost two
Levants—so like in light and loveliness°
That even heaven falls in love with earth
　　As once it did when those first branches greened
That in my heart have roots; more than myself 10
Since then I've always loved another one.
　　If two opposing hours treat me thus,
I'm right to yearn for one that makes me calm,
And fear and hate the one that brings me woe.

256

　　If only I could take revenge on her,
Who melts me with her glances and her speech,
Then to my greater sorrow, hides and flees,
Concealing such sweet wicked eyes from me.
　　And so my spirits, weary and distressed, 5
She saps as she consumes them bit by bit,
And over my heart like a lion fierce
Roars in the night when I should have repose.
　　My soul, whom death pursues from its abode,
Departs from me, and from that bond set free 10
Goes straightaway to her who threatens it.
　　Indeed, I am amazed that, sometimes, while
It speaks to her, weeps, then embraces her,
Her sleep's not shattered, if she gives it ear.

257

In quel bel viso ch'i' sospiro et bramo,
fermi eran li occhi desïosi e 'ntensi,
quando Amor porse, quasi a dir «che pensi?»,
quella honorata man che second' amo.

Il cor, preso ivi come pesce a l'amo,   5
onde a ben far per vivo exempio viensi,
al ver non volse li occupati sensi,
o come novo augello al visco in ramo.

Ma la vista, privata del suo obiecto,
quasi sognando si facea far via,   10
senza la qual è 'l suo bene imperfecto.

L'alma tra l'una et l'altra gloria mia
qual celeste non so novo dilecto
et qual strania dolcezza si sentia.

258

Vive faville uscian de' duo bei lumi
ver' me sí dolcemente folgorando,
et parte d'un cor saggio sospirando
d'alta eloquentia sí soavi fiumi,

che pur il rimembrar par mi consumi   5
qualor a quel dí torno, ripensando
come venieno i miei spirti mancando
al varïar de' suoi duri costumi.

L'alma, nudrita sempre in doglia e 'n pene
(quanto è 'l poder d'una prescritta usanza!),   10
contra 'l doppio piacer sí 'nferma fue,

ch'al gusto sol del disusato bene,
tremando or di paura or di speranza,
d'abandonarme fu spesso entra due.

259

Cercato ò sempre solitaria vita
(le rive il sanno, et le campagne e i boschi)
per fuggir questi ingegni sordi et loschi,
che la strada del cielo ànno smarrita;

et se mia voglia in ciò fusse compita,   5
fuor del dolce aere de' paesi toschi
anchor m'avria tra' suoi bei colli foschi
Sorga, ch'a pianger et cantar m'aita.

Ma mia fortuna, a me sempre nemica,
mi risospigne al loco ov'io mi sdegno   10
veder nel fango il bel tesoro mio.

257

On that fair face for which I long and sigh,
My urgent and impassioned eyes had paused
When Love, as if to say: "What do you think?"
Stretched forth that hand revered, my second love.

    My heart, caught fish-like on a hook, or like   5
A fledgling on a lime-smeared bough, enthralled
By such a living instance of good works,
Turned not distracted senses toward the truth,

    Yet sight, denied its object, still contrived
To find that pathway—as if in a dream—   10
Without which its well-being is impaired.

    Between my glories two, this one and that,
My soul experienced I know not what
New joy celestial, and what sweetness rare.

258

    From two fair eyes toward me flew living sparks
So sweetly flashing, and such gentle streams
Of lofty eloquence flowed sighing from
A heart that's wise, that just remembering

    It seems I am consumed, when to that day   5
I turn again, whenever I recall
the way my spirits quailed and fainted at
That variation from her usage cruel.

    My soul, forever fed on woe and pain
(How great's the power of a habit fixed!)   10
Against that double pleasure was so weak

    That merely tasting that unwonted good
And trembling now for fear and now for hope,
Oft it near stranded me between the two.

259

    I've ever sought the solitary life
(The banks of streams, the fields and woods know that)
To flee those squint-eyed and unhearing wits
Who've wandered from the way that leads to heaven.

    And if my will in this had been fulfilled,   5
Far from the Tuscan countryside's sweet air,
Then still, to help me weep and sing, would Sorgue°
Keep me amidst its fair and hazy hills.

    My fortune, though, who ever was my foe,
To that place goads me where I grow enraged   10
To see my lovely treasure in the mire.

A la man ond'io scrivo è fatta amica
a questa volta, et non è forse indegno:
Amor sel vide, et sa 'l madonna et io.

260

In tale stella duo belli occhi vidi,
tutti pien' d'onestate et di dolcezza,
che presso a quei d'Amor leggiadri nidi
il mio cor lasso ogni altra vista sprezza.
    Non si pareggi a lei qual piú s'aprezza,   5
in qual ch'etade, in quai che strani lidi:
non chi recò con sua vaga bellezza
in Grecia affanni, in Troia ultimi stridi;
    no la bella romana che col ferro
apre il suo casto et disdegnoso petto;   10
non Polixena, Ysiphile et Argia.
    Questa excellentia è gloria, s'i' non erro,
grande a Natura, a me sommo diletto,
ma' che vèn tardo, et súbito va via.

261

Qual donna attende a glorïosa fama
di senno, di valor, di cortesia,
miri fiso nelli occhi a quella mia
nemica, che mia donna il mondo chiama.
    Come s'acquista honor, come Dio s'ama,   5
come è giunta honestà con leggiadria,
ivi s'impara, et qual è dritta via
di gir al ciel, che lei aspetta et brama.
    Ivi 'l parlar che nullo stile aguaglia,
e 'l bel tacere, et quei cari costumi,   10
che 'ngegno human non pò spiegar in carte;
    l'infinita belleza ch'altrui abbaglia,
non vi s'impara: ché quei dolci lumi
s'acquistan per ventura et non per arte.

262

—Cara la vita, et dopo lei mi pare
vera honestà, che 'n bella donna sia.
—L'ordine volgi: e' non fur, madre mia,
senza honestà mai cose belle o care,
    et qual si lascia di suo honor privare,   5
né donna è piú né viva; et se qual pria
appare in vista, è tal vita aspra et ria

But this time, now, my writing hand has she
Befriended, not unworthily, perhaps.
That Love saw, and my lady and I know.

260

Two lovely eyes, all filled with sweetness and
With chastity I saw in such a star
That near those winsome nests of Love my heart,
Worn out, disdains all other sights but this.

She has no peer, no matter how much prized   5
In other ages or on foreign strands;
Not she who with her beauty's wanton charm°
Brought woe to Greece, to Troy its last shrill cries.

Nor that fair Roman who with iron unsealed°
Her chaste and scornful breast, nor Argia,   10
Nor Polyxena nor Hypsipyle.°

This excellence, to Nature glory great—
If I err not—to me is highest joy,
But it comes late, and passes soon away.

261

A lady seeking glorious renown
For judgment, valor, or for courtesy,
Can gaze deep in the eyes of this my foe,
This one who's called my lady by the world.

How one gains honor and how one loves God,   5
How chastity and gracefulness are joined
She there will learn, and what's the straightest path
To take to Heaven, which waits and yearns for her;

There speech unmatched by any style she'll learn,
And that fair silence, and those habits dear   10
That human skill in pages can't explain;

That beauty infinite which dazzles men,
There she'll not learn, because those sweet lights are
Acquired through destiny, and not through art.

262

"Life is most precious; next, true chastity
In a fair lady, as it seems to me."
"You twist the order, mother mine; unchaste,
There never were things precious, never fair;

"And she who lets her chastity be stripped   5
No more a lady is, nor does she live;
If she seems as before, far harsher is

via piú che morte, et di piú pene amare.
    Né di Lucretia mi meravigliai,
se non come a morir le bisognasse   10
ferro, et non le bastasse il dolor solo.—
    Vengan quanti philosophi fur mai,
a dir di ciò: tutte lor vie fien basse;
et quest'una vedremo alzarsi a volo.

263

    Arbor victorïosa trïumphale,
honor d'imperadori et di poeti,
quanti m'ài fatto dí dogliosi et lieti
in questa breve mia vita mortale!
    vera donna, et a cui di nulla cale,   5
se non d'onor, che sovr'ogni altra mieti,
né d'Amor visco temi, o lacci o reti,
né ngano altrui contr'al tuo senno vale.
    Gentileza di sangue, et l'altre care
cose tra noi, perle et robini et oro,   10
quasi vil soma egualmente dispregi.
    L'alta beltà ch'al mondo non à pare
noia t'è, se non quanto il bel thesoro
di castità par ch'ella adorni et fregi.

264

    I' vo pensando, et nel penser m'assale
una pietà sí forte di me stesso,
che mi conduce spesso
ad altro lagrimar ch'i' non soleva:
ché, vedendo ogni giorno il fin piú presso,   5
mille fiate ò chieste a Dio quell'ale
co le quai del mortale
carcer nostro intelletto al ciel si leva.
Ma infin a qui nïente mi releva
prego o sospiro o lagrimar ch'io faccia: 10
e cosí per ragion conven che sia,
ché chi, possendo star, cadde tra via,
degno è che mal suo grado a terra giaccia.
Quelle pietose braccia
in ch'io mi fido, veggio aperte anchora,   15
ma temenza m'accora
per gli altrui exempli, et del mio stato tremo,
ch'altri mi sprona, et son forse a l'extremo.

Such life than death—more ill, more bitter pain.
    "Nor did I wonder at Lucretia,°
Except she needed iron to die, and that   10
Her sorrow by itself did not suffice."
    Though all philosophers who ever lived
Dispute of this, their methods will creep low;
This reasoning we'll see rise up in flight.

263

    O you victorious and triumphal tree,
Glory of poets, and of emperors,
How many doleful days, and happy too
You've caused me in my brief and mortal life!
    True lady, only honor do you prize,   5
And far above the rest you garner it;
Love's birdlime you fear not, no springes, nets;°
No ruse against your judgment can avail.
    Nobility of birth, those other things
Precious to us, like rubies, pearls, and gold,   10
You equally disparage as vile dross.
    Your lofty beauty, peerless in the world,
Proves vexing but as it seems to adorn
And grace your treasure fair of chastity.

264

    I wander thinking, and within my thoughts
Such fierce self-pity lays me siege that I
Am often led to tears
Much different from the ones I used to weep.
For, seeing every day my end more near,   5
A thousand times I've begged God for those wings
On which our intellect
May fly this mortal prison up to heaven.
But nothing up till now has brought relief—
No prayer, no sigh, no tears that I bring forth;   10
And properly, for whosoever can
Stand firm, yet falls along the way, deserves
Despite himself to lie inert on earth.
Those arms compassionate,
In which I trust, I see still open wide,   15
But fear my heart transfixes
At others' plights, and for my state I quake;
They spur me on, and near my end I seem.

L'un penser parla co la mente, et dice:
—Che pur agogni? onde soccorso attendi?   20
Misera, non intendi
con quanto tuo disnore il tempo passa?
Prendi partito accortamente, prendi;
e del cor tuo divelli ogni radice
del piacer che felice   25
nol pò mai fare, et respirar nol lassa.
Se già è gran tempo fastidita et lassa
se' di quel falso dolce fugitivo
che 'l mondo traditor può dare altrui,
a che ripon' piú la speranza in lui,   30
che d'ogni pace et di fermezza è privo?
Mentre che 'l corpo è vivo,
ài tu 'l freno in bailia de' penser' tuoi:
deh stringilo or che pôi,
ché dubbioso è 'l tardar come tu sai,   35
e 'l cominciar non fia per tempo omai.
    Già sai tu ben quanta dolcezza porse
agli occhi tuoi la vista di colei
la qual ancho vorrei
ch'a nascer fosse per piú nostra pace.   40
Ben ti ricordi, et ricordar te 'n dêi,
de l'imagine sua quand'ella corse
al cor, là dove forse
non potea fiamma intrar per altrui face:
ella l'accese; et se l'ardor fallace   45
durò molt'anni in aspectando un giorno,
che per nostra salute unqua non vène,
or ti solleva a piú beata spene,
mirando 'l ciel che ti si volve intorno,
immortal et addorno: 50
ché dove, del mal suo qua giú sí lieta,
vostra vaghezza acqueta
un mover d'occhi, un ragionar, un canto,
quanto fia quel piacer, se questo è tanto?—
    Da l'altra parte un pensier dolce et agro,   55
con faticosa et dilectevol salma
sedendosi entro l'alma,
preme 'l cor di desio, di speme il pasce;
che sol per fama glorïosa et alma
non sente quand'io agghiaccio, o quand'io flagro,   60
s'i' son pallido o magro;
et s'io l'occido piú forte rinasce.

One thought discourses with my mind, and says:
"What do you covet still? Whence succor wait?   20
Wretch, do you fathom not
With what dishonor to you time goes by?
With wisdom make your mind up! Make it up!
And from your heart each root of joy rip out,
Joy that can never make   25
It happy, and that never lets it breathe.
If long you've been offended, and indeed
Worn down by sweetness false and fugitive—
Such as this traitor world can give mankind—
Why any longer rest your hope in that,   30
Devoid of peace and all stability?
While still the body lives
You have in charge the reins of your own thought:
Ah, curb it while you can;
Delay is dangerous as you well know,   35
And to begin now will be none too soon.
     "Indeed, you well know how much joy the sight
Of her has brought your eyes—she who I wish,
For our much greater peace,
Had yet still to be born. Well you recall—   40
And well you must recall—her image when
It rushed into your heart, there where perhaps
No other torch's flame
Could enter in: She kindled it, and if
Misleading ardor for so many years   45
Endured in expectation of a day,
One which for our salvation does not come,
Now raise yourself to a more blissful hope
Watching the heavens that, immortal and
Bespangled, round you wheel.   50
For if, so joyful in its ill down here,
Your longing's quieted
By glancing eyes, or discourse, or a song,
How great will be that joy if this is such?"
     Then on the other side, a bitter thought   55
And sweet, with weary, pleasing weight sits down
Within my soul; my heart
It crushes with desire, yet feeds it hope;
On glorious, life-giving fame's account
Alone, it feels not when I freeze or blaze,   60
Or if I'm wan and thin;
And if I kill it, stronger it's reborn.

Questo d'allor ch'i' m'addormiva in fasce
venuto è di dí in dí crescendo meco,
e temo ch'un sepolcro ambeduo chiuda.   65
Poi che fia l'alma de le membra ignuda,
non pò questo desio piú venir seco;
ma se 'l latino e 'l greco
parlan di me dopo la morte, è un vento:
ond'io, perché pavento   70
adunar sempre quel ch'un'ora sgombre,
vorre' 'l ver abbracciar, lassando l'ombre.

    Ma quell'altro voler di ch'i' son pieno,
quanti press'a lui nascon par ch'adugge;
e parte il tempo fugge   75
che, scrivendo d'altrui, di me non calme;
e 'l lume de' begli occhi che mi strugge
soavemente al suo caldo sereno,
mi ritien con un freno
contra chui nullo ingegno o forza valme.   80
Che giova dunque perché tutta spalme
la mia barchetta, poi che 'nfra li scogli
è ritenuta anchor da ta' duo nodi?
Tu che dagli altri, che 'n diversi modi
legano 'l mondo, in tutto mi disciogli,   85
Signor mio, ché non togli
omai dal volto mio questa vergogna?
Ché 'n guisa d'uom che sogna
aver la morte inanzi gli occhi parme;
et vorrei far difesa, et non ò l'arme.   90

    Quel ch'i' fo veggio, et non m'inganna il vero
mal conosciuto, anzi mi sforza Amore,
che la strada d'onore
mai nol lassa seguir, chi troppo il crede;
et sento ad ora ad or venirmi al core   95
un leggiadro disdegno aspro et severo
ch'ogni occulto pensero
tira in mezzo la fronte, ov'altri 'l vede:
ché mortal cosa amar con tanta fede
quanta a Dio sol per debito convensi,   100
piú si disdice a chi piú pregio brama.
Et questo ad alta voce ancho richiama
la ragione svïata dietro ai sensi;
ma perch'ell'oda, et pensi
tornare, il mal costume oltre la spigne,   105
et agli occhi depigne

From when I slept in swaddling clothes, this thought
Within me has been growing day by day;
One sepulchre will cover both, I fear.   65
For when my soul is naked of its flesh,
No longer can this passion go with it.
If Latins and if Greeks
Speak of me after death, it's but a wind;
Thus since I ever fear   70
To store up what one hour can sweep away,
Truth I'd embrace, and shadows I'd forsake.

    But yet that other wish by which I'm filled
Blights everything born near it, as it seems,
And meanwhile my time flies,   75
For, writing of her, I heed not myself.
And too, the light that from those lovely eyes
Melts me so gently with its radiant warmth
Now checks me with a rein
Against which skill or force avails me not.   80
What benefit, therefore, if my small boat
Is cleaned and caulked, when 'midst these shoals it's still
Detained by two such knots. You who from all
The other ties that variously bind
The world have set me free, why not, my lord,   85
Now rid my countenance
Of this disgrace of mine? For in the guise
Of one who dreams, I've death
Before my eyes, it seems, and I desire
To make defence, but yet I have no arms.   90

    I know what I am doing; misperceived
Truth tricks me not; but yet love forces me—
He never lets one follow
Honor's road who too much credits him.
And hour by hour I feel grow in my heart   95
A worthy scorn, severe and harsh, which sets
Forth all my secret thoughts
Upon my brow for others to observe.
Indeed, to love a mortal thing with faith
As great as that due but to God, is most   100
Denied him who the most for merit yearns.
Aloud this calls my reason back once more,
Gone straying after sense; but though it hears,
And aims still to return,
Habit evil forces it far on,   105
And paints before my eyes

quella che sol per farmi morir nacque,
perch'a me troppo, et a se stessa, piacque.
    Né so che spatio mi si desse il cielo
quando novellamente io venni in terra   110
a soffrir l'aspra guerra
che 'ncontra me medesmo seppi ordire;
né posso il giorno che la vita serra
antiveder per lo corporeo velo;
ma varïarsi il pelo   115
veggio, et dentro cangiarsi ogni desire.
Or ch'i' mi credo al tempo del partire
esser vicino, o non molto da lunge,
come chi 'l perder face accorto et saggio,
vo ripensando ov'io lassai 'l vïaggio   120
da la man destra, ch'a buon porto aggiunge:
et da l'un lato punge
vergogna et duol che 'ndietro mi rivolve;
dall'altro non m'assolve
un piacer per usanza in me sí forte   125
ch'a patteggiar n'ardisce co la morte.
    Canzon, qui sono, ed ò 'l cor via piú freddo
de la paura che gelata neve,
sentendomi perir senz'alcun dubbio:
ché pur deliberando ò vòlto al subbio   130
gran parte omai de la mia tela breve;
né mai peso fu greve
quanto quel ch'i' sostengo in tale stato:
ché co la morte a lato
cerco del viver mio novo consiglio,   135
et veggio 'l meglio, et al peggior m'appiglio.

265
    Aspro core et selvaggio, et cruda voglia
in dolce, humile, angelica figura,
se l'impreso rigor gran tempo dura,
avran di me poco honorata spoglia;
    ché quando nasce et mor fior, herba et foglia,   5
quando è 'l dí chiaro, et quando è notte oscura,
piango ad ognor: ben ò di mia ventura,
di madonna et d'Amore onde mi doglia.
    Vivo sol di speranza, rimembrando
che poco humor già per continua prova   10
consumar vidi marmi et pietre salde.
    Non è sí duro cor che, lagrimando,

Her who was only born to make me die
Because she pleased me—and herself—too much.
     And I know not what span Heav'n planned for me
When newly to this earth I came, so I   110
Could suffer this harsh war
That I knew how to wage against myself.
What day will seal my life, I can't foresee
Because of my corporeal veil,
But I see my hair graying   115
And in me every passion's changing too.
Now that I think my parting time at hand
Or not so very far away, like one
Whom loss has made alert and wise, I go
Recalling where I left the right hand course   120
That leads to that good port. And on one hand°
Shame goads me, and regret,
So I'm turned back, yet on the other hand
I have not been released
From joy, since habit's grown in me so strong   125
It ventures to negotiate with Death.
     Song, I am here; and colder far with fear
Is my heart than is frozen snow; without
A doubt I feel that I am perishing,
For, while deliberating, I have wound   130
A great part now of my brief thread upon
The beam; nor was a weight
As heavy, ever, as this one I bear
In such a plight; with Death
At hand, new counsel for my life I seek.   135
The best I see, yet seize upon the worst.

265

     A stern and savage heart and cruel desire
In an angelic figure, modest, sweet—
If harshness once begun should long endure—
Will get but little glorious spoils from me.
     For when leaves, blooms, and grass spring forth and die 5
When day is clear, and when the night's obscure,
I always weep; yes, I have cause to mourn
For Love, and for my lady, and my lot.
     On hope alone I live, when I recall
I've seen a little liquid's constant trial   10
Wear solid stone and marble quite away.
     No heart is so unyielding that sometimes

pregando, amando, talor non si smova,
né sí freddo voler, che non si scalde.

266

Signor mio caro, ogni pensier mi tira
devoto a verder voi, cui sempre veggio:
la mia fortuna (or che mi pò far peggio?)
mi tene a freno, et mi travolve et gira.

Poi quel dolce desio ch'Amor mi spira   5
menami a morte, ch'i' non me n'aveggio;
et mentre i miei duo lumi indarno cheggio,
dovunque io son, dí et notte si sospira.

Carità di signore, amor di donna
son le catene ove con molti affanni   10
legato son, perch'io stesso mi strinsi.

Un lauro verde, una gentil colomna,
quindeci l'una, et l'altro diciotto anni
portato ò in seno, et già non mi scinsi.

267

Oimè il bel viso, oimè il soave sguardo,
oimè il leggiadro portamento altero;
oimè il parlar ch'ogni aspro ingegno et fero
facevi humile, ed ogni huom vil gagliardo!

et oimè il dolce riso, onde uscío 'l dardo   5
di che morte, altro bene omai non spero:
alma real, dignissima d'impero,
se non fossi fra noi scesa sí tardo!

Per voi conven ch'io arda, e 'n voi respire,
ch'i' pur fui vostro; et se di voi son privo,   10
via men d'ogni sventura altra mi dole.

Di speranza m'empieste et di desire,
quand'io partí' dal sommo piacer vivo;
ma 'l vento ne portava le parole.

268

Che debb'io far? che mi consigli, Amore?
Tempo è ben di morire,
et ò tardato piú ch'i' non vorrei.
Madonna è morta, et à seco il mio core;
et volendol seguire,   5
interromper conven quest'anni rei,
perché mai veder lei
di·qua non spero, et l'aspettar m'è noia.

It is not swayed by tears and prayers and love,
No will so cold that it may not be warmed.

266

My precious lord, by each devoted thought°
I'm drawn to see you, whom I ever see;
My fortune, though (how can it treat me worse?)
Holds me in check and whirls and turns me round.
   Then that sweet yearning Love breathes into me   5
Pulls me toward death when I am least on guard,
And while my two lights vainly I invoke,
Wherever day or night I am, I sigh.
   Devotion to my lord and love for my
Dear lady are the links I've forged with pains,   10
For I myself have wound them close about.
   A laurel green, a column nobly born,
Fifteen the one, the other eighteen years
I've borne within my breast and never shirked.

267

Alas, that lovely face, alas, that gentle look,
Alas, that comely, graceful carriage proud;
Alas, that speech that humbled every wild
Stern intellect, each abject man made strong.
   And that sweet laugh, alas, whence flew the dart   5
From which I hope for no good else but death.
O queenly spirit, worthiest to rule,
Had you not late descended in our midst!
   For you I can but burn, and in you breathe;
For I was yours indeed; deprived of you,   10
Beyond all other sorrows I am grieved.
   You filled me with desire and hope when I
Departed from the highest joy alive,
But the wind blew all those words of it away.°

268

What must I do? What do you counsel, Love?
The time for dying's come,
And I have waited longer than I'd wish.
My lady's dead; she has with her my heart,
And I, who'd follow it,   5
Must interrupt this round of evil years,
For never can I hope
To see her here, and waiting wearies me.

Poscia ch'ogni mia gioia
per lo suo dipartire in pianto è volta,   10
ogni dolcezza de mia vita è tolta.
        Amor, tu 'l senti, ond'io teco mi doglio,
quant'è 'l damno aspro et grave;
e so che del mio mal ti pesa et dole,
anzi del nostro, perch'ad uno scoglio   15
avem rotto la nave,
et in un punto n'è scurato il sole.
Qual ingegno a parole
poria aguagliare il mio doglioso stato?
Ahi orbo mondo, ingrato,   20
gran cagion ài di dever pianger meco,
ché quel bel ch'era in te, perduto ài seco.
        Caduta è la tua gloria, et tu nol vedi,
né degno eri, mentr'ella
visse qua giú, d'aver sua conoscenza,   25
né d'esser tocco da' suoi sancti piedi,
perché cosa sí bella
devea 'l ciel adornar di sua presenza.
Ma io, lasso, che senza
lei né vita mortal né me stesso amo,   30
piangendo la richiamo:
questo m'avanza di cotanta spene,
et questo solo anchor qui mi mantene.
        Oïmè, terra è fatto il suo bel viso,
che solea far del cielo   35
et del ben di lassú fede fra noi;
l'invisibil sua forma è in paradiso,
disciolta di quel velo
che qui fece ombra al fior degli anni suoi,
per rivestirsen poi   40
un'altra volta, et mai piú non spogliarsi,
quando alma et bella farsi
tanto piú la vedrem, quanto piú vale
sempiterna bellezza che mortale.
        Piú che mai bella et piú leggiadra donna   45
tornami inanzi, come
là dove piú gradir sua vista sente.
Questa è del viver mio l'una colomna,
l'altra è 'l suo chiaro nome,
che sona nel mio cor sí dolcemente.   50
Ma tornandomi a mente
che pur morta è la mia speranza, viva

Since now my every joy
Is turned by her departure to lament,   10
All sweetness from my life is torn away.
    You feel it, Love, so I complain to you.
How harsh and grave this wound!
I know my sorrow grieves and burdens you—
Our sorrow, rather, for one same shoal   15
Our vessel we have wrecked,
And suddenly our sun has been obscured.
What skill in shaping words
Could equal, in its sorrow, all my woe?
Ah, ingrate world bereaved,   20
You have much cause that you should weep with me;
What beauty you possessed, you've lost with her.
    Your glory's fallen, and you see it not,
Nor did you merit her
Acqaintance while she lived upon the earth,   25
Unworthy for her sacred feet to touch,
Because a being so fine
With her fair presence should adorn the Heavens.
Ah me, without her I
Who love not mortal life nor yet myself—   30
In tears I call her back.
Nothing but this remains of all that hope,
And this alone sustains me here a while.
    Oh, into earth is turned that lovely face
Whose look once gave us faith   35
In Heaven, and faith in happiness above.
Invisible, her form's in paradise,
Released, now, from the veil
That shaded here the flower of her years.
In that veil she'll be clothed   40
Yet once again, to cast it off no more.
Holier, more caring
We shall see her then, more fair in that degree
That eternal beauty mortal worth exceeds.
    Now more than ever graceful, and more fair,   45
My lady comes to me,
Just where she knows her likeness pleases most.
Her image is one pillar of my life;
The other her bright name
That in my heart with sweetness still resounds.   50
To me the thought returns
That hope—once living while she flourished—now

[313]

allor ch'ella fioriva,
sa ben Amor qual io divento, et (spero)
vedel colei ch'è or sí presso al vero.   55
    Donne, voi che miraste sua beltate
et l'angelica vita
con quel celeste portamento in terra,
di me vi doglia, et vincavi pietate,
non di lei ch'è salita   60
a tanta pace, et m'à lassato in guerra:
tal che s'altri mi serra
lungo tempo il camin da seguitarla,
quel ch'Amor meco parla,
sol mi riten ch'io non recida il nodo.   65
Ma e' ragiona dentro in cotal modo:
    —Pon' freno al gran dolor che ti trasporta,
ché per soverchie voglie
si perde 'l cielo, ove 'l tuo core aspira,
dove è viva colei ch'altrui par morta,   70
et di sue belle spoglie
seco sorride, et sol di te sospira;
et sua fama, che spira
in molte parti anchor per la tua lingua,
prega che non extingua,   75
anzi la voce al suo nome rischiari,
se gli occhi suoi ti fur dolci né cari.—
    Fuggi 'l sereno e 'l verde,
non t'appressare ove sia riso o canto,
canzon mia no, ma pianto: 80
non fa per te di star fra gente allegra,
vedova, sconsolata, in vesta negra.

269

    Rotta è l'alta colonna e 'l verde lauro
che facean ombra al mio stanco pensero;
perduto ò quel che ritrovar non spero
dal borrea a l'austro, o dal mar indo al mauro.
    Tolto m'ài, Morte, il mio doppio thesauro,   5
che mi fea viver lieto et gire altero,
et ristorar nol pò terra né impero,
né gemma orïental, né forza d'auro.
    Ma se consentimento è di destino,
che posso io piú, se no aver l'alma trista,   10
humidi gli occhi sempre, e 'l viso chino?
    O nostra vita ch'è sí bella in vista,

Is really dead. How well
Love knows what I've become, and she (I hope)
Can see it too; she is so near the truth.   55
     You ladies who her beauty once admired,
And her angelic life
And heavenly comportment here on earth,
O, grieve for me! Let pity conquer you—
Not for her who, to peace   60
So great rose up and left me in this war.
Indeed, should others bar
Me long from following upon her road,
Then only what Love says
Can stop my cutting through life's knot,   65
For in this way he reasons here within:
     "Check that great grief which carries you away;
For your desires too great
Will lose that Heaven where your heart aspires,
Where she who, seeming dead to others, lives.   70
About her fair remains
She smiles within, but sighs on your behalf.
And her renown, which still
Your words breathe forth on every side,
She prays you won't extinguish;   75
Her name instead make brighter with your voice,
If her eyes precious were, or sweet to you."
     Flee clear sky, flee green earth;
Where song and laughter are, do not approach,
My song—no, my lament;   80
To dwell with joyous people will not do,
Widow disconsolate, in weeds of black.°

269

     That column high, that laurel green as well°
Which to my weary reverie gave shade,
Are felled; I've lost what I can't hope to find
From north to south, Indic to Moorish seas.
     My double treasure, Death, you've snatched away;   5
It made me live in joy and walk in pride;
No country and no realm can give it back,
Nor oriental jewel, nor power of gold.
     But if this is with destiny's consent,
Can I do more than have a spirit sad,   10
Have eyes forever wet, a face cast down?
     O, life of ours that is so fair to view,

com perde agevolmente in un matino
quel che 'n molti anni a gran pena s'acquista!

270

Amor, se vuo' ch'i' torni al giogo anticho,
come par che tu mostri, un'altra prova
meravigliosa et nova,
per domar me, conventi vincer pria.
Il mio amato tesoro in terra trova,   5
che m'è nascosto, ond'io son sí mendico,
e 'l cor saggio pudico,
ove suol albergar la vita mia;
et s'egli è ver che tua potentia sia
nel ciel sí grande come si ragiona,   10
et ne l'abisso (perché qui fra noi
quel che tu val' et puoi,
credo che 'l sente ogni gentil persona),
ritogli a Morte quel ch'ella n'à tolto,
et ripon' le tue insegne nel bel volto.   15
 Riponi entro 'l bel viso il vivo lume
ch'era mia scorta, et la soave fiamma
ch'anchor, lasso, m'infiamma
essendo spenta: or che fea dunque ardendo?
E' non si vide mai cervo né damma   20
con tal desio cercar fonte né fiume,
qual io il dolce costume
onde ò già molto amaro; et piú n'attendo,
se ben me stesso et mia vaghezza intendo,
che mi fa vaneggiar sol del pensero,   25
et gire in parte ove la strada manca,
et co la mente stanca
cosa seguir che mai giugner non spero.
Or al tuo richiamar venir non degno,
ché segnoria non ài fuor del tuo regno.   30
 Fammi sentir de quell'aura gentile
di for, sí come dentro anchor si sente;
la qual era possente,
cantando, d'acquetar li sdegni et l'ire,
di serenar la tempestosa mente   35
et sgombrar d'ogni nebbia oscura et vile,
ed alzava il mio stile
sovra di sé, dove or non poria gire.
Aguaglia la speranza col desire;
et poi che l'alma è in sua ragion piú forte,   40

In just one morn how easily you lose
What at great cost was gained through many years.

270

    If in your ancient yoke you want me back
Love, as it seems, some other marvellous
And rare ordeal you must
First undertake if you're to master me:
Find my dear treasure in the earth, where she's   5
Concealed from me and whence I'm beggared thus;
Find that sage, modest heart
Where my life sheltered once; and if it's true
That your authority's as great in Heaven
As we esteem it, and in the Abyss   10
(Since here among us both your might
And worthiness are felt
By every courtly person, I believe)
Take back from Death that which she's reft from us,
Again in that fair face your ensign set.   15
    In that fair look put back the living light
That was my guide; replace the sweet flame that
Though spent, alas, inflames
Me still (while yet it burned what it could do!)
One never sees a hart or hind seek spring   20
Or stream with such desire as I seek that
Sweet comportment, whence I've had
Much bitterness, indeed, and more await.
If well I know myself and my desire
That with mere thought makes me delirious,   25
In trackless regions makes me stray, and makes
My weary mind pursue
A thing I'll never hope to gain, now at
Your call I do not deign to come, because
Beyond your realm, no lordship do you hold.   30
    Make me feel from without that noble breeze
Just as, within, I feel it still; for it
Had power in its song
To quieten disdain, to placate wrath,
To make the storm-tossed mind grow tranquil, and   35
To sweep all dark and wretched fogs away;
My style it raised to heights
Beyond itself, where now it cannot go.
Make hope the equal of desire, and since
The soul is strongest in its sphere, once more   40

rendi agli occhi, agli orecchi il proprio obgetto,
senza qual imperfetto
è lor oprare, e 'l mio vivere è morte.
Indarno or sovra me tua forza adopre,
mentre 'l mio primo amor terra ricopre.   45

    Fa' ch'io riveggia il bel guardo, ch'un sole
fu spora 'l ghiaccio ond'io solea gir carco;
fa' ch'i' ti trovi al varco,
onde senza tornar passò 'l mio core;
prendi i dorati strali, et prendi l'arco,   50
et facciamisi udir, sí come sòle,
col suon de le parole
ne le quali io imparai che cosa è amore;
movi la lingua, ov'erano a tutt'ore
disposti gli ami ov'io fui preso, et l'ésca   55
ch'i' bramo sempre; e i tuoi lacci nascondi
fra i capei crespi et biondi,
ché 'l mio volere altrove non s'invesca;
spargi co le tue man'le chiome al vento,
ivi mi lega, et puo'mi far contento.   60

    Dal laccio d'òr non sia mai chi me scioglia,
negletto ad arte, e 'nnanellato et hirto,
né de l'ardente spirto
de la sua vista dolcemente acerba,
la qual dí et notte piú che lauro o mirto   65
tenea in me verde l'amorosa voglia,
quando si veste et spoglia
di fronde il bosco, et la campagna d'erba.
Ma poi che Morte è stata sí superba
che spezzò il nodo ond'io temea scampare,   70
né trovar pôi, quantunque gira il mondo,
di che ordischi 'l secondo,
che giova, Amor, tuoi ingegni ritentare?
Passata è la stagion, perduto ài l'arme,
di ch'io tremava: ormai che puoi tu farme?   75

    L'arme tue furon gli occhi, onde l'accese
saette uscivan d'invisibil foco,
et ragion temean poco,
ché 'ncontra 'l ciel non val difesa humana;
il pensar e 'l tacer, il riso e 'l gioco,   80
l'abito honesto e 'l ragionar cortese,
le parole che 'ntese
avrian fatto gentil d'alma villana,
l'angelica sembianza, humile et piana,

Restore their proper object to my eyes
And ears, for without that
Their action is impaired, and my life death.
Now idly you employ your strength on me
As long as earth is covering my first love.   45
    Show me once more the fair gaze that was sun
Upon the ice that used to burden me;
In that strait way through which
My heart passed and returned no more, let me
Discover you; take golden darts and bow,   50
And make me hear the music of her words.
Where, as before, I learned
What thing love is; make speak that tongue
Where always those hooks were set out, the ones
That caught me with the bait I ever crave;   55
Conceal as well your snares from view amidst
That blond and curling hair,
For my will can be caught no other place;
Her locks with your own hand strew to the wind;
There tie me fast, and you'll make me content.   60
    No one will ever free me from that snare
Of gold, ruffled and curled, with art unkempt,
Nor from the ardent spirit
Of her face, sweetly cruel, which night and day
Maintained that longing amorous in me,   65
More green than laurel or than myrtle when
Woods have put on and shed
Their leaves, and meadowland its grass.
But since Death was so arrogant that she
Cut through the knot I feared to fly, and since   70
Though you roam all the world, you cannot find
That which you need to wreathe
A second, what use Love, to try your tricks
Again? The season's past; you've lost those arms
I quaked at; what now can you do to me?   75
    Your weapons were her eyes, whence issued shafts
Ablaze with unseen fire, and reason they
But little feared, for no
Defence of man's has force against the heavens;
Her thoughtfulness and silence, laugh and play,   80
Her forthright nature, discourse courteous,
Those words that, grasped, would have
Enobled any soul though lowly bred,
Her countenance, angelic, modest, calm,

ch'or quinci or quindi udia tanto lodarsi;   85
e 'l sedere et lo star, che spesso altrui
poser in dubbio a cui
devesse il pregio di piú laude darsi.
Con quest'armi vincevi ogni cor duro:
or se' tu disarmato; i' son securo.   90

Gli animi ch'al tuo regno il cielo inchina
leghi ora in uno et ora in altro modo;
ma me sol ad un nodo
legar potêi, ché 'l ciel di piú non volse.
Quel'uno è rotto; en 'n libertà non godo   95
ma piango et grido: «Ahi nobil pellegrina,
qual sententia divina
me legò inanzi, et te prima disciolse?
Dio, che sí tosto al mondo ti ritolse,
ne mostrò tanta et sí alta virtute   100
solo per infiammar nostro desio».
Certo omai non tem'io,
Amor, de la tua man nove ferute;
indarno tendi l'arco, a voito scocchi:
sua virtú cadde al chiuder de' begli occhi.   105

Morte m'à sciolto, Amor, d'ogni tua legge:
quella che fu mia donna al ciel è gita,
lasciando trista et libera mia vita.

271

L'ardente nodo ov'io fui d'ora in hora,
contando, anni ventuno interi preso,
Morte disciolse, né già mai tal peso
provai, né credo ch'uom di dolor mora.

Non volendomi Amor perdere anchora,   5
ebbe un altro lacciuol fra l'erba teso,
et di nova ésca un altro foco acceso,
tal ch'a gran pena indi scampato fôra.

Et se non fosse experïentia molta
de' primi affanni, i' sarei preso et arso,   10
tanto piú quanto son men verde legno.

Morte m'à liberato un'altra volta,
et rotto 'l nodo, e 'l foco à spento et sparso:
contra la qual non val forza né 'ngegno.

272

La vita fugge, et non s'arresta una hora,
et la morte vien dietro a gran giornate,

Which near and far one heard so greatly praised.   85
The way, too, that she sat, the way she stood—
They often left in doubt
Which should receive reward of greatest praise:
With these arms each unyielding heart you won,
But now you are disarmed; I am secure.   90
    Those souls that heaven bends beneath your sway
First one way then another you bind up,
But only in one knot
Could you tie me, for heaven willed no more.
That knot is severed; yet in freedom I   95
Do not rejoice, but weep and cry aloud:
"Ah, noble pilgrim, what
Divine pronouncement in times past bound me
And first released you? God, who took you from
The world so soon, showed us such lofty and   100
Great virtue only to inflame desire
In us." Love, I fear not
New injuries, indeed, at your hand now.
You shoot at naught and draw your bow in vain;
Its virtues failed when those fair eyes were closed.   105
    Death from your every law has freed me, Love;
That one who was my lady passed to heaven,
And left my life in grief and liberty.

271

    That burning knot in which I was ensnared
For one and twenty years, reckoned by hours,
Death has undone; I never bore such weight
Nor do I think a man can die of woe.
    Not wishing, yet, to lose me, Love laid down   5
Another snare for me within the grass,
And with new tinder lit another fire
So great I barely could escape from it.
    Had it not been for much experience
In former trials, I'd have been caught and burnt—   10
So much the more since I am seasoned wood.
    Death's liberated me yet one more time,
Has cut the knot, has quenched and strewn the fire;
Against that one avails not strength nor wit.

272

    Life flees and will not be delayed an hour,
And, by forced marches, Death pursues apace,

et le cose presenti et le passate
mi dànno guerra, et le future anchora;
    e 'l rimembrare et l'aspettar m'accora,
or quinci or quindi, sí che 'n veritate,
se non ch'i' ò di me stesso pietate,
i' sarei già di questi pensier' fora.
    Tornami avanti, s'alcun dolce mai
ebbe 'l cor tristo; et poi da l'altra parte
veggio al mio navigar turbati i vènti;
    veggio fortuna in porto, et stanco omai
il mio nocchier, et rotte arbore et sarte,
e i lumi bei che mirar soglio, spenti.

273

    Che fai? che pensi? che pur dietro guardi
nel tempo, che tornar non pote omai?
Anima sconsolata, che pur vai
giugnendo legne al foco ove tu ardi?
    Le soavi parole e i dolci sguardi
ch'ad un ad un descritti et depinti ài,
son levati de terra; et è, ben sai,
qui ricercarli intempestivo et tardi.
    Deh non rinovellar quel che n'ancide,
non seguir piú penser vago, fallace,
ma saldo et certo, ch'a buon fin ne guide.
    Cerchiamo 'l ciel, se qui nulla ne piace:
ché mal per noi quella beltà si vide,
se viva et morta ne devea tôr pace.

274

    Datemi pace, o duri miei pensieri:
non basta ben ch'Amor, Fortuna et Morte
mi fanno guerra intorno e 'n su le porte,
senza trovarmi dentro altri guerreri?
    Et tu, mio cor, anchor se' pur qual eri,
disleal a me sol, che fere scorte
vai ricettando, et se' fatto consorte
de' miei nemici sí pronti et leggieri?
    In te i secreti suoi messaggi Amore,
in te spiega Fortuna ogni sua pompa,
et Morte la memoria di quel colpo
    che l'avanzo di me conven che rompa;
in te i vaghi pensier' s'arman d'errore:
perché d'ogni mio mal te solo incolpo.

And present deeds, and matters past, as well
As what's to come—all these make war on me!
    And it afflicts me to remember them—   5
And wait for them, first here, then there, so that
In truth, if piety did not prevent,
Beyond these cares I would already be.
    If something sweet my wretched heart once had
Comes to my mind, then on the other hand   10
My sailing winds become tumultuous,
    I see a storm in harbor, and by now
My pilot's wearied, split my masts and sails,
And those fair lights I steered for are snuffed out.

273

    What do you do? What think? Why always peer
Back into time that never can return,
Despondent spirit who forever strays
And on the fire wherein you burn heaps fuel.
    The soft words and sweet glances, one by one   5
Described and pictured by you are raised up
From earth; for it's too late, you surely know,
And no time now to seek them here again.
    Ah, don't revive what kills us; trace no more
That vague, deceitful thought, but firm and sure,   10
Pursue what to a good end leads us on.
    Let us seek heaven if nothing please us here:
For we perceived that beauty to our ill
If live and dead it must prevent our peace.

274

    My unrelenting cares, O, grant me peace!
Won't it suffice that Fortune, Love and Death
Make war all round me—at my portals too—
Without my finding other foes within?
    And you, my heart: are you still what you were,   5
Traitor to me alone? What savage troops
Do you recruit? And are you fellow to
My enemies so eager and so quick?
    In you love stores his secret messages,
Fortune in you her every pomp unfolds,   10
And Death hoards up the memory of that blow
    Which now must ravage what is left of me.
In you my wandering thoughts don error's arms;
So you alone I blame for every ill.

Occhi miei, oscurato è 'l nostro sole;
anzi è salito al cielo, et ivi splende:
ivi il vedremo anchora, ivi n'attende,
et di nostro tardar forse li dole.

Orecchie mie, l'angeliche parole   5
sonano in parte ove è chi meglio intende.
Pie' miei, vostra ragion là non si stende
ov'è colei ch'exercitar vi sòle.

Dunque perché mi date questa guerra?
Già di perdere a voi cagion non fui   10
vederla, udirla et ritrovarla in terra:

Morte biasmate; anzi laudate Lui
che lega et scioglie, e 'n un punto apre et serra
e dopo 'l pianto sa far lieto altrui.

Poi che la vista angelica, serena,
per súbita partenza in gran dolore
lasciato à l'alma e 'n tenebroso horrore,
cerco parlando d'allentar mia pena.

Giusto duol certo a lamentar mi mena: 5
sassel chi n'è cagione, et sallo Amore,
ch'altro rimedio non avea 'l mio core
contra i fastidi onde la vita è piena.

Questo un, Morte, m'à tolto la tua mano;
et tu che copri et guardi et ài or teco, 10
felice terra, quel bel viso humano,

me dove lasci, sconsolato et cieco,
poscia che 'l dolce et amoroso et piano
lume degli occhi miei non è piú meco?

S'Amor novo consiglio non n'apporta,
per forza converrà che 'l viver cange:
tanta paura et duol l'alma trista ange,
che 'l desir vive, et la speranza è morta;

onde si sbigottisce et si sconforta   5
mia vita in tutto, et notte et giorno piange,
stanca senza governo in mar che frange,
e 'n dubbia via senza fidata scorta.

Imaginata guida la conduce,
ché la vera è sotterra, anzi è nel cielo, 10
onde piú che mai chiara al cor traluce:

O eyes of mine, our sun has been obscured;
To heaven's ascended rather; there it shines.
There we shall see it yet; it waits us there.
Perhaps it sorrows at our tardiness.

My ears, angelic speeches sound in realms   5
Where one now dwells who better understands.
My feet, your range extends not to the place
Where she abides who tried your every power.

Come then, why do you thus make war on me?
It was not I indeed who made you lose   10
Her sight, her sound, and meeting her on earth.

Reproach Death then—or rather, give her praise
Who binds and frees, unseals and shuts at once,
And, after grief, knows how to bring one joy.

276

Because that sight, angelic and serene,
Has by its sudden passing left my soul
In sombre horror and in bitter grief,
I seek by speaking to relieve my pain.

A just woe surely leads me to complain: 5
The one who caused it knows it, and Love knows
That my heart had no other remedy
Against the cares with which my life is filled.

Your hand has robbed me, Death, of that one cure,
And you who shelter, watch, and keep with you   10
That lovely human face now, happy earth,

Ah where, unseeing and disconsolate,
Will you desert me, since my eyes' clear light
So sweet and amorous from me is gone.

277

If Love will offer me no new advice,
I must perforce transform my way of life;
Great fear and grief afflict my sorrowing soul
Because desire still lives, and hope is dead;

And so my life is anguished and dismayed   5
At every turn, and weeps by night and day,
Weary amidst the breakers, rudderless,
On doubtful course, without a faithful guide.

A pilot that I picture guides my life:
The real one's in the earth—that is, in heaven,   10
Whence, brighter than before, she lights my heart.

agli occhi no, ch'un doloroso velo
contende lor la disïata luce,
et me fa sí per tempo cangiar pelo.

278

Ne l'età sua piú bella et piú fiorita,
quando aver suol Amor in noi piú forza,
lasciando in terra la terrena scorza,
è l'aura mia vital da me partita,
    et viva et bella et nuda al ciel salita: 5
indi mi signoreggia, indi mi sforza.
Deh perché me del mio mortal non scorza
l'ultimo dí, ch'è primo a l'altra vita?
    Ché, come i miei pensier' dietro a lei vanno,
cosí leve, expedita et lieta l'alma   10
la segua, et io sia fuor di tanto affanno.
    Ciò che s'indugia è proprio per mio damno,
per far me stesso a me piú grave salma.
O che bel morir era, oggi è terzo anno!

279

Se lamentar augelli, o verdi fronde
mover soavemente a l'aura estiva,
o roco mormorar di lucide onde
s'ode d'una fiorita et fresca riva,
    là 'v'io seggia d'amor pensoso et scriva,   5
lei che 'l ciel ne mostrò, terra n'asconde,
veggio, et odo, et intendo ch'anchor viva
di sí lontano a' sospir' miei risponde.
    «Deh, perché inanzi 'l tempo ti consume?
—mi dice con pietate—a che pur versi   10
degli occhi tristi un doloroso fiume?
    Di me non pianger tu, ché' miei dí fersi
morendo eterni, et ne l'interno lume,
quando mostrai de chiuder, gli occhi apersi».

280

Mai non fui in parte ove sí chiar vedessi
quel che veder vorrei poi ch'io nol vidi,
né dove in tanta libertà mi stessi,
né 'mpiessi il ciel de sí amorosi stridi;
    né già mai vidi valle aver sí spessi   5
luoghi da sospirar riposti et fidi;
né credo già ch'Amore in Cipro avessi,

But not my eyes, because a veil of grief
Cuts off from them that light so much desired,
And makes my hair grow gray before its time.

278

In her most flowering season and most fair,
When Love in us has more than usual force,
Abandoning in earth her earthly chaff,
That gentle breeze, which gave me life, left me
    And rose to heaven, living, lovely, free;   5
Thence she commands me, thence she urges me.
Ah, why am I not stripped of mortal flesh
By that last day, the first of future life?
    For, just as my thoughts run on after her,
So follows her my soul, light, joyous, quick,   10
And I may be set free me from such great pain.
    What holds me back is surely to my cost,
And makes me a great burden to myself.
Ah, she died well, three years ago today!

279

Where some hear mourning birds, or verdant fronds
That rustle softly in the summer breeze,
Or quiet murmuring of lucent waves,
Beside a cool and flowering bank, there I
    Sit lost in thoughts of love, and write; there I   5
See her, and hear, and understand; for she
Whom heaven showed us, whom the earth conceals,
Yet lives; my sighs she answers from afar.
    "Alas, before your time, why waste away?"
She asks me with compassion, "Why still do   10
Your mournful eyes spill forth a woeful stream?
    "Weep not for me! Lo, dying makes my day
Eternal; to that inner light my eyes,
When I appeared to close them, opened wide."

280

In no place else could I so clearly see
That vision which I sought, but did not find,
Nor could I live in liberty so great,
Nor heaven fill with cries so full of love;
    Nor have I ever seen a vale so full   5
Of safe, secluded places to breathe sighs;
Nor do I think Love had on Cyprus or

o in altra riva, sí soavi nidi.

L'acque parlan d'amore, et l'òra e i rami
et gli augelletti e i pesci e i fiori et l'erba,   10
tutti inseme pregando ch'i' sempre ami.

Ma tu, ben nata che dal ciel mi chiami,
per la memoria di tua morte acerba
preghi ch'i' sprezzi 'l mondo e i suoi dolci hami.

281

Quant fïate, al mio dolce ricetto
fuggendo altrui et, s'esser pò, me stesso,
vo con gli occhi bagnando l'erba e 'l petto,
rompendo co' sospir' l'aere da presso!

Quante fïate sol, pien di sospetto,   5
per luoghi ombrosi et foschi mi son messo,
cercando col penser l'alto diletto
che Morte à tolto, ond'io la chiamo spesso!

Or in forma di nimpha o d'altra diva
che del piú chiaro fondo di Sorga esca,   10
et pongasi a sedere in su la riva;

or l'ò veduto su per l'erba fresca
calcare i fior' com'una donna viva,
mostrando in vista che di me le 'ncresca.

282

Alma felice che sovente torni
a consolar le mie notti dolenti
con gli occhi tuoi che Morte non à spenti,
ma sovra 'l mortal modo fatti adorni:

quanto gradisco che' miei tristi giorni   5
a rallegrar de tua vista consenti!
Cosí comincio a ritrovar presenti
le tue bellezze a' suoi usati soggiorni,

là 've cantando andai di te molt'anni,
or, come vedi, vo di te piangendo: 10
di te piangendo no, ma de' miei danni.

Sol un riposo trovo in molti affanni,
che, quando torni, te conosco e 'ntendo
a l'andar, a la voce, al volta, a' panni.

283

Discolorato ài, Morte, il piú bel volto
che mai si vide, e i piú begli occhi spenti;
spirto piú acceso di vertuti ardenti

On any other shore more pleasant nests.
    The waters talk of love, the breeze, the boughs,
And little birds and fish, the flowers, grass,   10
All pray together I may ever love.
    But you, well born, who call to me from heaven,
Through recollection of your bitter death
You pray I'll scorn the world and its sweet snares.

281

    How many times into my refuge sweet
Fleeing the crowd and, if I could, myself,
Have I escaped, eyes watering grass and breast,
Disturbing with my sighs the ambient air!
    How many times alone and full of doubt   5
Have I set out through shaded, misty spots,
In my thoughts searching for that lofty joy
Whom Death has snatched; there oft I summon her;
    Now in a nymph- or other goddess-shape
She comes forth from the clearest depths of Sorgue,   10
And there upon its bank she seats herself.
    Just now I've seen her tread upon new grass
And, like a woman living, through the flowers,
Her face revealing that she pities me.

282

    O blissful soul, how often you return
To comfort these afflicted nights of mine
With your eyes Death has not extinguished, but,
Which passing mortal fashion, has made fair.
    How welcome that, appearing thus, you cheer   5
So willingly my melancholy days;
Your beauties I discover once again
Close by where you accustomed sojourn made.
    There, singing of you, many years I strayed,
Now weeping for you, as you see, I pass—   10
No, weeping not for you, but for my harms.
    A single solace 'midst much grief I find:
When you return, I recognize you by
Your pace, your voice, your countenance, your clothes.

283

    You, Death, have painted dark the fairest face
Ever beheld, put out the finest eyes;
That soul with burning virtues most alight

del piú leggiadro et piú bel nodo ài sciolto.
	In un momento ogni mio ben m'ài tolto, 5
post'ài silentio a' piú soavi accenti
che mai s'udiro, et me pien di lamenti:
quant'io veggio m'è noia, et quant'io ascolto.
	Ben torna a consolar tanto dolore
madonna, ove Pietà la riconduce: 10
né trovo in questa vita altro soccorso.
	Et se come ella parla, et come luce,
ridir potessi, accenderei d'amore,
non dirò d'uom, un cor di tigre o d'orso.

284

	Sí breve è 'l tempo e 'l penser sí veloce
che mi rendon madonna cosí morta,
ch'al gran dolor la medicina è corta:
pur, mentr'io veggio lei, nulla mi nòce.
	Amor, che m'à legato et tienmi in croce, 5
trema quando la vede in su la porta
de l'alma ove m'ancide, anchor sí scorta,
sí dolce in vista et sí soave in voce.
	Come donna in suo albergo altera vène,
scacciando de l'oscuro et grave core   10
co la fronte serena i pensier' tristi.
	L'alma, che tanta luce non sostene,
sospira et dice:—O benedette l'ore
del dí che questa via con li occhi apristi!—

285

	Né mai pietosa madre al caro figlio
né donna accesa al suo sposo dilecto
die' con tanti sospir', con tal sospetto
in dubbio stato sí fedel consiglio,
	come a me quella che 'l mio grave exiglio 5
mirando dal suo eterno alto ricetto,
spesso a me torna co l'usato affecto,
et di doppia pietate ornata il ciglio:
	or di madre, or d'amante; or teme, or arde
d'onesto foco; et nel parlar mi mostra   10
quel che 'n questo vïaggio fugga o segua,
	contando i casi de la vita nostra,
pregando ch'a levar l'alma non tarde:
et sol quant'ella parla, ò pace o tregua.

You've freed from its most lovely, graceful bond.
    With one stroke you've bereft me of all good,   5
Have stilled the gentlest accents ever heard
And left me filled with wailing. What I see
And hear—how dreary for me it's become!
    My lady, to assuage such bitter grief
Returns where mercy leads her back once more;   10
I find no other succor in this life.
    If I could only reproduce her speech,
How she brings light, I should inflame with love—
No, not a man's—but tiger's heart, or bear's.

284

    So short the time, so rapid is the thought,
Which bring my lady back to me, though dead;
And thus the cure for my deep grief is quick:
For while I see her, nothing troubles me.
    Love quakes, when having bound and fixed me on   5
A cross, he sees her at the portal of
My soul, where I am slain—she still so wise,
So sweet to see, so gentle in her voice.
    Just like a stately matron to her home
She comes, and drives from my dark, burdened heart   10
All mournful thoughts before her brow serene.
    My soul, which such great light cannot sustain,
Speaks out, and sighs: "O, let the hours be blest
Of that day when your eyes unsealed this path."

285

    Never did pious mother to dear son
Nor blushing lady to beloved spouse
With greater sighs and with such diffidence,
Give surer counsel in a doubtful state
    Than she gave me, who sees my exile grave   5
From her eternal refuge high; to me
She oft returns with her accustomed care;
And has with double pity graced her brow.
    Now like the mother, the beloved now
She either fears, or with a chaste fire burns,   10
Tells what to flee on this journey or to seek,
    And citing the disasters of our life,
She prays I'll not be slow to lift my soul.
And I have peace or rest just when she speaks.

286

Se quell'aura soave de' sospiri
ch'i' odo di colei che qui fu mia
donna, or è in cielo, et anchor par qui sia,
et viva, et senta, et vada, et ami, et spiri,

    ritrar potessi, or che caldi desiri   5
movrei parlando! sí gelosa et pia
torna ov'io son, temendo non fra via
mi stanchi, o 'ndietro o da man manca giri.

    Ir dritto, alto, m'insegna; et io, che 'ntendo
le sue caste lusinghe e i giusti preghi   10
col dolce mormorar pietoso et basso,

    secondo lei conven mi regga et pieghi,
per la dolcezza che del suo dir prendo,
ch'avria vertú di far piangere un sasso.

287

Sennuccio mio, benché doglioso et solo
m'abbi lasciato, i' pur mi riconforto,
perché del corpo ov'eri preso et morto
alteramente se' levato a volo.

    Or vedi inseme l'un et l'altro polo,   5
le stelle vaghe et lor vïaggio torto,
et vedi il veder nostro quanto è corto,
onde col tuo gioir tempro 'l mio duolo.

    Ma ben ti prego che 'n la terza spera
Guitton saluti, et messer Cino, et Dante,   10
Franceschin nostro, et tutta quella schiera.

    A la mia donna puoi ben dire in quante
lagrime io vivo; et son fatt' una fera,
membrando il suo bel viso et l'opre sante.

288

I' ò pien di sospir' quest'aere tutto,
d'aspri colli mirando il dolce piano
ove nacque colei ch'avendo in mano
meo cor in sul fiorire e 'n sul far frutto,

    è gita al cielo, ed àmmi a tal condutto,   5
col súbito partir, che, di lontano
gli occhi miei stanchi lei cercando invano,
presso di sé non lassan loco asciutto.

    Non è sterpo né sasso in questi monti,
non ramo o fronda verde in queste piagge,   10
non fiore in queste valli o foglia d'erba,

286

Could I but render that soft, sighing breeze
I hear from her, who, though in heaven now,
Was here my lady, here still seems to be,
To live, to feel, to walk, to love and breathe—
    Now what warm passions would I stir with speech!   5
So zealous and devout she comes to me,
Afraid lest I grow weary on my way,
Turn back, or toward the wrong. Straight to the heights
    She teaches me to go; and I who hear
Her righteous prayers and her chaste blandishments   10
In murmurs sweet and pitying and low—
    I must, on her advice, subdue and rule
Myself, through sweetness taken from her speech,
For it has power to make a stone shed tears.

287

    Sennuccio mine, though you've left me alone°
And sorrowful, still once more I take heart
For from that flesh where captive you were held
And dead, you've risen proudly up in flight.
    Now both our poles together you can see,   5
The errant stars and all their twisting voyage;
How brief our vision is you see as well,
For which my woe I temper with your joy.
    Indeed, I pray that in the third sphere you
Will greet Guittone, Master Cino, Dante,   10
Our Franceschin' and all that company.°
    Yes, you can tell my lady in what tears
I live, how I become a beast when I
Recall her lovely face and sacred works.

288

    All of the air here I've filled up with sighs
While gazing from rough hills at that sweet plain
Where she was born, who kept within her hand
My heart, both when she bloomed and then bore fruit.
    To heaven she's gone; in such a plight I'm left   5
At her quick parting that my weary eyes,
While seeking her from far off and in vain,
Leave no place dry in their vicinity.
    Throughout these hills, there's not a stump or stone
No bough or verdant frond upon these slopes,   10
No flower in these vales, or leaf of grass,

stilla d'acqua non vèn di queste fonti,
né fiere àn questi boschi sí selvagge,
che non sappian quanto è mia pena acerba.

289

L'alma mia fiamma oltra le belle bella,
ch'ebbe qui 'l ciel sí amico et sí cortese,
anzi tempo per me nel suo paese
è ritornata, et a la par sua stella.

Or comincio a svegliarmi, et veggio ch'ella   5
per lo migliore al mio desir contese,
et quelle voglie giovenili accese
temprò con una vista dolce et fella.

Lei ne ringratio, e 'l suo alto consiglio,
che col bel viso et co' soavi sdegni   10
fecemi ardendo pensar mia salute.

O leggiadre arti et lor effetti degni,
l'un co la lingua oprar, l'altra col ciglio,
io gloria in lei, et ella in me virtute!

290

Come va 'l mondo! or mi diletta et piace
quel che piú mi dispiaque; or veggio et sento
che per aver salute ebbi tormento,
et breve guerra per eterna pace.

O speranza, o desir sempre fallace,   5
et degli amanti piú ben per un cento!
O quant'era il peggior farmi contento
quella ch'or siede in cielo, e 'n terra giace!

Ma 'l ceco Amor et la mia sorda mente
mi travïavan sí, ch'andar per viva   10
forza mi convenia dove morte era.

Benedetta colei ch'a miglior riva
volse il mio corso, et l'empia voglia ardente
lusingando affrenò perch'io non pèra.

291

Quand'io veggio dal ciel scender l'aurora
co la fronte di rose et co' crin' d'oro,
Amor m'assale, ond'io mi discoloro,
et dico sospirando: Ivi è Laura ora.

O felice Titon, tu sai ben l'ora   5
da ricovrare il tuo caro tesoro:
ma io che debbo far del dolce alloro?

No drop of water flowing from these springs,
Nor any beasts so savage in these woods
That they don't know how bitter is my pain.

289

Life-giving flame of mine, past beauty fair,
To whom heaven was so gracious here, so kind,
For me too early towards her homeland has
She turned again, gone back to her twin star.
    Now I begin to waken, and I see   5
That for the best my passion she withstood,
And all those burning, juvenile desires
She tempered with a face sweet, yet severe.
    For that I thank her, and for counsel high,
Since with her mild disdain and fair face she   10
Made me, though burning, think of being saved.
    O graceful arts and their benign effects;
One crafts with speech, the other with her brow,
I shape her glory; virtue she in me!

290

How this world goes! What once displeased me most
Now pleases and delights me; now I see
And feel that torment was to save my soul,
That brief war was to bring eternal peace.
    O hope, O ever false desire, indeed   5
For lovers by a hundred fold more false!
O how much worse had she made me content—
She, seated now in heaven and laid in earth!
    But my unhearing mind and blind love too
Misled me so, spurred on by vital force,   10
I was compelled to journey where Death dwelt.
    Bless her who toward the best shore set my course,
Who curbed with blandishments my ardent will,
So impious, that I might not be lost.

291

When I see dawn descend from heaven above
With rosy brow and with her locks of gold,
Love launches his assault on me, and I
Grow pale and, sighing, say: "There's Laura now."
    Happy Tithonus! O you know full well°   5
What hour brings again your treasure dear,
About sweet laurel, though, what must I do,

che se 'l vo' riveder, conven ch'io mora.

    I vostri dipartir' non son sí duri,
ch'almen di notte suol tornar colei   10
che non â schifo le tue bianche chiome:

    le mie notti fa triste, e i giorni oscuri,
quella che n'à portato i penser' miei,
né di sé m'à lasciato altro che 'l nome.

292

    Gli occhi di ch'io parlai sí caldamente,
et le braccia et le mani e i piedi e 'l viso,
che m'avean sí da me stesso diviso,
et fatto singular da l'altra gente;

    le crespe chiome d'òr puro lucente   5
e 'l lampeggiar de l'angelico riso,
che solean fare in terra un paradiso,
poca polvere son, che nulla sente.

    Et io pur vivo, onde mi doglio et sdegno,
rimaso senza 'l lume ch'amai tanto,   10
in gran fortuna e 'n disarmato legno.

    Or sia qui fine al mio amoroso canto:
secca è la vena de l'usato ingegno,
et la cetera mia rivolta in pianto.

293

    S'io avesse pensato che sí care
fossin le voci de' sospir' miei in rima,
fatte l'avrei, dal sospirar mio prima,
in numero piú spesse, in stil piú rare.

    Morta colei che mi facea parlare,   5
et che si stava de' pensier' miei in cima,
non posso, et non ò piú sí dolce lima,
rime aspre et fosche far soavi et chiare.

    Et certo ogni mio studio in quel tempo era
pur di sfogare il doloroso core   10
in qualche modo, non d'acquistar fama.

    Pianger cercai, non già del pianto honore:
or vorrei ben piacer; ma quella altera
tacito stanco dopo sé mi chiama.

294

    Soleasi nel mio cor star bella et viva,
com'alta donna in loco humile et basso:
or son fatto io per l'ultimo suo passo

Since if I want to see it, I must die?
    Your separations aren't so difficult,
For every night, at least, to you returns   10
She whom your hoary locks do not offend.
    My nights she saddens and obscures my days—
That one who bore away my thoughts, and left
Me nothing of herself except her name.

292
    Those eyes I spoke so passionately of,
Those arms and hands, the feet and face that from
My self have cut me off so, have as well
From other people set me quite apart.
    That twining hair of pure and lucent gold,   5
The lightning of her smile angelic, which
Once used to make a paradise on earth
Are now a little dust that senses naught.
    Yet I live angry; grieved am I at that,
Left here without the light I loved so much   10
In a great storm, a ship without a mast.
    Here let me finish now my amorous song;
The well-spring of accustomed skill is dry,
And my lyre is to lamentation turned.

293
    Had I but thought the chorus of my sighs
In rhyme would be so precious, from the first
A greater number of them I'd have made
And would have made them rarer in their style.
    That one is dead who caused me to speak out,   5
Who occupied the summit of my thoughts—
I can't, since I no longer own so sweet
A file, make gloomy, harsh rhymes soft and bright.
    And, certainly, my every study in
That time was still to ease my woeful heart   10
Some way and not to garner any fame.
    I sought release, not honor in my tears;
Now I should like to please; but that proud one
Summons me, worn and silent, after her.

294
    Alive and fair she once dwelt in my heart—
High lady in a low and humble place.
Now not just mortal, dead I'm made by her

non pur mortal, ma morto, et ella è diva.
    L'alma d'ogni suo ben spogliata et priva,   5
Amor de la sua luce ignudo et casso,
devrian de la pietà romper un sasso,
ma non è chi lor duol riconti o scriva:
    ché piangon dentro, ov'ogni orecchia è sorda,
se non la mia, cui tanta doglia ingombra,   10
ch'altro che sospirar nulla m'avanza.
    Veramente siam noi polvere et ombra,
veramente la voglia cieca e 'ngorda,
veramente fallace è la speranza.

295

    Soleano i miei penser; soavemente
di lor obgetto ragionare inseme:
—Pietà s'appressa, e del tardar si pente;
forse or parla di noi, o spera, o teme.—
    Poi che l'ultimo giorno et l'ore extreme   5
spogliâr di lei questa vita presente,
nostro stato dal ciel vede, ode et sente:
altra di lei non è rimaso speme.
    O miracol gentile, o felice alma,
o beltà senza exempio altera et rara,   10
che tosto è ritornata ond'ella uscío!
    Ivi à del suo ben far corona et palma
quella ch'al mondo sí famosa et chiara
fe' la sua gran vertute, e 'l furor mio.

296

    I' mi soglio accusare, et or mi scuso,
anzi me pregio et tengo assai piú caro,
de l'onesta pregion, del dolce amaro
colpo, ch'i' portai già molt'anni chiuso.
    Invide Parche, sí repente il fuso   5
troncaste, ch'attorcea soave et chiaro
stame al mio laccio, et quello aurato et raro
strale, onde morte piacque oltra nostro uso!
    Ché non fu d'allegrezza a' suoi dí mai,
di libertà, di vita alma sí vaga,   10
che non cangiasse 'l suo natural modo,
    togliendo anzi per lei sempre trar guai
che cantar per qualunque, e di tal piaga
morir contenta, et vivere in tal nodo.

Last step, and she a goddess has become.
　My soul, deprived and stripped of every good,　　　　5
And Love, cashiered, of his light destitute,
Must for the pity of it split a stone,
But no one will recount or write their woe,
　Because they weep within, where every ear
Is deaf but mine, I'm laden with such grief　　　　10
That, but for sighing, nothing's left to me.
　In truth we are but shadows, only dust,
In truth the will is gluttonous and blind,
In truth is expectation treacherous.

295

　My thoughts were once accustomed to converse
About their object gently 'midst themselves:
"Pity is near, and she repents delay;
She may now speak of us, may hope or fear."
　But since that final day, and that last hour　　　　5
Have stripped away from her this present life,
From heaven she sees and hears and feels our plight,
And here no other hope of her is left.
　O noble miracle, exultant soul,
O beauty rare and lofty with no peer,　　　　10
Which early has returned to where it sprung!
　For good deeds, there she has a crown and palm,
That one who to the world her virtue great
Made clear and famous—and my frenzy too.

296

　I used to blame myself, now I excuse—
That is, I prize, more precious hold myself
Because of that chaste prison, and the sweet
Sharp wound I've borne in secret many years.
　You jealous Fates, so unexpectedly　　　　5
You broke the spindle that spun soft, bright wool
For my snare, broke that rare and golden dart,
So that against all nature Death pleased me!
　For in its time there never was a soul
Joy charmed so much, or liberty, or life,　　　　10
That it would not exchange its natural way,
　Instead preferring ever to lament
For her, than sing for someone else—so hurt,
To die content and live ensnared like that.

297

Due gran nemiche inseme erano agiunte,
Bellezza et Honestà, con pace tanta,
che mai rebellïon l'anima santa
non sentí poi ch'a star seco fur giunte;

et or per Morte son sparse et disgiunte: 5
l'una è nel ciel, che se ne gloria et vanta;
l'altra sotterra, che' begli occhi amanta,
onde uscîr già tant'amorose punte.

L'atto soave, e 'l parlar saggio humile
che movea d'alto loco, e 'l dolce sguardo   10
che piagava il mio core (anchor l'acenna),

sono spariti; et s'al seguir son tardo
forse averrà che 'l bel nome gentile
consecrerò con questa stanca penna.

298

Quand'io mi volgo indietro a mirar gli anni
ch'ànno fuggendo i miei penseri sparsi,
et spento 'l foco ove agghiacciando io arsi,
et finito il riposo pien d'affanni,

rotta la fe' degli amorosi inganni,   5
et sol due parti d'ogni mio ben farsi,
l'una nel cielo et l'altra in terra starsi,
et perduto il guadagno de' miei damni,

i' mi riscuoto, et trovomi sí nudo,
ch'i' porto invidia ad ogni extrema sorte: 10
tal cordoglio et paura ò di me stesso.

O mia stella, o Fortuna, o Fato, o Morte,
o per me sempre dolce giorno et crudo,
come m'avete in basso stato messo!

299

Ov'è la fronte, che con picciol cenno
volgea il mio core in questa parte e 'n quella?
Ov'è 'l bel ciglio, et l'una et l'altra stella
ch'al corso del mio viver lume denno?

Ov'è 'l valor, la conoscenza e 'l senno?   5
L'accorta, honesta, humil, dolce favella?
Ove son le bellezze accolte in ella,
che gran tempo di me lor voglia fenno?

Ov'è l'ombra gentil del viso humano
ch'òra et riposo dava a l'alma stanca,   10
et là 've i miei pensier' scritti eran tutti?

297

Two mighty foes together were allied,
Beauty and Chastity, in such accord
That once they had combined to dwell in her,
That holy soul rebellion never knew.

    They're scattered and disjoined in death now, one's   5
In heaven, which glories and which boasts of it;
The other's under earth that hides fair eyes
From which once flew so many amorous darts.

    Her gentle deeds, her sage and modest speech
That issued from on high, and her sweet glance   10
That pierced my heart (and still it bears the scar)

    Have vanished; if I'm slow to follow, it
May come to pass that her fair noble name
I shall make sacred with this weary pen.

298

When I turn back to wonder at the years
That, fleeing, have dispersed my every thought
And quenched the fire in which I, freezing, burned,
And put an end to trouble-filled repose,

    And breached the faith of amorous deceits   5
And left my every good in but two parts—
One in heaven, and one on earth remains,
And lost is what I won by suffering—

    I rouse myself, and find I am so poor
I come to envy any dreadful fate;   10
Such fear and sorrow for myself I feel.

    O star of mine, O Fortune, Fate, O death
O day forever sweet and cruel to me,
In what a lowly plight you've set me down!

299

Where is that brow which with a little hint
Could turn my heart first this way and then that?
Where is that eyelash fair? Where both those stars
That shed light on the progress of my life?

    Where is that virtue, knowledge, and that wit?   5
That language, trenchant, modest, chaste, and sweet?
Where are those beauties gathered up in her,
Which for a long time worked their will in me?

    Where is the noble shadow of that face
So gracious, which to my tired soul brought ease,   10
Brought rest, there where my thoughts were all set forth?

Ov'è colei che mia vita ebbe in mano?
Quanto al misero mondo, et quanto manca
agli occhi miei che mai non fien asciutti!

300

Quanta invidia io ti porto, avara terra,
ch'abbracci quella cui veder m'è tolto,
et mi contendi l'aria del bel volto,
dove pace trovai d'ogni mia guerra!

    Quanta ne porto al ciel, che chiude et serra   5
et sí cupidamente à in sé raccolto
lo spirto da le belle membra sciolto,
et per altrui sí rado si deserra!

    Quanta invidia a quell'anime che 'n sorte
ànno or sua santa et dolce compagnia   10
la qual io cercai sempre con tal brama!

    Quant'a la dispietata et dura Morte,
ch'avendo spento in lei la vita mia,
stassi ne' suoi begli occhi, et me non chiama!

301

Valle che de' lamenti miei se' piena,
fiume che spesso del mio pianger cresci,
fere selvestre, vaghi augelli et pesci,
che l'una et l'altra verde riva affrena,

    aria de' miei sospir' calda et serena,   5
dolce sentier che sí amaro rïesci,
colle che mi piacesti, or mi rincresci,
ov'anchor per usanza Amor mi mena:

    ben riconosco in voi l'usate forme,
non, lasso, in me, che da sí lieta vita   10
son fatto albergo d'infinita doglia.

    Quinci vedea 'l mio bene; et per queste orme
torno a vedere ond'al ciel nuda è gita,
lasciando in terra la sua bella spoglia.

302

Levommi il mio penser in parte ov'era
quella ch'io cerco, et non ritrovo in terra:
ivi, fra lor che 'l terzo cerchio serra,
la rividi piú bella et meno altera.

    Per man mi prese, et disse:—In questa spera   5
sarai anchor meco, se 'l desir non erra:
i' so' colei che ti die' tanta guerra,

Where's she who held my life within her hand?
How much this wretched world lacks, and how much
My eyes, which never will be dry again.

300

How much I envy you, O greedy earth,
For her whose sight is reft from me you clasp,
And to me you forbid the air around
Her fair face, where from all war I found peace!
How much I envy heaven, which shuts and seals,   5
And which so avidly has welcomed to
Itself that spirit freed from lovely limbs,
Although, for others, seldom it's unlocked!
How much those souls now destined to enjoy
Her sweet and sacred company, for which   10
With such great yearning I forever searched!
How much I envy merciless, hard death,
Which, having quite snuffed out with her my life,
Stands fixed in her fair eyes, and calls me not.

301

O vale, so full of my lamenting cries,
And stream that often rises with my tears,
You forest beasts, you straying birds, you fish
Restrained by these two verdant river banks,
O air, made warm and cloudless by my sighs,   5
Sweet path that has so bitter grown for me,
Once pleasing hills that cause me now regret—
Where still love leads me, as his custom is.
I recognize in you your wonted forms;
Woe, not in me! Once joyous in my life,   10
The home of boundless sorrow I've become.
From here I saw my love, and with these steps
Return to see whence, naked, she has passed
To heaven and left her fair remains in earth.

302

My thought raised me to regions where she dwelt,
She whom I seek, but find no more on earth;
Amidst those whom the third sphere circles, there
Again I saw her, fairer and less proud.
She took my hand and said: "In this sphere yet   5
You'll be with me, if such desire's not wrong;
I'm she who brought such war to you, and who

[343]

et compie' mia giornata inanzi sera.
　　Mio ben non cape in intelletto humano:
te solo aspetto, et quel che tanto amasti　　　　　　10
e là giuso è rimaso, il mio bel velo.—
　　Deh perché tacque, et allargò la mano?
Ch'al suon de' detti sí pietosi et casti
poco mancò ch'io non rimasi in cielo.

303
　　Amor che meco al buon tempo ti stavi
fra queste rive, a' pensier' nostri amiche,
et per saldar le ragion' nostre antiche
meco et col fiume ragionando andavi;
　　fior', frondi, herbe, ombre, antri, onde, aure soavi,　　5
valli chiuse, alti colli et piaggie apriche,
porto de l'amorose mie fatiche,
de le fortune mie tante, et sí gravi;
　　o vaghi habitator' de' verdi boschi,
o nimphe, et voi che 'l fresco herboso fondo　　　　10
del liquido cristallo alberga et pasce:
　　i dí miei fur sí chiari, or son sí foschi,
come Morte che 'l fa; cosí nel mondo
sua ventura à ciaschun dal dí che nasce.

304
　　Mentre che 'l cor dagli amorosi vermi
fu consumato, e 'n fiamma amorosa arse,
di vaga fera le vestigia sparse
cercai per poggi solitarii et hermi;
　　et ebbi ardir cantando di dolermi　　　　　　　　5
d'Amor, di lei che sí dura m'apparse:
ma l'ingegno et le rime erano scarse
in quella etate ai pensier' novi e 'nfermi.
　　Quel foco è morto, e 'l copre un picciol marmo:
che se col tempo fossi ito avanzando　　　　　　　10
(come già in altri) infino a la vecchiezza,
　　di rime armato, ond'oggi mi disarmo,
con stil canuto avrei fatto parlando
romper le pietre, et pianger di dolcezza.

305
　　Anima bella da quel nodo sciolta
che piú bel mai non seppe ordir Natura,
pon' dal ciel mente a la mia vita oscura,

Completed my day's task ere evening fell.
   "No human mind can grasp my peace; for you
Alone I wait, and—what you loved so much—   10
My lovely veil, which there below remained."°
   Ah, why did she fall silent and let go
My hand? For at the sound of words so chaste
And pious, I in heaven nearly stayed.

303
   You, Love, who in that glad time stood with me
Upon these shores—these friends to all our thoughts—
Then, to resolve our ancient arguments,
Walked in debate with me, and with this stream,
   You fronds, flowers, grass, caves, gentle breezes, shades,
You waves, closed vales, high hills, and sunny slopes,
O haven from my drudgery for love,
And port in all my many grievous storms.
   O wandering dwellers in the verdant woods,
O nymphs, and you who dwell and feed within   10
The liquid crystal's cool and grassy deeps,
   My days, which were so bright, are now as dark
As Death who makes them so; thus in this world
Each has his fortune from his day of birth.

304
   As long as worms of love devoured my heart,
And it was burning in an amorous flame,
I sought the scattered vestiges of that
Fair wild one through remote, secluded hills.
   And, singing, I had courage to complain   5
Of love, of her who seemed to me so hard,
But I lacked skill, and rhymes were all too scarse
At that age, for my thoughts infirm and new.
   That fire is dead; a little marble now
Stands over it, but if it had with time   10
Kept growing till old age (in some it does)
   Then armed with rhymes—of which I'm now disarmed—
In style mature, with speech I could have made
Stones split apart and weep for tenderness.

305
   O lovely soul, freed from that bond more fair
Than any Nature earlier could wreathe:
My darkened life now from such joyful thoughts

da sí lieti pensieri a pianger volta.
La falsa opinïon dal cor s'è tolta,
che mi fece alcun tempo acerba et dura
tua dolce vista: omai tutta secura
volgi a me gli occhi, e i miei sospiri ascolta.
Mira 'l gran sasso, donde Sorga nasce,
et vedra'vi un che sol tra l'erbe et l'acque
di tua memoria et di dolor si pasce.
Ove giace il tuo albergo, et dove nacque
il nostro amor, vo' ch'abbandoni et lasce,
per non veder ne' tuoi quel ch'a te spiacque.

306

Quel sol che mi mostrava il camin destro
di gire al ciel con glorïosi passi,
tornando al sommo Sole, in pochi sassi
chiuse 'l mio lume e 'l suo carcer terrestro:
ond'io son fatto un animal silvestro,
che co' pie' vaghi solitarii et lassi
porto 'l cor grave et gli occhi humidi et bassi
al mondo, ch'è per me un deserto alpestro.
Cosí vo ricercando ogni contrada
ov'io la vidi; et sol tu che m'affligi,
Amor, vien' meco, et mostrimi ond'io vada.
Lei non trov'io: ma suoi santi vestigi
tutti rivolti a la superna strada
veggio, lunge da' laghi averni et stigi.

307

I' pensava assai destro esser su l'ale,
non per lor forza, ma di chi le spiega,
per gir cantando a quel bel nodo eguale
onde Morte m'assolve, Amor mi lega.
Trovaimi a l'opra via piú lento et frale
d'un picciol ramo cui gran fascio piega,
et dissi:—A cader va chi troppo sale,
né si fa ben per huom quel che 'l ciel nega.—
Mai non poria volar penna d'ingegno,
nonché stil grave o lingua, ove Natura
volò, tessendo il mio dolce ritegno.
Seguilla Amor con sí mirabil cura
in adornarlo, ch'i' non era degno
pur de la vista: ma fu mia ventura.

To weeping turned, from Heaven keep in mind.
That misconception from your heart is plucked   5
That made your sweet face hard toward me at times,
And bitter; now, entirely certain, cast
Your eyes on me, and to my sighs give ear.
O gaze on that great rock whence springs the Sorgue;
Between the grass and water there see one   10
Who feeds but on your memory, and woe.
The place your home stands, where our love was born,
I want you to abandon, leave it, so
You won't see in your own what you regret.

306

That sun which set me on the proper path
Toward heaven, with glorious steps returning to
The Highest Sun, sealed up with but few stones
Both her terrestrial prison and my light.
Thus, I've become a forest creature who   5
On straying, worn, and solitary feet
With tearful, downcast eyes bears through this world—
This desert wild for me—a heart oppressed.
Thus I comb every stretch of country where
I saw her; and you, vexing Love, alone   10
Walk by my side and show me where I go.
I find her not, but see blest vestiges
Of her, all pointing to that road divine°
Far from Avernian and Stygian lakes.°

307

I thought myself so expert on my wings—
Not by their strength, but his who spreads them wide—
I'd soar while singing fitly of that knot
Whence Death will free me, where Love binds me fast.
Far slower at that work, I found myself,   5
More frail than a small bough by great weight bent;
I said: "Who climbs too high is bound to fall,
Nor must man do, indeed, what Heaven forbids."
No artful quill—much less a weighty style
Or speech—could wing its way where Nature flew   10
As she was weaving my restraint so sweet.
Love followed, with such admirable care
Adorning her that I did not deserve
To see her, really; yet such was my fate.

308

Quella per cui con Sorga ò cangiato Arno,
con franca povertà serve richezze,
volse in amaro sue sante dolceze,
ond'io già vissi, or me ne struggo et scarno.

Da poi piú volte ò riprovato indarno   5
al secol che verrà l'alte belleze
pinger cantando, a ciò che l'ame et preze:
né col mio stile il suo bel viso incarno.

Le lode mai non d'altra, et proprie sue,
che 'n lei fur come stelle in cielo sparte,   10
pur ardisco ombreggiare, or una, or due:

ma poi ch'i' giungo a la divina parte
ch'un chiaro et breve sole al mondo fue,
ivi manca l'ardir, l'ingegno et l'arte.

309

L'alto et novo miracol ch'a' dí nostri
apparve al mondo, et star seco non volse,
che sol ne mostrò 'l ciel, poi sel ritolse
per adornarne i suoi stellanti chiostri,

vuol ch'i' depinga a chi nol vide, e 'l mostri,   5
Amor, che 'n prima la mia lingua sciolse,
poi mille volte indarno a l'opra volse
ingegno, tempo, penne, carte e 'nchiostri.

Non son al sommo anchor giunte le rime:
in me il conosco; et proval ben chiunque   10
è 'nfin a qui, che d'amor parli o scriva.

Chi sa pensare, il ver tacito estime,
ch'ogni stil vince, et poi sospire:—Adunque
beati gli occhi che la vider viva.—

310

Zephiro torna, e 'l bel tempo rimena,
e i fiori et l'erbe, sua dolce famiglia,
et garrir Progne et pianger Philomena,
et primavera candida et vermiglia.

Ridono i prati, e 'l ciel si rasserena;   5
Giove s'allegra di mirar sua figlia;
l'aria et l'acqua et la terra è d'amor piena;
ogni animal d'amar si riconsiglia.

Ma per me, lasso, tornano i piú gravi
sospiri, che del cor profondo tragge   10

308

That one for whom I changed Arno for Sorgue,°
Left servile riches for free poverty,
Has turned to gall her sacred sweetness that
I lived by; by it now I'm melted, flayed.

Since then, in song I've often vainly tried   5
To sketch her lofty beauties for the age
To come, so it may love and value them,
Yet her fair face my style can't body forth.

Those praises—no one else's, hers alone—
Which in her were like scattered stars in heaven,   10
I dare to shadow forth still—one or two;

But when I come to what's divine in her
Who was a bright, brief sun to all the world,
There courage falters, skill and art as well.

309

That high, rare miracle which in our day
Appeared here, but would not dwell in this world—
Whom heaven only showed us, and away
Then took, its starry cloisters to adorn,

Love who first loosed my tongue would have me sketch,
And show her to whoever's seen her not;
A thousand times in vain, then, has he set
To work my skill, time, papers, pens, and inks.

But rhyming has not reached perfection yet;
I know it in myself, and so do all   10
Who spoke of love or wrote of it till now.

May thinking men esteem the silent truth
That conquers every style, and sighing, say:
"Let eyes that saw her living, then, be blest."

310

Zephyr returns and brings fine weather back,°
Brings flowers and grass, all his sweet family,
And warbling Procne, weeping Philomel,°
And lovely Spring, pure white and brilliant red.

The meadows laugh, and bright sky shines serene;   5
To gaze upon his daughter Jove delights,°
And full of love are water, earth, and air;
All creatures once again take love's advice.

But, woe, to me the gravest sighs return,
From my heart's deepest places drawn by one   10

quella ch'al ciel se ne portò le chiavi;
　　et cantar augelletti, et fiorir piagge,
e 'n belle donne honeste atti soavi
sono un deserto, et fere aspre et selvagge.

311

　　Quel rosignuol, che sí soave piagne
forse suoi figli, o sua cara consorte,
di dolcezza empie il cielo et le campagne
con tante note sí pietose et scorte,
　　et tutta notte par che m'accompagne,　　　　　5
et mi rammente la mia dura sorte:
ch'altri che me non ò di ch'i' mi lagne,
ché 'n dee non credev'io regnasse Morte.
　　O che lieve è inganar chi s'assecura!
Que' duo bei lumi assai piú che 'l sol chiari　　10
chi pensò mai veder far terra oscura?
　　Or cognosco io che mia fera ventura
vuol che vivendo et lagrimando impari
come nulla qua giú diletta et dura.

312

　　Né per sereno ciel ir vaghe stelle,
né per tranquillo mar legni spalmati,
né per campagne cavalieri armati,
né per bei boschi allegre fere et snelle;
　　né d'aspettato ben fresche novelle　　　　　5
né dir d'amore in stili alti et ornati
né tra chiare fontane et verdi prati
dolce cantare honeste donne et belle;
　　né altro sarà mai ch'al cor m'aggiunga,
sí seco il seppe quella sepellire　　　　　　10
che sola agli occhi miei fu lume et speglio.
　　Noia m'è 'l viver sí gravosa et lunga
ch'i' chiamo il fine, per lo gran desire
di riveder cui non veder fu 'l meglio.

313

　　Passato è 'l tempo omai, lasso, che tanto
con refrigerio in mezzo 'l foco vissi;
passato è quella di ch'io piansi et scrissi,
ma lasciato m'à ben la penna e 'l pianto.
　　Passato è 'l viso sí leggiadro et santo,　　　　5
ma passando i dolci occhi al cor m'à fissi:

Who's borne away with her the keys to heaven.
    And little singing birds and flowering slopes,
Fair ladies' chaste and gentle courtesies
Are desert wastes, and savage creatures fierce.

311
    That nightingale that weeps so gently for
His children, or his precious mate perhaps,
With sweetness fills the heavens and the fields
With many well tuned notes, so full of woe.
    It seems he keeps me company all night   5
And of my bitter lot puts me in mind,
For no one but myself have I to blame:
I thought that death could not rule goddesses.
    Oh, one who's sure is easy to deceive!
Who ever thought to see those two fair eyes,   10
More brilliant than the sun, become dark earth?
    For, now I understand, my savage fate
Would have it that alive, in tears, I learn
How, down here, nothing both delights and lasts.

312
    No errant star will wend through skies serene,
Nor through a tranquil ocean ply tarred ships,
Nor through the fields go armored cavaliers,
Nor, through fair forests, gay and nimble beasts,
    Nor go fresh tidings of expected good,   5
Nor songs of love in lofty styles ornate
Nor 'midst clear fountains and green meadowlands
Sound forth sweet songs of women chaste and fair,
    Nor will another ever touch my heart;
How to inter it with her, she knew well,   10
She, the sole light and mirror for my eyes.
    To live so long and sadly vexes me,
So for life's end I call, through great desire
Once more to see her I'd best not have seen.

313
    Passed by now is that time, alas, when I
Lived so refreshed and cool amidst the fire;
Passed too is she for whom I wept and wrote,
But, truly, pen and tears she left behind.
    That blithesome face so holy passed as well,   5
But, passing, its sweet eyes transfixed my heart;

al cor già mio, che seguendo partissi
lei ch'avolto l'avea nel suo bel manto.

Ella 'l se ne portò sotterra, e 'n cielo
ove or trïumpha, ornata de l'alloro   10
che meritò la sua invicta honestate.

Cosí disciolto dal mortal mio velo
ch'a forza mi tien qui, foss'io con loro
fuor de' sospir' fra l'anime beate!

314
Mente mia, che presaga de' tuoi damni,
al tempo lieto già pensosa et trista,
sí 'ntentamente ne l'amata vista
requie cercavi de' futuri affanni,

agli atti, a le parole, al viso, ai panni,   5
a la nova pietà con dolor mista,
potêi ben dir, se del tutto eri avista:
Questo è l'ultimo dí de' miei dolci anni.

Qual dolcezza fu quella, o misera alma!
Come ardavamo in quel punto ch'i' vidi   10
gli occhi i quai non devea riveder mai,

quando a lor come a' duo amici piú fidi
partendo in guardia la piú nobil salma,
i miei cari penseri e 'l cor, lasciai!

315
Tutta la mia fiorita et verde etade
passava, e 'ntepidir sentia già 'l foco
ch'arse il mio core, et era giunto al loco
ove scende la vita ch'al fin cade.

Già incominciava a prender securtade   5
la mia cara nemica a poco a poco
de' sùoi sospetti, et rivolgeva in gioco
mie pene acerbe sua dolce honestade.

Presso era 'l tempo dove Amor si scontra
con Castitate, et agli amanti è dato   10
sedersi inseme, et dir che lor incontra.

Morte ebbe invidia al mio felice stato,
anzi a la speme; et feglisi a l'incontra
a mezza via come nemico armato.

316
Tempo era omai da trovar pace o triegua
di tanta guerra, et erane in via forse,

That heart, once mine, has left to follow her—
She who had lapped it in her lovely cloak.

Beneath the earth she bore it, and to heaven
Where she now triumphs, with that laurel crowned   10
Which her unconquered chastity deserves.

Set free thus from my mortal veil that holds
Me here by force, would I were there with them
Amidst the blessed spirits, past all sighs.

314

My mind, you had foretold your injuries—
Already sad and pensive in glad times—
From future torments you so earnestly
Sought out repose in her beloved sight;

Marking her deeds and words, her face and robes,   5
Her new compassion mingled with her woe,
You truly might have said (had you known all)
"This is the final day of my sweet years."

What tenderness was there! O my poor soul;
How, in that instant when I saw those eyes   10
That I must never see again, we flamed.

When, as to two most trusted friends, I left
At parting, in their care that noblest charge:
My precious thoughts, and left my heart as well.

315

All my green, flow'ring years were passing by;
Indeed, I felt the fire that burned my heart
Grow cool, and I had come to that place where
Life slips away, till at the end it fails.

Already, bit by bit, my precious foe   5
Began to feel more trust, despite her doubts,
And into playfulness her virtue sweet
Had started to transform my bitter pain.

That time when chastity falls in with Love
Was near, and when together lovers may   10
Sit down to talk of anything they like.

Death envied me this happy state—that is,
The hope of it, and, like a well-armed foe,
Fell on it as it went along its way.

316

The time was right for finding peace or truce
In such war; I'd have found a way, perhaps,

se non che' lieti passi indietro torse
chi le disaguaglianze nostre adegua:
    ché, come nebbia al vento si dilegua,   5
cosí sua vita súbito trascorse
quella che già co' begli occhi mi scorse,
et or conven che col penser la segua.
    Poco avev' a 'ndugiar, ché gli anni e 'l pelo
cangiavano i costumi: onde sospetto   10
non fôra il ragionar del mio mal seco.
    Con che honesti sospiri l'avrei detto
le mie lunghe fatiche, ch'or dal cielo
vede, son certo, et duolsene anchor meco!

317

    Tranquillo porto avea mostrato Amore
a la mia lunga et torbida tempesta
fra gli anni de la età matura honesta
che i vicii spoglia, et vertú veste e honore.
    Già traluceva a' begli occhi il mio core,   5
et l'alta fede non piú lor molesta.
Ahi Morte ria, come a schiantar se' presta
il frutto de molt'anni in sí poche hore!
    Pur vivendo veniasi ove deposto
in quelle caste orecchie avrei parlando   10
de' miei dolci pensier' l'antiqua soma;
    et ella avrebbe a me forse resposto
qualche santa parola sospirando,
cangiati i volti, et l'una et l'altra coma.

318

    Al cader d'una pianta che si svelse
come quella che ferro o vento sterpe,
spargendo a terra le sue spoglie excelse,
mostrando al sol la sua squalida sterpe,
    vidi un'altra ch'Amor obiecto scelse,   5
subiecto in me Callïope et Euterpe;
che 'l cor m'avinse, et proprio albergo felse,
qual per trunco o per muro hedera serpe.
    Quel vivo lauro ove solean far nido
li alti penseri, e i miei sospiri ardenti,   10
che de' bei rami mai non mossen fronda,
    al ciel translato, in quel suo albergo fido
lasciò radici, onde con gravi accenti
è anchor chi chiami, et non è chi responda.

If one who levels our disparities
Had not turned back my joyous steps again.

    For just as fog is scattered by the wind   5
Thus suddenly did her life pass away—
That one who led me with her lovely eyes,
And who I'm forced to follow now in thought,

    Not long had she to wait; for with my hair,
The years had changed my ways, and she need not   10
Have feared that I'd debate my ills with her.

    With what chaste sighs would I have told her of
My efforts long, which now I'm sure she sees
From Heaven, and sorrows for them still with me.

317

    Love pointed out a peaceful harbor from
My long and troubled tempest, in those years
Of chaste and seasoned age, when vices are
Sloughed off, and virtuous honor is put on.

    Already my heart shone in her fair eyes,   5
And perfect faith no longer troubled them.
Ah, wicked Death, how quick you are to crush
The fruit of many years in so few hours!

    Had she still lived, it might have come to pass
That speaking to those chaste ears I'd have set   10
Aside my ancient burden of sweet thought.

    And she might have replied to me, perhaps,
Some holy, sighing words—our faces changed,
And changed the color of our locks as well.

318

    When one tree fell, ripped out as if it were
By wind uprooted, or dislodged by iron,
Strewing its lofty foliage on the earth,
While showing to the sun its death-white root,

    I saw a tree next Love chose as my goal,   5
And Calliope and Euterpe as my theme,°
It won my heart, and there it made its home,
As ivy twines upon a trunk or wall.

    That living laurel, where my lofty thoughts
Once nested with those ardent sighs of mine,   10
Which never stirred a leaf on those fair boughs,

    Removed to heaven, has left its roots in this
Its loving home, where one still dwells who calls
In accents grave, though no one answers him.

I dí miei piú leggier' che nesun cervo
fuggîr come ombra, et non vider piú bene
ch'un batter d'occhio, et poche hore serene,
ch'amare et dolci ne la mente servo.

    Misero mondo, instabile et protervo,   5
del tutto è cieco chi 'n te pon sua spene:
ché 'n te mi fu 'l cor tolto, et or sel tene
tal ch'è già terra, et non giunge osso a nervo.

    Ma la forma miglior, che vive anchora,
et vivrà sempre, su ne l'alto cielo,   10
di sue bellezze ognor piú m'innamora;

    et vo, sol in pensar, cangiando il pelo,
qual ella è oggi, e 'n qual parte dimora,
qual a vedere il suo leggiadro velo.

    Sento l'aura mia anticha, e i dolci colli
veggio apparire, onde 'l bel lume nacque
che tenne gli occhi mei mentr'al ciel piacque
bramosi et lieti, or li tèn tristi et molli.

    O caduche speranze, o penser' folli!   5
Vedove l'erbe et torbide son l'acque,
et vòto et freddo 'l nido in ch'ella giacque,
nel qual io vivo, et morto giacer volli,

    sperando alfin, da le soavi piante
et da' belli occhi suoi, che 'l cor m'ànn'arso,   10
riposo alcun de le fatiche tante.

    O servito a signor crudele et scarso:
ch'arsi quanto 'l mio foco ebbi davante,
or vo piangendo il suo cenere sparso.

    È questo 'l nido in che la mia fenice
mise l'aurate et le purpuree penne,
che sotto le sue ali il mio cor tenne,
et parole et sospiri ancho ne elice?

    O del dolce mio mal prima radice,   5
ov'è il bel viso onde quel lume venne
che vivo et lieto ardendo mi mantenne?
Sol' eri in terra; or se' nel ciel felice.

    Et m'ài lasciato qui misero et solo,
talché pien di duol sempre al loco torno   10
che per te consecrato honoro et còlo;

319

My days, more swift than any deer that flees
Away like shadow, no more good have seen
Than one blink of an eye, a few bright hours,
Which, sweet and bitter, in my mind I store.

Poor arrogant, unstable world, to all   5
One's blind who rests his hope in you. In you
My heart was seized, and now is held by one
Already earth, with flesh disjoined from bone.

Her better form, though, living even now,
Which will forever live in Heaven above,   10
Still makes me love her beauties more and more.

I wander, turning gray, and only think
Of what she is today, of where she dwells
And what it's like to see her graceful veil.

320

That ancient breeze I feel, and those sweet hills
I see appear, where that fair light was born
Which kept my glad eyes yearning, while it so
Pleased Heaven; now it keeps them tearful, sad.

O fleeting hopes, O thoughtless lunacy!   5
The grass is widowed, waters have grown dark,
Empty and cold the nest in which she lay,
In which I live, in which I dead would lie,

Expecting at the last from her soft feet
And hoping from her fair eyes, which so parched   10
My heart, to have some rest from such great trials.

O, I have served a cruel and stingy lord,°
For while my fire before me blazed, I burned;
Now I go weeping for its scattered ash.

321

Is this the nest in which my phoenix poised
Those crimson, golden pinions that beneath
Her wings restrained my heart, and that can still
Draw forth from it both words and sighs as well?

O root of my first evil sweet, where is   5
The lovely face from which that light came forth
Which kept me burning, joyous and alive?
Unique on earth, you're happy now in heaven.

You've left me wretched, lonely here; so I
Return, forever woeful, to that place   10
You hallowed, which I honor and revere.

veggendo a' colli oscura notte intorno
onde prendesti al ciel l'ultimo volo,
et dove li occhi tuoi solean far giorno.

322

Mai non vedranno le mie luci asciutte
con le parti de l'animo tranquille
quelle note ov'Amor par che sfaville,
et Pietà di sua man l'abbia construtte.
Spirto già invicto a le terrene lutte,   5
ch'or su dal ciel tanta dolcezza stille,
ch'a lo stil, onde Morte dipartille,
le disvïate rime ài ricondutte:
di mie tenere frondi altro lavoro
credea mostrarte; et qual fero pianeta   10
ne 'nvidiò inseme, o mio nobil tesoro?
Chi 'nnanzi tempo mi t'asconde et vieta,
che col cor veggio, et co la lingua honoro,
e 'n te, dolce sospir, l'alma s'acqueta?

323

Standomi un giorno solo a la fenestra,
onde cose vedea tante, et sí nove,
ch'era sol di mirar quasi già stancho,
una fera m'apparve da man destra,
con fronte humana, da far arder Giove,   5
cacciata da duo veltri, un nero, un biancho;
che l'un et l'altro fiancho
de la fera gentil mordean sí forte,
che 'n poco tempo la menaro al passo
ove, chiusa in un sasso,   10
vinse molta bellezza acerba morte:
et mi fe' sospirar sua dura sorte.
Indi per alto mar vidi una nave,
con le sarte di seta, et d'òr la vela,
tutta d'avorio et d'ebeno contesta;   15
e 'l mar tranquillo, et l'aura era soave,
e 'l ciel qual è se nulla nube il vela,
ella carca di ricca merce honesta:
poi repente tempesta
orïental turbò sí l'aere et l'onde,   20
che la nave percosse ad uno scoglio.
O che grave cordoglio!
Breve hora oppresse, et poco spatio asconde,

I watch the night grow dark upon the hills
From which you made your final flight to heaven,
And where your eyes once used to make it day.

322
Ah, never will I look with peaceful mind
Or dry eyes on those verses, where it seems
That Love is shining, and which it appears
Compassion might have shaped with his own hand.
    Indeed, to earthly grief invincible   5
You, spirit, now distill from heaven above
Such sweetness, you've led back my wayward rhymes
To that style from which Death had parted them.
    My noble treasure, I'd show you, I thought,
Another labor of my budding leaves;   10
What planet fierce grudged our companionship?
    To me untimely who forbids you? hides
Whom my heart sees, and my tongue honors so,
And in whom, sighing sweet, my soul is calmed?

323
While one day at my window as I stood
Alone, I saw so many novel sights
That merely gazing almost wearied me:
At my right hand appeared a creature wild,
With human features that could Jove inflame;   5
Two hounds pursued her—one was black, one white;
They tore first one flank, then
The other ravened till, in a short time,
They brought that gentle beast to such a pass
That there, enclosed with stone,   10
Was beauty great by bitter death laid low,
Which left me sighing at its grievous fate.
    Then on the high seas I beheld a ship
With silken rigging and a sail of gold,
All framed of ivory and ebony;   15
The sea was tranquil, and the breeze was soft,
As when heaven glows, veiled not by any cloud;
Freighted she was with rich and virtuous goods;
A sudden eastern storm
Then cast into great tumult wind and waves,   20
And so the vessel splintered on a reef.
Oh, insupportable woe!
Brief hour o'erwhelmed and little space concealed

l'alte ricchezze a nul'altre seconde.
In un boschetto novo, i rami santi   25
fiorian d'un lauro giovenetto et schietto,
ch'un delli arbor' parea di paradiso;
et di sua ombra uscian sí dolci canti
di vari augelli, et tant'altro diletto,
che dal mondo m'avean tutto diviso;   30
et mirandol io fiso,
cangiossi 'l cielo intorno, et tinto in vista,
folgorando 'l percosse, et da radice
quella pianta felice
súbito svelse: onde mia vita è trista,   35
ché simile ombra mai non si racquista.
Chiara fontana in quel medesmo bosco
sorgea d'un sasso, et acque fresche et dolci
spargea, soavemente mormorando;
al bel seggio, riposto, ombroso et fosco,   40
né pastori appressavan né bifolci,
ma nimphe et muse a quel tenor cantando:
ivi m'assisi; et quando
piú dolcezza prendea di tal concento
et di tal vista, aprir vidi uno speco,   45
et portarsene seco
la fonte e 'l loco: ond'anchor doglia sento,
et sol de la memoria mi sgomento.
Una strania fenice, ambedue l'ale
di porpora vestita, e 'l capo d'oro,   50
vedendo per la selva altera et sola,
veder forma celeste et immortale
prima pensai, fin ch'a lo svelto alloro
giunse, et al fonte che la terra invola:
ogni cosa al fin vola;   55
ché, mirando le frondi a terra sparse,
e 'l troncon rotto, et quel vivo humor secco,
volse in se stessa il becco,
quasi sdegnando, e 'n un punto disparse:
onde 'l cor di pietate et d'amor m'arse.   60
Alfin vid'io per entro i fiori et l'erba
pensosa ir sí leggiadra et bella donna,
che mai nol penso ch'i' non arda et treme:
humile in sé, ma 'ncontra Amor superba;
et avea indosso sí candida gonna,   65
sí texta, ch'oro et neve parea inseme;
ma le parti supreme

Those noble riches, next in rank to none.
    In a new-planted grove, a laurel bloomed   25
With hallowed limbs so young and pure, it seemed
A tree of those that grow in Paradise;
And from its shade there issued such sweet songs
Of divers birds, and other great delight,
That I was carried wholly from the world.   30
While, marveling, I stared,
The sky above was altered—overcast;
Flashing, it struck and by the roots at once
Tore up that happy plant,
And ever since, my life's been full of woe,   35
For shade like that I'll never find again.
    In that same wood a crystal fountain flowed
Out of a stone, and waters cool and sweet
Came gushing, murmuring delightfully;
To that fair seat, hidden, shaded, and dark,   40
No country folk nor shepherds ventured near,
But nymphs and muses singing harmony;
There I sat down; as I
Most sweetness took from such a melody—
And such a view—I saw a chasm yawn,   45
And borne away within
The fountain and the place: still I feel pain;
By that mere memory am I dismayed.
    Observing a rare phoenix in the woods
Alone and proud, with both her wings attired   50
In purple, and in gold her head, I thought
At first to view her heavenly, deathless form
Till she to that uprooted laurel came
And to that fountain swallowed by the earth:
All, in the end, takes flight.   55
For, seeing scattered leaves upon the ground,
The broken trunk, that living liquid dry,
Upon herself her beak
She turned as in disdain, and vanished all
At once; whence love and pity sear my heart.   60
    At last amidst the grass and flowers I saw
A pensive lady go, so graceful, fair,
That just to think of her I burn and quake:
One humble in herself, against Love proud;
And she was wearing such a flawless gown,   65
Woven to seem of gold and snow at once,
But yet her crowning parts

eran avolte d'una nebbia oscura:
punta poi nel tallon d'un picciol angue,
come fior colto langue, 70
lieta si dipartio, nonché secura.
Ahi, nulla, altro che pianto, al mondo dura!
    Canzon, tu puoi ben dire:
—Queste sei visïoni al signor mio
àn fatto un dolce di morir desio.— 75

324

    Amor, quando fioria
mia spene, e 'l guidardon di tanta fede,
tolta m'è quella ond'attendea mercede.
    Ahi dispietata morte, ahi crudel vita!
L'una m'à posto in doglia, 5
et mie speranze acerbamente à spente;
l'altra mi tèn qua giú contra mia voglia,
et lei che se n'è gita
seguir non posso, ch'ella nol consente.
Ma pur ognor presente 10
nel mezzo del meo cor madonna siede,
et qual è la mia vita, ella sel vede.

325

    Tacer non posso, et temo non adopre
contrario effecto la mia lingua al core,
che vorria far honore
a la sua donna, che dal ciel n'ascolta.
Come poss'io, se non m'insegni, Amore, 5
con parole mortali aguagliar l'opre
divine, et quel che copre
alta humiltate, in se stessa raccolta?
Ne la bella pregione, onde or è sciolta,
poco era stato anchor l'alma gentile, 10
al tempo che di lei prima m'accorsi;
onde súbito corsi,
ch'era de l'anno et di mi' etate aprile,
a coglier fiori in quei prati d'intorno,
sperando a li occhi suoi piacer sí addorno. 15
    Muri eran d'alabastro, e 'l tetto d'oro,
d'avorio uscio, et fenestre di zaffiro,
onde 'l primo sospiro
mi giunse al cor, et giugnerà l'extremo:
inde i messi d'Amor armati usciro 20

Were all enfolded in a mist obscure;
Then a small serpent pricked her heel, and as
A gathered flower wilts,   70
She passed not only certain, but in joy.
Woe! Nothing, save for tears, in this world lasts.
    Song, you may surely say:
All these six visions of my master have
Produced in him a sweet desire for death.   75

324

    O Love, when my hope blossomed—
The recompense for such great faith—that one
To whom I'd looked for grace was reft from me.
    Ah, Death relentless! Cruel Life, alas!
The one brought woe to me,   5
And bitterly extinguished all my hopes;
Against my will, the other holds me here,
And I can't follow her
Who's gone before, since Life will not consent.
But ever present still,   10
Within my heart my lady has her home
And what my life is, she herself can see.

325

    I can't keep silent, yet fear lest my tongue
Shape some result displeasing to my heart,
Who would do honor to
His lady, who from heaven hears him now.
How can I, if you do not teach me, Love,   5
Make mortal words match works divine—match what
Is hidden by the high
Humility that is stored up in her?
In her fair prison—whence now she is free—
Her noble spirit had but little dwelt   10
When I at first became aware of her.
And so I ran at once—
Both my life's April and the year's it was—
To gather blossoms in the meadows round,
Hoping, so garlanded, to please her eyes.   15
    The walls were alabaster, gold the roof,
With ivory gate and sapphire windowpanes,
Whence that first sigh came to
My heart, and whence the final one will come.
Thence issued forth love's messengers with arms   20

di saette et di foco, ond'io di loro,
coronati d'alloro,
pur come or fusse, ripensando tremo.
D'un bel diamante quadro, et mai non scemo,
vi si vedea nel mezzo un seggio altero   25
ove, sola, sedea la bella donna:
dinanzi, una colonna
cristallina, et iv'entro ogni pensero
scritto, et for tralucea sí chiaramente,
che mi fea lieto, et sospirar sovente.   30
    A le pungenti, ardenti et lucide arme,
a la victorïosa insegna verde,
contra cui in campo perde
Giove et Apollo et Poliphemo et Marte,
ov'è 'l pianto ognor fresco, et si rinverde,   35
giunto mi vidi; et non possendo aitarme,
preso lassai menarme
ond'or non so d'uscir la via né l'arte.
Ma sí com'uom talor che piange, et parte
vede cosa che li occhi e 'l cor alletta,   40
cosí colei per ch'io son in pregione,
standosi ad un balcone,
che fu sola a' suoi dí cosa perfetta,
cominciai a mirar con tal desio
che me stesso e 'l mio mal posi in oblio.   45
    I' era in terra, e 'l cor in paradiso,
dolcemente oblïando ogni altra cura,
et mia viva figura
far sentia un marmo e 'mpiér di meraviglia,
quando una donna assai pronta et secura,   50
di tempo anticha, et giovene del viso,
vedendomi sí fiso
a l'atto de la fronte et de le ciglia:
«Meco—mi disse—, meco ti consiglia,
ch'i' son d'altro poder che tu non credi;   55
et so far lieti et tristi in un momento,
piú leggiera che 'l vento,
et reggo et volvo quanto al mondo vedi.
Tien' pur li occhi come aquila in quel sole:
parte da' orecchi a queste mie parole.   60
    Il dí che costei nacque, eran le stelle
che producon fra voi felici effecti
in luoghi alti et electi,
l'una ver' l'altra con amor converse:

Of darts and fire, and when I think again
Of them with laurel crowned,
I tremble still as if it happened now.
And in the midst a lofty throne was seen,
One made from precious diamond, flawless, square,   25
And there, alone, the lovely lady sat.
Before her rose a column
Crystalline, and there each thought set down
Inside, shone through outside so brilliantly,
It gave me joy, and often made me sigh.   30
    And so those piercing, fiery, brilliant arms,
And that victorious banner green, against
Which in the field Jove fails—
Apollo, Polyphemus, Mars as well—°
Where weeping, ever fresh, springs forth again,   35
I saw that I had reached; I could not help
Myself, but let myself
Be taken; now I know no way, no art
To lead me out. But as a man who weeps
At parting sometimes sees what lures his eyes   40
And heart, thus I began to gaze with such
Desire on her who stood
Upon a balcony, who in her day
Was solely perfect, for whom I'm enslaved,
That I forgot my evil and myself.   45
    On earth was I, my heart in paradise.
Forgetting sweetly every other care
And filled with awe, I sensed
My living figure into marble turn
When a most eager lady, one assured°   50
And old in years, but in her visage young,
Perceiving me so rapt
By the expression of my brow and eyes,
Called out aloud, "With me! Consult with me!
For I have power beyond your credence, and   55
Can in one instant gladden and make sad
More swiftly than the wind;
What in this world you see, I rule, I turn.
Still eagle-like your eyes fix on that sun
And meanwhile lend your ears to these my words.   60
    "The day that she was born, those stars that cause
Felicitous effects among you, were
In high auspicious places,
Aligned one with the other lovingly.

Venere e 'l padre con benigni aspecti   65
tenean le parti signorili et belle,
et le luci impie et felle
quasi in tutto del ciel eran disperse.
Il sol mai sí bel giorno non aperse:
l'aere et la terra s'allegrava, et l'acque   70
per lo mar avean pace et per li fiumi.
Fra tanti amici lumi,
una nube lontana mi dispiacque:
la qual temo che 'n pianto si resolve,
se Pietate altramente il ciel non volve.   75
        Com'ella venne in questo viver basso,
ch'a dir il ver non fu degno d'averla,
cosa nova a vederla,
già santissima et dolce anchor acerba,
parea chiusa in òr fin candida perla;   80
et or carpone, or con tremante passo,
legno, acqua, terra o sasso
verde facea, chiara, soave, et l'erba
con le palme o coi pie' fresca et superba,
et fiorir coi belli occhi le campagne,   85
et acquetar i vènti et le tempeste
con voci anchor non preste,
di lingua che dal latte si scompagne:
chiaro mostrando al mondo sordo et cieco
quanto lume del ciel fusse già seco.   90
        Poi che, crescendo in tempo et in virtute,
giunse a la terza sua fiorita etate,
leggiadria né beltate
tanta non vide 'l sol, credo, già mai:
li occhi pien' di letitia et d'onestate,   95
e 'l parlar di dolcezza et di salute.
Tutte lingue son mute,
a dir di lei quel che tu sol ne sai.
Sí chiaro à 'l volto di celesti rai,
che vostra vista in lui non pò fermarse;   100
et da quel suo bel carcere terreno
di tal foco ài 'l cor pieno,
ch'altro piú dolcemente mai non arse:
ma parmi che sua súbita partita
tosto ti fia cagion d'amara vita».   105
        Detto questo, a la sua volubil rota
si volse, in ch'ella fila il nostro stame,
trista et certa indivina de' miei danni:

Both father Jove and Venus with kind looks 65
Held sway in those fair lordly regions, and
Wicked impious stars
In almost all of heaven were put to flight.
    "Never began the sun so fair a day:
The air and earth rejoiced, and in the sea 70
And in the streams the waters were at peace.
Amidst so many friendly lights
One distant cloud distressed me, which I fear
Will be dissolved in tears if heaven's wheel
Is not by Pity turned some other way. 75
    "When in this base life (which to speak the truth
Did not deserve to have her) she arrived,
How rare a thing to see!
Already sweet, most sacred, though still young,
She seemed a pure white pearl in fine gold set; 80
On hands and knees, and then with toddling steps
She made the woods turn green,
Made water, earth, and stone grow gentle, and
With palms or feet made grass grow fresh and proud,
Made meadows blossom with her lovely eyes, 85
And quieted the tempests and the winds
With still unskillful words
Upon a tongue unweaned from milk as yet,
Thus showing clearly to a deaf, blind, world
What heavenly light so early shone in her. 90
    "In virtue growing, in her years as well,
She came into her third, her blooming time;
Such beauty and such grace
I think the sun had never seen before;
Her eyes with joy and chastity were filled, 95
With sweetness and salvation, too, her speech.
All tongues grow mute that try
To tell of her what you uniquely know.
So bright her visage with celestial beams
That on her face you can't let your gaze pause, 100
And from her fair, corporeal prison such
A fire has filled your heart,
No other fire more sweet has ever burned.
But, as it seems, her sudden parting will
Occasion soon a bitter life for you." 105
    This said, to her inconstant wheel she turned—
The one where she spins out our thread of life—
Unerring, sad diviner of my loss;

ché, dopo non molt'anni,
quella per ch'io ò di morir tal fame, 110
canzon mia, spense Morte acerba et rea,
che piú bel corpo occider non potea.

326

Or ài fatto l'extremo di tua possa,
o crudel Morte; or ài 'l regno d'Amore
impoverito; or di bellezza il fiore
e 'l lume ài spento, et chiuso in poca fossa;
   or ài spogliata nostra vita et scossa 5
d'ogni ornamento et del sovran suo honore:
ma la fama e 'l valor che mai non more,
non è in tua forza; abbiti ignude l'ossa:
   ché l'altro à 'l cielo, et di sua chiaritate,
quasi d'un piú bel sol, s'allegra et gloria, 10
et fi' al mondo de' buon' sempre in memoria.
   Vinca 'l cor vostro, in sua tanta victoria,
angel novo, lassú, di me pietate,
come vinse qui 'l mio vostra beltate.

327

L'aura et l'odore e 'l refrigerio et l'ombra
del dolce lauro et sua vista fiorita,
lume et riposo di mia stanca vita,
tolt' à colei che tutto 'l mondo sgombra.
   Come a noi il sol se sua soror l'adombra, 5
cosí l'alta mia luce a me sparita,
i' cheggio a Morte incontra Morte aita,
di sí scuri penseri Amor m'ingombra.
   Dormit' ài, bella donna, un breve sonno:
or se' svegliata fra li spirti electi, 10
ove nel suo factor l'alma s'interna;
   et se mie rime alcuna cosa ponno,
consecrata fra i nobili intellecti
fia del tuo nome qui memoria eterna.

328

L'ultimo, lasso, de' miei giorni allegri,
che pochi ò visto in questo viver breve,
giunto era, et facto 'l cor tepida neve
forse presago de' dí tristi et negri.
   Qual à già i nervi e i polsi e i penser' egri, 5
cui domestica febbre assalir deve,

Not many years, my Song,
Had passed till one for whom I hunger so   110
To die, was snuffed out by vile, bitter Death
Who could no fairer body have destroyed.

326

Now you have done the worst within your power,
O cruel Death: made love's realm destitute;
Now you've cut off both beauty's bloom and light,
And in a little grave you've sealed them up.

Our life you have despoiled and from it stripped   5
Its sovereign honor, every ornament,
But in your power undying fame lies not,
Nor merit; for yourself the bare bones take.

For Heaven has the rest and in her clear light joys
And glories as if in a sun more fair;   10
In good folks' memory she'll always be.

New angel, in your victory great above,
There let compassion for me win your heart
As, here, your loveliness mine overcame.

327

The breeze, the scent, and the refreshing shade
Of laurel sweet, her flowering countenance,
Respite and light in my exhausted life,
Has that one seized who sweeps clear all the world.

As when his sister hides the sun from us,   5
So my exalted light has disappeared;
I beg for Death's assistance against Death,
For love with thoughts so dark has weighed me down.

A brief sleep, lovely lady, you have slept;
'Midst spirits elect now you have wakened where,   10
In its Creator, one's soul is absorbed.

And, if my rhymes have any influence,
Your name here among noble minds will be
Held sacred in eternal memory.

328

The last of all my joyous days had come,
Alas, for few I've seen in this brief life,
And changed my heart to melting snow, of black
And dismal days an augury perhaps.

Like one with sinews, pulse, and thoughts infirm,   5
And whom the quartan ague soon must strike,°

tal mi sentia, non sappiend'io che leve
venisse 'l fin de' miei ben' non integri.
    Li occhi belli, or in ciel chiari et felici
del lume onde salute et vita piove,
lasciando i miei qui miseri et mendici,
    dicean lor con faville honeste et nove:
—Rimanetevi in pace, o cari amici.
Qui mai piú no, ma rivedrenne altrove.—

             329
    O giorno, o hora, o ultimo momento,
o stelle congiurate a 'mpoverirme!
O fido sguardo, or che volei tu dirme
partend'io per non esser mai contento?
    Or conosco i miei danni, or mi risento:
ch'i' creveda (ahi credenze vane e 'nfirme!)
perder parte, non tutto, al dipartirme;
quante speranze se ne porta il vento!
    Ché già 'l contrario era ordinato in cielo,
spegner l'almo mio lume ond'io vivea,
et scritto era in sua dolce amara vista;
    ma 'nnanzi agli occhi m'era post'un velo
che mi fea non veder quel ch'i' vedea,
per far mia vita súbito piú trista.

             330
    Quel vago, dolce, caro, honesto sguardo
dir parea:—To' di me quel che tu pôi,
ché mai piú qui non mi vedrai da poi
ch'avrai quinci il pe' mosso, a mover tardo.—
    Intellecto veloce piú che pardo,
pigro in antivedere i dolor' tuoi,
come non vedestú nelli occhi suoi
quel che ved' ora, ond'io mi struggo et ardo?
    Taciti sfavillando oltra lor modo,
dicean:—O lumi amici che gran tempo
con tal dolcezza feste di noi specchi,
    il ciel n'aspetta: a voi parrà per tempo;
ma chi ne strinse qui, dissolve il nodo,
e 'l vostro per farv' ira vuol che 'nvecchi.—

             331
    Solea da la fontana di mia vita
allontanarme, et cercar terre et mari,

I felt myself; nor did I know how fast
An end to my unstable state might come.
　　Those fair eyes, bright and happy now in heaven
With that light from which health and life rain down,　　10
On having left mine begging, wretched here,
　　To them spoke thus, aglow with virtue rare:
"Now stay at peace, dear friends; here never, no,
But elsewhere we shall once more meet again."

329

　　O day, O hour, O final instant, O
You stars, how you conspire to make me poor!
Devoted look, what did you long to say
At parting, so I'd never be content?
　　Aware at last, my injuries I know;　　5
For once I thought (ah, vain, infirm belief!)
To lose a part, not all, when I went forth;
How many hopes are blown away by wind!
　　Ere then, had Heaven decreed the opposite—
To quench that kindly light by which I lived—　　10
In her sweet face severe it was inscribed.
　　A veil then had been drawn before my eyes
That caused me not to see that which I saw,
To make my life grow, all at once, more sad.

330

　　It seemed that lovely sweet, chaste, precious look
Spoke thus: "What you are able, take from me,
For never more you'll see me here, once from
This place you stir your hesitating foot."
　　Ah, swifter than a leopard, intellect:　　5
How slow you are your own woes to foresee!
Why, in her eyes, did you not then perceive
What now you see, what burns and lays me waste?
　　Aglow more than their custom was, they spoke
In silence: "O you friendly lights that long　　10
Your mirrors sweetly made of us, now Heaven
　　Awaits us; it will seem too soon to you,
But he who tied us here unties my knot,
And to aggrieve you, wants yours to grow old."

331

　　Far distant from the fountain of my life
I used to wander, searching lands and seas,

non mio voler, ma mia stella seguendo;
et sempre andai, tal Amor diemmi aita,
in quelli exilii quanto e' vide amari,   5
di memoria et di speme il cor pascendo.
Or, lasso, alzo la mano, et l'arme rendo
a l'empia et vïolenta mia fortuna,
che privo m'à di sí dolce speranza.
Sol memoria m'avanza,   10
et pasco 'l gran desir sol di quest'una:
onde l'alma vien men frale et digiuna.
    Come a corrier tra via, se 'l cibo manca,
conven per forza rallentare il corso,
scemando la vertú che 'l fea gir presto,   15
cosí, mancando a la mia vita stanca
quel caro nutrimento in che di morso
die' chi 'l mondo fa nudo e 'l mio cor mesto,
il dolce acerbo, e 'l bel piacer molesto
mi si fa d'ora in hora, onde 'l camino   20
sí breve non fornir spero et pavento.
Nebbia o polvere al vento,
fuggo per piú non esser pellegrino:
et cosí vada, s'è pur mio destino.
    Mai questa mortal vita a me non piacque   25
(sassel' Amor con cui spesso ne parlo)
se non per lei che fu 'l suo lume, e 'l mio:
poi che 'n terra morendo, al ciel rinacque
quello spirto ond'io vissi, a seguitarlo
(licito fusse) è 'l mi' sommo desio.   30
Ma da dolermi ò ben sempre, perch'io
fui mal accorto a proveder mio stato,
ch'Amor mostrommi sotto quel bel ciglio
per darmi altro consiglio:
ché tal morí già tristo et sconsolato,   35
cui poco inanzi era 'l morir beato.
    Nelli occhi ov'habitar solea 'l mio core
fin che mia dura sorte invidia n'ebbe,
che di sí ricco albergo il pose in bando,
di sua man propria avea descritto Amore   40
con lettre di pietà quel ch'averrebbe
tosto del mio sí lungo ir desïando.
Bello et dolce morire era allor quando,
morend'io, non moria mia vita inseme,
anzi vivea di me l'optima parte: 45
or mie speranze sparte

Not my desire pursuing, but my star.
And Love so helped me that I ever went
Into that exile (grievous as he sees)   5
Feeding my heart on memory and hope.
Alas, I raise my hand now, and give up
My arms to Fortune, wicked, violent,
Who has bereft me of my hope so sweet.
Just memory remains;   10
On this alone I feed the great desire
And thus my frail and fasting soul grows weak.
    Just as along his way a courier must,
If he lacks food, perforce run slower when
The strength that made him quick diminishes,   15
Thus lacking in my weary life is that
Dear sustenance that one consumes who strips
The world bare, and casts down my heart, who turns
The sweet to bitter, and makes pleasure fair
An hourly vexation: I expect,   20
I fear, I'll not complete my course so brief.
I'm fog or dust in wind
And flee so I won't be a wanderer more.
Thus it must be, if truly that's my fate.
    This mortal life has never brought me joy   25
If not through her who was Love's light and mine
(Love knows that; oft with him I've talked of it);
Since, dead on earth, in Heaven reborn is she,
That spirit by whom I lived, to follow her
(If that's permissible) is my supreme   30
Desire. But I must ever mourn, for I
Was ill equipped to prophesy my plight
That, under that fair eyebrow, love displayed
To give me different counsel:
For some have died disconsolate and sad   35
Whom death a little sooner would have blest.
    In those eyes where my heart made its abode—
Until my bitter fate grew envious
And banished it from such a precious home—
In letters of compassion, Love set down   40
In his own hand what soon would happen on
My wanderings, so long and passionate:
Then fair and sweet would it have been to die,
When, had I died, I'd not have lost my life;
Instead my best part would have lived. My hopes   45
Now Death has scattered far; my good

à Morte, et poca terra il mio ben preme;
et vivo; et mai nol penso ch'i' non treme.

Se stato fusse il mio poco intellecto
meco al bisogno, et non altra vaghezza   50
l'avesse disvïando altrove vòlto,
ne la fronte a madonna avrei ben lecto:
—Al fin se' giunto d'ogni tua dolcezza
et al principio del tuo amaro molto.—
Questo intendendo, dolcemente sciolto   55
in sua presentia del mortal mio velo
et di questa noiosa et grave carne,
potea inanzi lei andarne,
a veder preparar sua sedia in cielo:
or l'andrò dietro, omai, con altro pelo.   60

Canzon s'uom trovi in suo amor viver queto,
di':—Muor' mentre se' lieto,
ché morte al tempo è non duol, ma refugio;
et chi ben pò morir, non cerchi indugio.—

332

Mia benigna fortuna e 'l viver lieto,
i chiari giorni et le tranquille notti
e i soavi sospiri e 'l dolce stile
che solea resonare in versi e 'n rime,
vòlti subitamente in doglia e 'n pianto,   5
odiar vita mi fanno, et bramar morte.

Crudele, acerba, inexorabil Morte,
cagion mi dài di mai non esser lieto,
ma di menar tutta mia vita in pianto,
e i giorni oscuri et le dogliose notti.   10
I mei gravi sospir' non vanno in rime,
e 'l mio duro martir vince ogni stile.

Ove è condutto il mio amoroso stile?
A parlar d'ira, a ragionar di morte.
U' sono i versi, u' son giunte le rime,   15
che gentil cor udia pensoso et lieto;
ove 'l favoleggiar d'amor le notti?
Or non parl'io, né penso, altro che pianto.

Già mi fu col desir sí dolce il pianto,
che condia di dolcezza ogni agro stile,   20
et vegghiar mi facea tutte le notti:
or m'è 'l pianger amaro piú che morte,
non sperando mai 'l guardo honesto et lieto,
alto sogetto a le mie basse rime.

A little earth weighs down; yet still I live,
Nor ever think of it that I don't quake.
    If my poor intellect had been with me
When needful, had no other grace turned it   50
Aside to make it lose its way, then I'd
Have surely read upon my lady's brow:
"The end of all your sweetness you have reached
And reached the start of your long bitterness."
Had I paid heed to this, before her eyes,   55
Freed sweetly from my mortal veil, and from
This troublesome and heavy flesh, ahead
Of her I could have gone,
Beheld her heavenly throne made ready there;
Now I shall come behind, with hair turned gray.   60
    Song, if one in his love finds quiet life,
Say: "Die while you are happy,
For timely death is refuge, not a grief;
Let one who can, die well—not seek to wait."

332

    My gracious fortune and my life so glad,
My clear and sunny days and peaceful nights,
And both my gentle sighing and sweet style
That used to sound in verses and in rhymes
Were turned at once to grieving and to tears;   5
They made me hate my life, and long for death.
    Cruel, premature, inexorable Death,
You give me reason never to be glad,
But rather all my life to lead in tears,
With dark and cloudy days and woeful nights.   10
My painful sighing won't turn into rhymes,
And my cruel torture conquers every style.
    To what has it been drawn, my amorous style?
To speak of rage, and discourse about death.
Where are the verses now, where are the rhymes   15
A noble heart heard once, one thoughtful, glad?
Where are the tales of love throughout the nights?
Of nothing now I speak or think but tears.
    Once, with desire, so sweet to me were tears,
They rendered sweeter every sour style   20
And caused me to be wakeful all those nights;
Now weeping is more bitter than is death
To me, since I hope never for that glad,
Chaste glance, the high theme of my lowly rhymes.

Chiaro segno Amor pose a le mie rime   25
dentro a' belli occhi, et or l'à posto in pianto,
con dolor rimembrando il tempo lieto:
ond'io vo col penser cangiando stile,
et ripregando te, pallida Morte,
che mi sottragghi a sí penose notti.   30
     Fuggito è 'l sonno a le mie crude notti,
e 'l suono usato a le mie roche rime,
che non sanno trattar altro che morte,
cosí è 'l mio cantar converso in pianto.
Non à 'l regno d'Amor sí vario stile,   35
ch'è tanto or tristo quanto mai fu lieto.
     Nesun visse già mai piú di me lieto,
nesun vive piú tristo et giorni et notti;
et doppiando 'l dolor, doppia lo stile
che trae del cor sí lacrimose rime.   40
Vissi di speme, or vivo pur di pianto,
né contra Morte spero altro che Morte.
     Morte m'à morto, et sola pò far Morte
ch'i' torni a riveder quel viso lieto
che piacer mi facea i sospiri e 'l pianto,   45
l'aura dolce et la pioggia a le mie notti,
quando i penseri electi tessea in rime,
Amor alzando il mio debile stile.
     Or avess'io un sí pietoso stile
che Laura mia potesse tôrre a Morte,   50
come Euridice Orpheo sua senza rime,
ch'i' viverei anchor piú che mai lieto!
S'esser non pò, qualchuna d'este notti
chiuda omai queste due fonti di pianto.
     Amor, i' ò molti et molt'anni pianto   55
mio grave danno in doloroso stile,
né da te spero mai men fere notti;
et però mi son mosso a pregar Morte
che mi tolla di qui, per farme lieto,
ove è colei ch'i' canto et piango in rime.   60
     Se sí alto pòn gir mie stanche rime,
ch'agiungan lei ch'è fuor d'ira e di pianto,
et fa 'l ciel or di sue bellezze lieto,
ben riconoscerà 'l mutato stile,
che già forse le piacque anzi che Morte   65
chiaro a lei giorno, a me fesse atre notti.
     O voi che sospirate a miglior' notti,
ch'ascoltate d'Amore o dite in rime,

A target bright Love set out for my rhymes   25
In fair eyes; now he places it in tears,
Remembering with sorrow times so glad,
For which I wander thoughtful, changing style,
And beseeching you again, O pallid Death,
To set me free from such afflicting nights.   30

　　All sleep has fled from my embittered nights,
And their accustomed tune from croaking rhymes,
For they can deal with nothing except Death;
So is my singing transformed into tears,
Nor has the realm of Love such varied style,   35
As woeful now as it was ever glad.

　　Than I, no one has ever lived more glad;
No one more woeful lives by day and night,
And twofold woe reduplicates my style
That from the heart draws forth such weeping rhymes.   40
I lived in hope, now still I live in tears
To counter Death I hope for naught but Death.

　　Ah Death has murdered me, and only Death
Can make see again that visage glad,
Which used to make me joy in sighs and tears,   45
That were sweet breeze and rainfall to my nights
When I was weaving lofty thoughts and rhymes
While Love was lifting up my feeble style.

　　Would I had now so piteous a style
That I could steal my Laura back from Death   50
As Orpheus his Eurydice, without rhymes,
For I would live then more than ever glad!
If that cannot occur, let any night
Close up at last these two well-springs of tears.

　　Love, for many a year have I shed tears   55
For my grave injuries in sorrowing style,
Nor from you do I ever hope for nights
Less savage; I am moved, thus, to pray Death
To snatch me hence to where (to make me glad)
She dwells, for whom I sing and weep in rhymes.   60

　　If so high they can soar, my weary rhymes,
That they reach her who's free from wrath and tears,
And now makes Heaven with her beauties glad,
She'll surely recognize my altered style
That gave her joy perhaps, before her death,   65
Made bright her day and, for me, black the nights.

　　O, all you folk who sigh for fairer nights,
Who hear of Love, or speak of him in rhymes,

pregate non mi sia piú sorda Morte,
porto de le miserie et fin del pianto;   70
muti una volta quel suo antiquo stile,
ch'ogni uom attrista, et me pò far sí lieto.

    Far mi pò lieto in una o 'n poche notti:
e 'n aspro stile e 'n angosciose rime
prego che 'l pianto mio finisca Morte.   75

333

    Ite, rime dolenti, al duro sasso
che 'l mio caro thesoro in terra asconde,
ivi chiamate chi dal ciel risponde,
benché 'l mortal sia in loco oscuro et basso.

    Ditele ch'i' son già di viver lasso,   5
del navigar per queste horribili onde;
ma ricogliendo le sue sparte fronde,
dietro le vo pur cosí passo passo,

    sol di lei ragionando viva et morta,
anzi pur viva, et or fatta immortale,   10
a ciò che 'l mondo la conosca et ame.

    Piacciale al mio passar esser accorta,
ch'è presso omai; siami a l'incontro, et quale
ella è nel cielo a sé mi tiri et chiame.

334

    S'onesto amor pò meritar mercede,
et se Pietà anchor pò quant'ella suole,
mercede avrò, ché piú chiara che 'l sole
a madonna et al mondo è la mia fede.

    Già di me paventosa, or sa (nol crede)   5
che quello stesso ch'or per me si vòle,
sempre si volse; et s'ella udia parole
o vedea 'l volto, or l'animo e 'l cor vede.

    Ond'i' spero che 'nfin al ciel si doglia
di miei tanti sospiri, et cosí mostra,   10
tornando a me sí piena di pietate;

    et spero ch'al por giú di questa spoglia
venga per me con quella gente nostra,
vera amica di Cristo et d'Onestate.

335

    Vidi fra mille donne una già tale,
ch'amorosa paura il cor m'assalse,
mirandola in imagini non false

Beg that no longer deaf to me is Death,
That port of wretchedness and end of tears;   70
This once let her transform her ancient style
That saddens all, but me can make so glad.

    Glad I can be in one or but few nights
And in rough style and agonizing rhymes
I pray my tears will have an end with Death.°   75

333

    Go forth, you woeful rhymes, to that hard stone
Which hides my precious treasure in the earth;
There summon one who will reply from Heaven,
Though what is mortal's in a dark, low place.

    Tell her, I now am weary of my life,   5
Of sailing through these waves so horrible;
And yet her scattered fronds I gather up,
And still come on behind her, step by step,

    And but of her I speak, alive and dead
(Instead, still living, and immortal now)   10
So that the world will know and cherish her.

    May she be pleased to note my passing, now
At hand, and meet me, draw and summon me
To be in heaven what she is herself.

334

    If love that's chaste can merit a reward,
And Pity still can do what once she could,
I shall have grace, for brighter than the sun
My faith is in my lady and the world.

    Once fearful of me, now she knows (not thinks)   5
What I today wish for myself is what
I ever wished; if then she heard my words
Or saw my face, now mind and heart she sees.

    And thus I hope that Heaven henceforth will grieve
For all my many sighs; and so it proves,   10
For, filled with pity, to me she returns.

    I hope, too, when I've shed this mortal flesh,
She'll come for me with all our company,
True friends of Chastity and friends of Christ.

335

    Amidst a thousand ladies I saw one
Indeed such that love's fear beseiged my heart
When I beheld in unfeigned images

a li spirti celesti in vista eguale.

Niente in lei terreno era o mortale,   5
sí come a cui del ciel, non d'altro, calse.
L'alma ch'arse per lei sí spesso et alse,
vaga d'ir seco, aperse ambedue l'ale.

Ma tropp' era alta al mio peso terrestre,
et poco poi n'uscí in tutto di vista: 10
di che pensando anchor m'aghiaccio et torpo.

O belle et alte et lucide fenestre,
onde colei che molta gente attrista
trovò la via d'entrare in sí bel corpo!

336

Tornami a mente, anzi v'è dentro, quella
ch'indi per Lethe esser non pò sbandita,
qual io la vidi in su l'età fiorita,
tutta accesa de' raggi di sua stella.

Sí nel mio primo occorso honesta et bella   5
veggiola, in sé raccolta, et sí romita,
ch'i' grido:—Ell'è ben dessa; anchor è in vita—,
e 'n don le cheggio sua dolce favella.

Talor risponde, et talor non fa motto.
I' come huom ch'erra, et poi piú dritto estima,   10
dico a la mente mia:—Tu se' 'ngannata.

Sai che 'n mille trecento quarantotto,
il dí sesto d'aprile, in l'ora prima,
del corpo uscío quell'anima beata.—

337

Quel, che d'odore et di color vincea
l'odorifero et lucido oriënte,
frutti fiori herbe et frondi (onde 'l ponente
d'ogni rara excellentia il pregio avea),

dolce mio lauro, ove habitar solea   5
ogni bellezza, ogni vertute ardente,
vedeva a la sua ombra honestamente
il mio signor sedersi et la mia dea.

Anchor io il nido di penseri electi
posi in quell'alma pianta; e 'n foco e 'n gielo   10
tremando, ardendo, assai felice fui.

Pieno era il mondo de' suoi honor' perfecti,
allor che Dio per adornarne, il cielo
la si ritolse: et cosa era da lui.

Her aspect like that of celestial sprites.

　　Nothing in her was mortal or mundane,　　　　　　　5
As suits one prizing Heaven, nothing else.
My soul, which for her often burned and froze,
Longing to go with her, spread both its wings.

　　Too high she flew, though, for my fleshly weight
And passed before long wholly from my view;　　　　10
I freeze still at the thought of it, grow numb.

　　O fair and lofty windows clear, through which
That one who saddens many people found
The way to enter into such fair flesh!

336

　　To my mind she returns—in fact, dwells there,
That one whom Lethe cannot banish thence—°
Just as I saw her at her blossoming,
All glowing with the splendor of her star,

　　Just so I chanced to meet her first; chaste, fair　　5
I see her, self-absorbed and so withdrawn,
I call out: "Yes, that's she! She's still alive,"
And beg her for the gift of her sweet speech.

　　She answers sometimes, sometimes says no word.
Like one who errs, and then corrects himself,　　　10
I tell my mind, "Ah, you have been deceived,

　　For you know that in thirteen forty-eight,
On April sixth, just at the hour of prime,°
That blest soul from its body issued forth."

337

　　That tree whose scent and color overcame
The fragrant, brilliant orient, the fruits,
Flowers, foliage, and boughs (for which the West
Has held the prize for each rare excellence),

　　My laurel sweet, where every beauty and　　　　5
Where every ardent virtue used to make
Its home, observed my lord together with
My goddess chastely sit within its shade.

　　Meanwhile the nest of all my chosen thoughts
I built in that life-giving tree; in fire,　　　　　　10
In ice, atremble and aflame, content

　　Was I. Its faultless glories filled the world,
When God, to deck out Heaven, took my tree
Again; for she was His indeed.

338

Lasciato ài, Morte, senza sole il mondo
oscuro et freddo, Amor cieco et inerme,
Leggiadria ignuda, le bellezze inferme,
me sconsolato et a me grave pondo,

    Cortesia in bando et Honestate in fondo.   5
Dogliom'io sol, né sol ò da dolerme,
ché svelt'ài di vertute il chiaro germe:
spento il primo valor, qual fia il secondo?

    Pianger l'aer et la terra e 'l mar devrebbe
l'uman legnaggio, che senz'ella è quasi   10
senza fior' prato, o senza gemma anello.

    Non la conobbe il mondo mentre l'ebbe:
conobbil'io, ch'a pianger qui rimasi,
e 'l ciel, che del mio pianto or si fa bello.

339

    Conobbi, quanto il ciel li occhi m'aperse,
quanto studio et Amor m'alzaron l'ali,
cose nove et leggiadre, ma mortali,
che 'n un soggetto ogni stella cosperse:

    l'altre tante sí strane et sí diverse   5
forme altere, celesti et immortali,
perché non furo a l'intellecto eguali,
la mia debile vista non sofferse.

    Onde quant'io di lei parlai né scrissi,
ch'or per lodi anzi a Dio preghi mi rende,   10
fu breve stilla d'infiniti abissi:

    ché stilo oltra l'ingegno non si stende;
et per aver uom li occhi nel sol fissi,
tanto si vede men quanto piú splende.

340

    Dolce mio caro et precïoso pegno
che Natura mi tolse, e 'l Ciel mi guarda,
deh come è tua pietà ver' me sí tarda,
o usato di mia vita sostegno?

    Già suo' tu far il mio sonno almen degno   5
de la tua vista, et or sostien' ch'i' arda
senz'alcun refrigerio: et chi 'l retarda?
Pur lassú non alberga ira né sdegno:

    onde qua giuso un ben pietoso core
talor si pasce delli altrui tormenti,   10
sí ch'elli è vinto nel suo regno Amore.

338

O Death, you've left the world dark, sunless, cold,
Left Love disarmed and blind, left elegance
Unclothed, left beauty frail, and comfortless
Left me, a grievous burden to myself;
   Courtesy banished, chastity sunk low,   5
I mourn alone, though not alone to mourn
Have I cause; Virtue's bright seed have you plucked;
Its greatest value gone, what will be next?
   Air, earth, and sea must weep for humankind,
Which lacking her is like a flowerless mead   10
Or like a ring whose gemstone has been lost.
   The world, while she was of it, knew her not,
I know her, and am left here to lament;
Heaven too, which with my tears is now made fair.

339

So wide had heaven opened up my eyes,
And diligence and Love so spread my wings,
I knew things graceful, rare, but mortal too,
Which on one being every star bestowed.
   Those many other lofty forms so strange,   5
Undying, heavenly, and singular,
Since they did not befit my intellect,
My feeble vision could not well endure.
   Thus everything I said or wrote of her
Who now pays back my praise with prayers to God,   10
Was but a droplet in the boundless deep.
   For style does not extend itself past wit,
And, when one has his eyes fixed on the sun,
As it shines brighter, so the less he sees.

340

My dear, sweet, precious pledge, which Nature stole
From me, and for me Heaven guards, ah how
To me does your true pity come so late,
O you accustomed buttress of my life?
   At least my sleep you once made worthy of   5
Your semblance; now you let me burn without
Relief; and who postpones it? Certainly
Above, there shelters no disdain or wrath;
   These sometimes cause a truly pious heart
Down here to feed on others' sufferings   10
So in his own realm, Love is overcome.

Tu che dentro mi vedi, e 'l mio mal senti,
et sola puoi finir tanto dolore,
con la tua ombra acqueta i miei lamenti.

341

Deh qual pietà, qual angel fu sí presto
a portar sopra 'l cielo il mio cordoglio?
ch'ancor sento tornar pur come soglio
madonna in quel suo atto dolce honesto
    ad acquetare il cor misero et mesto,   5
piena sí d'umiltà, vòta d'argoglio,
e 'nsomma tal ch'a morte i' mi ritoglio,
et vivo, e 'l viver piú non m'è molesto.
    Beata s'è, che pò beare altrui
co la sua vista, over co le parole,   10
intellecte da noi soli ambedui:
    —Fedel mio caro, assai di te mi dole,
ma pur per nostro ben dura ti fui,—
dice, et cos' altre d'arrestare il sole.

342

Del cibo onde 'l signor mio sempre abonda,
lagrime et doglia, il cor lasso nudrisco,
et spesso tremo et spesso impallidisco,
pensando a la sua piaga aspra et profonda.
    Ma chi né prima simil né seconda   5
ebbe al suo tempo, al lecto in ch'io languisco
vien tal ch'a pena a rimirar l'ardisco,
et pietosa s'asside in su la sponda.
    Con quella man che tanto desïai,
m'asciuga li occhi, et col suo dir m'apporta   10
dolcezza ch'uom mortal non sentí mai.
    «Che val—dice—a saver, chi si sconforta?
Non pianger piú: non m'ài tu pianto assai?
ch'or fostú vivo, com'io non son morta!»

343

Ripensando a quel, ch'oggi il cielo honora,
soave sguardo, al chinar l'aurea testa,
al volto, a quella angelica modesta
voce che m'adolciva, et or m'accora,
    gran meraviglia ò com'io viva anchora: 5
né vivrei già, se chi tra bella e honesta,
qual fu piú, lasciò in dubbio, non sí presta

Ah, you who see within me, know my ills,
And who alone can end such sorrowing,
Bring peace to my lamenting with your shade.

341

What pity, ah what angel was so quick
To carry my affliction up to Heaven?
As ever, still I see come back again
My lady, with her virtuous, sweet air,
    To calm my wretched and dejected heart;   5
She's filled with modesty, devoid of pride,
She's such, in short, that I'm set free from Death
And live, and life no longer vexes me.
    How blest is she who can bless others with
Her semblance or her conversation, which   10
Is understood by just the two of us:
    "My faithful, dear one, much I'm grieved for you,
Though with you I was stern for both our good,"
She says, and other things to stay the sun.

342

On food that my lord ever freely shares—
Sorrow and tears—my weary heart is fed,
And oft I quake and often I turn pale
In thinking of my heart's deep, bitter wound.
    But she, in her time peerless, unapproached,   5
So fair I hardly dare to look on her,
Comes to the bed where I lie languishing,
In pity, she sits down upon the edge,
    And with that hand I longed for so, she dries
My eyes, and with her words more sweetness brings   10
Than mortal ever sensed. "What use," she says,
    "Is knowing to the comfortless? Shed tears
No more. Have you not wept enough for me?
You should be living now, as I'm not dead!"

343

Recalling that soft look which Heaven reveres
Today, the tilting of that golden head,
That face, that modest and angelic voice
Which once assuaged, but pierces now my heart,
    I wonder greatly that I'm living still,   5
Nor would I be if she who left in doubt
Whether she was more fair or chaste, were not

fusse al mio scampo, là verso l'aurora.

O che dolci accoglienze, et caste, et pie;
et come intentamente ascolta et nota
la lunga historia de le pene mie!

Poiché 'l dí chiaro par che la percota,
tornasi al ciel, ché sa tutte le vie,
humida li occhi et l'una et l'altra gota.

344

Fu forse un tempo dolce cosa amore,
non perch'i' sappia il quando: or è sí amara,
che nulla piú; ben sa 'l ver chi l'impara
com'ò fatt'io con mio grave dolore.

Quella che fu del secol nostro honore,   5
or è del ciel che tutto orna et rischiara,
fe' mia requie a' suoi giorni et breve et rara;
or m'à d'ogni riposo tratto fore.

Ogni mio ben crudel Morte m'à tolto:
né gran prosperità il mio stato adverso   10
pò consolar di quel bel spirto sciolto.

Piansi et cantai: non so piú mutar verso;
ma dí et notte il duol ne l'alma accolto
per la lingua et per li occhi sfogo et verso.

345

Spinse amor et dolor ove ir non debbe
la mia lingua avïata a lamentarsi,
a dir di lei per ch'io cantai et arsi
quel che, se fusse ver, torto sarebbe:

ch'assai 'l mio stato rio quetar devrebbe   5
quella beata, e 'l cor racconsolarsi
vedendo tanto lei domesticarsi
con Colui che vivendo in cor sempre ebbe.

Et ben m'acqueto, et me stesso consolo;
né vorrei rivederla in questo inferno,   10
anzi voglio morire et viver solo:

ché piú bella che mai con l'occhio interno
con li angeli la veggio alzata a volo
a pie' del suo et mio Signore eterno.

346

Li angeli electi et l'anime beate
cittadine del cielo, il primo giorno
che madonna passò, le fur intorno

So quick to save me as the dawn draws near.
O what sweet greetings, chaste, and reverent;
And how attentively she hears and marks 10
The lengthy history of my travail!
Then, when broad daylight seems to touch her, she
Returns to heaven (for she knows every way),
With tearful eyes, and both cheeks wet as well.

344

Perhaps there was a time when love was sweet,
Not that I know just when; more bitter now
Can nothing be; that truth one clearly knows
Who learns it, as have I, to my deep grief.
The glory of our age—of Heaven now, 5
Which she completely brightens and adorns—
She made my rest both brief and rare in life,
And now has taken me from all repose.
My every good from me cruel Death has reft,
And great prosperity no comfort brings 10
In my sad plight, now her fair spirit's freed.
I wept and sang—can no more change my mode—
But day and night, the woe pent in my soul
I vent upon my tongue, pour through my eyes.

345

Both Love and Grief had forced my tongue to go
Where it ought not when it set forth, to mourn,
To tell of her for whom I sang and burned,
What, if it were the truth, would be unjust.
For much my plight unhappy should be eased 5
And much my heart take comfort, when I see
That blessed one a confidant of His,
Who in her life, was ever in her heart.
Indeed, I'm soothed and I am comforted,
Nor would I see her in this hell again, 10
Instead I wish to die and live alone.
For, more than ever fair, with inward eye
I see her soar in flight with angels, to
The feet of her eternal Lord, and mine.

346

Those chosen angels and those blessed souls,
And citizens of Heaven on that first day
My lady passed away, around her flocked

piene di meraviglia et di pietate.

«Che luce è questa, et qual nova beltate?   5
—dicean tra lor—perch'abito sí adorno
dal mondo errante a quest'alto soggiorno
non salí mai in tutta questa etate».

Ella, contenta aver cangiato albergo,
si paragona pur coi piú perfecti,   10
et parte ad or ad or si volge a tergo,

mirando s'io la seguo, et par ch'aspecti:
ond'io voglie et pensier' tutti al ciel ergo
perch'i' l'odo pregar pur ch'i' m'affretti.

347

Donna che lieta col Principio nostro
ti stai, come tua vita alma rechiede,
assisa in alta et glorïosa sede,
et d'altro ornata che di perle o d'ostro,

o de le donne altero et raro mostro,   5
or nel volto di Lui che tutto vede
vedi 'l mio amore, et quella pura fede
per ch'io tante versai lagrime e 'nchiostro;

et senti che ver' te 'l mio core in terra
tal fu, qual ora è in cielo, et mai non volsi   10
altro da te che 'l sol de li occhi tuoi:

dunque per amendar la lunga guerra
per cui dal mondo a te sola mi volsi,
prega ch'i' venga tosto a star con voi.

348

Da' piú belli occhi, et dal piú chiaro viso
che mai splendesse, et da' piú bei capelli,
che facean l'oro e 'l sol parer men belli,
dal piú dolce parlare et dolce riso,

da le man', da le braccia che conquiso   5
senza moversi avrian quai piú rebelli
fur d'Amor mai, da' piú bei piedi snelli,
da la persona fatta in paradiso,

prendean vita i miei spirti: or n'à diletto
il Re celeste, i Suoi alati corrieri;   10
et io son qui rimaso ignudo et cieco.

Sol un conforto a le mie pene aspetto:
ch'ella, che vede tutti miei penseri,
m'impetre gratia, ch'i' possa esser seco.

All full of wonder and of piety.
    "What light is this, and what new loveliness?"   5
They said among themselves, "For qualities
So graceful from an errant world to this
High mansion never rose in all this age."
    Contented to have changed her dwelling place,
The peer is she of those perfected ones,   10
Yet looks behind from time to time to see
    If I am following, and it seems she waits,
So all my longing thoughts I raise to Heaven,
Because I hear her pray that I make haste.

347

    O Lady, with our Maker you rejoice,
As your life-giving life has merited,
And, seated on a lofty, glorious throne,
You're graced with more than pearls and crimson garb.
    O marvel among women, rare, sublime,   5
Now in the countenance of Him who sees
All things, you see my love and that pure faith
For which I spent much ink, so many tears,
    You know on earth my heart felt toward you as
It does in Heaven now, and never longed   10
For more from you than sunshine from your eyes;
    And so, in recompense for that long war
Which turned me from the world to you alone,
Pray that I soon may hasten to your side.

348

    From fairest eyes and from the brightest face
That ever shone, and from the loveliest hair
That made gold seem less lovely—and the sun—
And from the sweetest speech and sweetest smile,
    From hands and arms that, without stirring, would   5
Have vanquished those who most rebelled 'gainst Love,
From those most lovely, agile feet and from
Her person, shaped in paradise, their life
    My spirits took; now joy in her the King
Celestial and His wingèd couriers take,   10
And naked here and blind I have remained.
    One solace only for my woes I wait:
That she who looks upon my every thought
Will gain me grace so I can be with her.

E' mi par d'or in hora udire il messo
che madonna mi mande a sé chiamando:
cosí dentro et di for mi vo cangiando,
et sono in non molt'anni sí dimesso,
    ch'a pena riconosco omai me stesso;   5
tutto 'l viver usato ò messo in bando.
Sarei contento di sapere il quando,
ma pur devrebbe il tempo esser da presso.
    O felice quel dí che, del terreno
carcere uscendo, lasci rotta et sparta   10
questa mia grave et frale et mortal gonna,
    et da sí folte tenebre mi parta
volando tanto su nel bel sereno,
ch'i' veggia il mio Signore et la mia donna.

Questo nostro caduco et fragil bene,
ch'è vento et ombra, et à nome beltate,
non fu già mai se non in questa etate
tutto in un corpo, et ciò fu per mie pene:
    ché Natura non vòl, né si convene,   5
per far ricco un, por li altri in povertate;
or versò in una ogni sua largitate
(perdonimi qual è bella, o si tene).
    Non fu simil bellezza anticha o nova,
né sarà, credo; ma fu sí coverta,   10
ch'a pena se n'accorse il mondo errante.
    Tosto disparve: onde 'l cangiar mi giova
la poca vista a me dal cielo offerta
sol per piacer a le sue luci sante.

Dolci durezze, et placide repulse,
piene di casto amore et di pietate;
leggiadri sdegni, che le mie infiammate
voglie tempraro (or me n'accorgo), e 'nsulse;
    gentil parlar, in cui chiaro refulse   5
con somma cortesia somma honestate;
fior di vertú, fontana di beltate,
ch'ogni basso penser del cor m'avulse;
    divino sguardo da far l'uom felice,
or fiero in affrenar la mente ardita   10
a quel che giustamente si disdice,

349

I seem to hear that envoy hourly
My lady sends to call me to herself;
So I go, changing both inside and out,
And in a few years have I so declined,
    That now I hardly recognize myself;   5
All my accustomed life I've put aside;
I would be happy if I knew the hour,
But certainly my time must be at hand.
    O happy day when I fare forth from this
Terrestrial prison, leave my mortal garb—   10
Enfeebled, heavy—scattered and in rags,
    And from such teeming darkness take my leave
And fly so far up through the bright, fair sky,
That I shall see my lady and my Lord.

350

Ah, this our fleeting, fragile blessing, which
Is wind and shadow—beauty, by its name—
Never but in this present age has dwelt
In just one flesh; and that was for my woe.
    For Nature does not want to make one rich   5
By making others poor, nor is it right;
Yet on one now all her largesse she's spent—
(Forgive me if you're fair, or think you are).
    Such beauty, new or ancient, never lived
Nor will, I think; but it was so concealed   10
This wayward world but little heeded it.
    Because too soon she vanished, I found joy
In changing just to please her holy eyes,
That vision brief which Heaven gave to me.

351

Those sweet severities and mild reproofs,
With chaste love filled, and piety as well,
That gracious scorn which tempered my desires,
Inflamed and witless (as I'm now aware),
    That noble speech where highest chastity   5
With highest courtesy shone forth so clear,
That bloom of virtue, fount of loveliness,
Which choked out every base thought of my heart,
    That look divine which makes a man content,
Now stern enough to urge my rash mind back   10
From that which rightly was forbidden it,

or presto a confortar mia frale vita:
questo bel varïar fu la radice
di mia salute, ch'altramente era ita.

352
Spirto felice che sí dolcemente
volgei quelli occhi, piú chiari che 'l sole,
et formavi i sospiri et le parole,
vive ch'anchor mi sonan ne la mente:
    già ti vid'io, d'onesto foco ardente,   5
mover i pie' fra l'erbe et le vïole,
non come donna, ma com'angel sòle,
di quella ch'or m'è piú che mai presente;
    la qual tu poi, tornando al tuo fattore,
lasciasti in terra, et quel soave velo   10
che per alto destin ti venne in sorte.
    Nel tuo partir, partí del mondo Amore
et Cortesia, e 'l sol cadde del cielo,
et dolce incominciò farsi la morte.

353
Vago augelletto che cantando vai,
over piangendo, il tuo tempo passato,
vedendoti la notte e 'l verno a lato
e 'l dí dopo le spalle e i mesi gai,
    se, come i tuoi gravosi affanni sai,   5
cosí sapessi il mio simile stato,
verresti in grembo a questo sconsolato
a partir seco i dolorosi guai.
    I' non so se le parti sarian pari,
ché quella cui tu piangi è forse in vita,   10
di ch'a me Morte e 'l ciel son tanto avari;
    ma la stagione et l'ora men gradita,
col membrar de' dolci anni et de li amari,
a parlar teco con pietà m'invita.

354
Deh porgi mano a l'affannato ingegno,
Amor, et a lo stile stancho et frale,
per dir di quella ch'è fatta immortale
et cittadina del celeste regno;
    dammi, signor, che 'l mio dir giunga al segno   5
de le sue lode, ove per sé non sale,
se vertú, se beltà non ebbe eguale

Now eager to sustain my fragile life:
This sweet variety became the root
Of my soul's health, which otherwise had failed.

352

Blest spirit, who so sweetly turned aside
Those eyes much brighter than the sun, who shaped
The sighs and vivid words that echo still
Within my mind: I looked upon you once,
  Aflame with honor's fire, stepping through grass   5
And violets—not as a lady treads,
But as an angel does—and with her feet
Who more than ever is present to me now.
  She whom, when to your Maker you returned
You left in earth, and left that gentle veil   10
Which by high destiny fell to your lot.
  And at your parting, Love, too, left the world,
And Courtesy; the sun fell from the sky,
And Death began to make herself seem sweet.

353

Ah, charming little bird that singing strays,
Or else strays weeping over times gone by,
At seeing night and winter near at hand,
Day past, and joyous months behind you now:
  If you could know my plight, so like your own,   5
As well as your own grievous woes you know,
You'd hasten to this breast disconsolate
To share with it that wretched sorrowing.
  I know not if our shares would be the same,
The one you weep for may be still alive—   10
That's why, toward me, so grudging are Death and Heaven.
  The season, though, and this unwelcome hour,
The memory of sweet and bitter years
With pity urge me to converse with you.

354

Ah, to my panting skill stretch forth your hand,
Love, help my feeble, weary style to speak
Of that one who's been made immortal now—
A citizen of the celestial realm;
  Lord, grant my words may reach the goal of praise   5
For her, to which, alone, they cannot rise;
Virtue and beauty like hers were peerless

il mondo, che d'aver lei non fu degno.
	Responde:—Quanto 'l ciel et io possiamo,
e i buon' consigli, e 'l conversar honesto,	10
tutto fu in lei, di che noi Morte à privi.
	Forma par non fu mai dal dí ch'Adamo
aperse li occhi in prima; et basti or questo:
piangendo i' 'l dico, et tu piangendo scrivi.—

355

O tempo, o ciel volubil, che fuggendo
inganni i ciechi et miseri mortali,
o dí veloci piú che vento et strali,
ora *ab experto* vostre frodi intendo:
	ma scuso voi, et me stesso riprendo,	5
ché Natura a volar v'aperse l'ali,
a me diede occhi, et io pur ne' miei mali
li tenni, onde vergogna et dolor prendo.
	Et sarebbe ora, et è passata omai,
di rivoltarli in piú secura parte,	10
et poner fine a li 'nfiniti guai;
	né dal tuo giogo, Amor, l'alma si parte,
ma dal suo mal: con che studio tu 'l sai;
non a caso è vertute, anzi è bell'arte.

356

L'aura mia sacra al mio stanco riposo
spira sí spesso, ch'i' prendo ardimento
di dirle il mal ch'i' ò sentito et sento,
che, vivendo ella, non sarei stat' oso.
	I' incomincio da quel guardo amoroso	5
che fu principio a sí lungo tormento,
poi seguo come misero et contento,
di dí in dí, d'ora in hora, Amor m'à roso.
	Ella si tace, et di pietà depinta
fiso mira pur me; parte sospira,	10
et di lagrime honeste il viso adorna:
	onde l'anima mia dal dolor vinta,
mentre piangendo allor seco s'adira,
sciolta dal sonno a se stessa ritorna.

357

Ogni giorno mi par piú di mill'anni
ch'i' segua la mia fida et cara duce,
che mi condusse al mondo, or mi conduce,

In this world, which to hold her was unfit.
    Love answers: "All that heaven and I can do,
And counsel wise, and conversation chaste,   10
All was in her whom Death has seized from us.
    "No form was ever like hers since that day
When Adam's eyes first opened; now enough:
In tears I say it, and in tears you write."

355

    O time, O wheeling heavens, which fleeing cheat
These mortal creatures miserable and blind;
O days, more fleet than arrows or the wind,
Put to the test, now your deceits I know.
    But I forgive you, and myself I blame,   5
For Nature spread your wings to fly, and gave
Me eyes, which on my wrongs I nonetheless
Kept fixed; from thence proceeds my grief and shame.
    It would be time, indeed the hour has passed,
To cast my eyes back to a surer place,   10
And put an end to their unending woe.
    Not from your yoke, Love, is my soul set free,
But from its ills, and with what pains you know;
From noble practice virtue springs, not chance.

356

    My Laura, sacred breeze, so often breathes
Upon my fitful rest that I make bold
To tell her of the woe I've felt and feel;
Which, while she lived, I'd never have presumed.
    So I begin first with that amorous glance   5
That was the source of such a torment long;
Next follows how I, wretched and content,
Was gnawed by Love each day and every hour.
    Flushed with compassion, silent she regards
Me steadily, a little sighs, and then   10
With seemly tears her countenance adorns.
    At that my soul, quite overwhelmed with grief,
Grows angry with itself although in tears,
And freed from sleep, comes to itself once more.

357

    Each day seems longer than a thousand years
Till I may follow my dear faithful guide;
Now she, who led me through the world, leads me

per miglior via, a vita senza affanni:
　　et non mi posson ritener li 'nganni　　　　　　　　5
del mondo, ch'i' 'l conosco; et tanta luce
dentro al mio core infin dal ciel traluce
ch'i' 'ncomincio a contar il tempo e i danni.
　　Né minaccie temer debbo, di morte,
che 'l Re sofferse con piú grave pena,　　　　　　　10
per farme a seguitar constante et forte;
　　et or novellamente in ogni vena
intrò di lei che m'era data in sorte,
et non turbò la sua fronte serena.

358

　　Non pò far Morte il dolce viso amaro,
ma 'l dolce viso dolce pò far Morte.
Che bisogn' a morir ben altre scorte?
Quella mi scorge ond'ogni ben imparo;
　　et Quei che del Suo sangue non fu avaro,　　　5
che col pe' ruppe le tartaree porte,
col Suo morir par che mi riconforte.
Dunque vien', Morte: il tuo venir m'è caro.
　　Et non tardar, ch'egli è ben tempo omai;
et se non fusse, e' fu 'l tempo in quel punto　　　10
che madonna passò di questa vita.
　　D'allor innanzi un dí non vissi mai:
seco fui in via, et seco al fin son giunto,
et mia giornata ò co' suoi pie' fornita.

359

　　Quando il soave mio fido conforto
per dar riposo a la mia vita stanca
ponsi del letto in su la sponda manca
con quel suo dolce ragionare accorto,
　　tutto di pieta et di paura smorto　　　　　　　　5
dico: «Onde vien' tu ora, o felice alma?»
Un ramoscel di palma
et un di lauro trae del suo bel seno,
et dice: «Dal sereno
ciel empireo et di quelle sante parti　　　　　　　10
mi mossi et vengo sol per consolarti».
　　In atto et in parole la ringratio
humilemente, et poi demando: «Or donde
sai tu il mio stato?» Et ella: «Le triste onde
del pianto, di che mai tu non se' satio,　　　　　　15

Along the best path, to untroubled life.
    The world's deceptions cannot hold me back;   5
I know them all, and such great light at last
From heaven now illuminates my heart
That I start reckoning the time, the costs.
    I must not fear the threat of death my King°
Endured with such grave suffering, so I   10
Could follow Him with constancy and strength—
    Nor death, which lately entered every vein
Of her whom destiny had given me,
And which did not disturb her peaceful brow.

358

    Ah, death cannot make harsh her lovely face,
Rather can her sweet visage sweeten death;
What need of other guide to face death well?
Since she escorts me, I'll learn every good.
    And He who was not sparing with His blood,   5
Who with His foot smashed Tartarean gates,°
Assures me by His death I am restored.
Come then, O Death; your coming is dear to me.
    And tarry not; the time is long since past,
And were it not, that moment was the time   10
In which my lady passed on from this life.
    And from that hour I never lived a day;
With her in life, linked with her at the end,
My journey I have finished in her steps.

359

    When that sweet faithful comforter of mine
Sits down upon the left side of my bed,
Bestowing on my weary life repose,
In conversation tender, skillful, wise,
I, pale with anguish and all wan with dread,   5
Inquire: "Whence come you now, O happy soul?"
A sprig of palm and one
Of laurel from her bosom fair she draws
And says: "From Heaven's bright
Empyrean those sacred fields I left,   10
And only to console you I have come."
    With words and posture, her I humbly thank;
I ask then, "How do you now know my plight?"
And she, "The mournful waves of tears with which
You never are content, that rush of sighs   15

coll'aura de' sospir', per tanto spatio
passano al cielo, et turban la mia pace:
sí forte ti dispiace
che di questa miseria sia partita,
et giunta a miglior vita;   20
che piacer ti devria, se tu m'amasti
quanto in sembianti et ne' tuoi dir' mostrasti».
    Rispondo: «Io non piango altro che me stesso
che son rimaso in tenebre e 'n martire,
certo sempre del tuo al ciel salire   25
come di cosa ch'uom vede da presso.
Come Dio et Natura avrebben messo
in un cor giovenil tanta vertute,
se l'eterna salute
non fusse destinata al tuo ben fare,   30
o de l'anime rare,
ch'altamente vivesti qui tra noi,
et che súbito al ciel volasti poi?
    Ma io che debbo altro che pianger sempre,
misero et sol, che senza te son nulla?   35
Ch'or fuss'io spento al latte e a la culla,
per non provar de l'amorose tempre!»
Et ella: «A che pur piangi et ti distempre?
Quanto era meglio alzar da terra l'ali,
et le cose mortali   40
et queste dolci tue fallaci ciance
librar con giusta lance,
et seguir me, s'è ver che tanto m'ami,
cogliendo omai qualchun di questi rami!»
    «I' volea demandar—respond'io allora—:   45
Che voglion importar quelle due frondi?»
Et ella: «Tu medesmo ti rispondi,
tu la cui penna tanto l'una honora:
palma è victoria, et io, giovene anchora,
vinsi il mondo et me stessa; il lauro segna   50
trïumpho, ond'io son degna,
mercé di quel Signor che mi die' forza.
Or tu, s'altri ti sforza,
a Lui ti volgi, a Lui chiedi soccorso,
sí che siam Seco al fine del tuo corso».   55
    «Son questi i capei biondi, et l'aureo nodo
—dich'io—ch'ancor mi stringe, et quei belli occhi
che fur mio sol?» «Non errar con li sciocchi,
né parlar—dice—o creder a lor modo.

As well, pass through enormous reaches up
To Heaven, and make turbulent my peace;
Are you so much displeased
That I have left behind this wretchedness
And reached a better life?   20
What pleasure you should feel, if you loved me,
As much as once your words and aspect showed."
    I answer: "For myself alone I weep,
For I remain in torment, in the dark,
But ever sure of your ascent to Heaven   25
As of a thing one sees before his eyes.
    "Oh how could God and Nature in the heart
Of one so young have placed such moral strength
Had not eternal Grace
Ordained it for the sake of your good works?   30
O most rare of spirits,
Who nobly lived among us here, and who
To Heaven then so quickly flew away!
    "What can I do then but forever weep—
Without you nothing, wretched and alone?   35
Had I but passed away ere I was weaned
Untempered in my cradle by Love's trials."
And she: "Why do you weep still, and dissolve?
Better it were to rise from earth on wings,
And weigh these mortal things,   40
Your charming and delusive nonsense too,
In honest scales, and me
To follow if in truth you love me so,
Plucking at last one of these boughs I bear."
    "I wish to ask you this," I then respond,   45
"What meaning should I draw from these two fronds?"
And she: "Reply to that yourself, O you
Whose quill to one of them such homage pays.
The palm means victory, for I, while young,
Subdued both world and self; the laurel stands   50
For triumph, which I earned;
For that I thank the Lord who gave me strength.
If some coerce you now,
Straight to Him turn, from Him implore relief,
Thus we shall be with Him at your life's end."   ·   55
    "Is this the blond hair, this the golden knot,"
I say, "that snares me still? and those fair eyes
That used to be my sun?" "Stray not with fools,"
She says, "Nor speak nor think like foolish ones.

Spirito ignudo sono, e 'n ciel mi godo: 60
quel che tu cerchi è terra, già molt'anni,
ma per trarti d'affanni
m'è dato a parer tale; et anchor quella
sarò, piú che mai bella,
a te piú cara, sí selvaggia et pia   65
salvando inseme tua salute et mia».
    I' piango; et ella il volto
co le sue man' m'asciuga, et poi sospira
dolcemente, et s'adira
con parole che i sassi romper ponno: 70
et dopo questo si parte ella, e 'l sonno.

360

    Quel'antiquo mio dolce empio signore
fatto citar dinanzi a la reina
che la parte divina
tien di nostra natura e 'n cima sede,
ivi, com'oro che nel foco affina,   5
mi rappresento carco di dolore,
di paura et d'orrore,
quasi huom che teme morte et ragion chiede;
e 'ncomincio:—Madonna, il manco piede
giovenetto pos'io nel costui regno,   10
ond'altro ch'ira et sdegno
non ebbi mai; et tanti et sí diversi
tormenti ivi soffersi,
ch'alfine vinta fu quell'infinita
mia patïentia, e 'n odio ebbi la vita.   15
    Cosí 'l mio tempo infin qui trapassato
è in fiamma e 'n pene: et quante utili honeste
vie sprezzai, quante feste,
per servir questo lusinghier crudele!
Et qual ingegno à sí parole preste,   20
che stringer possa 'l mio infelice stato,
et le mie d'esto ingrato
tante et sí gravi et sí giuste querele?
O poco mèl, molto aloè con fele!
In quanto amaro à la mia vita avezza   25
con sua falsa dolcezza,
la qual m'atrasse a l'amorosa schiera!
Che s'i' non m'inganno, era
disposto a sollevarmi alto da terra:
e' mi tolse di pace et pose in guerra.   30

Spirit unfleshed am I; In heaven I joy;   60
She whom you seek is earth these many years;
But, to abate your grief,
Thus I am allowed to seem—and that one
Shall I be, fairer far,
To you more dear—so untamed and devout—   65
Preserving your salvation and mine too."
    I weep; and with her hands
She dries my face; and then she sweetly sighs
But then grows wroth, with words
That could split stones apart; and after this   70
She slips away from me, and sleep departs.

360

    When that sweet wicked ancient lord of mine
Is summoned to appear before the queen°
Who in our nature rules
The part divine and on its utmost height
Holds court, then there like gold in fire refined   5
I represent myself, weighed down with pain,
With horror, and with fear,
Like one who pleads for justice and fears death;
Thus I begin: "My lady, my left foot,°
In tender youth I set within his realm.   10
From this naught have I known
But anger and disdain; there I've endured
So many torments cruel
That finally my patience infinite
Was overcome, and life grew odious.   15
    "So up till now my time here has been spent
In fire and grief: what useful paths and chaste,
How many joys I scorned
In serving this deceiver harsh and cruel!
What intellect possesses words so prompt   20
That it can summarize my wretched plight
And my great, very grave,
And just complaint against this thankless one.
But little honey, aloes much with gall!
To what great bitterness has he inured my life   25
With his sweetness false,
By which he lured me to his amorous troop!
For, if I do not err,
High from the earth I was prepared to rise;
He stole my peace from me, set me at war.   30

[401]

Questi m'à fatto men amare Dio
ch'i' non deveva, et men curar me stesso:
per una donna ò messo
egualmente in non cale ogni pensero.
Di ciò m'è stato consiglier sol esso,   35
sempr' aguzzando il giovenil desio
a l'empia cote, ond'io
sperai riposo al suo giogo aspro et fero.
Misero, a che quel chiaro ingegno altero,
et l'altre doti a me date dal cielo?   40
ché vo cangiando 'l pelo,
né cangiar posso l'ostinata voglia:
cosí in tutto mi spoglia
di libertà questo crudel ch'i' accuso,
ch'amaro viver m'à vòlto in dolce uso.   45
    Cercar m'à fatto deserti paesi,
fiere et ladri rapaci, hispidi dumi,
dure genti et costumi,
et ogni error che' pellegrini intrica,
monti, valli, paludi et mari et fiumi,   50
mille lacciuoli in ogni parte tesi;
e 'l verno in strani mesi,
con pericol presente et con fatica:
né costui né quell'altra mia nemica
ch'i' fuggia, mi lasciavan sol un punto;   55
onde, s'i' non son giunto
anzi tempo da morte acerba et dura,
pietà celeste à cura
di mia salute, non questo tiranno
che del mio duol si pasce, et del mio danno.   60
    Poi che suo fui non ebbi hora tranquilla,
né spero aver, et le mie notti il sonno
sbandiro, et piú non ponno
per herbe o per incanti a sé ritrarlo.
Per inganni et per forza è fatto donno   65
sovra miei spirti; et non sonò poi squilla,
ov'io sia, in qual che villa,
ch'i' non l'udisse. Ei sa che 'l vero parlo:
ché legno vecchio mai non róse tarlo
come questi 'l mio core, in che s'annida,   70
et di morte lo sfida.
Quinci nascon le lagrime e i martiri,
le parole e i sospiri,
di ch'io mi vo stancando, et forse altrui.

"This one caused me, less than I ought, to love
My God, and to myself to pay less heed;
And for a lady's sake
Each care I have neglected equally.
To that end, only he has counselled me,   35
While ever honing on an evil stone
My youthful passion; yet
In his cruel, rugged yoke, I'd hoped for rest.
Poor wretch! For what was bright and lofty wit
And other talents given me by heaven?   40
Although my hair is changing
I cannot force my stubborn will to change.
In every way he steals
My freedom, this cruel one that I accuse;
To sweet use he has turned my bitter life!   45
     "He's driven me to seek out desert lands,
Wild creatures, thieves rapacious, bristling thorns,
Harsh people and harsh ways,
All waywardness that pilgrims leads astray—
Mountains, valleys, quagmires, rivers, seas—   50
A thousand snares he set on every side;
Brought winter in strange months,
With danger ever-present, and fatigue:
Not for one instant did he leave me free,
No more will she, that other foe I fly.   55
So, if I have not met
Before my time a harsh and bitter death,
Celestial grace has cared
For my well being, not this tyrant, he
Who feeds himself upon my woe and pain.   60
     "Since I was his, I've had no tranquil hour,
Nor do I hope to have; and sleep my nights
Have exiled; no more can
They recover it with herbs or spells.
Deceit and force have made him ruler of   65
My spirits; when I stay within some town,
There rings no midnight bell
That I hear not. He sees that I speak truth,
For no worm ever bored old wood as these
Two gnawed upon my heart, in which they nest;   70
They threaten it with death.
In it are born the tears and sufferings,
The words and sighs, that have
Exhausted me, and others too perhaps.

Giudica tu, che me conosci et lui.— 75
    Il mio adversario con agre rampogne
comincia:—O donna, intendi l'altra parte,
che 'l vero, onde si parte
quest'ingrato, dirà senza defecto.
Questi in sua prima età fu dato a l'arte 80
da vender parolette, anzi menzogne;
né par che si vergogne,
tolto da quella noia al mio dilecto,
lamentarsi di me, che puro et netto,
contra 'l desio che spesso il suo mal vòle, 85
lui tenni, ond'or si dole,
in dolce vita, ch'ei miseria chiama:
salito in qualche fama
solo per me, che 'l suo intellecto alzai
ov'alzato per sé non fôra mai. 90
    Ei sa che 'l grande Atride et l'alto Achille,
et Hanibàl al terren vostro amaro,
et di tutti il piú chiaro
un altro et di vertute et di fortuna,
com'a ciascun le sue stelle ordinaro, 95
lasciai cader in vil amor d'ancille:
et a costui di mille
donne electe, excellenti, n'elessi una,
qual non si vedrà mai sotto la luna,
benché Lucretia ritornasse a Roma; 100
et sí dolce ydïoma
le diedi, et un cantar tanto soave,
che penser basso o grave
non poté mai durar dinanzi a lei.
Questi fur con costui li 'nganni mei. 105
    Questo fu il fel, questi li sdegni et l'ire,
piú dolci assai che di null'altra il tutto.
Di bon seme mal frutto
mieto: et tal merito à chi 'ngrato serve.
Sí l'avea sotto l'ali mie condutto, 110
ch'a donne et cavalier' piacea il suo dire;
et sí alto salire
i' 'l feci, che tra' caldi ingegni ferve
il suo nome et de' suoi detti conserve
si fanno con diletto in alcun loco; 115
ch'or saria forse un roco
mormorador di corti, un huom del vulgo:
i' l'exalto et divulgo,

Pass judgment, you who know both him and me."   75
   With sharp reproofs my adversary starts:
"O lady, understand the other side
That truth, away from which
This ingrate strays, will speak without defect.
He practiced in his early youth, the art   80
Of selling pretty words, or, rather, lies;
Nor did he seem ashamed
When drawn from boredom into my delights,
To make complaint of me who held him pure
And clean of that desire which its own ill   85
Oft seeks. This he regrets
In this sweet life he now calls misery.
Some fame he has achieved
Through me alone; his intellect I raised
Where by itself, it never would have climbed.   90
   "About great Atrides, Achilles high,
And Hannibal, one bitter to your land,
And—most renowned of all—
Another both of fortune and of worth,°
He knows how all his stars ordained that I   95
Let him sink low in passion for a slave;
Yet for this man I picked
One from a thousand ladies choice and rare,
Whose like will not be seen beneath the moon
Although Lucretia should return to Rome.°   100
So sweet the turn of phrase
I gave to her, and such a gentle song
No grievous thought or low
Could in her presence possibly endure,
And such were my deceptions with this man.   105
   "This was the gall, this was the scorn, the ire,
More sweet than any other woman's best.
Good seed yields me bad fruit,
And one who aids the thankless merits it.
I even led him forth beneath my wings   110
To make his speech please ladies and their knights;
So high I made him climb
That 'midst the brightest talents his name burns,
And his songs are remembered with delight
In places; now perhaps he would become   115
In courts a grumbler hoarse,
Would be the rabble's man, but I exalt
And I distinguish him

per quel ch'elli 'mparò ne la mia scola,
et da colei che fu nel mondo sola.						120
    Et per dir a l'extremo il gran servigio,
da mille acti inhonesti l'ò ritratto,
ché mai per alcun pacto
a lui piacer non poteo cosa vile:
giovene schivo et vergognoso in acto					125
et in penser, poi che fatto era huom ligio
di lei ch'alto vestigio
li 'mpresse al core, et fecel suo simíle.
Quanto à del pellegrino et del gentile,
da lei tene, et da me, di cui si biasma.					130
Mai nocturno fantasma
d'error non fu sí pien com'ei ver' noi:
ch'è in gratia, da poi
che ne conobbe, a Dio et a la gente.
Di ciò il superbo si lamenta et pente.					135
    Anchor, et questo è quel che tutto avanza,
da volar sopra 'l ciel li avea dat' ali,
per le cose mortali,
che son scala al fattor, chi ben l'estima:
ché, mirando ei ben fiso quante et quali					140
eran vertuti in quella sua speranza,
d'una in altra sembianza
potea levarsi a l'alta cagion prima;
et ei l'à detto alcuna volta in rima,
or m'à posto in oblio con quella donna					145
ch'i' li die' per colonna
de la sua frale vita.—A questo un strido
lagrimoso alzo et grido:
—Ben me la die', ma tosto la ritolse.—
Responde:—Io no, ma Chi per sé la volse.—				150
    Alfin ambo conversi al giusto seggio,
i' con tremanti, ei con voci alte et crude,
ciascun per sé conchiude:
—Nobile donna, tua sententia attendo.—
Ella allor sorridendo:							155
—Piacemi aver vostre questioni udite,
ma piú tempo bisogna a tanta lite.—

361

Dicemi spesso il mio fidato speglio,
l'animo stanco, et la cangiata scorza,
et la scemata mia destrezza et forza:

By that which in my school he learned, learned from
That one who was unique in all the world.   120
    "To mention last my greatest help to him,
I've saved him from a thousand unchaste acts,
For in no circumstance
Could he be pleased by an unworthy thing—
A bashful youth, and timid in his deeds   125
And thoughts—then he became her liegeman true;
With her high image graven
Upon his heart, and in her likeness formed,
What rare and noble qualities are his,
From her he holds them, from me whom he blames.   130
Ne'er nighttime spectre was
As full of error as he is towards us!
For since he's known us he
Has stood in grace with people and with God,
For that this proud one wails and has regrets!   135
    "Yet more, and this surpasses all, I gave
Him wings to soar above the heavens through
Things mortal, valued right
A stairway to our Maker; so when he
Gazed fixedly upon the number and   140
The kind of virtues in his hoped-for one,
From one resemblance to the next
He could have risen to the high First Cause,
As he has sometimes said himself in rhyme.
Now with that lady, he's consigned me to   145
Oblivion, I gave
Her as a pillar for his feeble life.
At that a tearful shriek
Rings out; I cry: "Yes, gave, but soon stole back."
"Not I, but One who wanted her Himself."   150
    At last the throne of reason both approach,
I with a quaking voice, his loud and harsh,
Each for himself concludes:
"O Noble dame, your verdict I await."
And then she, smiling, says: 155
"That I have heard your lawsuits pleases me,
But such great litigation needs more time."°

361

    My trusted mirror often says to me—
As do my weary mind and altered look,
My worn dexterity and failing strength—

—Non ti nasconder piú: tu se' pur vèglio.
　　Obedir a Natura in tutto è il meglio,　　　　　　5
ch'a contender con lei il tempo ne sforza.—
Súbito allor, com'acqua 'l foco amorza,
d'un lungo et grave sonno mi risveglio:
　　et veggio ben che 'l nostro viver vola
et ch'esser non si pò piú d'una volta;　　　　　　10
e 'n mezzo 'l cor mi sona una parola
　　di lei ch'è or dal suo bel nodo sciolta,
ma ne' suoi giorni al mondo fu sí sola,
ch'a tutte, s'i' non erro, fama à tolta.

362

　　Volo con l'ali de' pensieri al cielo
sí spesse volte che quasi un di loro
esser mi par ch'àn ivi il suo thesoro,
lasciando in terra lo squarciato velo.
　　Talor mi trema 'l cor d'un dolce gelo　　　　　　5
udendo lei per ch'io mi discoloro
dirmi:—Amico, or t'am'io et or t'onoro
perch'à' i costumi varïati, e 'l pelo.—
　　Menami al suo Signor: allor m'inchino,
pregando humilemente che consenta　　　　　　10
ch'i' stia a veder et l'uno et l'altro volto.
　　Responde:—Egli è ben fermo il tuo destino;
et per tardar anchor vent'anni o trenta,
parrà a te troppo, et non fia però molto.—

363

　　Morte à spento quel sol ch'abagliar suolmi,
e 'n tenebre son li occhi interi et saldi;
terra è quella ond'io ebbi et freddi et caldi;
spenti son i miei lauri, or querce et olmi:
　　di ch'io veggio 'l mio ben, et parte duolmi.　　　　　　5
Non è chi faccia et paventosi et baldi
i miei penser', né chi li agghiacci et scaldi,
né chi gli empia di speme, et di duol colmi.
　　Fuor di man di colui che punge et molce,
che già fece di me sí lungo stratio,　　　　　　10
mi trovo in libertate, amara et dolce;
　　et al Signor ch'i' adoro et ch'i' ringratio,
che pur col ciglio il ciel governa et folce,
torno stanco di viver, nonché satio.

"No more conceal it from yourself: you're old.
　"Obeying Nature in all things is best,　　　　　　　5
For time constrains us from opposing her."
Then suddenly, as water quenches fire
I waken from a long and heavy sleep,
　And clearly see that our life flies away
And that no more than once can we exist;　　　　10
And then, within my heart, one word resounds
　About her who, now freed from her fair bond,
Was in her life on earth so singular
That, if I err not, she plucked fame from all.

362

　Upon the wings of thought I fly to heaven
So often that I almost seem to be
One of those who have their treasure there,
They who have left their rent veils in the earth.
　At times a sweet chill shivers through my heart　　5
On hearing her, for whom I blanch, tell me,
"My friend, I love you now and honor you,
For as your hair has changed, so have your ways."
　She leads me to her Lord, then I bow down,
And humbly pray for His consent that I　　　　10
May there remain to see her face, and His.
　He answers me: "Your destiny is fixed;
Though still to tarry twenty, thirty years
Will seem too much to you, it won't be long."

363

　That sun which dimmed my sight, Death has put out
In darkness are those chaste and steadfast eyes;
She now is earth who chilled me, made me burn;
My laurels, withered, turn to oaks and elms:
　My benefit I see there, yet lament.　　　　　　5
No one who lives can stir my thoughts with fear
And gallantry, nor make them freeze and scald,
Nor fill them full of hope, and me with pain.
　Loosed from his hand who stings and mollifies,
Who once for me shaped such a torment long,　　10
I find myself in freedom, bitter-sweet.
　And to the Lord I worship, whom I thank,
Who merely with an eyelash orders heaven,
I turn, life-weary, not just satiate.

364

Tennemi Amor anni ventuno ardendo,
lieto nel foco, et nel duol pien di speme;
poi che madonna e 'l mio cor seco inseme
saliro al ciel, dieci altri anni piangendo.

Omai son stanco, et mia vita reprendo   5
di tanto error che di vertute il seme
à quasi spento, et le mie parti extreme,
alto Dio, a te devotamente rendo:

pentito et tristo de' miei sí spesi anni,
che spender si deveano in miglior uso,   10
in cercar pace et in fuggir affanni.

Signor che 'n questo carcer m'ài rinchiuso,
tràmene, salvo da li eterni danni,
ch'i' conosco 'l mio fallo, et non lo scuso.

365

I' vo piangendo i miei passati tempi
i quai posi in amar cosa mortale,
senza levarmi a volo, abbiend'io l'ale,
per dar forse di me non bassi exempi.

Tu che vedi i miei mali indegni et empi,   5
Re del cielo invisibile immortale,
soccorri a l'alma disvïata et frale,
e 'l suo defecto di Tua gratia adempi:

sí che, s'io vissi in guerra et in tempesta,
mora in pace et in porto; et se la stanza   10
fu vana, almen sia la partita honesta.

A quel poco di viver che m'avanza
et al morir, degni esser Tua man presta:
Tu sai ben che 'n altrui non ò speranza.

366

Vergine bella, che di sol vestita,
coronata di stelle, al sommo Sole
piacesti sí, che 'n te Sua luce ascose,
amor mi spinge a dir di te parole:
ma non so 'ncominciar senza tu' aita,   5
et di Colui ch'amando in te si pose.
Invoco lei che ben sempre rispose,
chi la chiamò con fede:
Vergine, s'a mercede
miseria extrema de l'humane cose   10
già mai ti volse, al mio prego t'inchina,

364

Love held me burning one-and-twenty years,
In fire elated, full of hope in pain;
And then my lady, my heart with her too,
Rose up to heaven—ten more tearful years.
    I'm weary now, and I reprove my life   5
For so much error, which has nearly spent
The seed of virtue; and my final days
Devotedly I yield you, God most high;
    Repenting sadly all my wasted years
That should in better service have been spent—   10
In fleeing sorrow and in seeking peace.
    Lord, you've enclosed me in this prisonhouse,°
Release me from it saved from endless pain;
I know my fault and offer no excuse.

365

    I wander weeping for my vanished hours,
For time spent loving a mere mortal thing,
Not rising up to fly, though I had wings
To give no base accounting of myself.
    And you who see my vile and impious deeds,   5
Invisible, immortal King of Heaven,
Bring succor to my frail and wayward soul,
And remedy its defect, by your grace.
    Thus, though I lived in tempest and at war,
May I yet die in harbor and at peace;   10
Though vain my stay, in virtue let me pass.
    In that small scrap of life that I have left,
And at my death, vouchsafe Your ready hand;
In others, well you know, I have no hope.

366

    O Virgin fair, in sunshine all arrayed,
Who, crowned with stars, so pleased the Highest Sun
That He concealed within you His own light,
To utter words of you Love presses me,
Yet, I cannot begin without your aid   5
And His who, loving, set Himself in you.
Her I invoke who always answered fair
One calling her with faith.
Virgin, if to compassion
The misery extreme of human things   10
Has ever turned you, to my prayer incline;

soccorri a la mia guerra,
bench'i' sia terra, et tu del ciel regina.
    Vergine saggia, et del bel numero una
de le beate vergini prudenti,   15
anzi la prima, et con piú chiara lampa;
o saldo scudo de l'afflicte genti
contra colpi di Morte et di Fortuna,
sotto 'l qual si trïumpha, non pur scampa;
o refrigerio al cieco ardor ch'avampa   20
qui fra i mortali sciocchi:
Vergine, que' belli occhi
che vider tristi la spietata stampa
ne' dolci membri del tuo caro figlio,
volgi al mio dubio stato,   25
che sconsigliato a te vèn per consiglio.
    Vergine pura, d'ogni parte intera,
del tuo parto gentil figliuola et madre,
ch'allumi questa vita, et l'altra adorni,
per te il tuo figlio, et quel del sommo Padre,   30
o fenestra del ciel lucente altera,
venne a salvarne in su li extremi giorni;
et fra tutti terreni altri soggiorni
sola tu fosti electra,
Vergine benedetta,   35
che 'l pianto d'Eva in allegrezza torni.
Fammi, ché puoi, de la Sua gratia degno,
senza fine o beata,
già coronata nel superno regno.
    Vergine santa d'ogni gratia piena,   40
che per vera et altissima humiltate
salisti al ciel onde miei preghi ascolti,
tu partoristi il fonte di pietate,
et di giustitia il sol, che rasserena
il secol pien d'errori oscuri et folti: 45
tre dolci et cari nomi ài in te raccolti,
madre, figliuola et sposa:
Vergine glorïosa,
donna del Re che nostri lacci à sciolti
et fatto 'l mondo libero et felice,   50
ne le cui sante piaghe
prego ch'appaghe il cor, vera beatrice.
    Vergine sola al mondo senza exempio,
che 'l ciel di tue bellezze innamorasti,
cui né prima fu simil né seconda,   55

Bring succor in my strife
Though I be earth, and you the Queen of Heaven.
  Wise Virgin, one among the company
Of blessed virgins provident,°   15
Indeed the first, and with the brightest lamp;
Against the strokes of Fortune and of Death
For this afflicted race the steady shield
Where we're not only saved, but triumph too;
O comfort for blind ardor blazing here   20
Among these mortal fools:
Virgin, those lovely eyes
That mourned to see the cruel wounds impressed
In the sweet limbs of your beloved Son,
Bend on my doubtful plight;   25
I comfortless, for counsel come to you.
  O Virgin pure, in every part complete,
Daughter and mother of your noble babe,
Who brightens this life, and the next adorns,
Through you your Son—the Highest Father's Son—   30
O heaven's window, shining and sublime,
Came down to save us in the final days,
And from all other shelters on the earth
You alone were chosen
Virgin consecrated,   35
O you who change Eve's weeping into joy.
As you can, make me worthy of His grace
O, ever blessed one,
Already crowned in that supernal realm.
  Virgin holy, filled with every grace,   40
With true humility most lofty you
Rose up to heaven, whence you hear my prayers,
You brought forth Pity's Fountain, and the Sun
Of Justice, who brings bright serenity
To this age, filled with thronging errors dark.   45
Three dear, sweet names you've gathered in yourself:
Mother, daughter, and bride;
Virgin with glory bright,
The Lady of that King who broke our bonds
And free and happy made this world; I pray   50
Upon His sacred wounds,
Content my heart, true bearer of my bliss.
  O Virgin peerless, in the world unique,
Who with your beauties did enamour heaven,
Whose like there neither was before nor since,   55

santi penseri, atti pietosi et casti
al vero Dio sacrato et vivo tempio
fecero in tua verginità feconda.
Per te pò la mia vita esser ioconda,
s'a' tuoi preghi, o Maria,   60
Vergine dolce et pia,
ove 'l fallo abondò, la gratia abonda.
Con le ginocchia de la mente inchine,
prego che sia mia scorta,
et la mia torta via drizzi a buon fine.   65

    Vergine chiara et stabile in eterno,
di questo tempestoso mare stella,
d'ogni fedel nocchier fidata guida,
pon' mente in che terribile procella
i' mi ritrovo sol, senza governo,   70
et ò già da vicin l'ultime strida.
Ma pur in te l'anima mia si fida,
peccatrice, i' nol nego,
Vergine; ma ti prego
che 'l tuo nemico del mio mal non rida: 75
ricorditi che fece il peccar nostro
prender Dio, per scamparne,
humana carne al tuo virginal chiostro.

    Vergine, quante lagrime ò già sparte,
quante lusinghe et quanti preghi indarno,   80
pur per mia pena et per mio grave danno!
Da poi ch'i' nacqui in su la riva d'Arno,
cercando or questa et or quel'altra parte,
non è stata mia vita altro ch'affanno.
Mortal bellezza, atti et parole m'ànno   85
tutta ingombrata l'alma.
Vergine sacra et alma,
non tardar, ch'i' son forse a l'ultimo anno.
I dí miei piú correnti che saetta
fra miserie et peccati   90
sonsen' andati, et sol Morte n'aspetta.

    Vergine, tale è terra, et posto à in doglia
lo mio cor, che vivendo in pianto il tenne
et de mille miei mali un non sapea:
et per saperlo, pur quel che n'avenne   95
fôra avenuto, ch'ogni altra sua voglia
era a me morte, et a lei fama rea.
Or tu donna del ciel, tu nostra dea
(se dir lice, et convensi),

Your sacred thoughts, deeds chaste, compassionate,
Have formed a hallowed living temple for
True God within your fruitful maiden womb.
Joyous my life can be because of you;
O Mary, by your prayers, 60
O Virgin, pious, sweet,
Where fault abounded once, now grace abounds.
And with my mind in prayerful attitude,
I beg you be my guide;
My tortuous way make straight to a good end. 65
    O Virgin bright, and fixed forevermore,
Above this ocean tempest-tossed the star—
For every trusty pilot, trusted guide,
Take heed in what a dreadful hurricane
I find myself alone and rudderless; 70
My final cries already are at hand.
But even so in you my soul confides—
A sinner, I admit,
But Virgin—I implore,
Let not your enemy deride my plight. 75
Remind yourself that sin of ours caused God,
So that He might deliver us, to don
Within your virgin cloister human flesh.
    Virgin, I have shed so many tears,
Scattered many coaxings, prayers in vain 80
All for my grief and my grave injury.
Since I was born upon the Arno's shore,
Searching first one place, then some other one,
In anguish I have ever spent my life.
Wholly have mortal beauty, deeds, and words 85
My spirit burdened down.
Sacred Virgin, nurturing,
Make haste, for in my final year, perhaps,
I am. My days more fleet than any dart
'Midst misery and sin 90
Were passed, and Death alone expects me now.
    Virgin, a certain one is earth; in pain
She left my heart. Alive, she held it weeping,
Though of my thousand woes she knew not one;
But when she found one out, the same thing came 95
To pass, for any other wish of hers
Was death for me and infamy for her.
Now you, Lady of Heaven; goddess ours
(If that is meet to say),

Vergine d'alti sensi, 100
tu vedi il tutto; et quel che non potea
far altri, è nulla a la tua gran vertute,
por fine al mio dolore;
ch'a te honore, et a me fia salute.

Vergine, in cui ò tutta mia speranza 105
che possi er vogli al gran bisogno aitarme,
non mi lasciare in su l'extremo passo.
Non guardar me, ma Chi degnò crearme;
no 'l mio valor, ma l'alta Sua sembianza,
ch'è in me, ti mova a curar d'uom sí basso. 110
Medusa et l'error mio m'àn fatto un sasso
d'umor vano stillante;
Vergine, tu di sante
lagrime et pïe adempi 'l meo cor lasso,
ch'almen l'ultimo pianto sia devoto, 115
senza terrestro limo,
come fu 'l primo non d'insania vòto.

Vergine humana, et nemica d'orgoglio,
del comune principio amor t'induca;
miserere d'un cor contrito humile. 120
Che se poca mortal terra caduca
amar con sí mirabil fede soglio,
che devrò far di te, cosa gentile?
Se dal mio stato assai misero et vile
per le tue man' resurgo, 125
Vergine, i' sacro et purgo
al tuo nome et penseri e 'ngegno et stile,
la lingua e 'l cor, le lagrime e i sospiri.
Scorgimi al miglior guado,
et prendi in grado i cangiati desiri. 130

Il dí s'appressa, et non pote esser lunge,
sí corre il tempo et vola,
Vergine unica et sola,
e 'l cor or conscïentia or morte punge.
Raccomandami al tuo figliuol, verace 135
homo et verace Dio,
ch'accolga 'l mïo spirto ultimo in pace.

Virgin of lofty vision,
You see all things, and what another could
Not do is nothing to your power great.
To my woe put an end;
For that would honor you and save me too.

    Virgin in whom I rest my every hope,
Who in great need both can and wants to aid,
Do not desert me at this final pass.
Not me, but Him who deigned to shape me, heed;
Let not my merit, but His likeness high
In me move you to care for one so low.
Medusa and my fault have made me stone,
Distilling idle tears.

With holy pious tears,
O Virgin, cause my weary heart to brim,
So my last cry at least may be devout,
Without the taint of earth
As was the first—of madness not devoid.

    Virgin human, foe of arrogance,
Be led by love of our shared origin;
Have mercy on a humble, contrite heart,
For if my habit is to love that small
Frail, mortal clay with such a wondrous faith,
What, noble creature, must I do for you?
If from my plight, so mean and vile, to life
By your hands I rise up,
Virgin, I will devote
To you, and in your name, I'll purify
My skill, thoughts, style, my tongue, heart, tears, and sighs.
Guide me to the better ford,
And, with good will, receive desire transformed.

    The day's at hand, it cannot be far off,
For time so hastes and flies;
Virgin unique, alone,
Conscience now pricks and death now stings my heart.
I pray that you commend me to your Son,
True man and truly God,
Who'll gather in my final breath in peace.°

100

105

110

115

120

125

130

135

Notes

1.1. Petrarch here initiates a structural counterpoint between themes of scattering and gathering that recurs throughout the *Rvf.* It achieves closure in the final line of the 366th poem with *accolga:* will gather.

2.1. Petrarch here uses a grammatical paradox in which subject and direct object are interchangeable. Its effect is to make Laura (the graceful one) the especially fitting instrument of Love's vengeance upon Petrarch for having earlier scorned that deity's power.

2.3. Love is envisioned as an armed assassin in keeping with a long-standing iconographic tradition.

2.5. Virtue is personified here as the goddess Virtute.

2.12. *high and weary hill:* the citadel of reason where the lover would be safe from Love's assault.

3.1. *day . . . rays paled:* Good Friday. Petrarch claims to have met Laura on April 6, 1327 at the Church of Santa Clara in Avignon. April 6 in the Christian tradition was the anniversary of the creation, the fall, Christ's crucifixion, and the day on which some expected the second coming.

4.4. Astrologically, Jupiter was a planet of more beneficent aspect than Mars.

4.5. The leaves of the scripture which revealed the truth as compared with the oak leaves, written upon and scattered by the Sybilline oracle, which concealed truth.

4.12. Laura is thought to have been born in the village of Carpentras, near Avignon. The circumstances of her birth recall Christ's birth and Petrarch's identification of Apollo, the sun god, with Christ.

Poem 5. Here Petrarch plays upon the syllables of the French form of Laura's name: LAU-RE-TA, LAU-RE-TA.

5.14. Throughout the *Rvf.*, Petrarch weaves the myth of Apollo and Daphne. Cupid, to avenge himself upon the taunting sun god, shot Apollo with his golden arrow and caused him to fall in love with the nymph Daphne, daughter of the river god Peneus. The love god struck Daphne, however, with his leaden arrow, which quenches love. Fleeing Apollo's importunate pursuit but about to be overtaken, Daphne prayed for transformation and was metamorphosed into a laurel tree. Disappointed in his desire for Daphne as his wife, Apollo adopted the laurel as his own tree, decorating it with his harp thus making it a symbol of poetic achievement, designating it the symbol of conquerors, and making it ever green, a symbol of immortality.

6.1. Desire is here figured forth as a run-away horse.

7.13. This is an epistolary sonnet, the first of many addressed to various persons, written to a friend to encourage him to follow the life of the mind.

8.4. The speakers in this poem appear to be captive animals or birds that Petrarch is sending as a gift with his poem to a friend.

9.4. *the planet that distinguishes*: the sun. The star Aldeberan is the tip of the horn of the constellation Taurus. In the spring it was thought to shed a seminal liquid which made the earth fecund.

9.9. *this fruit*: possibly truffles. This is another epistolary sonnet accompanying a gift to a friend.

10.1. Stefano Colonna, the elder, a friend, patron, and protector of Petrarch.

11.14. This poem is a ballata. In its questioning of sanity it reflects Petrarch's recognition of classical manifestations of love as distinct from the medieval ones that appear in the idea of all-consuming devotion and in the poem's death imagery.

14.14. This poem is a ballata.

16.10. *the true likeness*: the Veronica (vera icon—true image), a veil venerated during the Middle Ages at St. Peter's in Rome and thought to portray a likeness of the features of Christ. Both parallel and paradox are implicit in Petrarch's comparison of his pilgrimage and quest for Laura with the old man's pilgrmage to Rome. Making Laura his goal both enobles Petrarch, as he improves himself by emulating her superior moral qualities, and makes him guilty of idolatry in substituting her image for that of Christ.

19.2. Eagles, which were thought to push out nestlings that could not gaze steadily on the sun's disk.

21.5. The personified heart.

22.39. This poem is a sestina. In it Petrarch explicitly introduces for the first time in the *Rvf.* references to the Apollo-and-Daphne myth as parallel to his quest for Laura (line 36).

23.2. *Grasstime*: spring—the time of the year when animals are at grass. Ital. *in erab*: this picks up the image of nourishing or feeding from the first poem of the collection.

23.48. *Peneus*: the river on whose banks Daphne was transformed. *statelier stream*: possibly the Rhone or the Durance. Petrarch portrays himself as undergoing a series of Ovidian metamorphoses: laurel, swan, stone, fountain, echo, and deer as detailed in Warkentin's introduction.

23.60. Petrarch here alludes to the myths of Cygnus and Phaethon. Cygnus was Phaethon's uncle who was inconsolable after Zeus struck Phaethon with a thunderbolt to keep the earth from being burned when the youth drove his father Apollo's chariot (and the sun) too near the planet. Undercurrents of the fall of Icarus may also be present. Icarus fell when he ignored his father Daedalus's advice and flew too near the sun, melting the wax that held on the wings his father had made for him so the two could escape from the tyranny of King Minos.

23.63. *alien voice*: the swan's.

23.160. Here Petrarch alludes to the myth of Actaeon who was punished for looking upon Diana bathing by being transformed into a stag and torn by his own hounds.

23.163. Here Petrarch alludes to the myth of Jove and Danaë. Danaë was locked in a tower to protect her chastity, but Jove found her out and, in the form of a shower of gold, impregnated her.

23.164. An allusion to the myth of Aegina, daughter of the river god Asopus; she was beloved by Jove, who appeared to her as a flame.

23.165. An eagle. Warkentin reminds us that Petrarch uses the eagle to suggest his soaring mastery of the art of poetry.

24.2. The laurel was thought to be immune from lightning strikes.

24.4. The laurel crown of the poet *laureate*. The muses.

24.5. The muses.

24.8. Athena/Minerva, goddess of wisdom.

26.14. A reference to Matt. 18:12, 13, and Luke 15:4, 7.

27.1. Philip VI, the king of France is the successor both of his father, Charles IV and of Charlemagne, both of whom are probably intended by P., but especially the latter, given the sonnet's connection with the crusades.

27.3. Baghdad, from a European perspective the seat of the Muslim faith.

27.5. Pope John XXII.

27.9. An allusion to Agnese Colonna who had prevailed over a group of the family's enemies.

27.13. The absent Pope.

28.1. This canzone is addressed to Cardinal Giacomo Colonna, encouraging him to provide leadership in mounting the crusade of 1333.

28.25. Philip IV of France.

28.38. *Oxcart*: the constellation Ursa Major, also called the "Wain." *Pillars*: the Pillars of Hercules at the straits of Gibraltar—the boundary of the Mediterranean and hence of the known world (see also poem 51, line 14).

28.40. Mt. Helicon was the home of the muses.

28.51. The Teutonic peoples. This view of the Germans has been widely held by Italic peoples since classical times.

28.69. Orpheus could charm animals and plants with his music, and Amphion could move stones.

28.79. Romulus, one of the mythic founders of Rome.

28.80. Caesar Augustus, first of the Roman emperors.

28.91. King of the Persians who bridged the Hellespont so that he could attack Europe with his forces.

28.100. *Marathon*: the battle (490 BCE) at which the Athenians and Plataeans defeated a vastly superior Persian force, killing some 6400 with the loss of only 192 Athenians.

28.101. Leonidas, Greek hero who defended to the death of the last man the pass at Thermopylae against a vastly superior Persian force in 480 BCE.

28.113. *kerchiefs*: Ital. *bende*—used here as a symbol for women—especially married or widowed women.

29.23. *black and white*: a recurrent image for Laura's eyes.

29.37. *one*: Dido, queen of Carthage, on being deserted by Aeneas.

30.39. This poem is a sestina.

31.1. The editorial tradition suggests that this sonnet may have been written during a grave illness that Laura suffered. Petrarch is imagining her untimely death, her subsequent stellification, and its potential consequences among the spheres of the Ptolomaic universe.

31.5. *third light*: Venus—i.e., in the sphere of the sun.

31.9. *fourth sphere*: Ital. *quarto nido*, literally "fourth nest."

31.10. *three lights*: the moon, Mercury, and Venus.

33.1. *amorous star*: Venus. *another in the north*: The most brilliant star in the early morning northern sky would have been Arcturus. The references to "whirling" and Juno confuse the issue. Petrarch probably had in mind a constellation rather than a single star. The one that best fits his description is Cassiopeia. The mythic beauty's pride in her luxuriant hair angered Juno. As a circumpolar constellation, Cassiopeia "whirls" about the northern sky. On several occasions during the time in which this poem was written, conditions were right for the observation that Petrarch here reports. (I am grateful to astronomy professor John Williams of Albion College for checking this.)

36.12. *unhearing one*: death. Petrarch is pale and wishing to die, but death refuses to take notice.

38.1. Orso dell'Anguillara, a Roman aristocrat and friend of P.

40.11. *father*: St. Augustine, who was Petrarch's favorite among the church fathers. The editorial tradition suggests that Petrarch had requested the loan of a book from a patron, perhaps Giacomo Colonna, while Petrarch, again perhaps, was working on his *Remedies*.

41.1. Daphne. *Phoebus* in the next line is another name for the sun god, Apollo.

41.4. *Sicilian Smith*: Vulcan, the blacksmith of the gods who fabricated Jove's thunderbolts.

41.6. *Caesar and Janus*: Julius Caesar and the Roman deity, Janus, whose names the months of July and January commemorate.

41.10. The constellation Orion was associated with storms.

41.12. Aeolus, god of the winds; Juno, goddess of the air.

41.13. Neptune, god of the sea.

42.3. Vulcan.

42.6. *Mongibello*: Mt. Aetna—the volcano thought to be Vulcan's forge.

42.7. Juno, Jove's sister and spouse.

43.1. Apollo, the sun god.

44.1. *man*: Julius Caesar who grieved over the death of Pompey, his daughter Julia's husband.

44.5. The biblical David.

45.1. *Enemy*: Laura's mirror. Though Dante's Beatrice displays exclusively celestial virtues, in the *Rvf.*'s poems *in vita*, Petrarch is only too aware of Laura's human qualities, including, as here perhaps, her vanity.

45.12. *Narcissus*: In classical mythology, Narcissus fell in love with his own reflection and pined away, finally being transformed into the flower that bears his name.

51.3. Daphne.

52.1. *Diana*: goddess of chastity; her lover was Acteon.

53.1. *Noble spirit*: a Roman senator, perhaps Bosone de' Raffaelli da Gubbio or, less likely, Cola di Rienzi, whose abortive attempt to restore the Roman republic Petrarch supported enthusiastically.

53.26. *race of Mars*: the Romans. Petrarch's admiration of ancient Roman virtue rested on the qualities he attributed to the Republic, not on the corruption of the empire.

53.37. *Brutus*: Junius Brutus who rebelled against Tarquin (Durling, 126) and who put his own sons to death for conspiring to restore the Tarquins; *Scipios*: the first Scipio ended the second punic war with his victory at Zama (202 BCE); the second (Scipio Africanus) destroyed Carthage (146 BCE).

53.41. *Fabritius*: ca. Fabricius Luscinus, victor over Pyrrhus (Durling, 126). Fabritius was celebrated for his incorruptibility.

53.60. *black friars . . . grey friars . . . white [friars]*: the Dominican, Franciscan, and Carmelite orders, respectively.

53.65. *Hannibal*: a Chartheginian general, the sworn enemy of Rome.

53.71. The animals in this list allude respectively to the families of the Orsini, branches of the Counts of Tuscolo (both eagles and wolves), the Savelli or perhaps the Annibaldi, and the Caetani—all adversaries of the Colonna—the "column" of the next line.

53.74. *lady*: Rome.

53.84. *greater Father*: the Pope, perhaps Benedict XII, who was busy building a palace at Avignon (1334–7).

53.99. *Tarpeian Mount*: "The Capitoline Hill in Rome where the Tarpeian Rock was located," (Durling, 130). Persons convicted of capital crimes were executed there—thus it was associated with the seat of judgment. The others of Rome's seven hills were: the Palatine, Aventine, Caelian, Esquiline, Viminal, and Quirinal. These hills (except the Aventine) were surrounded by a sacred enclosure (the *pomoerium*) and together they constituted the city of Rome at the time of the Republic.

53.100. Probably Cola di Rienzi who had been knighted.

54.10. This poem is a madrigal.

58.2. *precious lord*: Agapito Colonna. This sonnet apparently accompanied the gift of a cushion and, perhaps, a sacred book whose message would help the reader avoid the pitfalls of the "left-hand path," and the gift of a chalice.

58.4. *Cruel one*: Love.

58.12. *me*: the sonnet.

58.13. *boatman*: Charon, who ferried the souls of the dead to the underworld.

61.13. *fame for her*: It is well to remember that Petrarch was already the most famous private person in Europe and that his poetic celebration of his love for Laura was widely circulated.

66.36. The critical tradition interprets this phrase as "thunder," and Durling apparently translates "cloud" throughout to accomodate this otherwise difficult image.

69.8. *Giglio, Elba*: Mediterranean islands.

70.10. The 10th line of each of the first three stanzas quotes a famous opening line from a predecessor's poem, and the final line quotes Petrarch's own opening line from poem 23 of this collection. Line 10, Petrarch thought, was a line of Arnault Daniel, though in fact it seems either anonymous or a line from Guillem de Saint-Gregori. Line 20 cites Guido Cavalcanti, line 30 cites Dante, and line 40 cites Cino da Pistoia. The 51st line is the opening line from his own canzone, *Rvf.* 23. The concatenation of these famous lines firmly establishes Petrarch's own perception of his place in the emergent vernacular canon.

71.108. This canzone and the two that follow comprise a set known as the "three sisters," thus Petrarch's references to "sisters" in these three poems are references to the songs themselves.

77.4. *Polyclitus*: a sculptor whose masterwork was the gold and ivory statue of Hera at Argos.

77.5. *Simone*: Simone Martini, who made a portrait of Laura for P.

78.12. *Pygmalion*: sculptor whose prayer Venus granted by bringing to life his gold and ivory statue, thereafter called Galatea, whom Pygmalion married.

81.5. *great friend*: Jesus Christ.

Poem 84. Dialogue between Petrarch and his Eyes.

91.1. *you*: probably Petrarch's brother, Gherardo, on the death of his beloved (Ponchioroli, 124).

92.4. This sonnet laments the death of Petrarch's friend the poet Cino da Pistoia (1270–1336).

94.14. This poem begins with an explanation, based on Renaissance physiology, of the mechanism of blanching or turning white when one falls in love at first sight. The beloved's image, arriving in the lover's heart by unknown but instantaneous means, drives out the soul, which ordinarily dwells in the heart. Unable to govern the vital spirits—the powers of motion that the soul confers upon the limbs—the soul is driven forth through the windows of the eyes, leaving the person temporarily immobile, thunderstruck, and, because the heart skips a beat or two, pale. But, once out, as I understand the conceit, the exiled soul of one lover encounters that of another who has suffered exactly the same sequence of events. The two souls then mingle happily, thereby having revenge on the usurping images. While the souls are mingling, the astonished lovers remain as pale as Petrarch usually is. It is pleasant amidst the sigh tempests and tear floods of the *Rvf.* to encounter occasional evidence of Petrarch's sense of ironic humor.

98.1. Orso dell'Anguillara, a friend of Petrarch.

102.1. *traitor.* Pompey: Gnaeus Pompeius (106–48 BCE). After sharing power with Julius Caesar for a time, Pompey, once married to Caesar's daughter, quarreled with Caesar, and was politically ruined by his defeat at Pharsalus (48 BCE), after which he fled to Egypt where he was treacherously murdered on landing by one of his old Centurions—to Caesar's ill-concealed relief. Ponchioroli (135) names Ptolemy as the Egyptian traitor.

102.5. *Hannibal*: Carthaginian general.

103.5. *she-bear.* alludes to the Orsini family, deafeated at San Cesario (22 May 1333) by Stefano Colonna, the recipient of this epistolary sonnet.

104.1. Pandolfo Malatesta (Ponchioroli, 137).

104.11. All the men named in this tercet were celebrated Roman generals.

104.13. Literary pursuit.

105.1. This poem is a *canzone frotolla*. It is characterized by shifting subjects, intentionally unclear references, internal rhyme, and uncontextualized maxims.

108.13. *Sennuccio*: Sennuccio del Bene, a friend of Petrarch's at Avignon.

112.1. *Sennuccio*: Sennuccio del Bene was Petrarch's best friend. In this epistolary sonnet Petrarch discusses deeply personal matters with him.

114.1. *Babylon*: the Papal court at Avignon, which Petrarch found morally corrupt.

114.5. *here*: Vaucluse, a lovely and isolated valley near the source of the Sorgue River, not far from Avignon. It was here Petrarch retired from the papal court that he had come to regard as Babylon and here that he apparently was sometimes visited by Laura in company with other ladies who had come to bathe in the Fountain of the Sorgue. The Sorgue gushes forth from a great rock—a mountain really—at the foot of which Petrarch built his house. The house still stands and can be visited. The river then takes its course through a narrow valley, closed off at one end by the rock wall. From this unusual geography the vale where Petrarch retired to the country takes its name, *Vaucluse*—closed valley. Many of the following poems are set there.

114.14. *him*: perhaps Giovanni Colonna (Ponchioroli, 150).

119.1. *lady*: Glory. This allegorical canzone was written after Petrarch's incoronation as poet laureate by the Roman Senate at Campidoglio on 8 April 1341 (Ponchiorli, 155).

119.60. *lady*: Virtue (Ponchioroli, 157).

119.111. *he who posed this task*: The poet, Petrarch himself, has imposed the task on his messenger, the song.

120.2. This sonnet is addressed to Antonio da Ferrara who, on hearing a rumor of Petrarch's death, composed a poem in his honor (Ponchioroli, 159).

124.4. *those . . . other shore*: those who have died and entered the other life.

126.37. *win me grace*: in this context, by saying a prayer for the soul of the departed.

128.1. This canzone, by consensus one of the noblest of the Italian language, is addressed to the contentious rulers of a divided Italy's petty principalities. The Germanic mercenaries hired by these leaders laid waste to the Italian countryside for many years.

128.45. *Marius*: Roman victor over the Teutons at Aquae Sextiae (modern Aix). The victory (102 BCE) was still celebrated in the vicinity until as late as the 18th century.

128.71. *matins until tierce*: Matins is the first cannonical hour. Technically midnight, it can also be observed at dawn. Tierce is the third canonical hour, 9 a.m. Thus, depending on what time he meant by "matins," Petrarch is suggesting that the warlords of Italy devote either all night or the morning hours to introspection.

129.43. *Leda*: raped by Zeus in the form of a swan, Leda gave birth to twins, Pollux and Castor, the latter of whom was fathered by Leda's husband on the same night as the rape. The daughter alluded to in the next line, Helen of Troy, was also fathered by Zeus on another occasion (*Oxford Classical Dictionary*, 492).

130.10. *Zeuxis* (420–390 BCE): a renowned Greek painter; *Praxiteles* (ca. 350 BCE) and *Phidias* (ca. 500–432? BCE): Greek sculptors. *Scythia* and *Numidia*: distant lands, the first between the Carpathian Mountains and the Don River and the second in North Africa near Egypt. The point is that he cannot travel far enough in his exile to escape Envy.

136.2. This sonnet and the two following were written to excoriate the Papal Court at Avignon for its corruption. Together they are known as the Babylonian sonnets.

137.4. The deities of amorous dalliance and drunkeness instead of those of wisdom and power.

138.13. *Constantine*: Flavius Valerius Aurelius Constantinus, Roman emperor (324–337 BCE) was thought to have corrupted the church by enriching it.

138.14. *sad world*: the Inferno. Dante mentions Constantine twice in the *Inferno* (19.115 and 27.94), though the pilgrim does not encounter him there.

139.7. Perhaps Venice (Ponchioroli, 194).

139.11. *Egypt*: like the ancient Hebrews, to servitude in Avignon.

142.3. *heaven*: the sphere of Venus.

145.3. *car*: in a preindustrial age, "car" and "chariot" were synonymous; the car of Phoebus Apollo was the chariot of the sun.

146.10. *Thule*: the northernmost limit of the world; *Bactria*: (Ital. *Battro*)—Ponchiorli glosses "Balkh," a river of Afghanistan. Balkh was also the name of the capital of ancient Bactria, which Durling selects to translate this nonce word. I follow Durling because the place names seem presented in groups: two distant lands; two rivers—the Tana (Don) and the Nile; and three quasi-mythical locales—Mt. Olympus, Mt. Atlas, and Calpe, the ancient name of the Rock of Gibraltar, one of the Pillars of Hercules.

146.14. Italy.

147.5. *He*: Will personified.

148.5. The principal rivers of the known world.

148.8. The Sorgue in Vaucluse.

Poem 150. Dialogue between Petrarch and his Soul.

166.2. Delphi (Ponchioroli, 222) or Mt. Parnassus (Durling, 166). Verona, Mantua, and Sessa Arunca are the respective birthplaces of the poets Catullus, Virgil, and Juvenal. The suggestion that Florence as yet has no poet significantly omits Dante.

166.11. *olive tree*: symbol of wisdom sacred to its inventress, Athena/Minerva.

176.1. This and the next sonnet concern the great forest at Ardennes and recall the allegorical force of wandering in forests as being lost in sin and waywardness.

179.1. *Geri*: this sonnet replies to another, written by Geri dei Gianfigliazzi, inquiring how to overcome a lady's scorn.

186.8. Aeneas, Achilles and Ulysses are the heroes of Virgil's *Aeneid* and of Homer's *Iliad* and *Odyssey*, respectively. (Petrarch regularly employs "*Ulixe*," the Latin form of "Odysseus." Though Petrarch owned a Greek manuscript Homer, he never learned to read the language.) Augustus Caesar ruled Rome for 56 years, and Aegisthus killed Agamemnon. The Italian syntax also makes possible a reading in which Orestes, the killer of Agamemnon, might be intended.

186.12. Quintus Ennius, a Roman poet (239–169 BCE) wrote about Scipio Africanus, the Roman conqueror of Carthage—a subject Petrarch treats in his *Africa*.

186.13. *other*: Laura.

187.9. *Orpheus*: archetypal Greek musician and poet whose music tamed wild beasts, caused plants to sway in time, and made stones weep.

187.10. Virgil, born at Mantova.

187.13. Petrarch himself.

189.3. Scylla and Charybdis: Literally, shoals and a whirlpool in the Strait of Messina between the Italian penninsula and Sicily. Ulysses (Odysseus) in Homer's *Odyssey* had to pass between them. Figuratively, a dilemma either of whose alternatives, if chosen, will prove unsatisfactory.

190.1. Another allegorical representation of Laura.

190.3. *rivers*: the Sorgue and the Durance.

190.11. Both Durling (336) and Ponchiorli (246) gloss this famous line by alluding to its source, Solinus, who, 300 years after Caesar's death, reported that a deer was found with a collar inscribed: "Noli me tangere, Caesaris sum," (Let no one touch me, I am Caesar's). While, as both these commentators note, Petrarch's "Caesar" may allude to God, it may also allude to Laura's husband and his well founded faith in her constancy and purity.

191.13. Pliny (*Nat. Hist.* 7.2.18 and 2.36) suggests that a people lived along the Ganges in India who subsisted on odor alone and that a tiny Cyprian salamander dwelt in flame.

194.1. *breeze*: Ital. *L'aura*—another manifestation of Petrarch's constant play on Laura's name.

197.5. *Medusa*: a mortal become Gorgon. The sight of Medusa turned into stone whoever looked on her, as it turned Atlas, the Titan who held up the world (the old giant Moor), into a mountain. Significantly, wheras Dante's Medusa, whom the pilgrim fears to encounter in hell lest he be turned to stone (*Inferno* 9.52–57), is distinct from the Dante pilgrim's inspiration and protectress, Beatrice, on the contrary, Petrarch's inspiration and figurative Medusa are one in the same and combined in the person of Laura.

203.8. *pity's fountain*: Ponchioroli takes this phrase to allude to Laura, but here as elsewhere there seems to me a Christologic *double entendre*.

206.27. Pharoh and the Egyptian host, following Moses and the Israelites, saw an east wind blow back the waters of the Red Sea, exposing dry land over which the Israelites passed. When Pharoh and his host tried to follow, they were drowned as the waters of the sea closed over them (Exod. 14:22–31).

206.49. The image here is of a trial by jousting combatants in which God will defend the right and truth will overthrow its adversary, falsehood.

206.55. Although Jacob had labored seven years in exchange for the hand of Rachel, her father, Laban, under cover of darkness, exchanged his elder daughter Leah for the bride agreed upon. When, after the wedding had been consumated, Jacob discovered his wife's identity and challenged Laban, he explained that custom demanded that the elder sister marry first. Jacob had to serve seven more years to win Rachel as his second wife (Gen. 29:13–30).

206.59. *Elijah*: a Hebrew prophet who was transported, living, to heaven in a chariot of fire (2 Kings 2:11).

208.2. *your name*: the Rhone river, Ital. *Rodano*, from the same etymological root as "rodent," thus the river that gnaws or erodes.

210.1. *Hydaspes*: the Jhellum river (Ponchioroli, 271).

210.5. These birds, flying on the right and left respectively, were thought to foretell good fortune.

210.6. *Fate*: in classical mythology the Moirai (or the Parcae, as Petrarch knew them from his Latin sources), daughters of Zeus and the Titan Themis (Hesiod) or of the Titan Themis, were Lachesis, Clotho, and Atropos. They respectively assigned the lot, spun the thread of human life, and snipped it off at death.

211.13. See the note to to the first line of poem 3 for the significance of April 6.

219.8. Because of his prematurely gray hair, Petrarch regularly identifies himself with Tithonus, human spouse of Aurora, goddess of the dawn. When Aurora wed Tithonus she asked Jove to grant him immortality but forgot to specify eternal youth. Jove granted her request precisely, so that Tithonus aged and aged and, in some versions of the myth, turned at last into a cricket. The poems of Petrarch's later years are written in the *stile canuto*—the "gray-haired" style.

Poem 222. Debate between Petrarch and Ladies.

225.4. Petrarch associates his having seen Laura (or imagined her) with other women in a small boat, and in a chariot in a triumphal procession with the voyage of Jason in search of the golden fleece, and with the victories of Achilles. Tiphys was the pilot of Jason's argonauts, and Automedon drove Achilles' chariot.

225.7. *shepherd*: Paris, son of Priam, king of Troy, had been a shepherd before being called into diplomatic service by his father, running off with Helen of Troy, and causing the Trojan War. A poisoned arrow fired by Paris wounded Achilles in his only vulnerable spot, his heel, and killed him. Paris in turn was wounded with a poisoned arrow of Hercules by the archer Philoctetes and eventually died of the wound.

230.13. *laurel, olive, palm*: complex symbols—laurel for fame and poetic achievement and a paranym for Laura; olive for reason and peace; palm for victory and salvation.

230.14. This sonnet and the succeeding two tempt one to posit a rapprochement between Petrarch and Laura to which someone, perhaps her husband, angrily (and effectively) objected.

232.14. This erudite series of *exempla* illustrates the danger of wrath recoiling fatally upon the wrathful. The son of Philip of Macedon, Alexander the Great, gave orders that only Appelles could paint his likeness, Pyrgoteles sculpt him in marble, and Lysippus engrave him in bronze (Pliny *Nat. Hist.* 7. 33; cited by Durling, 388 and Ponchioroli, 294). Tydeus (Statius *Thebiad* 8.752ff.; Durling, 338 and Ponchioroli, 294; Dante, *Inferno* 32.130–31) became so angry at Menalippus, whom Tydeus had killed but who had also mortally wounded him, that he gnawed at his enemy's severed head, a crime against the gods. Sulla and Valentinianus, Roman heads of state, died of apoplexy, and the Greek warrior Ajax committed suicide in a fit of pique. Perhaps the person for whom this poem is intended is the one who has prevented Petrarch from seeing Laura.

237.31. *lover of the moon*: Endymion, a Latmian shepherd who wooed Selene (later identified with Diana) the moon goddess with a fleece of wool and became her paramour. Discovered by Jupiter, Endymion had the choice between dying by any means he preferred and living but sleeping eternally. He chose the latter and continued to be visited by the moon goddess. Petrarch's sexual repression surfaces more clearly, perhaps, in this poem than in any other of the collection.

238.4. *nature regal*: a royal personnage who visited Avignon—perhaps Charles of Luxemburg (Ponchioroli, 301).

239.8. *Breeze*: Ital. L'aura, a paranym for Laura.

Poem 242. Petrarch debates with himself.

244.3. *you*: Giovanni Dondi dell'Orologio, whose sonnet this one answers (Durling, 244).

246.9. Premonitions of Laura's death begin to appear in this poem, but Petrarch thinks that he, her elder, will die first.

247.11. The places named are the actual or putative birthplaces of Demosthenes, Cicero, Virgil, Homer, Pindar, and Horace; the lyres represent the poetic traditions of Greece and Rome (Durling, 408; Ponchioroli, 311).

249.13. More premonitions of Laura's impending death.

255.7. *Levants*: two easts from which two suns rise. The word "Levant," designating the Orient, is etymologically related to "lever"—to rise; thus the Levant is the place where the sun comes up.

259.7. *Sorgue*: the river that has its source at Vaucluse.

260.7. Helen of Troy.

260.9. *fair Roman*: Lucretia, who committed suicide rather than suffer the shame she felt at being raped.

260.11. *Argia*: Oedipus' daughter-in-law, Polynices' wife. (Statius *Thebiad* 2.266); Polyxena: Trojan princess betrothed to Achilles and who was either sacrificed on his grave (Ovid *Metam.* 13.440ff.) or committed suicide on his tomb (Philostratus *Heroica*, 20–18); Hypsipyle: Lemnian princess who nursed Opheltes (Statius *Thebiad*, 4.739ff.). All were extraordinary but ill-fated women.

262.9. See note to poem 260 above.

263.7. *birdlime*: pitch or other sticky substance spread on branches to catch small birds; *springes*: snares.

264.121. *course . . . port*: the straight and narrow path to heaven.

266.1. *precious lord*: Cardinal Giovanni Colonna, whose surname means column. The poem dates from 1345, eighteen years after Petrarch met Laura and fifteen after meeting Colonna.

267.14. Poem 267 marks the division often observed by Italian editors of the poems *in vita della Madonna Laura* (during Laura's lifetime) and those *in morte* following her death. Petrarch annotated his beloved copy of Virgil, preserved in the Ambrosiana Library in Milan, with a Latin inscription saying that he first met Laura on April 6, 1327 at the church of St. Claire at 7 a.m. She died of the plague in Avignon at the same hour on April 6, 1348. News of her death reached Petrarch in Parma on May 19.

268.82. *widow*: Petrarch addresses the poem itself.

269.1. *column high*: Petrarch's patron and friend, Cardinal Giovanni Colonna died July 7, 1348.

287.1. Petrarch's friend Sennuccio del Bene died in the autumn of 1349. This sonnet was written in November of that year (Carducci and Ferrari, 399).

287.11. *Guittone, Cino, Dante, Franceschin'*: Petrarch and Sennuccio del Bene's predecessor poets in the Italian amorous tradition. Guittone d'Arezzo, d. 1294; Cino da Pistoia, d. late 1336 or early 37; Dante Alighieri, d. 1321; and Franceschino degli Albizzi, d. 1328.

291.5. *Tithonus*: human husband of the goddess of the dawn, Aurora—his treasure dear. Petrarch seems especially to identify with them owing to the characteristic of gray hair that the poet shared with Tithonus.

302.11. *veil*: Laura's body which she will resume on judgment day.

306.13. *road divine*: the way that leads to eternal salvation.

306.14. *Avernian and Stygian lakes*: Lake Avernus, located in an area of active vulcanism north of Naples and not far from Mt. Vesuvius, lies near the mouth of the Avernian Sibyl's cave that was thought to be the entrance to the underworld. *Stygian lake*: the River Styx—one of the four rivers of hell, over which Charon ferried the souls of the damned.

308.1. Petrarch elected to live a solitary existence in the country in Vaucluse on the banks of the Sorgue river rather than return to Florence, on the Arno's banks, where wealth might have awaited him.

310.1. *Zephyr*: the personfied west wind of classical mythology, harbinger of the spring.

310.3. *Procne and Philomel*: sisters who had been metamorphosed into the swallow and the nightingale—birds that return with spring but that are also associated with tragedy. Ovid tells their story in *Metam.* 6.424ff.

310.6. This line suggests simultaneously that Jove delights in gazing upon his daughter by Ceres, Proserpina, returned for six months to the upper world (Venafro cited in Carducci and Ferrari, 424–25) and perhaps that the planets Jupiter and Venus are near one another in the spring skies with a favorable astrological aspect (Leopardi cited in Carducci and Ferrari, 424 and Durling, 488).

318.6. *Calliope and Euterpe*: the muses of epic and lyric poetry, respectively.

320.12. *lord*: Love.

325.34. Lines 31–34 suggest that Love's arms and Laura's beauty can overcome Jove's power, Apollo's light, Mars' strength and valor, and Polyphemus's (the Cyclops of Homer's *Odyssey*) roughness and ill manners (Tassoni, cited in Carducci and Ferrari, 449).

325.50. *lady*: Fortune—the goddess Fortuna, God's agent in controlling the affairs of the world.

328.6. *quartan ague*: a fever that recurs every fourth day. Ital: *domestica febbre*.

332.75. This poem is a double sestina.

336.2. *Lethe*: the river of the underworld whose waters make those who drink of them forget everything.

336.13. *prime*: the second of the seven canonical hours, the first being matins.

357.9. *King*: Christ.

358.6. *smashed . . . gates*: alludes to Christ's harrowing of hell when, after the crucifixion, he released from hell those who had died before his coming who were worthy of salvation—principally persons from the Old Testament.

360.2. *queen*: usually interpreted as reason by the commentators.

360.9. *left foot*: the weaker and more wayward foot.

360.94. Atrides, Achilles, Hannibal, Another (Scipio Africanus): Atrides (Agamemnon) and Achilles quarreled over the love of the Trojan captive Chryseis or Briseis (Chaucer's Criseyde and Shakespeare's Cressida); Hannibal, the Cartheginian general, and Scipio Africanus, the Roman conqueror of Carthage loved unworthy objects of their affections.

360.100. *Lucretia*: Roman matron honored for her chastity and courage.

360.157. This canzone recalls Petrarch's early legal training and gives evidence of a puckish sense of humor. He also uses the device of debating before an allegorical judge in two voices in his *Secretum*, where a persona named Petrarch debates another named St. Augustine in the presence of Truth.

364.12. *prisonhouse*: Petrarch's body.

366.15. *virgins provident*: an allusion to the parable of the wise and foolish virgins in Matt. 25:1–13.

366.137. As the first line of the collection begins with the image of scattering, the last ends with one of gathering. Both images allude to prophetic texts—the scattered leaves of the pagan oracles, and the gathered codex of the Christian Bible.

Selected Reading

The most useful introductory guide to Petrarchan bibliography for an English reader is to be found in Nicholas Mann, *Petrarch* (1984), 115–18. Mann stresses scholarly editions and sources; for a list of critical studies, chiefly Italian, see Peter Hainsworth, *Petrarch the Poet* (1988); both are noted below. In addition, we list the major studies cited in the text, plus a selection of recent translations and useful and/or recent critical material.

Barolini, Teodolinda. "The making of a Lyric Sequence: Time and Narrative in Petrarch's *Rerum vulgarium fragmenta*." *Modern Language Notes* 104 (1989): 1–38.

Bergin, Thomas G. *Petrarch*. Twayne's World Authors Series. Boston: Twayne Publishers, 1970.

Bernardo, Aldo. "Dramatic Dialogue in the Prose Letters of Petrarch." *Symposium* 5 (1951): 302–16.

———. "Dramatic Dialogue and Monologue in Petrarch's Works—II." *Symposium* 7 (1953): 92–119.

———. "The Importance of the Non-Love Poems in Petrarch's *Canzoniere*." *Italica* 27 (1950): 302–12.

———. *Petrarch, Laura, and the Triumphs*. Albany: State Univ. of New York Press, 1974.

———. *Petrarch, Scipio, and the Africa*. Baltimore: Johns Hopkins, 1962.

Billanovich, Giuseppe. "Da Dante al Petrarca," *Accademia Nazionale dei Lincei: Adunanze Straordinarie per il conferimento dei premi della Fondazione A. Feltrinelli* 1. fasc. 3 (1966): 63–67.

———. *Petrarca letterato 1: lo scrittoio del Petrarca*. Rome: Edizioni storia e letteratura, 1947.

———. *La tradizione del testo di Livio et le origini dell'Umanesimo*. 2 vols. Padua: Editrice Antenore, 1981.

—————. "L'Orazio Morgan e gli studi del giovane Petrarca." In *Tradizione classica e letteratura umanistica per Alessandro Perosa*, edited by Roberto Cardini, Eugenio Garin, Lucia Cesarini Martinelli and Giovanni Pascucci, 121–38. Rome: Bulzoni editore, 1985.

Boyle, Marjorie O'Rourke. *Petrarch's Genius: Pentimento and Prophecy*. Berkeley: Univ. of California Press, 1991.

Brugnolo, Furio. "Il libro di poesia nel trecento." In *Il libro di poesie dal copista al tipografo*, edited by Marco Santagata and Amedeo Quondam, 9–23. Modena: Edizioni Panini, 1989.

Cerquiglini, Jacqueline. *"Un engin si soutil": Guillaume de Machaut et l'éscriture au XIV siècle*. Geneva-Paris: Editions Slatkine, 1985.

—————. "Ethique de la totalisation et esthetique de la rupture dans le *Voir-Dit* de Guillaume de Machaut." In *Guillaume de Machaut, Colloque-Table Ronde*, Université de Reims, April 19–22, 1978, 253–62. Paris: Editions Klincksieck, 1982.

Cook, James Wyatt. "'For not just under kerchiefs [*bende*] Love resides ...' Tone, Lexicon, Context, and Symbol in a Petrarchan Crux Word." *Quaderni d' Italianistica* 14.1 (1993): 121–25.

—————. "Petrarch's Mirrors of Love and Hell: *Canzoniere* 45 and 46." *Italian Culture* 3 (1981): 47–62.

—————. and Germaine Warkentin. "Toward Making a New Verse *Canzoniere*." *Yale Italian Studies* 1 (1980): 23–43.

Draper, William H., trans. *Petrarch's Secret: or The Soul's Conflict With Passion*. London: Chatto and Windus, 1911.

Durling, Robert M. *The Figure of the Poet in Renaissance Epic*. Cambridge, Mass.: Harvard Univ. Press, 1965.

—————. "Petrarch's 'Giovane donna sotto un verde lauro,'" *Modern Language Notes* 86 (1971): 1–20.

—————, trans. *Petrarch's Lyric Poems: the Rime Sparse and Other Lyrics*. Cambridge, Mass.: Harvard Univ. Press, 1976.

Dutschke, Dennis. *Francesco Petrarca: Canzone XXIII from First to Final Version*. Ravenna: Longo editore, 1977.

Feo, Michele. "Petrarca ovvero l'avanguardia del trecento," *Quaderni petrarcheschi* I (1983): 1–22.

Foster, Kenelm. *Petrarch: Poet and Humanist*. Edinburgh: Edinburgh Univ. Press, 1984.

Freccero, John. "The Fig-Tree and the Laurel: Petrarch's Poetics." In *Literary Theory / Renaissance Texts*, edited by Patricia Parker and David Quint, 20–32. Baltimore: Johns Hopkins Univ. Press, 1986.

Galbiati, Giovanni, ed. *Francisci Petrarcae Vergilianus codex.* ... Milan: U. Hoepli, 1930.

Gorni, Guglielmo. "Metamorfosi e redenzione in Petrarca. Il senso della forma Correggio del Canzoniere." *Lettere italiane* 30 (1983): 3–16.

Greene, Thomas M. *The Light in Troy: Imitation and Discovery in Renaissance Poetry.* New Haven: Yale Univ. Press, 1982.

Hainsworth, Peter. "The Myth of Daphne in the *Rerum Vulgarium Fragmenta*," *Italian Studies* 34 (1979): 28–44.

———. *Petrarch the Poet: An Introduction to the Rerum Vulgarium Fragmenta.* London and New York: Routledge, 1988.

Huot, Sylvia. *From Song to Book: The Poetics of Writing in Old French Lyric and Lyrical Narrative Poetry.* Ithaca and London: Cornell Univ. Press, 1987.

Jones, F. J. "Further Evidence of the Identity of Petrarch's Laura." *Italian Studies* 39 (1984): 27–46.

———. "Laura's Date of Birth and the Calendrical System Implicit in the Canzoniere." *Modern Language Review* 79 (1984): 579–88.

———. "Petrarch's Methods of Dating and Time-Telling in Vat. Lat. 3196 and in his Correspondence." *Modern Language Review* 80 (1985): 586–93.

Kahn, Victoria. "The Figure of the Reader in Petrarch's *Secretum*." *Publications of the Modern Language Association of America* 100 (1985): 154–66.

Kilmer, Nicholas, trans. *Francis Petrarch: Songs and Sonnets from Laura's Lifetime.* San Francisco: North Point Press, 1981.

Kleinhenz, Christopher. "Petrarch and the Art of the Sonnet." In *Francis Petrarch, Six Centuries Later,* edited by Aldo Scaglione, 189–90. Chapel Hill: Department of Romance Languages, Univ. of North Carolina, and Chicago: Newberry Library, 1975.

Mann, Nicholas. "The Making of Petrarch's 'Bucolicum Carmen': a Contribution to the History of the Text." *Italia medioevale e umanistica* 20 (1977): 127–82.

———. *Petrarch.* Past Masters Series. Oxford: Oxford Univ. Press, 1984.

Martellotti, Guido. *Scritti petrarcheschi.* Eds. Michele Feo and Sylvia Rizzo. Padua: Editrice Antenore, 1983.

Martinelli, Bortolo. "L'ordinamento morale del *Canzoniere* del petrarca." *Studi petrarcheschi* 8 (1976): 93–167.

———. *Petrarca e il Ventoso.* Bergamo: Minerva italica, 1977.

Mazzotta, Giuseppe. "The Canzoniere and the Language of the Self." *Studies in Philology* 75 (1978): 271–96.

Musa, Mark, trans. *Selections from the Canzoniere and Other Works.* Oxford: Oxford Univ. Press, 1985.

Nicholson, G. R., trans. *Sonnets for Laura.* London: Autolycus, ca. 1981.

Noferi, Adelia. "Il Canzoniere del Petrarca: scrittura del desiderio e desiderio della scrittura," *Paragone* 296 (October 1974): 3–24.

————. *L'esperienza poetica del Petrarca*. Florence: Le Monnier, 1962.

Nolhac, Pierre de. *Pétrarque et l'Humanisme* (1907). 2 vols. Paris: Librairie Honoré Champion, 1965.

Patterson, Lee. *Chaucer and the Subject of History*. Madison: Univ. of Wisconsin Press, 1991.

Petrarca, Francesco. *Letters on Familiar Matters: Rerum familiarium libri*, 3 vols. Trans. Aldo S. Bernardo. Vol 1: Albany: State Univ. of New York Press, 1975. Vols. 2 and 3: Baltimore and London: The Johns Hopkins Univ. Press, 1975–85.

————. *Letters of Old Age: Rerum senilium libri I–XVII*, 2 vols. Trans. Aldo S. Bernardo, Saul Levin, and Reta A. Bernardo. Baltimore and London: The Johns Hopkins Univ. Press, 1992.

Petrie, Jennifer. *Petrarch, the Augustan Poets, the Italian Tradition and the Canzoniere*. Dublin: Irish Academic Press, 1983.

Petronio, G. "Storicità della lirica politica del Petrarca." *Studi petrarcheschi* 7 (1961): 247–64.

Porena, Manfredi, ed. *Il codice vaticano lat. 3196, autografo del Petrarca*. Roma: R. Accademia d'Italia, 1941.

Pötters, Wilhelm. *Chi era Laura? Strutture linguistiche e matematiche nel "Canzoniere" di Francesco Petrarca*. Bologna: Società editrice il Mulino, 1987.

Rico, Francisco. "'Rime Sparse', 'Rerum Vulgarium Fragmenta'. Para el titulo y el primer sonetto del 'Canzoniere'," *Medioevo Romanzo* 3 (1976): 101–38.

Robertis, Domenico de, ed. *Il Codice Chigiano L. V. 176: Autografo di Giovanni Boccaccio*. Rome: Archivi edizioni, 1974.

Roche, Thomas P., Jr. "The Calendrical Structure of Petrarch's Canzoniere." *Studies in Philology* 71 (1974): 152–72.

————. *Petrarch and the English Sonnet Sequences*. New York: AMS Press, 1989.

Romanò, Angelo. *Il codice degli abbozzi (Vat. Lat. 3196) di Francesco Petrarca*. Rome: Giovanni Bardi editore, 1955.

Santagata, Marco. *Dal sonetto al canzoniere*. Padua: Liviana editrice, 1979.

————. *I frammenti dell'anima: storia e racconto nel Canzoniere di Petrarca*. Bologna: il Mulino, 1992.

————. *Per moderne carte: la biblioteca volgare di Petrarca*. Bologna: il Mulino, 1990.

————. "Presenze di Dante 'Comico' nel 'Canzoniere' del Petrarca," *Giornale Storico della Letteratura Italiano* 146 (1969): 163–211.

Schiaffini, Alfredo. "Il lavorio della forma in Francesco Petrarca." In his *Momenti di storia della lingua italiana*. 2d ed. Rome: Editrice Studium (1953), 67.

Shapiro, Marianne. *Hieroglyph of Time: the Petrarchan Sestina*. Minneapolis: Univ. of Minnesota, 1980.

Shore, Marion. *For Love of Laura: Poetry of Petrarch*. Fayetteville: Univ. of Arkansas Press, 1987.

Sturm-Maddox, Sara. *Petrarch's Metamorphoses: Text and Subtext in the Rime Sparse*. Columbia, Mo.: Univ. of Missouri Press, 1985.

———. *Petrarch's Laurels*. University Park, Pa.: Pennsylvania State Univ. Press, 1992.

Trovato, Paolo. *Dante in Petrarca. Per un inventario dei dantismi nei Rerum vulgarium fragmenta*. Biblioteca dell' *Archivum Romanicum* 1.149. Florence: L. Olschki, 1979.

Velli, Giuseppe. *Petrarca e Boccaccio. Tradizione memoria scrittura*. Padua: Editrice Antenore, 1979.

Vickers, Nancy J. "Diana Described: Scattered Woman and Scattered Rhyme." *Critical Inquiry* 8 (1981): 265–79.

Wack, Mary Frances. *Lovesickness in the Middle Ages: the Viaticum and its Commentaries*. Philadelphia: Univ. of Pennsylvania Press, 1990.

Warkentin, Germaine. "The Form of Dante's 'Libello' and Its Challenge to Petrarch." *Quaderni d' Italianistica* 2.2 (Autumn, 1981): 160–70.

Wilkins, E. H. "Petrarch's Coronation Oration." In *Studies in the Life and Works of Petrarch*, 300–13 (Cambridge, Mass.: Medieval Academy of America, 1955.

———. *Life of Petrarch*. Univ. of Chicago Press, 1961.

———. *The Making of the Canzoniere and Other Petrarchan Studies*. Rome: Edizioni di storia e letteratura, 1951.

Index of First Lines

O blissful soul, how often you return   329
O Column glorious, on whom depends   37
O day, O hour, O final instant, O   371
O Death, you've left the world dark, sunless, cold   383
O envy, virtue's foe, one who to fair   227
O eyes of mine, our sun has been obscured   325
O fair and blessed soul whom Heaven awaits   57
O flowered, verdant, fresh and shady hill   287
O glances sweet, O clever little words   295
O ladies weep, and may Love weep with you   139
O Lady, with our Maker you rejoice   389
O little room, you sometimes were a port   279
O Love, when my hope blossomed   363
O Love, who clearly sees my every thought   221
O lovely hand, you clasp my heart so fast   247
O lovely soul, freed from that bond more fair   345
O noble soul with ardent virtue graced   207
O scattered steps, O longing thoughts alert   219
O time, O wheeling heavens, which fleeing cheat   395
O vale, so full of my lamenting cries   343
O Virgin fair, in sunshine all arrayed   411
O vital Sun, the only tree I love   239
O weep, my eyes; accompany my heart   133
O woe! Unhappy vision horrible   293
O you that hear in scattered rhymes the sound   31
O you victorious and triumphal tree   303
On food that my lord ever freely shares   385
On reaching fierce Achilles' famous tomb   237
On that fair face for which I long and sigh   299
Orso, there never was a stream nor pond   77
Passed by now is that time, alas, when I   351
Perhaps there was a time when love was sweet   387
Po, you can bear my body easily   233
Rapacious Babylon has stuffed her sack   201
Recalling that soft look which Heaven reveres   385
See now, Love, how a youthful lady slights   167
Sennuccio, I desire that you should know   157
Sennuccio mine, though you've left me alone   333
Seventeen years by now the heavens have rolled   169
Simone, when he found that high conceit   127
Since, by my destiny   121
Since Mercy's path is barred to me, along leads   191
Since you and I so frequently have proved   143
So feeble is the thread by which is held   73
So many fish dwell not in ocean's waves   281

Petrarch's *Canzoniere* (more formally known as *Rerum vulgarium fragmenta*), a body of 366 poems, mostly sonnets but including other forms such as madrigals and *canzoni*, is a central document in the development of the sensibility and the literature of western culture. This work marked the intellectual and cultural dividing line between the Middle Ages and the Renaissance. It has been seminal in the development of European and American lyric poetry for the ways in which the poems closely scrutinize the artistic, emotional, intellectual, and spiritual life of the poet. In this body of poetry, a kind of literary autobiography, Petrarch adumbrated the modern mind.

Petrarch's Songbook is a complete verse translation of this remarkable work. But this is not simply a verse rendering. James Wyatt Cook's songbook addresses a remarkable array of poetic elements, including the deceptive simplicity of Petrarch's vocabulary; the cultural context of the work—rendered here as broadly modern rather than facilely archaic; and the elegance of Petrarch's poetic diction.

Because the poetry of Cook's translation reflects Petrarch's poetic creations in carefully considered ways, this volume presents the original Italian text and English verse translation on facing pages.

ꟼRTS

ꟽEDIEVAL & RENAISSANCE TEXTS & STUDIES
is the publishing program of the
Center for Medieval and Early Renaissance Studies
at the State University of New York at Binghamton.

ꟽRTS emphasizes books that are needed —
texts, translations, and major research tools.

ꟽRTS aims to publish the highest quality scholarship
in attractive and durable format at modest cost.